Pro .NET 2.0 XML

Bipin Joshi

Apress®

Pro .NET 2.0 XML

ISBN-13 (pbk): 978-1-59059-825-2

ISBN-10 (pbk): 1-59059-825-3

Printed and bound in the United States of America 9 8 7 6 5 4 3 2 1

Lead Editors: Ewan Buckingham and Matthew Moodie
Technical Reviewer: Fabio Claudio Ferracchiati
Editorial Board: Steve Anglin, Ewan Buckingham, Gary Cornell, Jason Gilmore, Jonathan Gennick, Jonathan Hassell, James Huddleston, Chris Mills, Matthew Moodie, Jeff Pepper, Paul Sarknas, Dominic Shakeshaft, Jim Sumser, Matt Wade
Project Manager: Laura Esterman
Copy Edit Manager: Nicole Flores
Copy Editor: Sharon Wilkey
Assistant Production Director: Kari Brooks-Copony
Production Editor: Ellie Fountain
Compositor: Pat Christenson
Proofreader: April Eddy
Indexer: Brenda Miller
Artist: Kinetic Publishing Services, LLC
Cover Designer: Kurt Krames
Manufacturing Director: Tom Debolski

Distributed to the book trade worldwide by Springer-Verlag New York, Inc., 233 Spring Street, 6th Floor, New York, NY 10013. Phone 1-800-SPRINGER, fax 201-348-4505, e-mail `orders-ny@springer-sbm.com`, or visit `http://www.springeronline.com`.

For information on translations, please contact Apress directly at 2560 Ninth Street, Suite 219, Berkeley, CA 94710. Phone 510-549-5930, fax 510-549-5939, e-mail `info@apress.com`, or visit `http://www.apress.com`.

The source code for this book is available to readers at `http://www.apress.com` in the Source Code/ Download section.

This work is dedicated to Lord Shiva,
who, I believe, resides in each one of us as
pure consciousness

Contents at a Glance

Contents

About the Author

BIPIN JOSHI is a trainer and consultant by profession and runs his own firm, BinaryIntellect Consulting. Bipin has been programming since 1995 and has worked with .NET ever since its beta release. Founder and web master of two community websites—DotNetBips.com and BinaryIntellect.net—he also contributes to printed magazines and other websites. He is the author or coauthor of half a dozen books, including his *Developer's Guide to ASP.NET 2.0*. Bipin is a Microsoft MVP and a member of ASPInsiders. His deep interest in yoga prompted him to start YogaVision.in, a website dedicated to yoga and spirituality. Having adopted a yoga way of life, he remains absorbed in practicing and studying yoga when not engaged with computers. His blog at bipinjoshi.com is his place to jot down thoughts about technology and life. He can also be reached there.

About the Technical Reviewer

FABIO CLAUDIO FERRACCHIATI is a senior developer for Brain Force (`http://www.brainforce.com`). A prolific writer on leading-edge technologies, he has contributed to more than a dozen books on .NET, C#, Visual Basic, and ASP.NET. His most recent books are *LINQ for Visual C# 2005* and *LINQ for VB 2005*. He's a .NET MCSD and lives in Milan, Italy. He can be reached at `http://www.ferracchiati.com`.

Acknowledgments

Though my name alone appears as the author, many have contributed directly or indirectly to this book. When I got a nod from Apress to begin this book, I was a bit worried because I had only five months in hand and there were many activities going on at my end, including training programs, writing for my websites, and development work. Today I feel satisfied to see the task accomplished on time.

First of all, I must express my feeling of devotion toward Lord Shiva. His yogic teachings have made me understand the real meaning of life. Without His blessings, this would not have been possible. I am also thankful to my parents and brother for their help and support in my activities at all levels.

Writing a book is about teamwork. Input from the technical reviewer, Fabio Claudio Ferracchiati, was very useful in rendering the book accurate. The whole team at Apress was very helpful. Ewan Buckingham provided very good coordination and input at the conceptualization and initial stage. Matthew Moodie kept an eagle's eye on the language consistency and overall format. Laura Esterman was always there to ensure that everything went as per the schedule. Thank you, team, for playing your part so wonderfully.

Finally, thanks to Sona (my dog). Each time I show her my book, she feels so proud! Thank you, Sona, for providing fun at the end of tiring work schedules.

Introduction

The Internet has brought a huge difference in the way we develop and use software applications. Applications are becoming more and more distributed, connecting heterogeneous systems. With such a radical change, the role of XML is highly significant. XML has already established itself as a standard way of data encoding and transfer. No wonder that Microsoft's .NET Framework provides such a strong support for XML. Data access, raw parsing, configuration, code documentation, and web services are some of the examples where .NET harnesses the power and flexibility of XML.

The .NET Framework comes with a plethora of classes that allow you to work with XML data. This book demystifies XML and allied technologies. Reading and writing XML data, using DOM, ADO.NET integration with XML, SQL Server XML features, applying XSLT style sheets, SOAP, web services, and configuration systems are some of the topics that this book explores in detail. Real-world examples scattered throughout the book will help you understand the practical use of the topic under consideration. The book will also act as a handy reference when developers go on the job.

Who Is This Book For?

This book is for developers who are familiar with the .NET Framework and want to dive deep into the XML features of .NET. This book will not teach you XML manipulation using non-Microsoft tools. All the examples in this book are presented in C#, and hence working knowledge of C# is also assumed. In some chapters, familiarity with ADO.NET and SQL Server is necessary, though I have provided a brief overview along with the respective topics.

Software Required

I have used Visual Studio 2005 as the IDE for developing various applications. However, for most of the examples you can use Visual C# Express Edition. In some samples you also need Visual Web Developer Express Edition, SQL Server 2005, and the Sandcastle help file generation tool.

Structure of the Book

The book is divided into twelve chapters and three appendixes. Chapters 1 to 4 talk about navigating, reading, and writing XML documents by using classes from the `System.Xml` namespace. In these chapters, you will learn to use classes such as `XmlDocument`, `XmlReader`, `XmlWriter`, and `XPathNavigator`.

Manipulating XML data is just one part of the story. Often you need to validate and transform it so that it becomes acceptable to your system. Chapters 5 and 6 deal with the issues of validating XML documents and applying XSLT transformations to them, respectively.

The .NET Framework itself uses XML in many places. This is often under the hood, but for any XML developer it is essential to know where this occurs. To that end, Chapters 7 to 9 cover topics such as ADO.NET integration with XML, XML serialization, and XML web services.

Microsoft has not limited the use of XML only to areas such as ADO.NET and web services. SQL Server 2005 incorporates many XML-related enhancements. These features are discussed in Chapter 10. Though this topic isn't strictly one of the XML features of .NET, many developers will find it useful. This is because many real-world projects developed by using the .NET Framework make use of SQL Server 2005 as a data store. Chapter 11 covers many other areas where the .NET Framework uses XML. Some of them include configuration files, ASP.NET server controls, and C# XML comments.

In the .NET Framework 3.0, Microsoft added a new component-development framework called Windows Communication Foundation (WCF). WCF allows you to develop service-oriented applications by using a unified programming model. It also uses XML heavily as a format of communication. Thus it is worthwhile to peek into this new framework, and Chapter 12 does exactly that.

Finally, the three appendixes supplement what you learned throughout the book by providing real-world case studies and resources.

Downloading the Source Code

The complete source of the book is available for download at the book's companion website. Just visit `http://www.apress.com` and download the zip file containing the code from the Source Code/Download area.

Contacting the Author

You can reach me via the DotNetBips.com discussion forums (`http://www.dotnetbips.com/forums`) or via my blog at `http://www.bipinjoshi.com`.

CHAPTER 1

Introducing XML and the .NET Framework

XML has emerged as a de facto standard for data representation and transportation. No wonder that Microsoft has embraced it fully in their .NET Framework. This chapter provides an overview of what XML is and how it is related to the .NET Framework. Many of the topics discussed in this chapter might be already familiar to you. Nevertheless, I will cover them briefly here so as to form a common platform for further chapters. Specifically you will learn about the following:

- Features and benefits of XML
- Rules of XML grammar
- Brief introduction to allied technologies such as DTD, XML schemas, parsers, XSLT, and XPath
- Overview of the .NET Framework
- Use of XML in the .NET Framework
- Introduction to Visual Studio

If you find the concepts already familiar, you may want to skip ahead to Chapter 2.

What Is XML?

XML stands for *Extensible Markup Language* and is a markup language used to describe data. It offers a standardized way to represent textual data. Often the XML data is also referred to as an XML document. The XML data doesn't perform anything on its own; to process that data, you need to use a piece of software called a *parser*. Unlike Hypertext Markup Language (HTML), which focuses on how to present data, XML focuses on how to represent data. XML consists of user-defined tags, which means you are free to define and use your own tags in the XML document. XML was approved as a recommendation by the World Wide Web Consortium (W3C) in February 1998. Naturally this very fact contributed a lot to such a wide acceptance and support of XML in the software industry.

Now that you have brief idea about XML, let's see a simple XML document, as illustrated in Listing 1-1.

Listing 1-1. *A Simple XML Document*

```
<?xml version="1.0"?>
<customers>
   <customer ID="C001">
      <name>Acme Inc.</name>
      <phone>12345</phone>
   </customer>
   <customer ID="C002">
      <name>Star Wars Inc.</name>
      <phone>23456</phone>
   </customer>
</customers>
```

There are many rules that govern the creation of such XML documents. But we will save them for later discussion.

Benefits of XML

Why did XML become so popular? Well, this question has many answers and I will present some of the important ones in this section.

XML Is an Industry Standard

As you learned previously, XML is a W3C recommendation. This means it is an industry standard governed by a vendor-independent body. History shows that vendor-specific proprietary standards don't get massive acceptance in the software industry. This nonacceptance affects overall cross-platform data sharing and integration. Being an industry standard has helped XML gain huge acceptance.

XML Is Self-Describing

XML documents are self-describing. Because of markup tags, they are more readable than, say, comma-separated values (CSV) files.

XML Is Extensible

Markup languages such as HTML have a fixed set of tags and attributes. You cannot add your own tags in such markup languages. XML, on the other hand, allows you to define your own markup tags.

XML Can Be Processed Easily

Traditionally, the CSV format was a common way to represent and transport data. However, to process such data, you need to know the exact location of the commas (,) or any other delimiter used. This makes reading and writing the document difficult. The problem becomes severe when you are dealing with a number of altogether different and unknown CSV files.

As I said earlier, XML documents can be processed by a piece of software called a parser. Because XML documents use markup tags, a parser can read them easily. Parsers are discussed in more detail later in this chapter.

XML Can Be Used to Easily Exchange Data

Integrating cross-platform and cross-vendor applications is always difficult and challenging. Exchanging data in heterogeneous systems is a key problem in such applications. Using XML as a data-exchange format makes your life easy. XML is an industry standard, so it has massive support and almost all vendors support it in one way or another.

XML Can Be Used to Easily Share Data

The fact that XML is nothing but textual data ensures that it can be shared among heterogeneous systems. For example, how can a Visual Basic 6 (VB6) application running on a Windows machine talk with a Java application running on a Unix box? XML is the answer.

XML Can Be Used to Create Specialized Vocabularies

As you already know, XML is an extensible standard. By using XML as a base, you can create your own vocabularies. Wireless Application Protocol (WAP), Wireless Markup Language (WML), and Simple Object Access Protocol (SOAP) are some examples of specialized XML vocabularies.

XML-Driven Applications

Now that you know the features and benefits of XML, let's see what all these benefits mean to modern software systems.

Figure 1-1 shows a traditional web-based application. The application consists of Active Server Pages (ASP) scripts hosted on a web server. The client in the form of a web browser requests various web pages. Upon receiving the requests, the web server processes them and sends the response in the form of HTML content. This architecture sounds good at first glance, but suffers from several shortcomings:

- It considers only web browsers as clients.
- The response from the web server is always in HTML. That means a desktop-based application may not render this response at all.
- The data and presentation logic are tightly coupled together. If we want to change the presentation of the same data, we need to make considerable changes.
- Tomorrow if some other application wants to consume the same data, it cannot be shared easily.

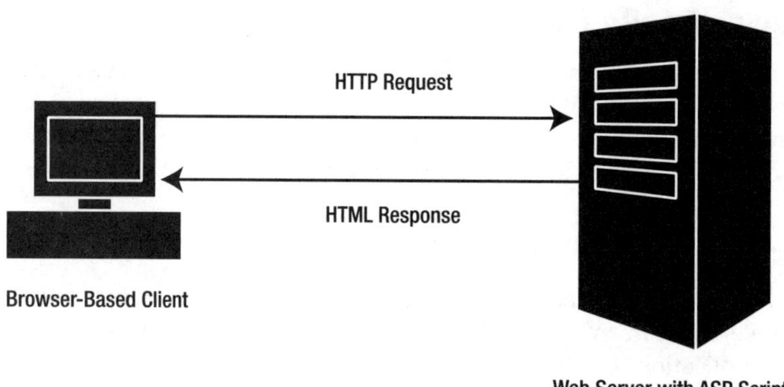

Figure 1-1. *Classic architecture for developing applications*

Now let's see how XML can come to the rescue in such situations.

Have a look at Figure 1-2. Here there are multiple types of clients. One is a web browser and the other is a desktop application. Both send a request to the server in the form of XML data. The server processes the request and sends the data in XML format. The web browser applies a style sheet (discussed later) to the XML data to render it as HTML content. The desktop application, on the other hand, parses the data by using an XML parser (discussed later) and displays it in a grid. Much more flexible than the previous architecture, isn't it? The advantages of the new architecture are as follows:

- The application has multiple types of clients. It is not tied only to web browsers.
- There is loose coupling between the client and the processing logic.
- New types of clients can be added at any time without changing the processing logic on the server.
- The data and the presentation logic are neatly separated from each other. Web clients have one set of presentation logic, whereas desktop applications have their own presentation logic.
- Data sharing becomes easy because the outputted data is in XML format.

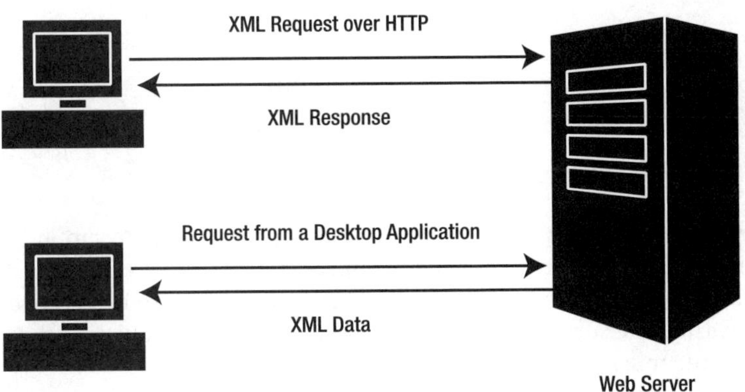

Figure 1-2. *XML-driven architecture*

Rules of XML Grammar

In the "What is XML?" section, you saw one example of an XML document. However, I didn't talk about any of the rules that you need to follow while creating it. It's time now to discuss those rules of XML grammar. If you have worked with HTML, you will find that the rules of XML grammar are more strict than the HTML ones. However, this strictness is not a bad thing, because these rules help ensure that there are no errors while we parse, render, or exchange data.

Before I present the rules in detail, you need to familiarize yourself with the various parts of an XML document. Observe Figure 1-3 carefully.

```
<?xml version="1.0" encoding="utf-8" ?>
<!-- This is list of customers -->
<customers>
  <customer ID="C001">
    <name>Acme Inc.</name>
    <phone>12345</phone>
    <comments>
      <![CDATA[Regular customer since 1995]]>
    </comments>
  </customer>
  <customer ID="C002">
    <name>Star Wars Inc.</name>
    <phone>23456</phone>
    <comments>
      <![CDATA[A small but healthy company.]]>
    </comments>
  </customer>
</customers>
```

Figure 1-3. *Parts of a typical XML document*

Line 1 is called a *processing instruction*. A processing instruction is intended to supply some information to the application that is processing the XML document. Processing instructions are enclosed in a pair of `<?` and `?>`. The `xml` processing instruction in Figure 1-3 has two attributes: `version` and `encoding`. The current W3C recommendations for XML hold version 1.0 and hence the `version` attribute must be set to `1.0`.

Line 2 represents a comment. A *comment* can appear anywhere in an XML document after the `xml` processing instruction and can span multiple lines.

Line 3 contains what is called the *document element* of the XML document. An XML document has one and only one document element. XML documents are like an inverted tree, and the document element is positioned at the root. Hence the document element is also called a *root element*. Each element (whether it is the document element or otherwise) consists of a start tag and end tag. The start tag is `<customers>`, and the end tag is `</customers>`.

It is worthwhile to point out the difference between three terms: element, node, and tag. When you say *element*, you are essentially talking about the start tag and the end tag of that element together. When you say *tag*, you are talking about either the start tag or end tag of the element, depending on the context. When you say *node*, you are referring to an element and all its inner content, including child elements and text.

Inside the `<customers>` element, you have two `<customer>` nodes. The `<customer>` element has one attribute called `ID`. The attribute value is enclosed in double quotes. The `<customer>` element has three child elements: `<name>`, `<phone>`, and `<comments>`. The text values inside elements such as `<name>` and `<phone>` are often called *text nodes*. Sometimes the text content that you want to put inside a node may contain special characters such as < and >. To represent such content, you use a character data (`CDATA`) section. Whatever you put inside the `CDATA` section is treated as a literal string. The `<comments>` tag shown in Figure 1-3 illustrates the use of a `CDATA` section.

Now that you have this background, you're ready to look at the basic rules of XML grammar. Any XML document that conforms to the rules mentioned next is called a *well-formed document*.

XML Markup Is Case Sensitive

Just like some programming languages, such as C#, XML markup is also case sensitive. That means `<customer>`, `<Customer>`, and `<CUSTOMER>` all are treated as different tags.

The XML Document Must Have One and Only One Root Element

An XML document must have one and only one root element. In the preceding example, the `<customers>` element is the root element. Note that it is mandatory for XML documents to have a root element.

The Start Tag Must Have an End Tag

Every start tag must have a corresponding end tag. In HTML, this rule is not strictly followed—for example, tags such as `<br>` (line break), `<hr>` (horizontal rule), and `<img>` (image) are often used with no end tag at all. In XML, that would be not be well formed. The end tag for elements that do not contain any child elements or text can be written by using shorter notation. For example, assuming that the `<customer>` tag doesn't contain any child elements, you could have written it as `<customer ID="C001"/>`.

The Start and End Tags Must Be Properly Nested

In HTML, this rule about nesting tags properly is not followed strictly. For example, the following markup shows up in the browser correctly:

```
<B><I>Hello World</B></I>
```

This, however, is illegal in XML. The nesting of start and end tags must be proper. The correct representation of the preceding markup in XML would be as follows:

```
<B><I>Hello World</I></B>
```

The Attribute Values Must Be Enclosed in Quotes

In HTML, you may or may not enclose the attribute values. For example, the following is valid markup in HTML:

```
<IMG SRC=myphoto.jpg>
```

However, this is illegal in XML. All the attribute values must be enclosed in quotes. Thus the accepted XML representation of the preceding markup would be as follows:

```
<IMG SRC="myphoto.jpg">
```

DTDs and XML Schemas

Creating well-formed XML documents is one part of the story. The other part is whether these documents adhere to an agreed structure, or *schema*. That is where Document Type Definitions (DTDs) and XML schemas come into the picture.

DTDs and XML schemas allow you to convey the structure of your XML document to others. For example, if I tell you to create an XML file, what structure will you follow? What is the guarantee that the structure that you create is the one that I have in mind? The problem is solved if I give you a DTD or schema for the document. Then you have the exact idea as to how the document should look and what its elements, attributes, and nesting are.

The XML documents that conform to some DTD or XML schema are called *valid documents*. Note that an XML document can be well formed, but it may not be valid if it doesn't have an associated DTD or schema.

DTDs are an older way to validate XML documents. Nowadays XML schemas are more commonly used to validate XML documents because of the advantages they offer. You will learn about the advantages of schemas over DTDs in Chapter 5. Throughout our discussion, when I talk about validating XML documents, I will be referring to XML schemas.

Parsing XML Documents

XML data by itself cannot do anything; you need to process that data to do something meaningful. As I have said, the software that processes XML documents is called a parser (or XML processor). XML parsers allow you read, write, and manipulate XML documents. XML parsers can be classified in two categories depending on how they process XML documents:

- DOM-based parsers (*DOM* stands for *Document Object Model*)
- SAX-based parsers (*SAX* stands for *Simple API for XML*)

DOM-based parsers are based on the W3C's Document Object Model recommendations and are possibly the most common and popular. They look at your XML document as an inverted tree structure. Thus our XML document shown in Figure 1-3 will be looked at by a DOM parser, as shown in Figure 1-4.

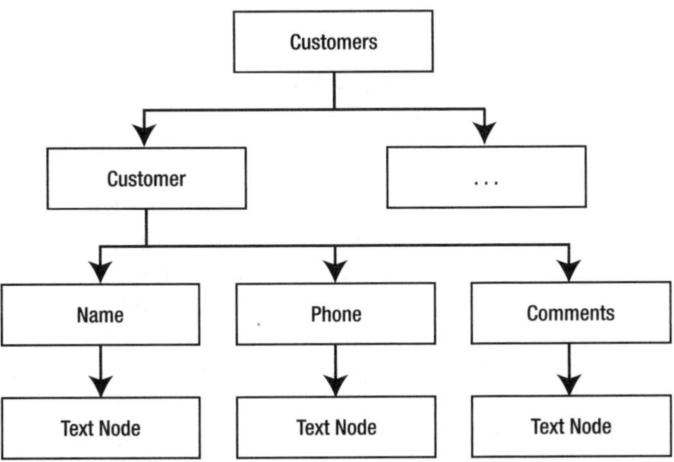

Figure 1-4. *The DOM representation of an XML document*

DOM-based parsers are read-write parsers, which means you can read as well as write to the XML document. They allow random access to any particular node of the XML document and as such they need to load the entire XML document in memory. This also implies that the memory footprint of DOM-based parsers is large. DOM-based parsers are also called *tree-based parsers* for obvious reasons.

Note Microsoft's DOM-based parser implementation is nothing but a COM component popularly known as Microsoft XML Core Services (MSXML).

SAX-based parsers do not read the entire XML document into memory at once. They essentially scan the document sequentially from top to bottom. When they encounter various parts of the document, they raise events, and you can handle these events to read the document. SAX parsers are read-only parsers, which means you cannot use them to modify an XML document. They are useful when you want to read huge XML documents and loading such documents into memory is not advisable. These types of parsers are also called *event-based parsers*.

Note MSXML includes a component that provides a SAX implementation of the parser.

Parsers can also be classified as validating and nonvalidating. *Validating parsers* can validate an XML document against a DTD or schema as they parse the document. On the other hand, *nonvalidating parsers* lack this ability.

XSLT

XML solves the problem of data representation and exchange. However, often we need to convert this XML data into a format understood by the target application. For example, if your target client application is a web browser, the XML data must be converted to HTML before display in the browser.

Another example is that of business-to-business (B2B) applications. Let's say that application A captures order data from the end user and represents it in some XML format. This data then needs to be sent to application B that belongs to some other business. It is quite possible that the XML format as generated by application A is different from that required by application B. In such cases, you need to convert the source XML data to a format acceptable to the target system. In short, in real-world scenarios you need to transform XML data from one form to another.

That is where XSLT comes in handy. *XSLT* stands for *Extensible Stylesheet Language Transformations* and allows you to transform XML documents from one form into another. Figure 1-5 shows how this transformation happens.

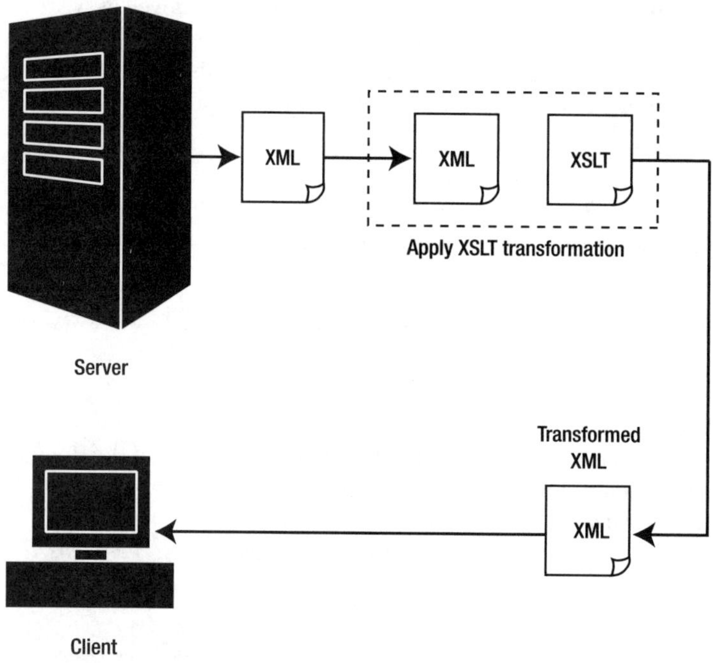

Figure 1-5. *XML transformation*

XPath

Searching for and locating certain elements within an XML document is a fairly common task. *XPath* is an expression language that allows you to navigate through elements and attributes in an XML document. XPath consists of various XPath expressions and functions that you can use to look for and select elements and attributes matching certain patterns. XPath is also a W3C recommendation. Figure 1-6 shows an example of how XPath works.

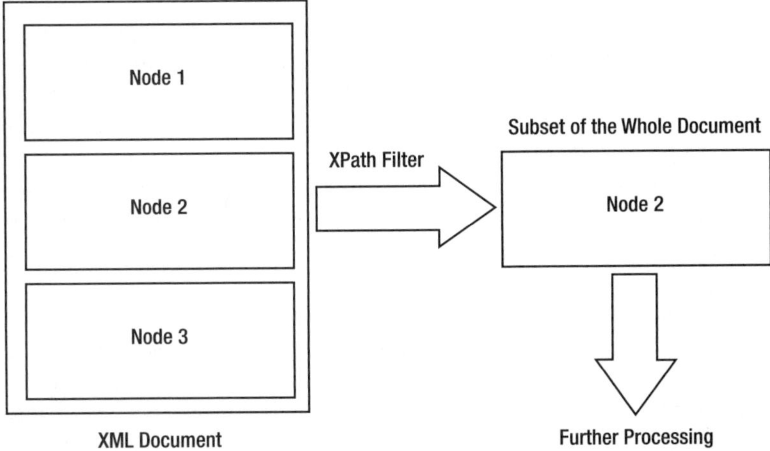

Figure 1-6. *Using XPath to select nodes*

The .NET Framework

Microsoft's *.NET Framework* is a platform for building Windows- and web-based applications, components, and services by using a variety of programming languages. Figure 1-7 shows the stack of the .NET Framework.

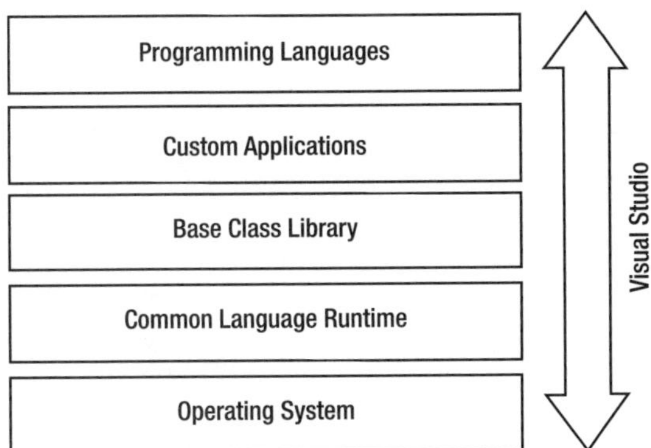

Figure 1-7. *Stack of the .NET Framework*

At the bottom level you have the operating system. As far as commercial application development using the .NET Framework is concerned, your operating system will be one of the various flavors of Windows (including Windows 2000, Windows 2003, Windows XP, or Windows Vista).

On top of the operating system, you have the common language runtime (CLR) layer. The CLR is the heart of the .NET Framework. It provides the executing environment to all the .NET applications, so in order to run any .NET applications you must have the CLR installed. The CLR does many things for your application, including memory management, thread management, and security checking.

On top of the CLR, a huge collection of classes called the Base Class Library gets installed. The Base Class Library provides classes to perform almost everything that you need in your application. It includes classes for file input/output (IO), database access, XML manipulation, web programming, socket programming, and many more things. If you are developing a useful application in .NET, the chances are that you will use one or another of the classes in the Base Class Library and hence your applications are shown sitting on top of it.

These applications can be developed using a variety of programming languages. Out of the box, the .NET Framework provides five programming languages: Visual Basic .NET, Visual C#, Managed C++, JScript .NET, and Visual J#. There are many other third-party compilers that you can use to develop .NET applications.

As a matter of fact, you can develop any .NET application by using Notepad and command-line compilers. However, most of the real-world applications call for a short development time, so that is where an integrated development environment (IDE) such as Visual Studio 2005 can be very helpful. It makes you much more productive than the Notepad approach. Features such as drag and drop, powerful debugging, and IntelliSense make application development much simpler and faster.

.NET and XML

The .NET Framework Base Class Library provides a rich set of classes that allows you to work with XML data. The relationship between the .NET Framework and XML doesn't end here. There are a host of other features that make use of XML. These features include the following:

- .NET configuration files
- ADO.NET
- ASP.NET server controls
- XML serialization
- Remoting
- Web services
- XML documentation
- SQL Server XML features
- XML parsing
- XML transformation

In this section, you will take a brief look at each of these features.

Assemblies and Namespaces

The core XML-related classes from the Base Class Library are physically found in an assembly called `System.Xml.dll`. This assembly contains several namespaces that encapsulate various XML-related classes. In the following text, you will take a brief look at some of the important namespaces.

System.Xml Namespace

The `System.Xml` namespace is one of the most important namespaces. It provides classes for reading and writing XML documents. Classes such as `XmlDocument` represent the .NET Framework's DOM-based parser, whereas classes such as `XmlTextReader` and `XmlTextWriter` allow you to quickly read and write XML documents. This namespace also contains classes that represent various parts of an XML document. These classes include `XmlNode`, `XmlElement`, `XmlAttribute`, and `XmlText`. We will be using many of these classes throughout the book.

System.Xml.Schema Namespace

The `System.Xml.Schema` namespace contains various classes that allow you to work with schemas. The entire Schema Object Model (SOM) of .NET is defined by the classes from this namespace. These classes include `XmlSchema`, `XmlSchemaElement`, `XmlSchemaComplexType`, and many others.

System.Xml.XPath Namespace

The `System.Xml.XPath` namespace provides classes and enumerations for finding and selecting a subset of the XML document. These classes provide a cursor-oriented model for navigating and editing through the selection. The classes include `XPathDocument`, `XPathExpression`, `XPathNavigator`, `XPathNodeIterator`, and more.

System.Xml.Xsl Namespace

The `System.Xml.Xsl` namespace provides support for XSLT transformations. By using the classes from this namespace, you can transform XML data from one form to another. The classes provided by this namespace include `XslCompiledTransform`, `XslTransform`, `XsltSettings`, and so on.

System.Xml.Serialization Namespace

The `System.Xml.Serialization` namespace provides classes and attributes that are used to serialize and deserialize objects to and from XML format. These classes are extensively used in web services infrastructures. The main class provided by this namespace is `XmlSerializer`. Some commonly used attributes classes such as `XmlAttributeAttribute`, `XmlRootAttribute`, `XmlTextAttribute`, and many others are also provided by this namespace.

The XML Parsing Model in the .NET Framework

The previous sections discussed two types of parsers: DOM- or tree-based parsers, and SAX- or event-based parsers. It would be reasonable for you to expect that the .NET Framework supports parsing models for both types of parsers. Though you won't be disappointed at their offering, there are some differences that you must know.

In the .NET Framework you can categorize the XML parsers into two flavors:

- Parsers based on DOM
- Parsers based on the reader model

The first thing that may strike you is the lack of a SAX-based parser. But don't worry, the new reader-based parsers provide similar functionality in a more efficient way. You can think of reader-based parsers as an alternative to traditional SAX-based parsers.

The DOM-based parser of the .NET Framework is represented chiefly by a class called `XmlDocument`. By using this parser, you can load, read, and modify XML documents just as you would with any other DOM-based parser (such as MSXML, for example).

The reader-based parsers use a cursor-oriented approach to scan the XML document. The main classes that are at the heart of these parsers are `XmlReader` and `XmlWriter`. These two classes are abstract classes, and other classes (such as `XmlTextReader` and `XmlTextWriter`) inherit from them. You can also create your own readers and writers if you so wish.

Thus to summarize, the .NET Framework supports DOM parsing and provides an alternate and more efficient way to carry out SAX-based parsing. I will be discussing these parsers thoroughly in subsequent chapters.

.NET Configuration Files

Almost all real-world applications require configuration, which includes things such as database connection strings, file system paths, security schemes, and role-based security settings. Prior to the introduction of the .NET Framework, developers often used .INI files or the Windows registry to store such configuration settings. Unfortunately, the simple task of storing configuration settings used to be cumbersome in popular tools such as Visual Basic 6. For example, VB6 doesn't have a native mechanism to read and write to .INI files. Developers often used Windows application programming interfaces (APIs) to accomplish this. VB6 does have some features to work with the Windows registry, but they are too limited for most scenarios. Moreover, storing data in the Windows registry always came with its own risks. In such cases, developers tend to rely on a custom solution. The impact was obvious: no standardization, more coding time, more efforts, and repeated coding for the same task.

Thankfully, the .NET Framework takes a streamlined and standardized approach to configuring the applications. It relies on XML-based files for storing configuration information. That means developers no longer need to write custom logic to read and write .INI files or even the Windows registry. Some of the advantages of using XML files instead of classic approaches are as follows:

- Because XML files are more readable, the configuration data can be stored in a neat and structured way.
- To read the configuration information, the .NET Framework provides built-in classes. That means you need not write any custom code to access the configuration data.
- Storing the configuration information in XML files makes it possible to deploy it easily along with the application. In the past, Windows registry-based configuration posed various deployment issues.
- There are no dangers in manipulating the XML configuration files for your application. In the past, tampering with the Windows registry involved risks and created unwanted results.
- .NET Framework configuration files are not limited to using the predefined XML tags. You can extend the configuration files to add custom sections.
- Sometimes the configuration information includes some confidential data. .NET Framework configuration files can be encrypted easily, giving more security to your configuration data. The encryption feature is a built-in part of the framework needing no custom coding from the developer's end.

The overall configuration files of the .NET Framework are of three types:

- Application configuration files
- Machine configuration files
- Security configuration files

Application configuration files store configuration information applicable to a single application. For Windows Forms and console-based applications, the name of the configuration file takes the following form:

```
<exe name>.exe.config
```

That means that if you are developing a Windows application called `HelloWorld.exe`, its configuration file name must be `HelloWorld.exe.config`. The markup from Listing 1-2 shows sample configuration information for a Windows Forms–based application.

Listing 1-2. *XML Markup from an Application Configuration File*

```
<?xml version="1.0" encoding="utf-8" ?>
<configuration>
  <appSettings>
    <add key="defaultemail"
         value="someone@somedomain.com"/>
  </appSettings>
</configuration>
```

On the other hand, a configuration file for a web application is called `web.config`. The markup from Listing 1-3 shows a sample `web.config` file.

Listing 1-3. *XML Markup from a web.config File*

```
<?xml version="1.0"?>
   <configuration>
       <connectionStrings>
         <add name="connstr"
                        connectionString="Data Source=.\SQLEXPRESS;
                        Integrated Security=True;
                       AttachDbFilename=|DataDirectory|AspNetDb.mdf"
                       providerName="System.Data.SqlClient"/>
      </connectionStrings>
   <system.web>
      <compilation debug="true"/>
      <authentication mode="Forms">
      <forms name="login" loginUrl="login.aspx">
      </forms>
      </authentication>
      <authorization>
         <deny users="?"/>
      </authorization>
      <membership defaultProvider="AspNetSqlProvider">
            <providers>
                  <add
                              name="AspNetSqlProvider"
                              type="System.Web.Security.SqlMembershipProvider"
                              connectionStringName="connstr"
                              passwordFormat="Clear"
                             enablePasswordRetrieval="true"
                            requiresQuestionAndAnswer="true"
                            maxInvalidPasswordAttempts="3">
                     </add>
              </providers>
      </membership>
   </system.web>
</configuration>
```

When you install the .NET Framework on a machine, a file named machine.config gets created in the installation folder of the .NET Framework. This file is the master configuration file and contains configuration settings that are applied to all the .NET applications running on that machine. The settings from machine.config can be overridden by using the application configuration file. Because the settings from machine.config are applied to all the .NET applications, it is recommended that you alter this file with caution. Generally, only server administrators and web-hosting providers modify this file.

The .NET Framework offers a secure environment for executing applications. It needs to check whether an assembly is trustworthy before any code in the assembly is invoked. To test the trustworthiness of an assembly, the framework checks the permission granted to it. Permissions granted to an assembly can be configured by using the security configuration files. This is called *Code Access Security*.

ADO.NET

For most business applications, data access is where the rubber meets the road. In .NET, *ADO.NET* is the technology for handling database access. Though ADO.NET sounds like it is the next version of classic ADO, it is, in fact, a complete rewrite for the .NET Framework.

ADO.NET gives a lot of emphasis to disconnected data access, though connected data access is also possible. A class called DataSet forms the cornerstone of the overall disconnected data architecture of ADO.NET. A DataSet class can be easily serialized as an XML document and hence it is ideal for data interchange, cross-system communications, and the like. A class called XmlDataDocument allows you to work with relational or XML data by using a DOM-based style. It can give a DataSet to you, which you can use further for data binding and related tasks. Another class called SqlCommand allows you to read data stored in Microsoft SQL Server and return it as an XmlReader. I am going to cover XML-related features of ADO.NET in detail in subsequent chapters.

ASP.NET Server Controls

You learned that the ASP.NET configuration file (web.config) is an XML file. The use of XML in ASP.NET doesn't end there. ASP.NET uses a special XML vocabulary to represent its server controls, which are programmable controls that can be accessed from server-side code. Consider the markup shown in bold in Listing 1-4.

Listing 1-4. *Server Control Markup*

```
<%@ Page Language="C#" %>
<script runat="server">
protected void Button1_Click(object sender, EventArgs e)
{
Label2.Text = TextBox1.Text;
}
</script>
```

```
<html xmlns="http://www.w3.org/1999/xhtml" >
<body>
<form id="form1" runat="server">
<asp:Label ID="Label1" runat="server" Text="Enter some text :"></asp:Label>
<asp:TextBox ID="TextBox1" runat="server"></asp:TextBox>
<asp:Button ID="Button1" runat="server" Text="Submit" OnClick="Button1_Click" />
<asp:Label ID="Label2" runat="server"></asp:Label>
</form>
</body>
</html>
```

The preceding fragment shows the markup of a few ASP.NET server controls. As you can see, a Label control is represented by the `<asp:Label>` markup tag. Similarly, a Button control is represented by the `<asp:Button>` markup tag. This is a special vocabulary of XML and follows all the rules of XML grammar.

XML Serialization

Modern applications seldom run on a single machine. They are distributed and span two or more machines. Figure 1-8 shows a simple distributed application spanning three machines.

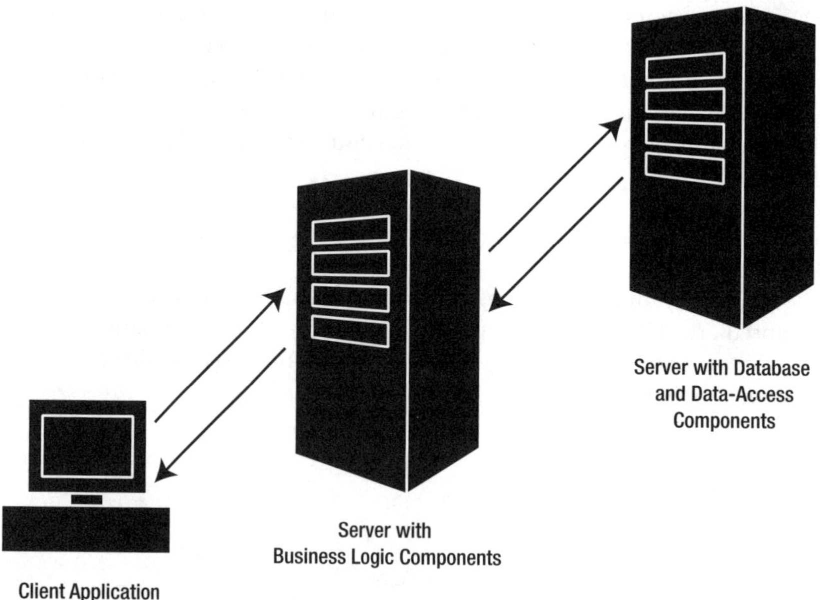

Figure 1-8. *A simple distributed application*

Here the database and data-access components are located on a separate server. Similarly, business logic components are located on their own server, and the client applications access these components through a network. Imagine that the client wants some data from the database to display to the end user. The data is pulled out from the database from data-access components. But how will it reach the client? That is where serialization comes into the picture.

Serialization is a process in which data is written to some medium. In the preceding example, the medium is a network—but it can be a file or any other stream also. The data-access components will serialize the requested data so that it can reach the client application. The client application then deserializes it—that is, it reads from the medium and reconstructs the data in an object or any other data structure. In the case of XML serialization, this data is serialized in the XML format. XML serialization is used extensively by web services. The `XmlSerializer` class provides a programmatic way to serialize and deserialize your objects.

Remoting

In the previous example, we simply assumed that components residing on different machines talk with each other. But how? Remoting is the answer. *.NET remoting* provides an infrastructure for building distributed applications. Though remoting can be used over the Internet, more commonly it is used when the network involved is a local area network (LAN). For Internet-driven communication, web services are more appropriate (see the next section).

You can think of remoting as a replacement for Distributed Component Object Model (DCOM) under .NET. It is clear that remote components must serialize and deserialize data being requested by the client applications. This serialization can be in binary format or in XML format. Moreover, the remoting configuration can be carried by using XML-based configuration files.

Web Services

With the evolution of the Internet, distributed applications are spanning different geographical locations. You may have one server residing in the United States with clients talking to it from India. It is quite possible that the clients and server are running two entirely different platforms (Windows and Unix, for example). In such cases it is necessary that a standard mode of communication be established between the server and clients so that communication can take place over the Internet. That is where web services come into the picture.

Formally speaking, *web services* are a programmable set of APIs that you can call over a network by using industry-standard protocols: HTTP, XML, and an XML-based protocol called SOAP (as noted earlier in this chapter, *SOAP* stands for *Simple Object Access Protocol*). You can think of a web service as a web-callable component.

Because a web service is supposed to serve cross-platform environments, it relies heavily on XML. HTTP, XML, and SOAP form the pillars of web services architecture. Web services are industry standards and just like XML they are standardized by the W3C and hence have massive industry support.

Have a look at Figure 1-8 again. Assume that the three machines involved are connected via the Internet and not a LAN. The components will now be replaced with web services and they will perform the same job as the components did previously. In such cases, the client will call a web service residing on the business logic server, which in turn calls a web service residing on the database server. The requested data is sent back to the client in XML format. It doesn't matter whether the client is a VB6 application, a VB.NET application, or a Java application. Powerful, isn't it? You will explore web services thoroughly in later chapters.

XML Documentation

Everybody knows the importance of well-documented code. However, this important task is often not given proper attention. One of the reasons is that comments left by the developer are not properly captured while creating program documentation or help files. C# as well as Visual Basic .NET supports a special commenting syntax that is based on XML. These XML comments can be converted into HTML documentation later. Just to give you a feel for how it works, see the C# code shown in Listing 1-5.

Listing 1-5. *XML Commenting Syntax*

```
/// <summary>
/// This is the starting point.
/// </summary>
/// <param name="args">
/// This parameter receives command line arguments.
/// </param>
static void Main(string[] args)
{
}
```

As you can see, the XML commenting syntax uses three slashes (///). The tags such as <summary> and <parameter> are built-in tags, and I will cover them in detail in subsequent chapters. To generate XML documentation out of this code, you need to choose project settings, as shown in Figure 1-9.

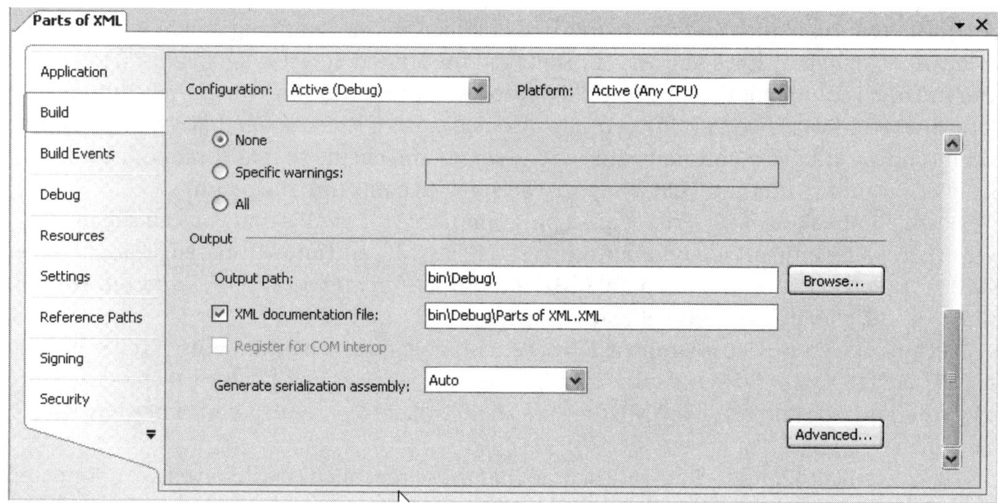

Figure 1-9. *Configuring a project for XML documentation*

Notice the check box titled XML Documentation File. After you select this check box and specify the output path, the compiler generates an XML file, as shown in Listing 1-6.

Listing 1-6. *Resultant XML Comments*

```
<?xml version="1.0"?>
<doc>
   <assembly>
      <name>Parts of XML</name>
   </assembly>
   <members>
      <member name="M:Parts_of_XML.Program.Main(System.String[])">
         <summary>
              This is the starting point.
         </summary>
         <param name="args">
             This parameter receives command line arguments.
         </param>
       </member>
   </members>
</doc>
```

You can now apply an Extensible Stylesheet Language (XSL) style sheet to the preceding XML file to get HTML documentation out of it.

SQL Server XML Features

SQL Server 2005 is one of the most powerful database engines used today. Moreover, it is from the creators of the .NET Framework. Naturally, you can expect good XML support in the product.

SQL Server 2005 provides some extensions to the `SELECT` statement, such as `FOR XML`, `AUTO`, `EXPLICIT`, `PATH`, and `RAW`, that return the requested data in XML form. The XML data returned by these queries can be retrieved by using the `ExecuteXmlReader()` method of the `SqlCommand` object. Further, Microsoft has released a set of managed classes called SQLXML that facilitate reading, processing, and updating data to and from SQL Server 2005 databases in XML format. Finally, SQL Server 2005 provides a new data type called `xml` to the standard data types. I will cover these features at length in Chapter 10.

Working with Visual Studio

Throughout the remainder of the book, you will be using Microsoft Visual Studio 2005 for developing various applications. Hence it is worthwhile to quickly illustrate how Visual Studio can be used to develop Windows and web applications. Note that this section is not intended to give you a detailed understanding of Visual Studio. I will restrict our discussions to the features that you need later in this book.

■ **Note** Though the examples in this book are developed by using Visual Studio 2005, for most of the Windows Forms examples you can also use Visual C# Express Edition. Similarly, for examples related to websites and web services, you can use Visual Web Developer (VWD). Visual C# Express Edition and Visual Web Developer can be downloaded from Microsoft's website free of charge.

Creating Windows Applications

In this section, you will learn how to create a Windows Forms–based application by using Visual Studio. To create a Windows Forms–based application, you need to create a project of type Windows Application. To begin creating such a project, click File ➤ New Project from the main menu. This opens the New Project dialog box, as shown in Figure 1-10.

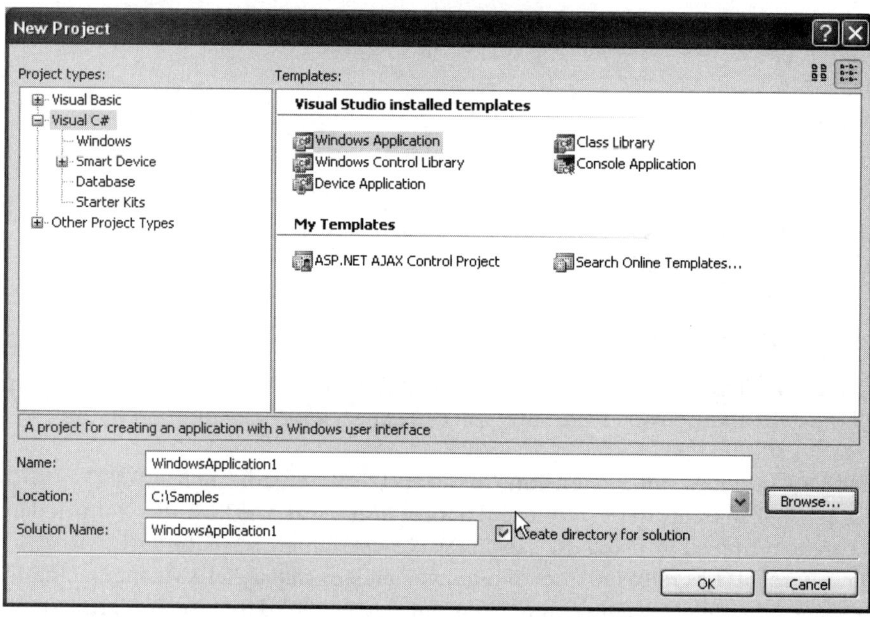

Figure 1-10. *Creating a Windows application in Visual Studio*

In the Project Types section, select Visual C#. This will display all the project templates applicable to the C# language. Now choose Windows Application from the templates. Name the project **HelloWindowsWorld**. Also, choose an appropriate location from your disk to store the project files. If you wish, you can also specify a solution name for the Visual Studio solution file. Finally, click the OK button to create the project.

Your Visual Studio IDE should resemble Figure 1-11.

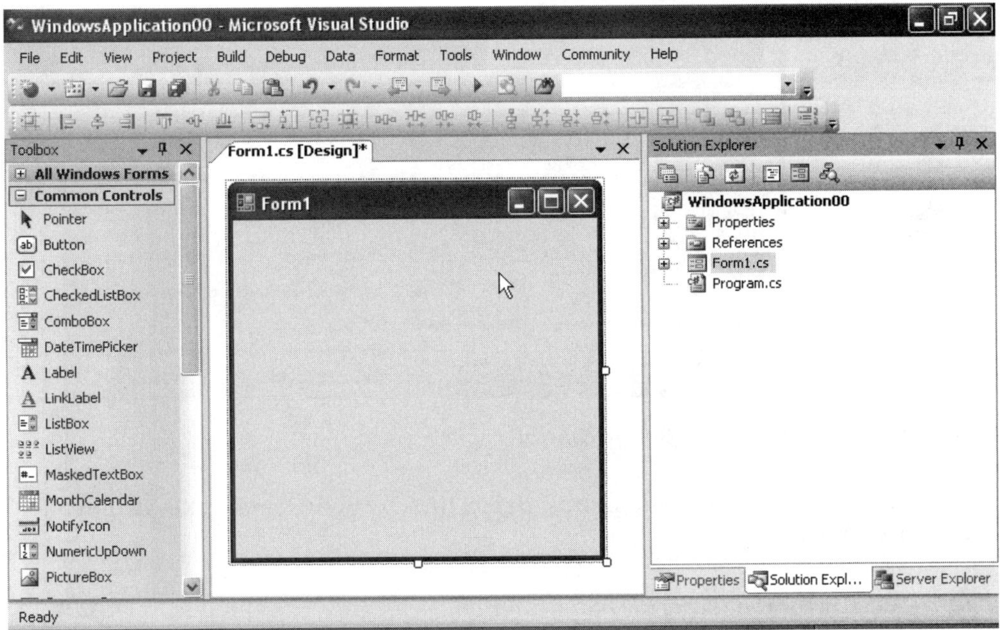

Figure 1-11. *A newly created Windows application in the Visual Studio IDE*

The project contains a single Windows form. You can drag and drop controls from the toolbox onto the form and handle their events. Just to illustrate how this is done, drag and drop a Button control on the form. Open the properties windows by using the View menu and set its Text property to **Click Me**. Your form should now look similar to Figure 1-12.

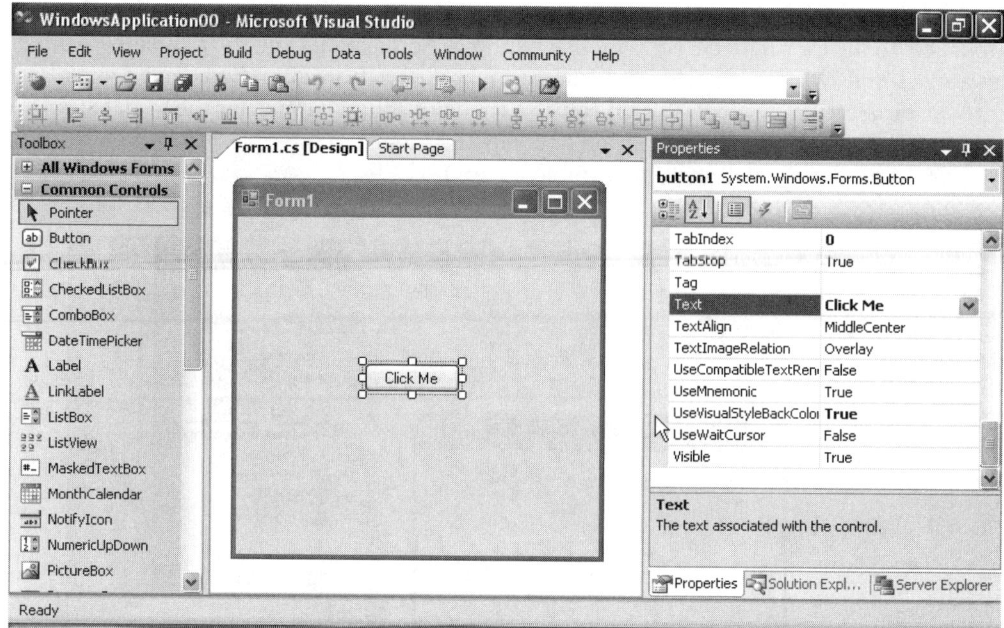

Figure 1-12. *Windows form with Button control*

Double-click the Click Me button so as to go in its `Click` event handler. Key in the code shown in Listing 1-7.

Listing 1-7. *Click Event Handler of the Button Control*

```
private void button1_Click(object sender, EventArgs e)
{
   MessageBox.Show("Hello from Windows Forms");
}
```

The code shows the `Click` event handler of the Button control. Notice the signature of the event handler carefully. Throughout the .NET Framework, Microsoft has maintained a uniform signature for event handlers. The first parameter of the event handler gives you the reference of the control (or object in general) that raised the event. The second parameter (often referred to as *event arguments*) supplies more information about the event, if any. The second parameter can be either an instance of the `EventArgs` class directly or of any other class inheriting from the `EventArgs` class.

Note You might be wondering why the sender parameter is needed. In the .NET Framework, one method can act as an event handler for multiple controls. For example, you can handle the `Click` event of two Button controls by writing just one event handler function. In such cases, the sender parameter can be used to identify the control that raised the event.

When you double-click on a control, Visual Studio automatically takes you to its default event handler. However, you can wire various events and their handlers manually by using properties windows. Figure 1-13 shows how this is done.

Figure 1-13. *Wiring events and their handlers manually*

Inside the event handler we have used the `MessageBox` class to display a message box. The `Show()` method of the `MessageBox` class has many overloads. We have used the one that accepts a message to be displayed to the user.

Now use the Build menu to compile the application. Compiling the application will create an .EXE-based (executable) .NET assembly. Though you can run the .EXE directly, you may prefer to run the application via the Visual Studio IDE so that you can debug it if required. To run the application, choose Debug ➤ Start Debugging from the menu. Figure 1-14 shows a sample run of the application.

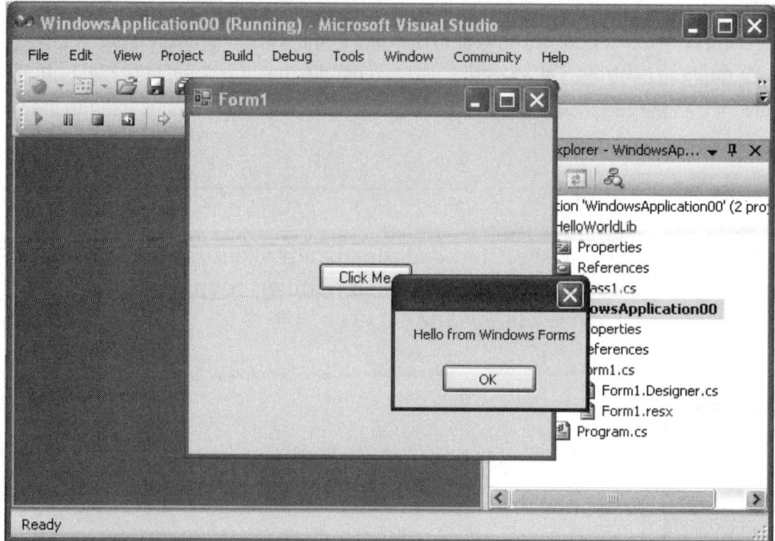

Figure 1-14. *Sample run of the application*

Creating Class Libraries

A project of type Windows Application outputs an .EXE assembly. Generally, such applications present some type of user interface to the user. However, at times you need to code functionality and create a component. Such components reside as dynamic link libraries (.DLL files) and generally do not include any presentation logic. To create dynamic link libraries by using Visual Studio, you need to create a project of type Class Library.

To learn how to create and consume class libraries, you will create a Class Library project. The resultant assembly will be consumed by the Windows application that you developed in the preceding section.

Again choose File ➤ New Project from the menu to open the New Project dialog box, as shown in Figure 1-15.

This time select the Class Library project template and name it **HelloWorldLib**. At the bottom of the dialog box, there is a combo box that allows you to add the new solution to the existing solution. Ensure that you choose Add to Solution in this combo box. Finally click the OK button. Your Visual Studio IDE should now resemble Figure 1-16.

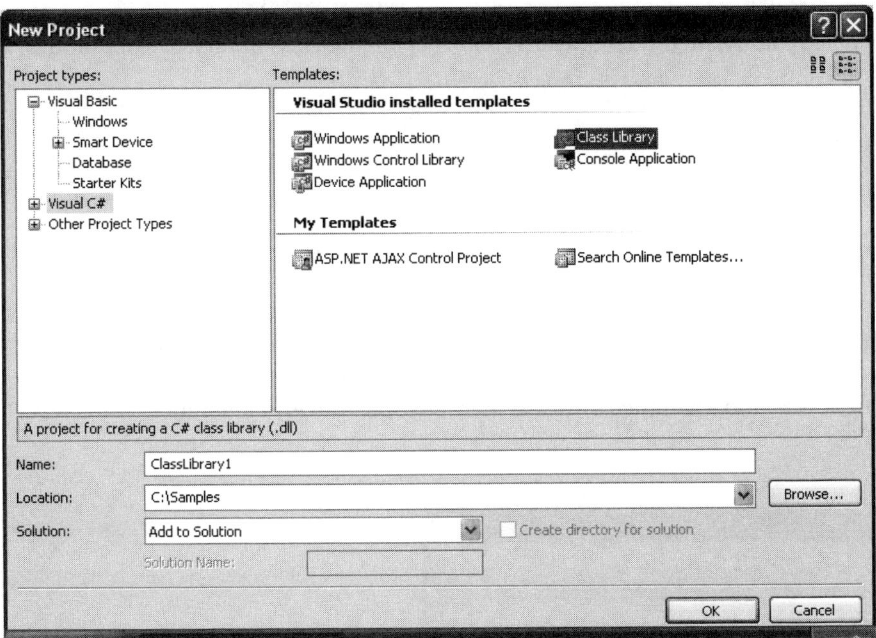

Figure 1-15. *Adding a Class Library project*

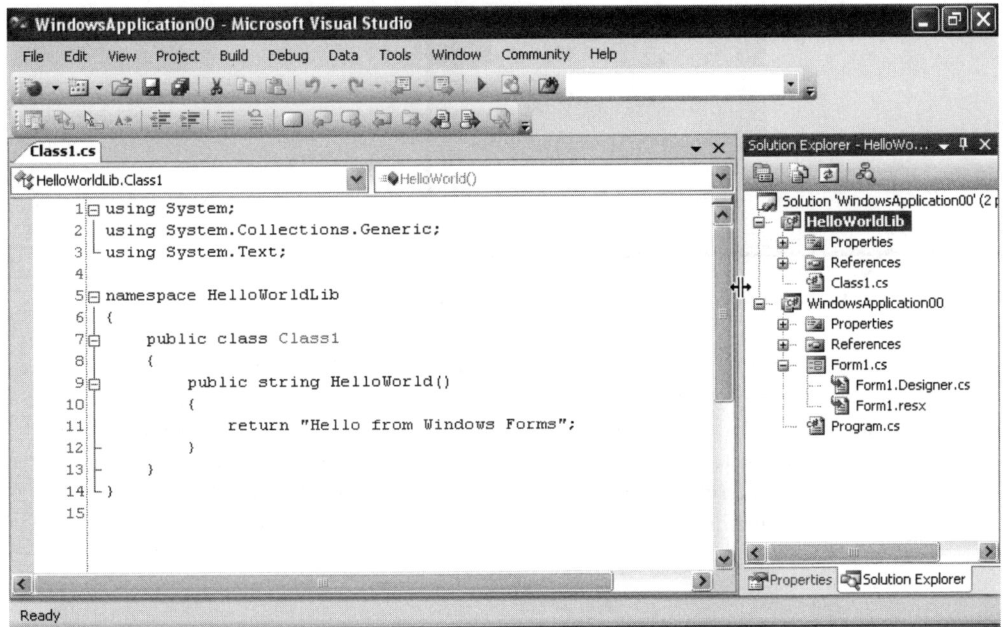

Figure 1-16. *The Visual Studio IDE after adding the Class Library project*

By default the class library contains one class. You can of course add more classes at a later stage if required. Now add a method named `HelloWorld()` in the class library. The method is shown in Listing 1-8.

Listing 1-8. *HelloWorld() Method*

```
public string HelloWorld()
{
            return "Hello from Windows Forms";
}
```

The method simply returns a string to the caller. Now compile the class library as outlined before. Our class library is now ready to be consumed in another application.

Choose Projects ➤ Add Reference from the menu to open the Add Reference dialog box (see Figure 1-17).

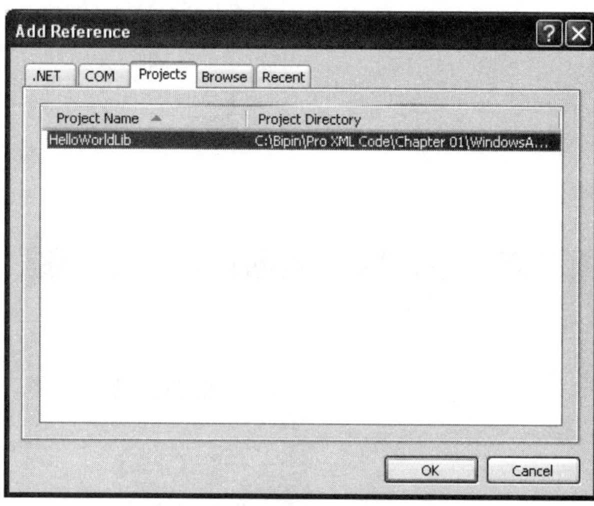

Figure 1-17. *Adding a reference through the Add Reference dialog box*

This dialog box contains several tabs. The .NET and COM tabs are used to add a reference to built-in .NET Framework assemblies and COM components, respectively. The Projects tab is used to add a reference to another project from the same solution. Finally, the Browse tab can be used to add a reference to assemblies located somewhere on your machine. In our example, you need to add a reference to the `HelloWorldLib` assembly from the Projects tab.

Now change the code of the Windows application, as shown in Listing 1-9.

Listing 1-9. *Modified Code of the Windows Application*

```
using System;
using System.Windows.Forms;
using HelloWorldLib;

namespace HelloWindowsWorld
{
    public partial class Form1 : Form
    {
        public Form1()
        {
            InitializeComponent();
        }

        private void button1_Click(object sender, EventArgs e)
        {
            Class1 obj = new Class1();
            MessageBox.Show(obj.HelloWorld());
        }
    }
}
```

Notice the code marked in bold. The code imports the `HelloWorldLib` namespace with the help of a `using` statement. In the `Click` event handler, an object of `Class1` from the `HelloWorldLib` project is created. `HelloWorld()` is then called on the instance and supplied to the `Show()` method of the `MessageBox` class.

If you run the application after modifying the code as shown in Listing 1-9, you should get the same result as before.

■ **Note** You will learn more about website and web service types of projects in Chapters 9 and 11.

Summary

XML is a de facto standard for representing, exchanging, and transporting data across heterogonous systems. All the members of the XML family of technologies (XML, XML Schema, XPath, XSL, and XSLT) are industry standards and hence enjoy massive support from all the leading vendors. Developing cross-platform applications becomes easy with the help of such standards.

Microsoft has harnessed the full potential of XML while developing the .NET Framework. The System.Xml namespaces and several sub-namespaces provide dozens of classes that allow you to read, write, and modify XML documents. The configuration files of .NET applications exclusively make use of XML markup. Distributed technologies such as remoting and web services also use XML heavily. The C# and VB.NET languages support XML commenting, which you can use to generate XML documentation for your applications. The .NET Framework also allows you to leverage XML-related features of SQL Server 2005 by exposing managed components such as SQLXML.

CHAPTER 2

■ ■ ■

Manipulating XML Documents by Using the Document Object Model

Chapter 1 discussed two flavors of parsers—tree-based parsers and event-based parsers. You also learned that the Document Object Model (DOM) is a set of APIs for manipulating XML documents. This chapter covers the following topics:

- `System.Xml` namespace classes related to DOM
- Knowing when to use DOM
- Reading an XML document by using DOM
- Writing XML documents by using DOM
- Creating a customized DOM-based parser by extending what is offered by .NET

Using the DOM Parser

The `System.Xml` namespace provides a set of classes that together allow DOM manipulation of an XML document. At the heart of DOM manipulation in .NET lies a class called `XmlDocument`. This class is the DOM parser of the .NET Framework. Just like any other DOM parser, `XmlDocument` looks at your XML file as a tree. It loads the XML document and builds its tree representation (consisting of elements, attributes, comments, and so on) in memory.

For example, consider Listing 2-1.

Listing 2-1. *Parts of a Typical XML Document*

```
<?xml version="1.0"?>
<customers>
   <customer CustomerID="C001">
      <name>Acme Inc.</name>
      <phone>12345</phone>
      <comments>Regular customer since 1995</comments>
   </customer>
   <customer CustomerID="C002">
      <name>Star Wars Inc.</name>
      <phone>23456</phone>
      <comments>A small but healthy company.</comments>
   </customer>
</customers>
```

The preceding XML document consists of the parts listed in Table 2-1.

Table 2-1. *Parts of the XML Document*

Part Name	Type of Part
`<?xml ...?>`	Processing instruction
`customers`	Document element or root node
`customer`	Element
`CustomerID`	Attribute of the `<customer>` element
`name`	Child element of the `<customer>` element
`phone`	Child element of the `<customer>` element
`comments`	Child element of the `<customer>` element

In addition to what is shown in the preceding table, the <name>, <phone>, and <comment> elements contain text values that are called text nodes.

The preceding document is loaded in memory by the DOM parser as a tree and resembles Figure 2-1.

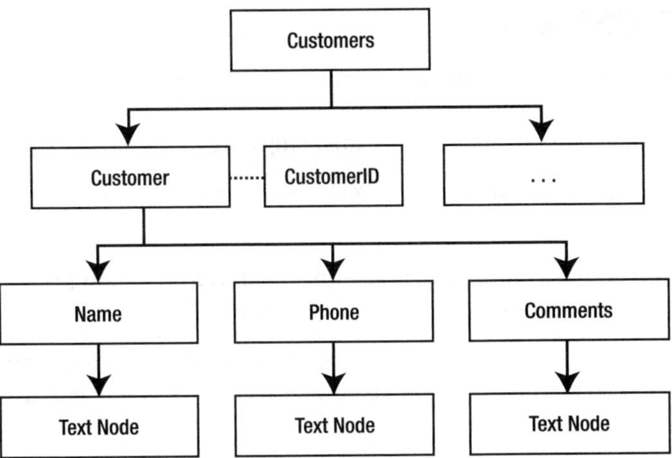

Figure 2-1. *Tree representation of an XML document*

Each part of the preceding diagram is actually a node. In .NET a node is represented by an abstract class called `XmlNode`. Even text values and attributes are nodes. They are of course handled differently from the other nodes.

Each of the parts mentioned in Table 2-1 is represented by a class, each of which is described in Table 2-2.

Table 2-2. *XML DOM Classes*

Part of XML Document	Class Representing the Part
Document element	`XmlElement`
Processing instructions	`XmlProcessingInstruction`
Element	`XmlElement`
Attribute	`XmlAttribute`
Text values	`XmlText`
Nodes	`XmlNode`

All of the classes in Table 2-2 inherit directly or indirectly from an abstract base class `XmlNode`. While using the `XmlDocument` class, you will often use one or another of the classes from Table 2-2.

Knowing When to Use DOM

Before you go ahead and use DOM for accessing your XML documents, you should understand the areas to which DOM is best suited and areas where its use should be avoided.

The decision of whether to use DOM is governed by the following core factors:

Read/write access: DOM allows you to read and write the XML document. But do you really need to change the underlying document?

Memory footprint: DOM loads the entire document in memory. Naturally the memory footprint of DOM is larger. Are your documents large, say over 100MB?

Type of access: DOM allows you to access any node randomly. This is possible because the entire document tree is available in memory. Do you need such access? Or is sequential access sufficient?

Answers to the preceding questions will help you to decide whether to use DOM. To summarize, DOM is best suited in the following scenarios:

- You want to modify the XML documents, that is, read-only access is not sufficient.
- You want to access various nodes randomly, that is, sequential access is not sufficient.
- You want to process documents that are small in size.
- The memory footprint is not a constraint.

A Sample XML Document

Throughout this chapter, we will be using an XML document that resides on the disk as a file named `Employees.xml`. The `Employees.xml` file is shown in Listing 2-2.

Listing 2-2. *A Sample XML Document*

```
<?xml version="1.0" encoding="utf-8" ?>
<!-- This is list of employees -->
<employees>
  <employee employeeid="1">
    <firstname>Nancy</firstname>
    <lastname>Davolio</lastname>
    <homephone>(206) 555-9857</homephone>
    <notes>
      <![CDATA[includes a BA in psychology from Colorado State University in
      1970. She also completed "The Art of the Cold Call." Nancy is a member of
      Toastmasters International.]]>
  </notes>
  </employee>
```

```
  <employee employeeid="2">
    <firstname>Andrew</firstname>
    <lastname>Fuller</lastname>
    <homephone>(206) 555-9482</homephone>
    <notes>
      <![CDATA[Andrew received his BTS commercial in 1974 and a Ph.D. in
      international marketing from the University of Dallas in 1981.  He is fluent
      in French and Italian and reads German. He joined the company as a sales
      representative, was promoted to sales manager in January 1992 and to vice
      president of sales in March 1993. Andrew is a member of the Sales
      Management Roundtable, the Seattle Chamber of Commerce, and the Pacific
      Rim Importers Association.]]>
    </notes>
  </employee>
  <employee employeeid="3">
    <firstname>Janet</firstname>
    <lastname>Leverling</lastname>
    <homephone>(206) 555-3412</homephone>
    <notes>
      <![CDATA[Janet has a BS degree in chemistry from Boston College (1984).
      She has also completed a certificate program in food retailing management.
      Janet was hired as a sales associate in 1991 and promoted to sales
      representative in February 1992.]]>
    </notes>
  </employee>
</employees>
```

This XML document represents a list of employees. The `<employees>` element forms the document element and contains three `<employee>` child elements. The `<employee>` element has an attribute called `employeeid` and four sub-elements: `<firstname>`, `<lastname>`, `<homephone>`, and `<notes>`. The `<notes>` element contains descriptive data that is stored as `CDATA`.

To create an XML file, you can enlist the help of the Visual Studio IDE, which enables you to quickly create XML documents by auto-completing end tags, putting attributes in quotes, and showing errors related to the document not being well formed. Because we will be using this file often, I recommend that you create it and keep it in a handy location on your hard disk.

Opening an Existing XML Document for Parsing

To open an existing XML document, you need to use the `XmlDocument` class. The `XmlDocument` class allows you to open XML documents in three common ways:

- You can specify the path to, or URL of, the XML file.
- You can use a stream object such as `FileStream` that contains the XML data.
- You can hold a string in memory that contains the XML data.

To see how each of the preceding approaches can be used, you need to develop a Windows application as shown in Figure 2-2.

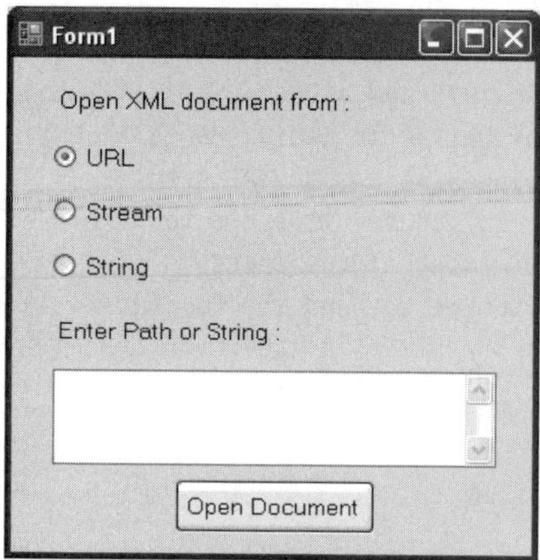

Figure 2-2. *Opening an XML document*

The application consists of three radio buttons for selecting the place from where the XML document is to be loaded. There is a text box for entering the file path, URL, or XML string. Finally, there is a button titled Open Document that opens the XML file depending on the selection and shows a message box with a success message.

Listing 2-3 shows the `Click` event handler of the button.

Listing 2-3. *Opening an XML Document*

```
private void button1_Click(object sender, EventArgs e)
{
try
{
  XmlDocument doc = new XmlDocument();
  if (radioButton1.Checked)
  {
    doc.Load(textBox1.Text);
  }
  if (radioButton2.Checked)
  {
    FileStream stream = new FileStream(textBox1.Text, FileMode.Open);
    doc.Load(stream);
    stream.Close();
  }
  if (radioButton3.Checked)
```

```
    {
      doc.LoadXml(textBox1.Text);
    }
    MessageBox.Show("XML Document Opened Successfully!");
  }
  catch(Exception ex)
  {
  MessageBox.Show(ex.Message);
  }
  }
```

The code creates an instance of the XmlDocument class. The XmlDocument class has two important methods: Load() and LoadXml(). The former method can take a file system path, URL, or stream object pointing to the XML document that you want to open. The latter method accepts a string containing the XML data to be loaded. Depending on the selection made by the user, either Load() or LoadXml() is called. Note that depending on the selection, your text box should contain a URL, a file system path, or raw XML data.

■ **Note** You must import the System.IO and System.Xml namespaces to successfully compile the code shown in Listing 2-3. This applies to most of the examples illustrated in this chapter.

You can run the application and supply the path of the Employees.xml file that we created earlier.

Navigating Through an XML Document

An XML document consists of one or more nodes, and nodes can be nested inside other nodes. Such nested nodes are called *child nodes*.

The XmlNode class has a collection called ChildNodes that contains a list of child nodes of the node under consideration. Note that most of the other DOM-related classes are inherited directly or indirectly from the XmlNode class and hence the ChildNodes collection is also available to them. Further, the XmlNode class has properties such as ParentNode, FirstChild, LastChild, NextSibling, and PreviousSibling that allow you to navigate to the corresponding node. Thus the ParentNode property will allow you to access the parent node of the current node, and the NextSibling property will allow you to access the next node at the same level as that of the current node.

To see how many of these properties can be used, we will develop a Windows application. The application navigates through the Employees.xml file and displays a TreeView control with various nodes nested as per the document structure.

The application is shown in Figure 2-3.

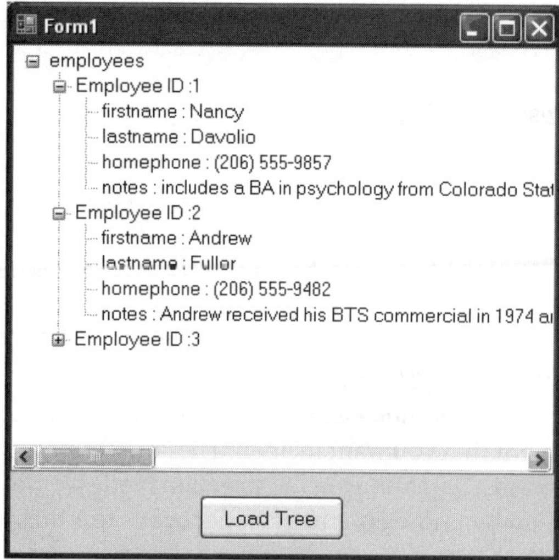

Figure 2-3. *Navigating through an XML document by using DOM*

The application consists of a TreeView control and a button titled Load Tree. After you click the button, the application loads the `Employees.xml` file by using the `XmlDocument` class. It then iterates through all the child nodes and reads the values of the attributes and nodes. The XML nodes are then added to the TreeView as TreeNodes.

Listing 2-4 shows the `Click` event handler of the Load Tree button.

Listing 2-4. *Loading the Tree*

```
private void button1_Click(object sender, EventArgs e)
{
  XmlDocument doc = new XmlDocument();
  doc.Load(Application.StartupPath + "/employees.xml");
  TreeNode root = new TreeNode(doc.DocumentElement.Name);
  treeView1.Nodes.Add(root);
  foreach (XmlNode node in doc.DocumentElement.ChildNodes)
  {
    TreeNode employee = new TreeNode("Employee ID :" +
      node.Attributes["employeeid"].Value);
    root.Nodes.Add(employee);
    if (node.HasChildNodes)
    {
      foreach (XmlNode childnode in node.ChildNodes)
```

```
            {
              TreeNode n2 = new TreeNode(childnode.Name + " : "+ childnode.InnerText);
              employee.Nodes.Add(n2);
            }
          }
        }
      }
```

The code creates an instance of the XmlDocument class and loads the Employees.xml file by using its Load() method. Then the code adds the root node of the TreeView. The XML document root node is <employees> and can be accessed by using the DocumentElement property of the XmlDocument class. The DocumentElement property is of type XmlElement. It has a property called Name that returns the name of the element (employees, in our case).

The <employees> node contains three <employee> child nodes, which can be accessed by using the ChildNodes property of the DocumentElement. A foreach loop then iterates through them. With each iteration, a new TreeNode is added to the TreeView with the employee ID as the text. To access the employeeid attribute, we use the Attributes collection of the XmlNode class. You can specify either an attribute's index or name to retrieve its value.

The code then checks whether the <employee> nodes have further child nodes by using a Boolean property of the XmlNode class called HasChildNodes. If this property returns true, another foreach loop iterates through the child nodes of the <employee> node. With each iteration, a new TreeNode is added with text equal to the name of the child node and its value. To retrieve the data inside nodes such as <firstname>, <lastname>, and so on, the code uses the InnerText() method of the XmlNode class. The InnerText() method returns concatenated values of the node and all its child nodes.

Looking for Specific Elements and Nodes

Often we are not interested in the entire XML document loaded in memory but a part of it. This requires us to search for a specific element or node for further processing. There are several methods used to search the XML document:

- Retrieving specific elements by using the GetElementByTagName() method
- Retrieving specific elements by using the GetElementById() method
- Selecting specific nodes by using the SelectNodes() method
- Selecting a single specific node by using the SelectSingleNode() method

Retrieving Specific Elements by Using the GetElementByTagName() Method

The `GetElementsByTagName()` method of the `XmlDocument` class accepts the name of the tag (excluding < and >) and returns all the nodes matching that tag name. The matching nodes are returned as an `XmlNodeList`. The `XmlNodeList` class represents a collection of `XmlNode` objects.

To see `GetElementsByTagName()` in action, we need to develop a Windows application as shown in Figure 2-4.

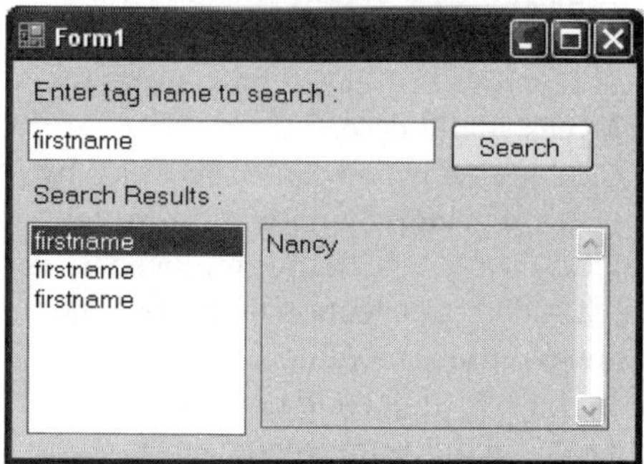

Figure 2-4. *Using the GetElementsByTagName() method*

The application consists of a text box to enter the tag name to look for. After you click the Search button, the matching tags are displayed in the list box. Selecting a tag from the list box displays its contents in a read-only text box.

The code that makes the preceding form work is given in Listing 2-5.

Listing 2-5. *Using the GetElementsByTagName() Method*

```
XmlNodeList list = null;

private void button1_Click(object sender, EventArgs e)
{
  XmlDocument doc = new XmlDocument();
  doc.Load(Application.StartupPath + "/employees.xml");
  list = doc.GetElementsByTagName(textBox1.Text);
  listBox1.Items.Clear();
  foreach (XmlNode node in list)
  {
    listBox1.Items.Add(node.Name);
  }
}
```

```
private void listBox1_SelectedIndexChanged(object sender, EventArgs e)
{
  textBox2.Text = list[listBox1.SelectedIndex].InnerXml;
}
```

The code declares a variable of type XmlNodeList at the form level. This variable needs to be declared at the form level because we need to access it in two event handlers.

In the Click event handler of the Search button, an XmlDocument instance is created. The Employees.xml file is loaded into it by using its Load() method. The code then calls the GetElementByTagName() method of the XmlDocument object, which accepts the tag name to look for. In our application, the tag is specified in textBox1. As mentioned earlier, the return value of the GetElementByTagName() method is of type XmlNodeList. The XmlNodeList class stores the collection of XmlNode objects. The code then iterates through the returned XmlNodeList and adds each node name into the list box.

The user can select any of the nodes displayed in the list box. In order to show the contents of the selected node, the code handles the SelectedIndexChanged event of the list box. Inside the SelectedIndexChanged event handler, the selected node is retrieved from the XmlNodeList we stored previously. The contents of the selected node are displayed by using the InnerXml property of the XmlNode class, which returns all the XML content that is inside the node under consideration.

To see how the application works, run it from the Visual Studio IDE. Enter **firstname** in the search text box and click the Search button. The list box should display three firstname entries. This is expected because our XML document contains three <employee> nodes, each having a <firstname> child element of its own. Click on any of the firstname entries from the list box. The text box beside the list box should show the value of the firstname node.

Retrieving Specific Elements by Using the GetElementById() Method

Often our XML elements have an attribute that is unique for each instance of that element in the XML document. We may want to look for a specific element based on this attribute value. This process is analogous to looking for a record in a database based on its primary key. The difference, however, is that the XmlDocument class does not know automatically that a specific attribute is acting as a primary key for that element. Formally such an attribute is called the *ID* of that element.

To convey this information, you must use a DTD or schema. Both of these techniques can mark an attribute as the ID of the element, and the XmlDocument class can then understand them as IDs. After you have a DTD or schema attached to your XML document, you can call the GetElementById() method of the XmlDocument class. The GetElementById() method accepts the ID of the element to search for and returns that element as an instance of the XmlElement class. You can then access the sub-elements or text inside this element.

To illustrate the use of the GetElementById() method, we will build an application as shown in Figure 2-5.

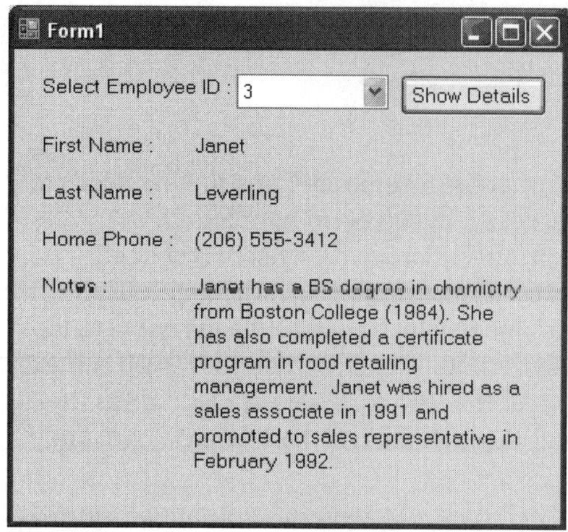

Figure 2-5. *Using the GetElementByID() method*

The application consists of a combo box showing a list of employee IDs. After you select an ID and click the Show Details button, the details such as `firstname`, `lastname`, `homephone`, and `notes` are displayed below.

Before you proceed with the application development, you must modify the `Employees.xml` file as shown in Listing 2-6.

Listing 2-6. *XML File with DTD*

```
<?xml version="1.0" encoding="utf-8" standalone="yes" ?>
<!-- This is list of employees -->
<!DOCTYPE employees [
  <!ELEMENT employees ANY>
  <!ELEMENT employee ANY>
  <!ELEMENT firstname ANY>
  <!ELEMENT lastname ANY>
  <!ELEMENT homephone ANY>
  <!ELEMENT notes ANY>
  <!ATTLIST employee employeeid ID #REQUIRED>
]>
```

```
<employees>
  <employee employeeid="1">
    <firstname>Nancy</firstname>
    <lastname>Davolio</lastname>
    <homephone>(206) 555-9857</homephone>
    <notes>
       <![CDATA[includes a BA in psychology from Colorado State University in
       1970. She also completed "The Art of the Cold Call." Nancy is a member of
       Toastmasters International.]]>
  </notes>
  </employee>
  <employee employeeid="2">
    <firstname>Andrew</firstname>
    <lastname>Fuller</lastname>
    <homephone>(206) 555-9482</homephone>
    <notes>
       <![CDATA[Andrew received his BTS commercial in 1974 and a Ph.D.
       in international marketing from the University of Dallas in 1981.
       He is fluent in French and Italian and reads German. He joined the company
       as a sales representative, was promoted to sales manager in January 1992
       and to vice president of sales in March 1993. Andrew is a member of the
       Sales Management Roundtable, the Seattle Chamber of Commerce,
       and the Pacific Rim Importers Association.]]>
    </notes>
  </employee>
  <employee employeeid="3">
    <firstname>Janet</firstname>
    <lastname>Leverling</lastname>
    <homephone>(206) 555-3412</homephone>
    <notes>
       <![CDATA[Janet has a BS degree in chemistry from Boston College (1984).
        She has also completed a certificate program in food retailing management.
       Janet was hired as a sales associate in 1991 and promoted to sales
       representative in February 1992.]]>
    </notes>
  </employee>
</employees>
```

The document looks almost identical to the original. However, an important piece is added at the top (see the markup shown in bold). We have added a DTD for our document. I will not go into the details of the DTD here, but suffice it to say that the ATTLIST section defines an attribute called employeeid for the <employee> element. More important, the employeeid attribute is marked as the ID and is also a REQUIRED attribute. This is how the XmlDocument class knows which attribute of an element is acting as an ID.

If you look at the source code of the application, you will see a form-level variable of type XmlDocument called doc:

```
XmlDocument doc = new XmlDocument();
```

The Load event handler of the form bears the code shown in Listing 2-7.

Listing 2-7. *Populating the Combo Box*

```
private void Form1_Load(object sender, EventArgs e)
{
  doc.Load(Application.StartupPath + "/employees.xml");
  foreach (XmlNode node in doc.DocumentElement.ChildNodes)
  {
    string employeeid = node.Attributes["employeeid"].Value;
    comboBox1.Items.Add(employeeid);
  }
}
```

The code loads the new Employees.xml file in the XmlDocument instance we created earlier by using its Load() method. A foreach loop then iterates over all the <employee> nodes. With each iteration, the employeeid attribute of the <employee> node is retrieved by using the Attributes collection of the XmlNode class. The attribute value is added to the combo box.

When the user selects a particular ID, the details of that employee are displayed. This is accomplished in the Click event handler of the Show Details button. The code inside the Click event handler is shown in Listing 2-8.

Listing 2-8. *Calling the GetElementById() Method*

```
private void button1_Click(object sender, EventArgs e)
{
  XmlElement ele= doc.GetElementById(comboBox1.SelectedItem.ToString());
  label6.Text = ele.ChildNodes[0].InnerText;
  label7.Text = ele.ChildNodes[1].InnerText;
  label8.Text = ele.ChildNodes[2].InnerText;
  label9.Text = ele.ChildNodes[3].InnerText;
}
```

The code calls the `GetElementById()` method of the `XmlDocument` class and passes the employee ID to look for. The `GetElementById()` method returns the matching element as an object of type `XmlElement`. Because the `XmlElement` class inherits from the `XmlNode` class, the `ChildNodes` collection is available to the `XmlElement` class also. To retrieve the values of the `<firstname>`, `<lastname>`, `<homephone>`, and `<notes>` nodes, the `ChildNodes` collection is accessed by using the index of the corresponding element. Finally, the `InnerText` property of each `XmlNode` gives the text inside the appropriate node.

Selecting Specific Nodes by Using the SelectNodes() Method

In complex cases, you may want to search for a node matching a pattern. This is accomplished with the help of XPath. Though XPath is not the subject of this chapter, I will give you a glimpse of how it can be used. I will explain XPath fully in Chapter 4.

The `XmlDocument` class has a method called `SelectNodes()` that accepts the XPath criteria for filtering the available nodes. It returns an `XmlNodeList` containing the matching nodes.

To see how the `SelectNodes()` method works, we need to develop a Windows application as shown in Figure 2-6.

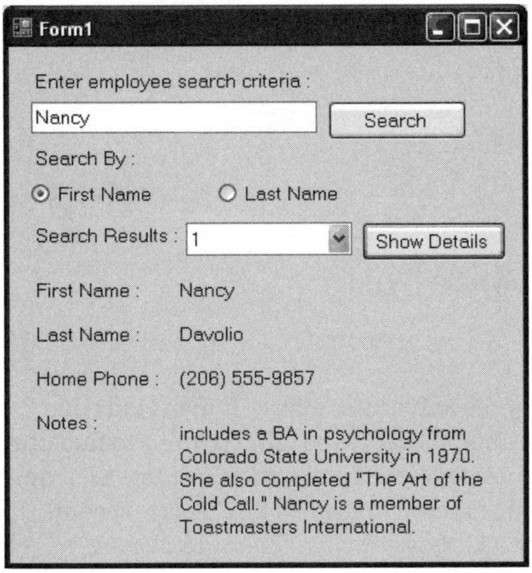

Figure 2-6. *Using the SelectNodes() method*

The application consists of a text box for entering the first name or last name of an employee. The radio buttons allow you to choose whether to look for matching first names or last names. Upon clicking the Search button, the `SelectNodes()` method is called. The returned `<employee>` nodes are collected in an `XmlNodeList`. The combo box displays the list of matching employee IDs. You can select an employee ID and click the Show Details button to display the employee details.

If you look at the source code of the application, you will find a declaration of a variable of type `XmlNodeList` at the form level:

```
XmlNodeList list = null;
```

We declare the variable at the form level because it is used in multiple event-handler functions.

The `Click` event handler of the Search button is shown in Listing 2-9.

Listing 2-9. *Using the SelectNodes() Method*

```
private void button1_Click(object sender, EventArgs e)
{
  XmlDocument doc = new XmlDocument();
  doc.Load(Application.StartupPath + "/employees.xml");
  if (radioButton1.Checked)
  {
    list = doc.SelectNodes(string.Format
   ("//employee[./firstname/text()='{0}']",textBox1.Text));
  }
  else
  {
    list = doc.SelectNodes(string.Format
   ("//employee[./lastname/text()='{0}']",textBox1.Text));
  }
  foreach (XmlNode node in list)
  {
    comboBox1.Items.Add(node.Attributes["employeeid"].Value);
  }
}
```

The preceding code first creates an instance of the `XmlDocument` class. It then loads the `Employees.xml` file by using the `Load()` method. Further, it checks the radio buttons to find out whether to search on the basis of first name or last name. We want to search `<employee>` nodes whose `<firstname>` or `<lastname>` matches the value entered in the text box. This is accomplished by calling the `SelectNodes()` method of the `XmlDocument` class. The `SelectNodes()` method takes the XPath string and returns an `XmlNodeList` containing the matching nodes. Look at the XPath syntax carefully. Because we want to select `<employee>` nodes, we specify `//employee`. But we are not interested in selecting all the `<employee>` nodes, so we place the filtering criterion in a pair of square brackets (`[]`). To represent the text value of the `<firstname>` and `<lastname>` nodes, we use the `text()` XPath function.

The code then iterates through the `XmlNodeList` and adds employee IDs to a combo box. The values of the `employeeid` attributes are retrieved by using the `Attributes` collection of the `XmlNode` class.

The user will select the employee ID whose details they want to see and will click the Show Details button. Listing 2-10 shows the code from the `Click` event handler of the Show Details button.

Listing 2-10. *Displaying Employee Details*

```
private void button2_Click(object sender, EventArgs e)
{
  label8.Text = list[comboBox1.SelectedIndex].ChildNodes[0].InnerText;
  label9.Text = list[comboBox1.SelectedIndex].ChildNodes[1].InnerText;
  label10.Text = list[comboBox1.SelectedIndex].ChildNodes[2].InnerText;
  label11.Text = list[comboBox1.SelectedIndex].ChildNodes[3].InnerText;
}
```

The code simply retrieves the desired `XmlNode` from the `XmlNodeList`. The child nodes of the node are accessed by using the `ChildNodes` collection. The `InnerText` property of the `XmlNode` class returns the text from each child node.

Selecting a Single Specific Node by Using the SelectSingleNode() Method

The `SelectSingleNode()` is very similar to the `SelectNodes()` method that we just learned, with one difference. Instead of returning a list of `XmlNode` objects in the form of an `XmlNodeList`, it simply returns the first matching `XmlNode`.

To test this method, you can modify the previous example as shown in Listing 2-11.

Listing 2-11. *Using the SelectSingleNode() Method*

```
XmlNode node = null;

private void button1_Click(object sender, EventArgs e)
{
  XmlDocument doc = new XmlDocument();
  doc.Load(Application.StartupPath + "/employees.xml");
  if (radioButton1.Checked)
  {
    node = doc.SelectSingleNode("//employee[./firstname/text()='" +
      textBox1.Text + "']");
  }
  else
  {
    node = doc.SelectSingleNode("//employee[./lastname/text()='" +
      textBox1.Text + "']");
  }
  if (node != null)
  {
    comboBox1.Items.Add(node.Attributes["employeeid"].Value);
  }
}
```

```
private void button2_Click(object sender, EventArgs e)
{
  label8.Text = node.ChildNodes[0].InnerText;
  label9.Text = node.ChildNodes[1].InnerText;
  label10.Text = node.ChildNodes[2].InnerText;
  label11.Text = node.ChildNodes[3].InnerText;
}
```

The code now declares a variable of type `XmlNode` at the form level. The `Click` event handler of the Search button calls the `SelectSingleNode()` method, which accepts the same XPath expression as in the previous example. This method returns the first matching node instead of an `XmlNodeList`, though our search criteria may not necessarily return any matching node. Therefore, the code accesses the `XmlNode` variable only if it is not null. In the `Click` event of the Show Details button, the `XmlNode` variable `node` is used to retrieve employee details.

Modifying XML Documents

Up until this point, we have seen how to read XML documents; how to navigate through them; and how to search them on the basis of tag names, IDs, and XPath expressions. But what about modifying them? That's the topic of this section.

Often business requirements call for modification of the underlying XML document. This modification can be an addition, a deletion, or a modification of nodes or attributes. As you saw previously, DOM is a read-write parser. That means DOM APIs also allow you to modify the document.

To illustrate the use of several `System.Xml` classes for modifying XML documents, we are going to develop a Windows application as shown in Figure 2-7.

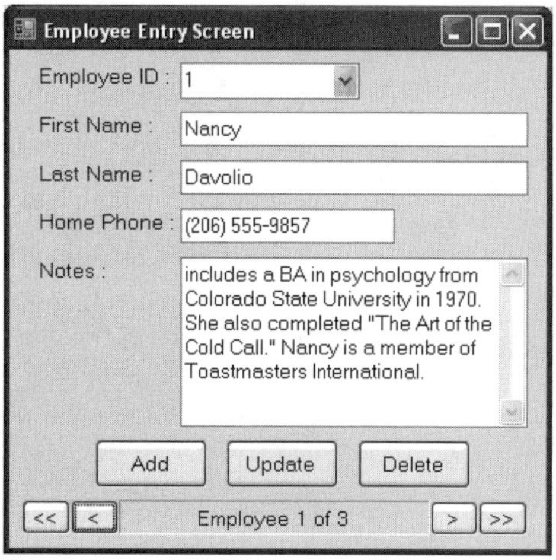

Employee Entry Screen

Employee ID : 1

First Name : Nancy

Last Name : Davolio

Home Phone : (206) 555-9857

Notes : includes a BA in psychology from Colorado State University in 1970. She also completed "The Art of the Cold Call." Nancy is a member of Toastmasters International.

Add | Update | Delete

<< < Employee 1 of 3 > >>

Figure 2-7. *Data entry screen for the Employees.xml file*

The application represents a complete data entry screen for the Employees.xml file. The application allows us to do the following tasks:

- Navigate among the available employees with the help of VCR buttons. (The buttons used to navigate to the previous, next, first, and last records are often called *VCR buttons*.)
- Add a new employee.
- Modify the details of a particular employee. The employee ID attribute acts like a primary key for our XML document and hence it cannot be changed.
- Delete an existing employee.

If you look at the source code of the preceding application, you will see two form-level variables as shown here:

```
XmlDocument doc = new XmlDocument();
int CurrentNodeIndex = 0;
```

The XmlDocument instance is used throughout the application. The integer variable CurrentNodeIndex is used to keep track of the current employee record that is being displayed (it is mainly used by the navigational buttons).

The Load event handler of the form is shown in Listing 2-12.

Listing 2-12. *Filling Controls*

```
private void Form1_Load(object sender, EventArgs e)
{
  doc.Load(Application.StartupPath + "/employees.xml");
  foreach (XmlNode node in doc.DocumentElement.ChildNodes)
  {
    comboBox1.Items.Add(node.Attributes["employeeid"].Value);
  }
  FillControls();
}
```

The preceding code loads the Employees.xml file by using the Load() method. It then iterates through all the <employee> nodes and fills the combo box with employee IDs. The employeeid attribute is retrieved by using the Attributes collection of the XmlNode class. Finally, the code calls a helper method called FillControls(). This method simply displays first name, last name, home phone, and notes from the current <employee> node in various text boxes. We will be looking at the FillControls() method shortly.

Navigating Between Various Nodes

The application allows you to navigate between various <employee> nodes with the help of VCR navigation buttons. Listing 2-13 shows how the navigation buttons work.

Listing 2-13. *Working of Navigation Buttons*

```
//go to first record
private void button4_Click(object sender, EventArgs e)
{
  CurrentNodeIndex = 0;
  FillControls();
}

//go to previous record
private void button5_Click(object sender, EventArgs e)
{
  CurrentNodeIndex--;
  if (CurrentNodeIndex < 0)
  {
    CurrentNodeIndex = 0;
  }
  FillControls();
}

//go to next record
private void button6_Click(object sender, EventArgs e)
{
  CurrentNodeIndex++;
  if (CurrentNodeIndex >= doc.DocumentElement.ChildNodes.Count)
  {
    CurrentNodeIndex = doc.DocumentElement.ChildNodes.Count-1;
  }
  FillControls();
}

//go to last record
private void button7_Click(object sender, EventArgs e)
{
  CurrentNodeIndex = doc.DocumentElement.ChildNodes.Count - 1;
  FillControls();
}
```

In the `Click` event of the First Record (<<) button, the code sets the `CurrentNodeIndex` variable to `0` and calls the `FillControls()` method. The `FillControls()` method then populates various controls based on the value of the `CurrentNodeIndex` variable.

The `Click` event handler of the Previous Record (<) button decrements the `CurrentNodeIndex` variable. If the value becomes less than 0, the event handler sets it to `0`. The `FillControls()` method is then called.

In the Click event handler of the Next Record (>) button, the code increments the CurrentNodeIndex variable. If the value goes beyond the total number of <employee> nodes, the event handler sets a new value of the total number of employee nodes minus 1. This is necessary because just like any other collection in .NET, the ChildNodes collection is zero based.

Finally, the Click event handler of the Last Record (>>) button sets the CurrentNodeIndex variable to the total number of employee nodes minus 1.

Now that you know how the navigation system of the application works, let's move on to the more interesting part—modifying, deleting, and adding XML content.

Modifying Existing Content

To modify an <employee> node, we first need to retrieve it from the list of <employee> nodes. The employee ID of the employee will be taken from the combo box. To retrieve the <employee> node, we can use the SelectNodes() or SelectSingleNode() method. In our example, because there can be only one <employee> node matching the given employee ID, SelectSingleNode() is a better choice. After a reference to the <employee> node is retrieved, we can change its child nodes. The complete code implementing this logic is given in Listing 2-14.

Listing 2-14. *Modifying Existing Content*

```
private void button2_Click(object sender, EventArgs e)
{
  XmlNode node=doc.SelectSingleNode("//employee[@employeeid='" +
    comboBox1.SelectedItem + "']");
  if (node != null)
  {
    node.ChildNodes[0].InnerText = textBox1.Text;
    node.ChildNodes[1].InnerText = textBox2.Text;
    node.ChildNodes[2].InnerText = textBox3.Text;
    XmlCDataSection notes = doc.CreateCDataSection(textBox4.Text);
    node.ChildNodes[3].ReplaceChild(notes, node.ChildNodes[3].ChildNodes[0]);
  }
  doc.Save(Application.StartupPath + "/employees.xml");
}
```

First, the code retrieves the <employee> node matching the selected employee ID by using the SelectSingleNode() method. Carefully note the XPath expression that is used. In XPath expressions, attributes are prefixed with the @ symbol. Thus @employeeid refers to the employeeid attribute of the <employee> node. The SelectSingleNode() method returns the selected node in the form of an XmlNode object. Before we proceed and change its contents, we need to ensure that the SelectSingleNode() has returned a node. This is done by checking whether the node returned is null or otherwise.

The XmlNode returned from the SelectSingleNode() method will be an <employee> node. That means it will have four child nodes: <firstname>, <lastname>, <homephone>, and <notes>. The InnerText property of these four child nodes is nothing but the text values of the corresponding node. Inside the if condition, the code sets the InnerText property of all four child nodes to the values from respective text boxes. There is one interesting thing to note here. The <notes> element contains free text that can feature special markup symbols such as <, >, and ". If we simply assign the InnerText property of the <notes> node to the new value, it can create problems when accessing the document later.

Remember that we have written the contents of the <notes> node as a CDATA section to avoid just such a problem, so we must write the new data as a CDATA section as well. The CDATA section is represented by a class called XmlCDataSection. The CreateCDataSection() method of the XmlDocument class creates a new CDATA section with the supplied text (the entire text supplied is placed within <![CDATA[...]]>). To change the content of an existing CDATA section, the code calls the ReplaceChild() method of the XmlNode class. The ReplaceChild() method accepts the new node and the old node as parameters. The old node is then replaced with the new node.

After you make any changes to an XML document, the entire document must be saved to disk in order to persist the changes. This is accomplished by using the Save() method of the XmlDocument class. The Save() method accepts the target path where you would like to save the file. In our example, because we want to overwrite the existing Employees.xml file with the modified version, we supply the same path as that of the original file.

Deleting Existing Content

Deleting an <employee> node requires finding it from the list of available employees based on the employee ID and then removing it from the document. The code that implements the delete feature is given in Listing 2-15.

Listing 2-15. *Deleting a Node*

```
private void button3_Click(object sender, EventArgs e)
{
  XmlNode node = doc.SelectSingleNode("//employee[@employeeid='" +
    comboBox1.SelectedItem + "']");
  if (node != null)
  {
    doc.DocumentElement.RemoveChild(node);
  }
  doc.Save(Application.StartupPath + "/employees.xml");
  UpdateLabel();
}
```

The code retrieves the node that we wish to delete by using the SelectSingleNode() method. To delete a node from the ChildNodes collection, the XmlNode class provides a method called RemoveChild(). The RemoveChild() method accepts a reference to the XmlNode that is to be removed from the ChildNodes collection. In our case, we wish to remove the entire <employee> node, which is a child node of the <employees> root element. Hence the code calls the RemoveChild() method on the DocumentElement, that is, the root node of the document.

After the node is deleted, the file is saved to disk by using the Save() method of the XmlDocument class. The UpdateLabel() helper method simply updates the current record number displayed on the status label.

Adding New Content

The code that adds a new employee is a bit lengthier than our previous examples. It is more interesting too. You will now learn how to create XML document contents from the ground up. Creating elements, attributes, text nodes, and CDATA sections will all be demystified in this section.

First of all, let's count the elements, attributes, and nodes that we need to create in order to add a new employee to our XML document. Here is a list of nodes that we need to add:

- An <employee> element
- A <firstname> element
- A <lastname> element
- A <homephone> element
- A <notes> element
- An employeeid attribute for the <employee> element
- A text node for the <firstname> value
- A text node for the <lastname> value
- A text node for the <homephone> value
- A CDATA section for the <notes> value

Note one important thing: the text that appears as the value of the <firstname>, <lastname>, <homephone>, and <notes> elements is also treated as a node.

The complete code that implements an employee addition is shown in Listing 2-16.

Listing 2-16. *Adding a New Node*

```
private void button1_Click(object sender, EventArgs e)
{
  XmlElement employee = doc.CreateElement("employee");
  XmlElement firstname = doc.CreateElement("firstname");
  XmlElement lastname = doc.CreateElement("lastname");
  XmlElement homephone = doc.CreateElement("homephone");
  XmlElement notes = doc.CreateElement("notes");

  XmlAttribute employeeid = doc.CreateAttribute("employeeid");
  employeeid.Value = comboBox1.Text;

  XmlText firstnametext = doc.CreateTextNode(textBox1.Text);
  XmlText lastnametext = doc.CreateTextNode(textBox2.Text);
  XmlText homephonetext = doc.CreateTextNode(textBox3.Text);
  XmlCDataSection notestext = doc.CreateCDataSection(textBox4.Text);

  employee.Attributes.Append(employeeid);
  employee.AppendChild(firstname);
  employee.AppendChild(lastname);
  employee.AppendChild(homephone);
  employee.AppendChild(notes);

  firstname.AppendChild(firstnametext);
  lastname.AppendChild(lastnametext);
  homephone.AppendChild(homephonetext);
  notes.AppendChild(notestext);

  doc.DocumentElement.AppendChild(employee);
  doc.Save(Application.StartupPath + "/employees.xml");

  UpdateLabel();
}
```

The code creates five elements by using the `CreateElement()` method of the `XmlDocument` class. These five elements are `<employee>`, `<firstname>`, `<lastname>`, `<homephone>`, and `<notes>`. The `CreateElement()` method accepts the tag name of the element and returns an object of type `XmlElement`. Note that `XmlElement` inherits from the `XmlNode` class.

An attribute is represented by the `XmlAttribute` class and is created by using the `CreateAttribute()` method of the `XmlDocument` class. The `CreateAttribute()` method accepts the attribute name as a parameter, in this case `employeeid`. The value of the attribute can be assigned by setting the `Value` property of the `XmlAttribute` class.

The code proceeds to create three text nodes that represent the values of the `<firstname>`, `<lastname>`, and `<homephone>` elements, respectively. Text nodes are represented by a class called `XmlText`. To create these text nodes, the code uses the `CreateTextNode()` method of the `XmlDocument` class. The `CreateTextNode()` method accepts the value of the text node as a parameter.

As I said earlier, the <notes> element contains character data (CDATA), and a CDATA section is represented by a class called XmlCDataSection. As we did before, we create the CDATA section by using the CreateCDataSection() method of the XmlDocument class.

This completes the element, attribute, and node creation. The code then proceeds to nest various elements as per the required XML structure.

All the attributes of an XmlNode are stored in its Attributes collection. To add the employeeid attribute to the <employee> element, the Append() method of Attributes collection is used. The Append() method accepts an instance of the XmlAttribute class.

The AppendChild() method of the XmlNode class accepts another XmlNode and makes it a child of the node on which AppendChild() has been called. The code calls the AppendChild() method on the <employee> element and adds all the remaining four elements as its children.

Next, the code adds all the text nodes and CDATA section to their respective parents by using the same AppendChild() method.

Finally, the entire <employee> node is appended to the DocumentElement, that is, the <employees> root node. Because we have added a brand new node to the document, the Save() method is needed to save the changed document to disk.

Using Helper Methods

In the preceding code, we frequently used two helper methods: FillControls() and UpdateLabel(). These methods are shown in Listing 2-17.

Listing 2-17. *Helper Methods Used in the Application*

```
private void FillControls()
{
  XmlNode node = doc.DocumentElement.ChildNodes[CurrentNodeIndex];
  comboBox1.Text = node.Attributes["employeeid"].Value;
  textBox1.Text = node.ChildNodes[0].InnerText;
  textBox2.Text = node.ChildNodes[1].InnerText;
  textBox3.Text = node.ChildNodes[2].InnerText;
  textBox4.Text = node.ChildNodes[3].InnerText;
  UpdateLabel();
}

private void UpdateLabel()
{
  label6.Text = "Employee " + (CurrentNodeIndex + 1) + " of " +
    doc.DocumentElement.ChildNodes.Count;
}
```

The FillControls() method retrieves a reference to the <employee> node to be displayed. The index for this node is indicated by the CurrentNodeIndex variable. The employeeid is retrieved from the Attributes collection of the node and displayed in the combo box. Other text boxes are populated with the InnerText of <firstname>, <lastname>, <homephone>, and <notes>, respectively.

The UpdateLabel() method simply sets the Text property of the navigation status label to the current employee index.

Dealing with White Space

You have learned how to read and write XML documents by using `XmlDocument` and associated classes. During various operations, we hardly bothered with white space. *White space* includes characters such as space, tab, carriage return, and so on. By default when you load the document (either via the `Load()` method or the `LoadXml()` method) or save the document (by using the `Save()` method), the `XmlDocument` class will ignore white space. You can toggle this behavior by using a Boolean property called `PreserveWhitespace`. Setting this property to `true` will preserve the white space, whereas setting it to `false` will ignore it.

To see what difference the `PreserveWhitespace` property makes, let's create a simple application as shown in Figure 2-8.

Figure 2-8. *Importance of the PreserveWhiteSpace property*

The application consists of a check box that allows you to toggle whether to preserve white space. When you click the Load Document button, it simply loads the `Employees.xml` file by using the `Load()` method and displays the entire content in a message box.

The code inside the `Click` event handler of the Load Document button is given in Listing 2-18.

Listing 2-18. *Loading a Document*

```
private void button1_Click(object sender, EventArgs e)
{
  XmlDocument doc = new XmlDocument();
  doc.PreserveWhitespace = checkBox1.Checked;
  doc.Load(Application.StartupPath + @"\employees.xml");
  MessageBox.Show(doc.InnerXml);
}
```

The code creates an instance of the `XmlDocument` class and sets its `PreserveWhitespace` property to the property selected via the check box. That means if the user selects the check box, `true` will be assigned; otherwise, `false` will be assigned. Then the `Employees.xml` file is loaded by using the `Load()` method. The complete content of the file is retrieved by using the `InnerXml` property of the `XmlDocument` instance and displayed in a message box.

Figure 2-9 shows the message box that is displayed when you deselect the check box. In contrast, Figure 2-10 shows the message box when the check box is selected.

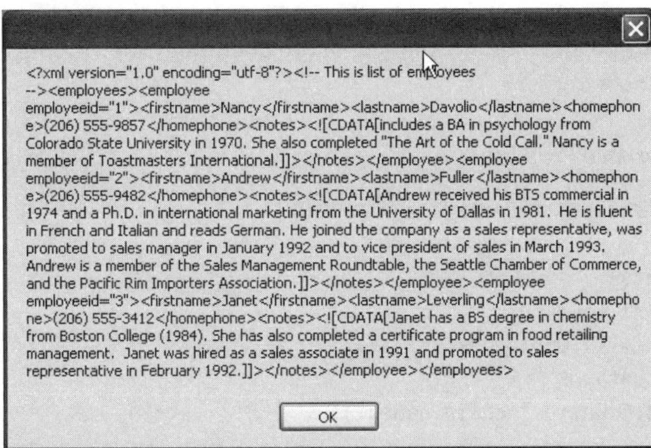

Figure 2-9. *Output with the PreserveWhitespace property set to false*

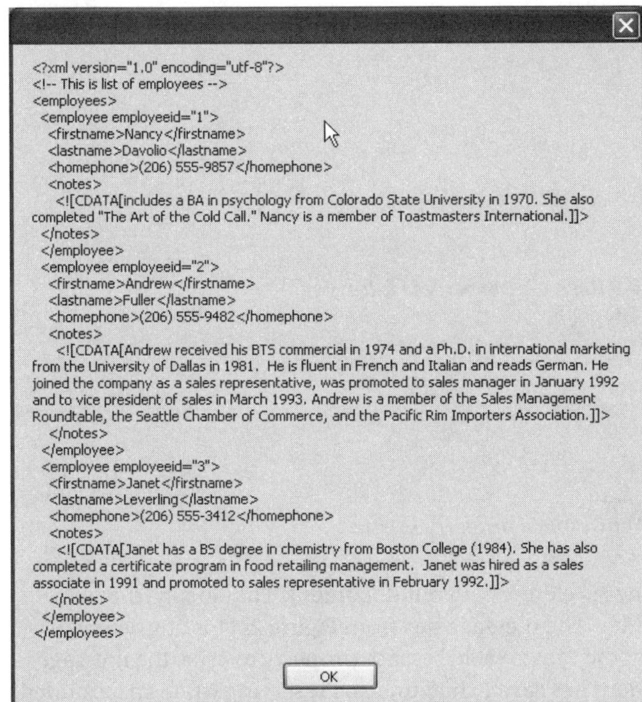

Figure 2-10. *Output with the PreserveWhitespace property set to true*

You can see the difference: the second message box shows that the white space is preserved.

Does the PreserveWhitespace property affect your parsing logic? The answer to this question is yes. To illustrate the effect of this property on the parsing of the document, let's modify the preceding application as shown in Listing 2-19.

Listing 2-19. *Effect of the PreserveWhitespace Property*

```
private void button1_Click(object sender, EventArgs e)
{
  XmlDocument doc = new XmlDocument();
  doc.PreserveWhitespace = checkBox1.Checked;
  doc.Load(Application.StartupPath + @"\employees.xml");
  MessageBox.Show("Employee node contains " +
    doc.DocumentElement.ChildNodes.Count + " child nodes");
}
```

The preceding code is almost identical to the previous example, but this time the message box shows the total number of child nodes of the document element, that is, the root node <employees>. See Figures 2-11 and 2-12 for the resulting message boxes with the PreserveWhitespace property set to false and true, respectively.

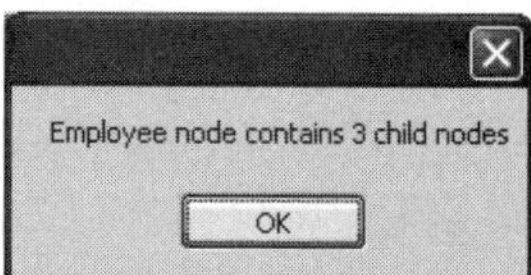

Figure 2-11. *Result when the PreserveWhitespace property is false*

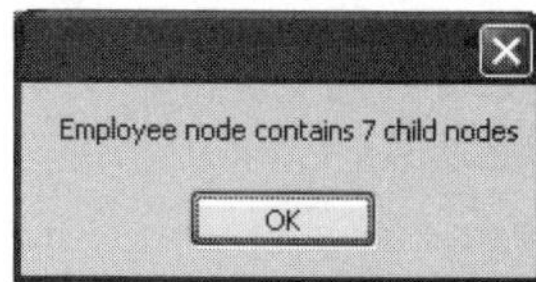

Figure 2-12. *Result when the PreserveWhitespace property is true*

Surprised? We have three <employee> elements in our document. That means the <employees> node has three child nodes. The message box from Figure 2-11 is consistent with this fact. However, when you set the PreserveWhitespace property to true, the message box shows that the <employees> element has seven child nodes. Preserving white space added four child nodes to the <employees> element. These extra nodes are of type XmlWhiteSpace. If you are accessing various nodes by their indexes, toggling white space can cause your logic to fail. There is one more class related to white space: `XmlSignificantWhitespace`. The `XmlSignificantWhitespace` class represents white space between markup in a mixed content node.

It is important to understand the difference between `XmlWhiteSpace` and `XmlSignificantWhitespace`. Consider the markup shown in Listing 2-20.

Listing 2-20. *Understanding the Difference Between the XmlWhiteSpace and XmlSignificantWhiteSpace Classes*

```
<?xml version="1.0" ?>
<root>
  <fullname>Nancy Davolio</fullname>
  <address>
    23143 Sagebrush
    Novi,
    MI 48375
    USA
  </address>
</root>
```

In the markup shown in Listing 2-20, there are several white spaces. First, there are white spaces between tags such as `<root>`, `<fullname>`, and `<address>`. Remember that in XML, carriage returns and line feeds are also considered white spaces. These white spaces between various elements are used mainly to improve readability of the document and are represented by the `XmlWhiteSpace` class. Second, there are white spaces embedded within the content of the `<address>` node. For example, there is a carriage return and line feed after the text `Novi` as well as `MI 48375`. These white spaces are represented by the `XmlSignificantWhiteSpace` class.

Dealing with Namespaces

The concept of XML namespaces is analogous to .NET namespaces. XML namespaces allow you to identify elements as part of a single group (a namespace) by uniquely qualifying element and attribute names used in an XML document. Each namespace is identified by a Uniform Resource Identifier (URI). This allows developers to combine information from different data structures in a single XML document without causing ambiguity and confusion among element names.

For example, assume that you have two XML fragments, one related to employees and another related to customers. Further assume that both fragments contain a tag called `<name>`. The problem is that when you mix them together, you have ambiguity for the `<name>` tag. XML namespaces come in handy in such situations.

To see how .NET provides support for XML namespaces, we will modify `Employees.xml` as shown in Listing 2-21.

Listing 2-21. *XML Document with Namespaces*

```
<?xml version="1.0" encoding="utf-8" ?>
<!-- This is list of employees -->
<emp:employees xmlns:emp="http://www.somedomain.com">
  <emp:employee employeeid="1">
    <emp:firstname>Nancy</emp:firstname>
    <emp:lastname>Davolio</emp:lastname>
    <emp:homephone>(206) 555-9857</emp:homephone>
    <emp:notes>
      <![CDATA[includes a BA in psychology from Colorado State University in
      1970. She also completed "The Art of the Cold Call." Nancy is a member of
      Toastmasters International.]]>
    </emp:notes>
  </emp:employee>
  <emp:employee employeeid="2">
    <emp:firstname>Andrew</emp:firstname>
    <emp:lastname>Fuller</emp:lastname>
    <emp:homephone>(206) 555-9482</emp:homephone>
    <emp:notes>
      <![CDATA[Andrew received his BTS commercial in 1974 and a Ph.D.
      in international marketing from the University of Dallas in 1981.  He is
      fluent in French and Italian and reads German. He joined the company as
      a sales representative, was promoted to sales manager in January 1992 and
      to vice president of sales in March 1993. Andrew is a member of the Sales
      Management Roundtable, the Seattle Chamber of Commerce, and the
      Pacific Rim Importers Association.]]>
    </emp:notes>
  </emp:employee>
  <emp:employee employeeid="3">
    <emp:firstname>Janet</emp:firstname>
    <emp:lastname>Leverling</emp:lastname>
    <emp:homephone>(206) 555-3412</emp:homephone>
    <emp:notes>
      <![CDATA[Janet has a BS degree in chemistry from Boston College (1984).
      She has also completed a certificate program in food retailing management.
      Janet was hired as a sales associate in 1991 and promoted to sales
      representative in February 1992.]]>
    </emp:notes>
  </emp:employee>
</emp:employees>
```

It's the same document, but we have added a namespace to it. Look at the markup shown in bold. In the root element `<employees>`, we specified an XML namespace called `emp` with a URI `http://www.somedomain.com`. Though it is a common practice to use URLs as namespace URIs, any unique string would work. Note how all the tag names are prefixed with `emp`. You can access namespace details by using three properties of the `XmlNode` class: `NamespaceURI`, `Prefix`, and `LocalName`.

To illustrate how these properties are used, we will develop an application as shown in Figure 2-13.

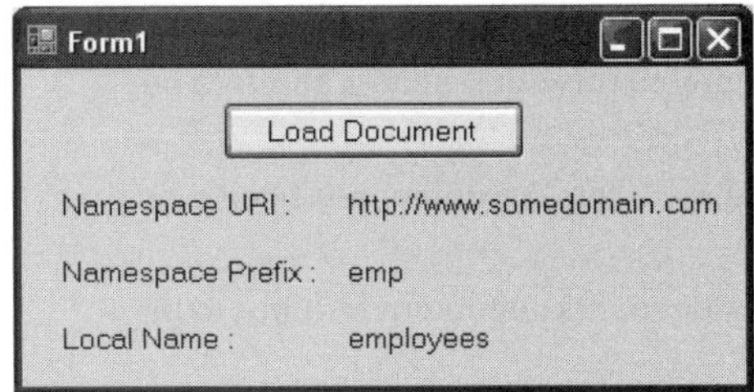

Figure 2-13. *Retrieving namespace details*

The application loads our new version of `Employees.xml` and extracts the `NamespaceURI`, `Prefix`, and `LocalName` properties of the document element. The namespace details are shown in labels. Listing 2-22 shows the `Click` event handler of the Load Document button.

Listing 2-22. *Retrieving Namespace Details*

```
private void button1_Click(object sender, EventArgs e)
{
  XmlDocument doc = new XmlDocument();
  doc.Load(Application.StartupPath + @"\employees.xml");
  label4.Text = doc.DocumentElement.NamespaceURI;
  label5.Text = doc.DocumentElement.Prefix;
  label6.Text = doc.DocumentElement.LocalName;
}
```

The code loads the `Employees.xml` file by using the `Load()` method. It then simply retrieves the value of the `NamespaceURI`, `Prefix`, and `LocalName` properties. One thing to note is that these three properties are read-only properties. If you want to write these details, you must supply them while creating attributes, elements, and nodes from the `XmlDocument` class. Methods of the `XmlDocument` class such as `CreateElement()` and `CreateAttribute()` have appropriate overloads that allow you to specify namespace details.

Understanding Events of the XmlDocument Class

Whenever you modify an XML document, the `XmlDocument` class raises several events. These events follow a pre and post pattern. Pre-events are raised prior to the actual operation, whereas post-events are raised after the operation is over. These events are summarized in Table 2-3.

Table 2-3. *Events of the XmlDocument Class*

Event Name	Description
`NodeChanging`	This event is raised when the value of a node belonging to this document is about to be changed.
`NodeChanged`	This event is raised when the value of a node belonging to this document has been changed.
`NodeRemoving`	This event is raised when a node belonging to this document is about to be removed from the document.
`NodeRemoved`	This event is raised when a node belonging to this document has been removed from its parent.
`NodeInserting`	This event is raised when a node belonging to this document is about to be inserted into another node.
`NodeInserted`	This event is raised when a node belonging to this document has been inserted into another node.

Each of the events specified in the preceding table receives an event argument parameter of type `XmlNodeChangedEventArgs`. The `XmlNodeChangedEventArgs` class provides several properties. Some of them are listed in Table 2-4.

Table 2-4. *Properties of the XmlNodeChangedEventArgs Class*

Property	Description
`Action`	Supplies information about the action that is causing the node to change. This property is an enumeration of type `XmlNodeChangedAction`. Possible values include `Change`, `Remove`, and `Insert`.
`OldParent`	Returns the parent `XmlNode` of the node being changed prior to the operation.
`NewParent`	Returns the parent `XmlNode` of the node being changed after the operation.
`OldValue`	Returns the value of the node prior to the operation.
`NewValue`	Returns the value of the node after the operation is complete.
`Node`	Returns an `XmlNode` object representing the node being affected.

To see some of these events in action, we will modify the same employee data-entry application that we developed previously.

Modify the `Form_Load` event handler as shown in Listing 2-23.

Listing 2-23. *Attaching Event Handlers*

```
private void Form1_Load(object sender, EventArgs e)
{
  doc.Load(Application.StartupPath + "/employees.xml");

  doc.NodeChanged += new XmlNodeChangedEventHandler(doc_NodeChanged);
  doc.NodeInserted += new XmlNodeChangedEventHandler(doc_NodeInserted);
  doc.NodeRemoved += new XmlNodeChangedEventHandler(doc_NodeRemoved);

  foreach (XmlNode node in doc.DocumentElement.ChildNodes)
  {
    comboBox1.Items.Add(node.Attributes["employeeid"].Value);
  }
  FillControls();
}
```

Note the lines marked in bold. The code attaches event handlers to `NodeChanged`, `NodeRemoved`, and `NodeInserted` events, respectively. These events are of delegate type `XmlNodeChangedEventHandler`.

The code in Listing 2-24 shows these event handlers.

Listing 2-24. *Handling Events of the XmlDocument Class*

```
void doc_NodeRemoved(object sender, XmlNodeChangedEventArgs e)
{
  MessageBox.Show("Node " + e.Node.Name + " removed successfully!");
}

void doc_NodeInserted(object sender, XmlNodeChangedEventArgs e)
{
  MessageBox.Show("Node " + e.Node.Name + " added successfully!");
}

void doc_NodeChanged(object sender, XmlNodeChangedEventArgs e)
{
  MessageBox.Show("Node " + e.Node.Name + " changed successfully!");
}
```

The code in each event handler simply displays the node being affected in a message box. To test these events, you need to run the application and try updating, deleting, and adding new employees. You will find that with every such operation, the `NodeChanging`, `NodeRemoving`, and `NodeInserting` events are raised. Figure 2-14 shows a sample run of the application.

Figure 2-14. *Handling events of the XmlDocument class*

Summary

This chapter presented a detailed examination of the `XMLDocument` class—the .NET DOM parser. You worked with several other classes including `XmlNode`, `XmlElement`, `XmlAttribute`, and `XmlText`. You learned how to load XML documents, how to navigate through them, how to read the content, and finally how to modify them. You also learned how white space and namespaces can be dealt with. Finally, you handled various events of `XmlDocument` that are raised when you change the document in some way.

You can build on what you have learned so far. For example, you can create your own custom extensions of `XmlDocument` and other classes by inheriting from them. Though the need to do so is rare, this task can be accomplished by inheriting from these classes and adding extra properties and methods.

CHAPTER 3

Reading and Writing XML Documents

Chapter 2 gave you a detailed understanding of the .NET Framework's DOM parser, that is, the `XmlDocument` class. You also learned when to use DOM parsers. In this chapter, you are going to learn about XML reader and writer classes. The topics discussed include the following:

- Using reader and writer classes
- Knowing when to use these classes instead of DOM
- Reading XML documents by using the `XmlTextReader` class
- Writing XML documents by using the `XmlTextWriter` class
- Working with a subset of XML documents and reader and writer classes

What Are XML Readers and Writers?

DOM-based parsers are best suited to modifying XML documents that are small. However, with huge XML documents, DOM access can pose problems in terms of memory footprint and performance. In such cases, an alternative must be adopted so that we can read and write XML documents without these limitations. Traditionally, event-based parsers based on the SAX specifications were used to deal with such scenarios. The .NET answer, however, is a bit different.

The .NET Framework provides a class called `XmlReader` that provides read-only access to XML documents in a forward-only fashion. Though SAX and `XmlReader` sound similar, they behave differently. Any SAX-based parser essentially raises events as various parts of the XML document are encountered. Thus it works on a push model. On the other hand, the `XmlReader` class allows you to iterate through the document and access the required content rather than raising events. Thus it uses a pull model. As you will see later, this pull model is more flexible from a development point of view. The `XmlReader` class does not load the entire document in memory, resulting in a small memory footprint. Because it is read-only, it is faster too.

Just as `XmlReader` allows you to read XML documents, a class called `XmlWriter` allows you to write XML documents. Like `XmlReader`, `XmlWriter` also uses a forward-only model. However, it offers write-only functionality.

The XmlReader and XmlWriter classes are abstract classes. That means you will not be able to instantiate and use them directly in your code. Fortunately, the System.Xml namespace contains two ready-to-use classes that inherit from these base classes. Those classes are XmlTextReader and XmlTextWriter. The former inherits from XmlReader, whereas the latter inherits from XmlWriter.

When to Use Readers and Writers

In the previous section, you learned that DOM parsers are a poor choice when working with huge XML documents. In general, you can say that XmlReader is better suited when

- You need to only read the document.
- The document is huge.
- You need to keep the memory footprint small.
- You want to work with many XML documents that are a reasonable size.
- You do not want to access various parts of the document randomly.

Similarly, XmlWriter is better suited when

- You want to only write content.
- You want to keep the memory footprint small.
- You are writing huge XML documents and looking for better performance.

Reader Classes

As you've seen, the XmlReader is an abstract class. That means you cannot instantiate it directly in your applications; you must inherit from it to make any use of it. Fortunately, the .NET Framework provides three implementations of the XmlReader class. These implementations are discussed briefly in this section.

The XmlTextReader Class

The XmlTextReader class can be used to parse XML documents. This class has very fast parsing abilities. It checks that the underlying documents are well formed but does not validate them against a DTD or schema.

The XmlValidatingReader Class

The XmlValidatingReader class can validate an XML document against a DTD or XML schema.

The XmlNodeReader Class

The `XmlNodeReader` class allows you to read XML data from the DOM tree. The constructor of `XmlNodeReader` takes a parameter of type `XmlNode`. This `XmlNode` can be obtained as a result of an XPath query or directly from a DOM document. In terms of properties and methods, the `XmlNodeReader` class closely resembles the `XmlTextReader` class.

Reading Documents by Using XmlTextReader

In this section, you will learn the following:

- How to open XML documents by using the `XmlTextReader` class
- How to read and access the content
- How to deal with white space
- How to work with name tables
- How to deal with namespaces

Let's begin by opening XML documents. Throughout our examples, we will be using the same `Employees.xml` file that we used earlier in the book.

Opening XML Documents

To illustrate how XML documents can be opened, we will develop a Windows application as shown in Figure 3-1.

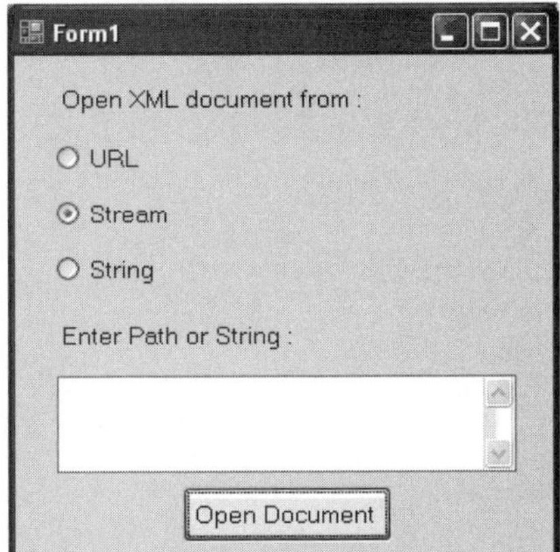

Figure 3-1. *Reading XML documents by using XmlTextReader*

The application allows you to choose the location from where the document is to be opened. The possible locations are URL, stream, or string. Depending on the choice, you need to enter the URL, filename, or XML string in the text box and click the Open Document button. Clicking the Open Document button opens the document and displays a success message box.

The `XmlReader` class can read an XML document from either a URL or a stream. The stream can by any kind of stream, such as a `FileStream` or `MemoryStream`. The `XmlReader` class cannot read XML strings directly. First, you need to read the string into a `MemoryStream` and then feed this `MemoryStream` to the `XmlReader` class. The code from Listing 3-1 shows these three techniques.

Listing 3-1. *Loading an XML Document in XmlTextReader*

```
private void button1_Click(object sender, EventArgs e)
{
  XmlTextReader reader;

  if (radioButton1.Checked)
  {
    reader = new XmlTextReader(textBox1.Text);
  }

  if (radioButton2.Checked)
  {
    FileStream stream=File.OpenRead(textBox1.Text);
    reader = new XmlTextReader(stream);
    //some processing code
    stream.Close();
    reader.Close();
  }

  if (radioButton3.Checked)
  {
    MemoryStream ms=new MemoryStream();
    byte[] data=ASCIIEncoding.ASCII.GetBytes(textBox1.Text);
    ms.Write(data,0,data.Length);
    reader = new XmlTextReader(ms);
    //some processing code
    ms.Close();
    reader.Close();
  }

  MessageBox.Show("XML Document Opened Successfully!");
}
```

■ **Note** Make sure to import the `System.Xml` and `System.IO` namespaces before writing the preceding code. The `XmlTextReader` class resides in the `System.Xml` namespace, and the `MemoryStream` class resides in the `System.IO` namespace.

The code declares a variable of type `XmlTextReader`. It then checks to see which radio button has been selected. If the user wants to use a URL, a new instance of `XmlTextReader` is created by passing the URL in the constructor.

If the user decides to read the file from disk, it is first read into a stream. This is done by using the `OpenRead()` method of the `File` class. The `OpenRead()` method opens the specified file in read-only mode. The resulting `FileStream` is then passed in the constructor of the `XmlTextReader` class.

You cannot directly pass an XML string to the `XmlTextReader` class. Hence the third condition reads the string into `MemoryStream`. Note the use of the `GetBytes()` method to convert a string into a byte array. The resulting byte array is written to the `MemoryStream` object. Finally, this `MemoryStream` instance is supplied to the constructor of the `XmlTextReader` class.

Reading Attributes, Elements, and Values

In this section, we are going to develop a Windows application that will display a tree of various elements and their values. In the process, you will learn how to read attributes, elements, and text nodes from an XML document by using the `XmlTextReader` class.

The application is shown in Figure 3-2.

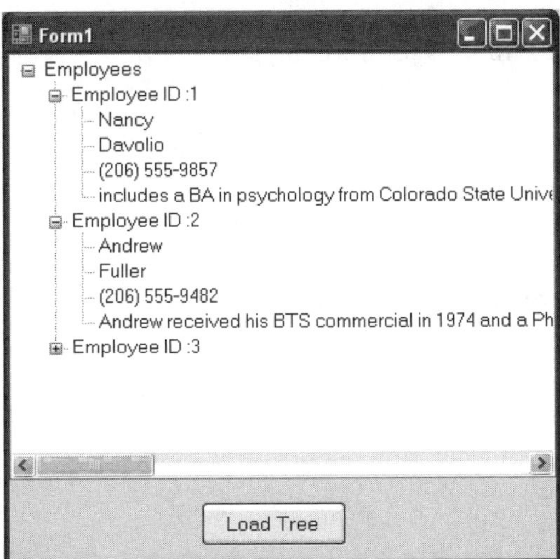

Figure 3-2. *Reading an XML document by using XmlTextReader*

The application consists of a TreeView control and a Button control. Clicking the Load Tree button displays the entire tree of nodes in the tree view as shown.

The core logic goes in the `Click` event handler of the Load Tree button and is shown in Listing 3-2.

Listing 3-2. *Loading the Tree*

```
private void button1_Click(object sender, EventArgs e)
{
  XmlTextReader reader =
    new XmlTextReader(Application.StartupPath + @"\employees.xml");
  reader.WhitespaceHandling = WhitespaceHandling.None;
  TreeNode employeenode=null;
  TreeNode rootnode = null;

  while (reader.Read())
  {
    if (reader.NodeType == XmlNodeType.Element)
    {
      if (reader.Name == "employees")
      {
        rootnode = treeView1.Nodes.Add("Employees");
      }

      if (reader.Name == "employee")
      {
        string employeeid = reader.GetAttribute("employeeid");
        employeenode = new TreeNode("Employee ID :" + employeeid);
        rootnode.Nodes.Add(employeenode);
      }

      if (reader.Name == "firstname")
      {
        string firstname = reader.ReadElementString();
        TreeNode node = new TreeNode(firstname);
        employeenode.Nodes.Add(node);
      }
```

```
        if (reader.Name == "lastname")
        {
          reader.Read();
          string lastname = reader.Value;
          TreeNode node = new TreeNode(lastname);
          employeenode.Nodes.Add(node);
        }

        if (reader.Name == "homephone")
        {
          string homephone = reader.ReadElementString();
          TreeNode node = new TreeNode(homephone);
          employeenode.Nodes.Add(node);
        }

        if (reader.Name == "notes")
        {
          string notes = reader.ReadElementString();
          TreeNode node = new TreeNode(notes);
          employeenode.Nodes.Add(node);
        }
      }
      reader.Close();
}
```

The code creates an instance of the XmlTextReader class by passing the path of the XML file. The WhitespaceHandling property of XmlTextReader governs the behavior of the reader while reading white space. This property is an enumeration of type WhitespaceHandling and has three possible values: All, None, or Significant. We set WhitespaceHandling to ignore any white space. This will simplify our coding.

A while loop repeatedly calls the Read() method of XmlTextReader. The Read() method reads the next node from the file and returns true if the next node can be read successfully; otherwise, it returns false.

Inside the while loop, the code retrieves the type of node by using the NodeType property of the XmlTextReader class. The NodeType property is an enumeration of type XmlNodeType and can have values such as Attribute, CDATA, Comment, Element, EndElement, Text, Whitespace, SignificantWhitespace, and so on. Note that the start and end elements are represented separately. This is because while scanning the document the XmlTextReader class reads start elements (for example, <employee>) and end elements (for example, </employee>) separately. In our example, we are interested only in start elements and therefore the if condition checks only for a node type of Element.

The code then checks the name of each element. This is done by checking the Name property of the XmlTextReader class and executing code depending on the element name:

- If the element name is employees, the code adds the root node of the TreeView control.
- If the element name is employee, the code retrieves the employeeid attribute. To retrieve attribute values, XmlTextReader provides a method called GetAttribute(), which accepts the name of the attribute whose value is to be retrieved and returns the value as a string. A tree node is then added for this employee.
- If the element name is firstname, the text value inside it needs to be retrieved. This is done with the help of the ReadElementString() method, which returns the text content within the current element. For us it will return the first name of the employee.
- The next if condition contains a variation on reading element values. It also illustrates the cursor-oriented model of XmlTextReader. When this if condition is triggered, the XmlTextReader is pointing to the <lastname> element. When we call the Read() method again, the cursor moves to the text node inside the <lastname> element. The Value property of XmlTextReader then returns the value of the text node.
- The values of the homephone and notes elements are read along the same lines.

Finally, the XmlTextReader is closed by using its Close() method.

Improving Performance by Using Name Tables

Whenever XmlTextReader parses any XML file, it creates a list of element names found in that document. This list is called a *name table*. Imagine that you are parsing dozens of separate files that have the same structure as that of Employees.xml. That means the XmlTextReader class needs to generate the same name table again and again. You can improve the efficiency of this process by supplying a ready-made name table, represented by the XmlNameTable class, for further parsing. The XmlNameTable class is an abstract class, but the .NET Framework provides a class called NameTable that inherits from it. You can therefore use this NameTable class in your code.

The code fragment in Listing 3-3 will make the use of name tables clear.

Listing 3-3. *Using Name Tables*

```
NameTable table = new NameTable();
XmlTextReader reader1 =
  new XmlTextReader(Application.StartupPath + @"\employees1.xml",table);
XmlTextReader reader2 =
  new XmlTextReader(Application.StartupPath + @"\employees2.xml",table);
XmlTextReader reader3 =
  new XmlTextReader(Application.StartupPath + @"\employees3.xml",table);
//process further
```

The code creates a new instance of the NameTable class, which will naturally be empty. Then an instance of XmlTextReader is created. This time the constructor takes two parameters: a filename and a NameTable. When you read the XML document for the first time, that is, using reader1, the supplied NameTable instance is populated. That means we have a NameTable ready for use. The same NameTable is supplied as a parameter to reader2 and reader3; they will in turn use this ready-made NameTable, thus improving the efficiency of the code.

Dealing with Namespaces

The XmlTextReader class has the same three XML namespace-related properties as the XmlNode class. The properties are NamespaceURI, Prefix, and LocalName. Their meaning is the same as already discussed in Chapter 2.

Moving Between Elements

In the previous example, you learned how to navigate through and read an XML document by using XmlTextReader. There are some additional methods of XmlTextReader that allow you to move between elements and read the content. This section presents these methods.

The ReadSubTree() Method

The ReadSubTree() method reads subnodes of the current node and returns the subtree as another XmlReader instance. This method is useful when you are parsing huge documents but want to work with a small section at a time. Figure 3-3 shows pictorially how this method works.

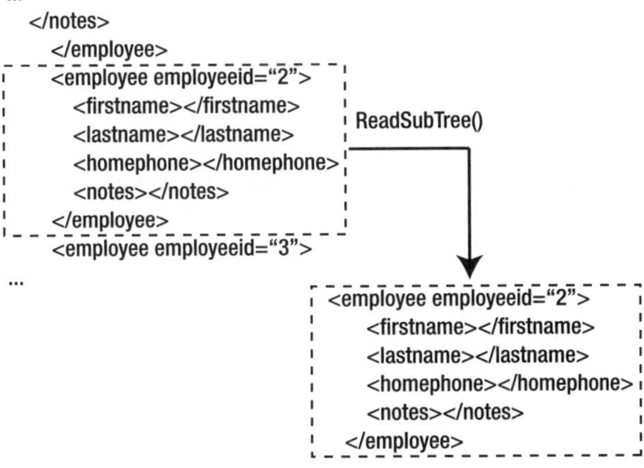

Figure 3-3. *Using the ReadSubTree() method*

From the figure you can see that if you call ReadSubTree() when your XmlTextReader is on an <employee> node of the document, the ReadSubTree() method returns another XmlReader containing that <employee> node and all its child nodes (that is, the subtree of the <employee> node).

The ReadToDescendant() Method

The ReadToDescendant() method advances the XmlTextReader to the next occurrence of the specified child node. This method comes in handy when you want to jump to a specific node rather than sequentially moving there. Figure 3-4 shows how this method works.

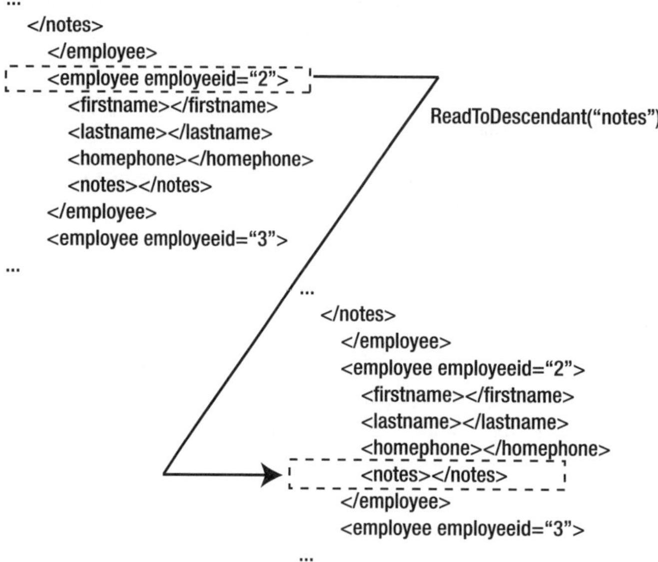

Figure 3-4. *Using the ReadToDescendant() method*

As shown in Figure 3-4, if you call the ReadToDescendant() method when you are on an <employee> node and specify notes as the target element, your reader jumps to the next <notes> element.

The ReadToFollowing() Method

The ReadToFollowing() method is very similar to the ReadToDescendant() method, with one difference. The ReadToDescendant() method can jump to the specified element only if it is a descendant of the current node, whereas the ReadToFollowing() method jumps to the first occurrence of the specified element, be it a descendant or not.

Note Notice the difference between the `ReadToDescendant()` and `ReadToFollowing()` methods. Assuming that you are on the `<firstname>` node of the second employee and wish to jump to the `<notes>` node of the same employee, you would use the `ReadToDescendant()` method. On the other hand, if you are on the `<firstname>` node of the second employee and wish to jump to the next occurrence of the `<firstname>` node, you would use the `ReadToFollowing()` method.

The ReadToNextSibling() Method

The `ReadToNextSibling()` method moves the reader from the current element to the next element at the same level. Figure 3-5 shows how this method works.

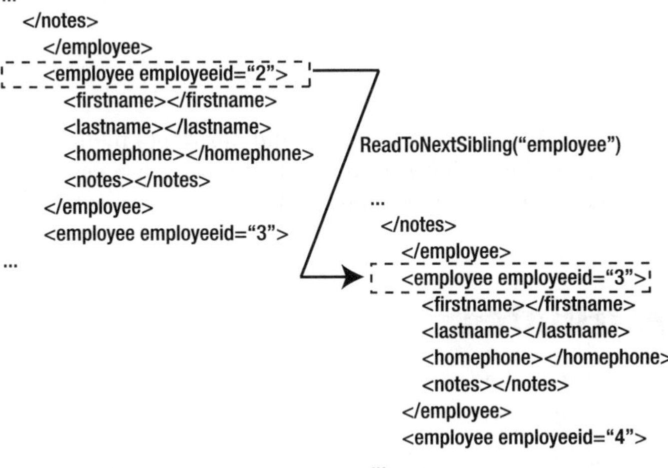

Figure 3-5. *Using the ReadToNextSibling() method*

As you can see in Figure 3-5, if you call `ReadToNextSibling()` when the reader is on the second `<employee>` node, the reader will jump to the third `<employee>` node because they are sibling nodes.

The Skip() Method

The `Skip()` method skips the child elements and jumps directly to the next element. `Skip()` comes in handy when you want to bypass child nodes depending on a certain condition. Figure 3-6 shows how this method works.

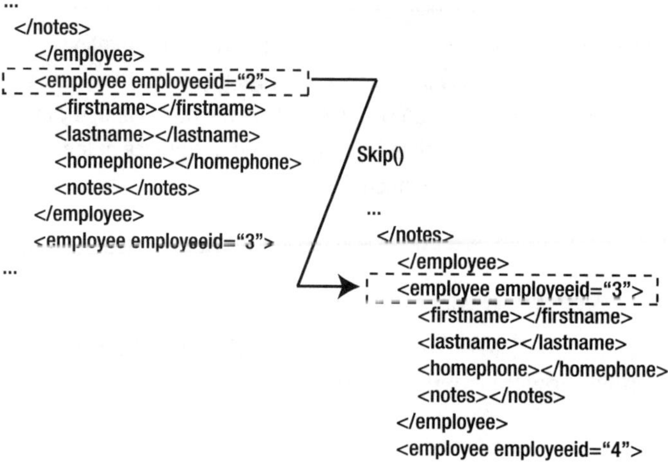

Figure 3-6. *Using the Skip() method*

Note the difference between the `ReadToNextSibling()` method and the `Skip()` method. The former advances the reader to the next sibling element, whereas the latter advances the reader to the next possible element (not necessarily a sibling node) after bypassing the child nodes.

Moving Between Attributes

The `XmlTextReader` class also provides four methods for moving between attributes. These methods, which are useful only for element nodes, are as follows:

- The `MoveToAttribute()` method accepts the index or name of the attribute to navigate to and moves the reader to the attribute.
- The `MoveToFirstAttribute()` method takes the reader to the first attribute of the current element.
- The `MoveToNextAttribute()` method moves the reader to the next attribute of the current element.
- The `MoveToElement()` method moves the reader back to the element node whose attributes were just read.

Figure 3-7 shows how all these methods work.

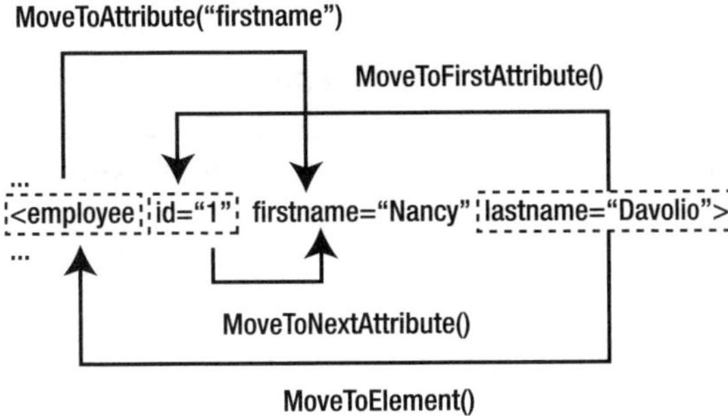

Figure 3-7. *Moving between attributes*

As you can see in Figure 3-7, if you call `MoveToAttribute()` by passing `firstname` as the parameter, the reader moves to the `firstname` attribute. When you are on the `lastname` attribute, calling `MoveToFirst()` will take the reader to the `id` attribute. Calling `MoveToNextAttribute()` when the reader is on the `id` attribute will advance the reader to the `firstname` attribute. Finally, calling `MoveToElement()` from any attribute will take the reader back to the `<employee>` element.

Reading Content

In our previous example, we used the `Value` property and the `ReadElementString()` method to read content from an element. In this section, you are going to see a few more ways to read the content.

The ReadInnerXml() Method

The `ReadInnerXml()` method reads all the XML content inside the current node and returns it as a string. The returned string does not contain the current node markup. For example, if you call `ReadInnerXml()` when your reader is on the first `<employee>` element, the method will return the markup as shown in Listing 3-4.

Listing 3-4. *Result of the ReadInnerXml() Method*

```
<firstname>Nancy</firstname>
<lastname>Davolio</lastname>
<homephone>(206) 555-9857</homephone>
<notes>
<![CDATA[includes a BA in psychology from Colorado State University in 1970. She
also completed "The Art of the Cold Call." Nancy is a member of Toastmasters
International.]]>
</notes>
```

The ReadOuterXml() Method

The `ReadOuterXml()` method is similar to the `ReadInnerXml()` method, but the difference is that it also includes the markup of the current element. For example, if you call `ReadOuterXml()` while the reader is on the first `<employee>` element, `ReadOuterXml()` will return the markup as shown in Listing 3-5.

Listing 3-5. *Result of the ReadOuterXml() Method*

```
<employee employeeid="1">
  <firstname>Nancy</firstname>
  <lastname>Davolio</lastname>
  <homephone>(206) 555-9857</homephone>
  <notes>
<![CDATA[includes a BA in psychology from Colorado State University in 1970. She
also completed "The Art of the Cold Call." Nancy is a member of Toastmasters
International.]]>
  </notes>
</employee>
```

The ReadString() Method

The `ReadString()` method reads the contents of an element or a text node as a string. It simply returns all the text from the element until any markup is encountered. For example, look at the XML markup shown here:

```
<node1>
  <node2>
    Hello World <node3>This is some text</node3>
  </node2>
</node1>
```

If you call `ReadString()` when the reader is on `<node2>`, `ReadString()` will return `Hello World` and not the remaining markup from `<node3>`.

Writing XML Documents

In the previous sections, you learned how `XmlTextReader` can be used to read XML documents in a serialized fashion. Reading XML documents is just half of the story; often you need to write XML documents also.

The counterpart of `XmlTextReader` is another class called `XmlTextWriter`. The `XmlTextWriter` class allows you to quickly serialize XML documents to a file or any stream. The `XmlTextWriter` class inherits from an abstract class: `XmlWriter`. In this section, you will learn how this class can be used to write XML documents.

To see the XmlTextWriter class in action, you will build a Windows application as shown in Figure 3-8.

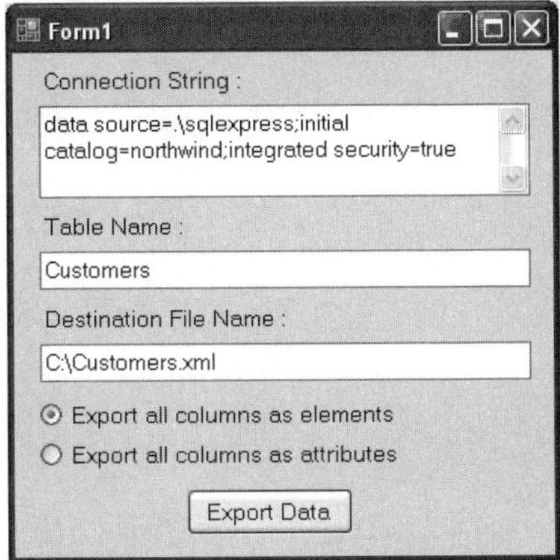

Figure 3-8. *Using the XmlTextWriter class*

The application allows you to export data from any table of SQL Server into an XML file. As shown in Figure 3-8, the application accepts a database connection string, a table name to export, and the destination XML filename where the data is to be exported. The two radio buttons allow you to select whether all the columns are to be exported as elements or attributes in the resultant document. Clicking the Export Data button exports the data to the specified file.

The code needs to import the following namespaces:

```
using System.Data.SqlClient;
using System.Xml;
```

The System.Data.SqlClient namespace represents the SQL Server Data Provider of the .NET Framework and supplies classes related to data access such as SqlConnection and SqlCommand.

The Click event handler of the Export Data button contains the code shown in Listing 3-6.

Listing 3-6. *Exporting Data*

```
private void button1_Click(object sender, EventArgs e)
{
            SqlConnection cnn=null;
            SqlCommand cmd=null;
            SqlDataReader reader=null;
            XmlTextWriter writer=null;
            try
```

```
{
    cnn = new SqlConnection(textBox1.Text);
    cmd = new SqlCommand();
    cmd.Connection = cnn;
    cmd.CommandText = "select * from " + textBox2.Text;
    cnn.Open();
    reader = cmd.ExecuteReader();
    writer = new XmlTextWriter(textBox3.Text, null);
    writer.WriteStartDocument();
    writer.WriteComment("File exported on " + DateTime.Now);
    writer.WriteStartElement("table");
    while (reader.Read())
    {
        if (radioButton1.Checked)
        {
            writer.WriteStartElement("row");
            for (int i = 0; i < reader.FieldCount; i++)
            {
                writer.WriteStartElement(reader.GetName(i));
                writer.WriteString(reader.GetValue(i).ToString());
                writer.WriteEndElement();
            }
            writer.WriteEndElement();
        }
        else
        {
            writer.WriteStartElement("row");
            for (int i = 0; i < reader.FieldCount; i++)
            {
                writer.WriteAttributeString(reader.GetName(i),
                reader.GetValue(i).ToString());
            }
            writer.WriteEndElement();
        }
    }
    writer.WriteEndElement();
}
catch (Exception ex)
{
    MessageBox.Show(ex.Message);
}
finally
```

```
            {
                writer.Close();
                reader.Close();
                cnn.Close();
            }
}
```

The code creates an instance of the `SqlConnection` class by passing a database connection string as the parameter. The `SqlConnection` class represents a database connection. In order to execute queries against a database, a `SqlCommand` object is created. The `Connection` property of `SqlCommand` represents the `SqlConnection` object through which the queries are to be executed. The `CommandText` property indicates the SQL query that is to be executed. In our example, we need to create a `SELECT` query by concatenating the name of the table as entered by the user.

The code then opens the connection with the help of the `Open()` method of `SqlConnection`. The `ExecuteReader()` method fires the `SELECT` statement as indicated by the `CommandText` property and returns a `SqlDataReader` object. The `SqlDataReader` object is like a read-only and forward-only cursor and allows you to iterate through the result set.

The code then proceeds to create an instance of the `XmlTextWriter` class, which can write directly to a disk file or to any stream. In our example, we write the data directly to the specified disk file. The second parameter of the constructor is the encoding of the data to be written. If this parameter is null, the `XmlTextWriter` writes the data as UTF-8 (Unicode Transformation Format, 8-bit encoding form) and omits the `encoding` attribute from the XML processing instruction. After the `XmlTextWriter` instance is ready, the actual writing process begins.

When the user selects to export all the columns as XML elements, the resultant document will bear the structure shown in Figure 3-9.

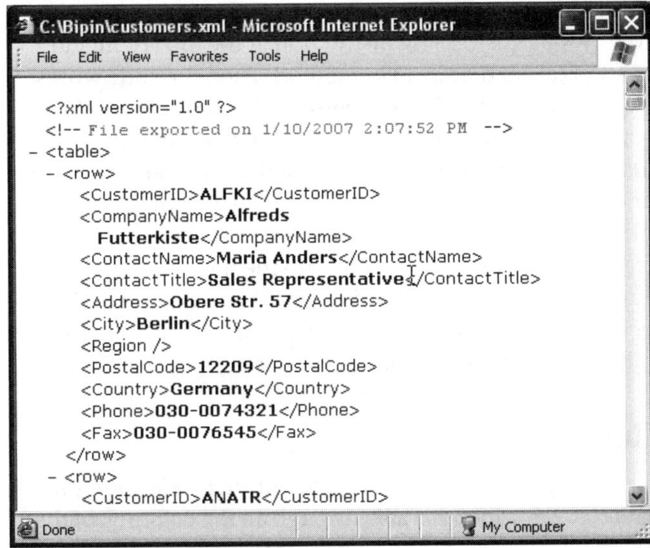

Figure 3-9. *Columns exported as elements*

The root element is `<table>`, which contains one or more `<row>` elements. Each `<row>` element further contains child elements, depending on the number of columns in the table. The child elements assume the same name as the database column name.

Similarly, when the user opts to export all the columns as attributes, the resultant document will bear the structure shown in Figure 3-10.

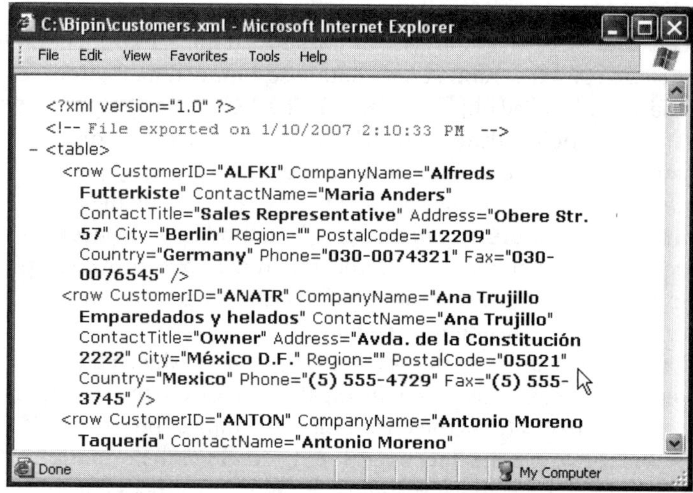

Figure 3-10. *Columns exported as attributes*

The root element is `<table>` again, which will contain one or more `<row>` elements. Each `<row>` element will have one or more attributes representing the column values. The attribute name will be the same as the column name.

All XML documents need to have the XML processing instruction at the top. To include this processing instruction, we call the `WriteStartDocument()` method. Then the code writes a comment specifying the date and time at which the file is exported. The `WriteComment()` method accepts the comment string and writes it into the document. The root element `<table>` is then written to the document by using the `WriteStartElement()` method, which accepts the name of the element to be written and writes it to the file. Note that you need not specify the < and > characters while specifying the element name. Thus, when you pass `table` as the parameter to the `WriteStartElement()` method, it writes `<table>` into the file.

The code now starts iterating through the available records. The `Read()` method of the `SqlDataReader` class advances the record pointer to the next row and reads values from that row. It returns `true` if the record can be read successfully; otherwise, it returns `false`.

Exporting Columns As Elements

If the columns are to be exported as elements (that is, the first radio button is selected), the `<row>` element will not have any attributes. A `for` loop iterates through all the columns of the current row. The `FieldCount` property of the `SqlDataReader` class returns the total number of columns in the result set. With each iteration of the `for` loop, a new element is created by using the WriteStartElement() method. This time the WriteStartElement() method accepts the column name returned by the GetName() method of the SqlDataReader class, which accepts the column index and returns the column name.

To write the actual value of the column, the WriteString() method is called. This method accepts the string to be written, which in our example is retrieved by using the GetValue() method of SqlDataReader. The GetValue() method accepts a column index and returns the contents as an object. The code then calls the ToString() method on the returned object to get its string representation.

After the element value is written, the code calls the WriteEndElement() method of XmlTextWriter to write the innermost end element to the file. The WriteEndElement() method correctly writes the end element depending on the nesting of the document.

When you run the application and export your table, your output should resemble Figure 3-9.

Exporting Columns As Attributes

If the column values are to be written as attributes instead of elements, a similar process is followed. This time, however, the code uses the WriteAttributeString() method of XmlTextWriter to write the attributes. The WriteAttributeString() method accepts two parameters: the name of the attribute and the value of the attribute.

After writing all the end elements, the code closes the XmlTextWriter by calling its Close() method. Similarly, SqlDataReader and SqlConnection are also closed.

When you run the application and export your table, your output should resemble Figure 3-10.

Specifying Character Encoding

In the previous example, we constructed the XmlTextWriter class by providing a filename and the character encoding. In this case, the encoding parameter was null, but there are four possible encoding options in the .NET Framework. They are available as properties of the Encoding class, which resides in the System.Text namespace. Each of these properties is shown in Table 3-1.

Table 3-1. *Properties of the Encoding Class*

Property	Class Name	Description
Encoding.ASCII	ASCIIEncoding	Represents ASCII encoding. This encoding encodes Unicode characters as single 7-bit ASCII characters.
Encoding.Unicode	UnicodeEncoding	Represents Unicode encoding. This scheme encodes Unicode characters as 2 bytes.
Encoding.UTF7	UTF7Encoding	Represents UTF-7 encoding. The characters are stored in 7-bit format.
Encoding.UTF8	UTF8Encoding	Represents UTF-8 encoding. The characters are stored in 8-bit format. This is the default scheme.

Formatting the Output

If you open the XML document that we created in our previous example in Notepad, it will look like Figure 3-11.

```
<?xml version="1.0"?><!--File exported on
talCode><Country>Mexico</Country><Phone>(5
lCode><Country>Germany</Country><Phone>062
Country>France</Country><Phone>91.24.45.40
010</PostalCode><Country>Argentina</Countr
32-043</PostalCode><Country>Brazil</Countr
alCode>44000</PostalCode><Country>France</
<Country>Brazil</Country><Phone>(11) 555-9
ntry>Sweden</Country><Phone>0695-34 67 21<
><Phone>011-4988260</Phone><Fax>011-498826
Code><Country>Spain</Country><Phone>(95) 5
y>Venezuela</Country><Phone>(2) 283-2951</
```

Figure 3-11. *XML document without any formatting*

What's the problem? Well, there is no problem as far as the document being well formed. It does follow all the rules of XML grammar. However, the document lacks proper formatting. Such documents are difficult for the human eye to read. Fortunately, the `XmlTextWriter` class provides several formatting options that help you create well-formatted documents.

To see how these formatting options work, you need to modify the previous application as shown in Figure 3-12.

Form1
Connection String :
data source=.\sqlexpress;initial catalog=northwind;integrated security=true
Table Name :
Customers
Destination File Name :
D:\bipin\customers.xml
Export all columns as elements
Export all columns as attributes
Format resultant XMLdocument
Indention 3
Indent Character
Space Tab
Export Data

Figure 3-12. *Formatting the XML document*

The application has a check box that toggles whether the document will be formatted. You can specify the indention as well as the indent character (space or tab).

The code in the `Click` event handler of the Export Data button needs to be modified as shown in Listing 3-7.

Listing 3-7. *Formatting XML Document While Writing*

```
private void button1_Click(object sender, EventArgs e)
{
  SqlConnection cnn = new SqlConnection(textBox1.Text);
  SqlCommand cmd = new SqlCommand();
  cmd.Connection = cnn;
  cmd.CommandText = "SELECT * FROM " + textBox2.Text;
  cnn.Open();
  SqlDataReader reader = cmd.ExecuteReader();
  XmlTextWriter writer = new XmlTextWriter(textBox3.Text, null);

  if(checkBox1.Checked)
  {
    writer.Formatting = Formatting.Indented;
    writer.Indentation = int.Parse(textBox4.Text);
    writer.IndentChar = (radioButton3.Checked ? ' ' : '\t');
  }

  writer.WriteStartDocument();
  writer.WriteComment("File exported on " + DateTime.Now);
  writer.WriteStartElement("table");

  while (reader.Read())
  {
    if (radioButton1.Checked)
    {
      writer.WriteStartElement("row");
      for (int i = 0; i < reader.FieldCount; i++)
      {
        writer.WriteStartElement(reader.GetName(i));
        writer.WriteString(reader.GetValue(i).ToString());
        writer.WriteEndElement();
      }
      writer.WriteEndElement();
    }
    else
    {
      writer.WriteStartElement("row");
      for (int i = 0; i < reader.FieldCount; i++)
```

```
            {
              writer.WriteAttributeString(reader.GetName(i),
                                          reader.GetValue(i).ToString());
            }
            writer.WriteEndElement();
          }
        }
        writer.WriteEndElement();
        writer.Close();
        reader.Close();
        cnn.Close();
      }
```

Note the code marked in bold. The `Formatting` property of `XmlTextWriter` governs whether the document will be formatted. The `Formatting` property is an enumeration of type `Formatting` and contains two possible values: `None` and `Indented`. The `Indentation` property of `XmlTextWriter` specifies the number of indent characters to be written in the document. This property is useful only if `Formatting` is set to `Indented`. The `IndentChar` property holds the character to be used for indentation. Though you can specify any valid character for `IndentChar`, space and tab are commonly used.

If you export the `Customers` table after making the preceding modifications, the resultant document should resemble Figure 3-13.

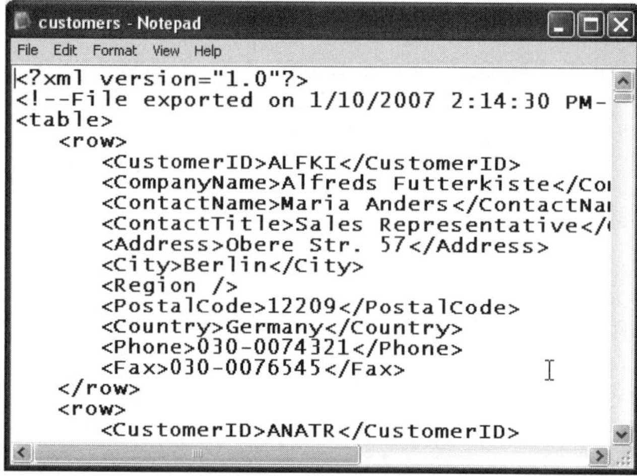

Figure 3-13. *Well-formatted XML document*

Much better than the previous one, isn't it?

Though not covered by our application, you can also set the `QuoteChar` property to decide which character to use for enclosing attribute values. The default value for `QuoteChar` is the double-quote character.

Including Namespace Support

Recall from Chapter 2 and earlier discussion in this chapter that XML namespaces provide a method for uniquely qualifying element and attribute names used in an XML document by associating them with a namespace. When you create XML documents by using `XmlTextWriter`, you may need to include namespace support for the resultant document. That is what you are going to see in this section.

Various methods of `XmlTextWriter`, such as `WriteStartElement()`, provide overloads that can be used to specify namespace and prefix information. To see how these overloads can be used, you need to modify the previous application as shown in Figure 3-14.

Figure 3-14. *Namespace support in XmlTextWriter*

As you can see in Figure 3-14, there are text boxes for accepting the namespace URI and prefix from the user. The modified code that adds namespace support is shown in Listing 3-8.

Listing 3-8. *Namespace Support in XmlTextWriter*

```
private void button1_Click(object sender, EventArgs e)
{
  SqlConnection cnn = new SqlConnection(textBox1.Text);
  SqlCommand cmd = new SqlCommand();
  cmd.Connection = cnn;
  cmd.CommandText = "SELECT * FROM " + textBox2.Text;
  cnn.Open();
  SqlDataReader reader = cmd.ExecuteReader();
```

```
    XmlTextWriter writer = new XmlTextWriter(textBox3.Text, null);
    writer.WriteStartDocument();
    writer.WriteComment("File exported on " + DateTime.Now);
    writer.WriteStartElement(textBox5.Text, "table", textBox4.Text);

    while (reader.Read())
    {
      if (radioButton1.Checked)
      {
        writer.WriteStartElement(textBox5.Text, "row", textBox4.Text);
        for (int i = 0; i < reader.FieldCount; i++)
        {
          writer.WriteStartElement(textBox5.Text, reader.GetName(i),
                                   textBox4.Text);
          writer.WriteString(reader.GetValue(i).ToString());
          writer.WriteEndElement();
        }
        writer.WriteEndElement();
      }
      else
      {
        writer.WriteStartElement(textBox5.Text, "row", textBox4.Text);
        for (int i = 0; i < reader.FieldCount; i++)
        {
          writer.WriteAttributeString(textBox5.Text, reader.GetName(i),
                                      textBox4.Text,
                                      reader.GetValue(i).ToString());
        }
        writer.WriteEndElement();
      }
    }
    writer.WriteEndElement();
    writer.Close();
    reader.Close();
    cnn.Close();
}
```

Notice the lines marked in bold. The `WriteStartElement()` and `WriteAttributeString()` methods have an overload that accepts a prefix and namespace URI. If you create XML documents by using these overloads, your document should resemble Figure 3-15.

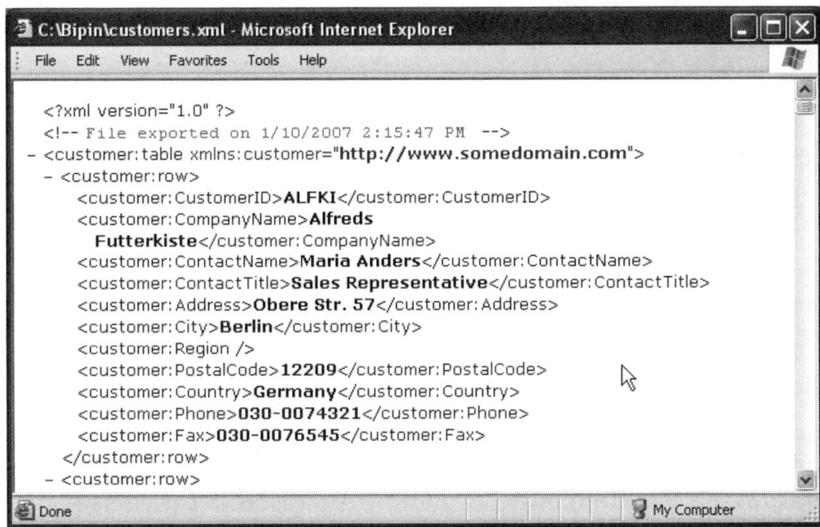

Figure 3-15. *XML document with namespaces and prefix added*

Notice how the namespace has been added to the `<table>` element. Also notice how each element now bears the prefix.

Dealing with Nontextual Data

Up until now, we have been using `XmlReader` and `XmlWriter` to read textual data. However, at times you may need to deal with nontextual data as well. For example, you may want to serialize image files or binary files as XML data in order to pass it over the Internet in a firewall-friendly way. Thankfully, both `XmlTextReader` and `XmlTextWriter` provide ways to handle such situations.

To help you understand how `XmlTextReader` and `XmlTextWriter` can be used to work with nontextual data, we will develop an application as shown in Figure 3-16.

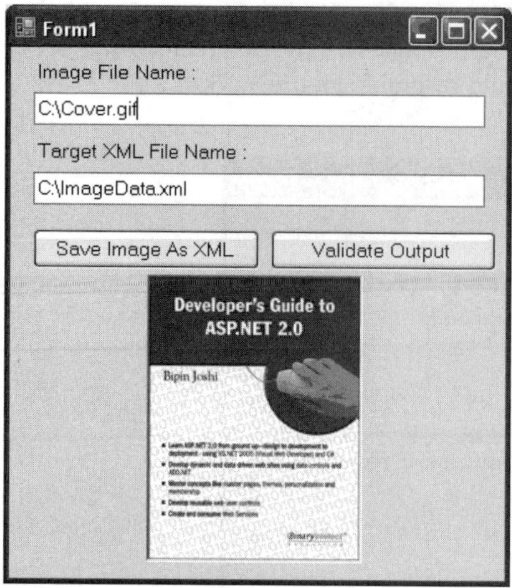

Figure 3-16. *Dealing with nontextual data*

The application allows you to read any image file and serialize it as an XML document. You can specify the source image filename and the destination XML filename in the text boxes. After you save the image as an XML document, you can validate whether the serialized image is correct by loading it in a picture box.

Serializing Data

Listing 3-9 shows the `Click` event handler of the Save Image as XML button.

Listing 3-9. *Writing Base64 Data*

```
private void button1_Click(object sender, EventArgs e)
{
  XmlTextWriter writer = new XmlTextWriter(textBox2.Text, null);
  FileStream fs = File.OpenRead(textBox1.Text);
  byte[] data = new byte[fs.Length];
  fs.Position = 0;
  fs.Read(data, 0, data.Length);
  fs.Close();
  writer.WriteStartDocument();
  writer.WriteStartElement("imagefile");
  writer.WriteAttributeString("filename", textBox1.Text);
  writer.WriteAttributeString("size", data.Length.ToString());
  writer.WriteBase64(data,0,data.Length);
  writer.WriteEndElement();
  writer.Close();
}
```

The code creates an `XmlTextWriter` object by passing the path of the destination XML file to the constructor. Then a `FileStream` is created for reading data from the image file. The contents of the file are read by using the `Read()` method of the `FileStream` class, which accepts three parameters: the byte array to read the data into, the start index in the byte array from where the writing should start, and the length of data to read. The `XmlTextWriter` then starts writing the document. It first writes the XML processing instruction and the `<imagefile>` element. The `<imagefile>` element has two attributes: `filename` and `size`. The `filename` attribute stores the complete path of the image file that is being serialized as XML. The `size` attribute contains the size of the source image file.

Image files contain nontextual data. You have a couple of options when you want to serialize nontextual data into XML files. You can use either hexadecimal encoding or Base64 encoding for the serialization. In our example, we use Base64 encoding. To write data into Base64 format, the `XmlTextWriter` class provides a method called `WriteBase64()`, which accepts three parameters: a byte array that contains the nontextual data, the index of the byte array from which the writing should start, and the length of data to write. The `WriteBase64()` method writes the supplied byte array as a Base64 string inside the destination XML element. Figure 3-17 shows how the XML file looks after serializing an image file.

Figure 3-17. *Image file serialized in Base64 format*

Now that you know how to write nontextual data by using `XmlTextWriter`, you're ready to see how to use `XmlTextReader` to read the document back.

Unserializing Data

The `Click` event handler of the Validate Document button contains the code shown in Listing 3-10.

Listing 3-10. *Reading Base64 Data*

```
private void button2_Click(object sender, EventArgs e)
{
  XmlTextReader reader = new XmlTextReader(textBox2.Text);
  reader.WhitespaceHandling = WhitespaceHandling.None;

  while (reader.Read())
  {
    if (reader.NodeType == XmlNodeType.Element)
    {
      if (reader.Name == "imagefile")
      {
        int length = int.Parse(reader.GetAttribute("size"));
        string filename = reader.GetAttribute("filename");
        byte[] data = new byte[length];
        string str = reader.ReadElementString();
        byte[] imagedata = Convert.FromBase64String(str);
        MemoryStream ms = new MemoryStream();
        ms.Write(imagedata, 0, imagedata.Length);
        Image image = Image.FromStream(ms);
        pictureBox1.Image = image;
        ms.Close();
      }
    }
  }
}
```

The code creates an instance of the XmlTextReader class by passing the XML document we just created. It then starts reading the document. If the element name is imagefile, the code reads the two attributes filename and size. Based on the value of the size attribute, a byte array is created with that much capacity. The contents of the <imagefile> element are read by using the ReadElementString() method.

■ **Note** The XmlTextReader class also provides a method called ReadContentAsBase64() that does the same job. The ReadContentAsBase64() method takes three parameters: a byte array into which the content is to be read, the index of the byte array from where writing should start, and the length of data to read.

The returned string will be in Base64 format and needs to be converted back into a byte array. This is done with the help of the FromBase64String() method of the Convert class, which accepts the Base64-encoded string and returns an equivalent byte array. The byte array returned from FromBase64String() is written to a MemoryStream object; the MemoryStream is then converted into an Image object. This is accomplished by using the FromStream() static method of the Image class, which returns an instance of the Image class constructed from the supplied stream. Finally, the Image instance is assigned to the Image property of the picture box control.

Summary

This chapter covered two important classes: `XmlTextReader` and `XmlTextWriter`. They are implementations of the abstract base classes `XmlReader` and `XmlWriter`, respectively. The `XmlTextReader` class represents a read-only parser that can parse XML documents very quickly. Because it does not load the entire XML document in memory, its memory footprint is small. It provides a cursor-oriented model to read the XML documents. The `XmlTextWriter` class allows you to quickly create XML documents and serialize nontextual data in hexadecimal or Base64 format. You can also create your own custom readers and writers by inheriting from the `XmlReader` and `XmlWriter` abstract classes.

CHAPTER 4

■ ■ ■

Accessing XML Documents by Using the XPath Data Model

In Chapters 2 and 3, you learned how to read and write XML documents by using the XmlDocument, XmlReader, and XmlWriter classes. These classes allow you to access the underlying documents, but by themselves they hardly provide a way to query and retrieve the data. That is why we need something that allows us to navigate, query, and retrieve data from XML documents easily and efficiently. The XPath standard is designed to do just that.

The .NET Framework namespace System.Xml.XPath provides a complete set of classes that allow you to query and retrieve data from an XML document by using the XPath data model. Recollect that in Chapter 2 we used the SelectNodes() and SelectSingleNode() methods that use XPath expressions. In this chapter, I will discuss XPath at length. Specifically, you will learn about the following:

- The location path, axis, and node tests
- The XPath built-in functions
- How to use the XPathNavigator class along with XPath
- How to read and write XML data by using the XPathNavigator class

Overview of XPath

XPath provides a way to query and select a part of an XML document. To work with XPath expressions, you must understand some of the basic terminology. Specifically, you must be comfortable with the following terms:

- Location path
- Axis
- Node tests
- Predicates

Location Path

We are all familiar with the Windows file system. In the file system, each file has a path and we denote that path by using a specific notation. Similarly, various parts of an XML document, such as elements and attributes, also have a location. The location is indicated by a specific XPath syntax called the *location path*, which allows you to select a set of nodes from an XML document. A location path consists of an axis, a node test, and predicates.

Axis

When dealing with file system paths, we normally start with the drive letter. Thus the drive letter forms the basis for locating the file. A similar role is played by the axis for XML documents. The *axis* partitions the XML document based on the current node, so by using an axis you specify the starting point to apply node tests and predicates. The available axes are listed in Table 4-1.

Table 4-1. *XPath Axes*

Axis	Description
Self	Represents the current node (often the context node)
Child	Represents the children of the context node
Parent	Represents the parent of the context node
Attribute	Represent attributes of the context node
Descendent	Represents all the child nodes of the context node
Ancestor	Represents parent, grandparent, and so on until the document root
Following	Represents all the nodes that come after the context node
Following-sibling	Represents the sibling nodes following the context node
Preceding	Represents all the nodes that come before the context node
Preceding-sibling	Represents the preceding sibling of the context node

Node Tests

Node tests allow you to test elements and node types for a certain condition and return the selected elements or nodes. You can use the asterisk (`*`) character to indicate all the nodes. Some of the commonly used node tests are as follows:

- Testing elements with the same name as the supplied element name
- Testing all the nodes of a specific axis
- Testing all the text elements of a specific axis
- Testing all the comments of a specific axis
- Testing all the processing instructions of a specific axis

Predicates

Predicates are Boolean expressions that are used to further filter the nodes selected by the axis and node test. The XPath specifications provide a good number of functions that you can use to form predicates. The return values of these functions can be compared or checked with the help of familiar operators, such as `=`, `!=`, `<`, `>`, `<=`, `>=`, and so on.

Putting It All Together

Now that you know the meaning of the XPath terms, let's see what a location path looks like. The general syntax of a location path is given here:

```
Axis::node-test[predicate]
```

The axis is separated from the rest of the path by the `::` operator. The node test typically contains a series of nodes, that is, a path. Finally, the predicate is specified in a set of square brackets. Here is an example of a location path:

```
following::employee[@employeeid='2']
```

The preceding location path points to the employee node following the current node whose `employeeid` attribute is `2`.

Here are the XPath expressions that we used in Chapter 2:

```
//employee[./firstname/text()='some_text']
//employee[@employeeid='1']
```

In both cases, the axis is the root node as indicated by `//`. The node test consists of a single node (`employee`). The predicate for the first expression tests whether the text value of the `firstname` node of the current employee node matches some specific text. The predicate for the second expression checks whether the `employeeid` attribute (the attribute axis can be abbreviated as `@`) of the current employee node is `1`.

XPath Functions

The XPath specification provides several built-in functions. These functions can be grouped in the following way:

- Functions that work on a set of nodes
- Functions that return a Boolean value
- Functions that work on strings
- Functions that work on numbers

These functions are listed in Tables 4-2 through 4-5.

Table 4-2. *Functions That Work on a Set of Nodes*

Function Name	Description
`last()`	Returns the number of nodes in the current node set
`position()`	Returns the index of the context node in the current node set
`count()`	Returns the total number of nodes in the given node set
`id()`	Returns a node set containing nodes with an ID attribute matching the specified value
`name()`	Returns the fully qualified name of the specified node
`text()`	Returns the text of the specified node
`local-name()`	Returns the local name of the node
`namespace-uri()`	Returns the namespace of the node

Table 4-3. *Functions That Return Boolean Values*

Function Name	Description
`not()`	Returns `true` if the supplied value is `false`; otherwise, returns `false`
`true()`	Returns `true`
`false()`	Returns `false`

Table 4-4. *Functions That Work on Strings*

Function Name	Description
`concat()`	Returns a concatenated string
`starts-with()`	Returns `true` if the string starts with the specified letters
`contains()`	Returns `true` if the string contains the specified string
`substring()`	Returns part of the specified string
`string-length()`	Returns the number of characters in the string
`translate()`	Replaces characters from a string with the specified characters

Table 4-5. *Functions That Work on Numbers*

Function Name	Description
`number()`	Converts the specified string to its equivalent number
`sum()`	Returns the sum of numbers
`floor()`	Returns a number rounded down to the next integer
`ceiling()`	Returns a number rounded up to the next integer
`round()`	Returns a number rounded to the nearest integer

Now that you have a good understanding of XPath, location paths, and XPath functions, let's delve further into the .NET Framework's XPath data model.

The XPath Data Model

The XPath data model of the .NET Framework relies on a class called `XPathNavigator` residing in the `System.Xml.XPath` namespace. The `XPathNavigator` class is an abstract class and provides a cursor-based navigation model for the underlying XML data. It also allows you to edit XML documents. You can obtain an `XPathNavigator` instance from any class that implements the `IXPathNavigable` interface. The classes that already implement this interface are `XmlDocument` and `XPathDocument`.

You have already worked with the `XmlDocument` class and hence it needs no explanation. The `XPathDocument` class, which resides in the `System.Xml.XPath` namespace, provides a read-only representation of an XML document by using the XPath data model. It loads the document in memory and naturally provides fast access to various parts of the document.

The `XPathNavigator` instance returned from `XmlDocument` is editable, whereas that returned by `XPathDocument` is read-only.

Creating XPathNavigator

You can obtain an instance of `XPathNavigator` from either `XmlDocument` or `XPathDocument`. Both of these classes implement the `IXPathNavigable` interface and provide a method called `CreateNavigator()` that creates and returns an object of type `XPathNavigator`.

To see how these classes can be used, you need to develop a Windows application as shown in Figure 4-1.

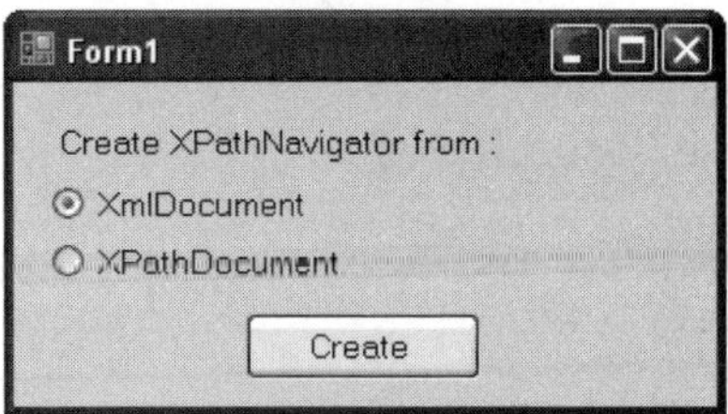

Figure 4-1. *Creating XPathNavigator*

The application consists of two radio buttons that allow you to select whether to use `XmlDocument` or `XPathDocument` for creating your `XPathNavigator`. When you click the Create button, the `XPathNavigator` instance is created depending on the selected radio button. Note that you need to import the `System.Xml` and `System.Xml.XPath` namespaces before you write any code. Listing 4-1 shows the code from the `Click` event handler of the Create button.

Listing 4-1. *Creating XPathNavigator*

```
private void button1_Click(object sender, EventArgs e)
{
  XPathNavigator navigator = null;
  if (radioButton1.Checked)
  {
    XmlDocument doc = new XmlDocument();
    doc.Load(Application.StartupPath + @"/employees.xml");
    navigator = doc.CreateNavigator();
  }
  else
  {
    XPathDocument doc =
      new XPathDocument(Application.StartupPath + @"/employees.xml");
    navigator = doc.CreateNavigator();
  }
  MessageBox.Show("Navigator created successfully!");
}
```

The code begins by declaring a variable of type `XPathNavigator` at the top of the event handler. It then checks which radio button is selected. If the `XPathNavigator` is to be created from `XmlDocument`, it creates an instance of the `XmlDocument` class. It then loads the `Employees.xml` file with the help of the `Load()` method of `XmlDocument`. The `XmlDocument` class has a method called `CreateNavigator()` that creates and returns an instance of the `XPathNavigator` class.

If the navigator is to be created from `XPathDocument`, the code creates an instance of the `XPathDocument` class. There are several overloads on the constructor of this class; our code uses the one that accepts the path to the XML file. The `CreateNavigator()` method of `XPathDocument` creates and returns an instance of `XPathNavigator`. Finally, a message box is displayed just to report the success of the operation.

Navigating an XML Document by Using XPathNavigator

In the previous section, you learned to create `XPathNavigator` from `XmlDocument` and `XPathDocument`. In this section, you will see how to use `XPathNavigator` and access various attributes and elements.

To work through this section, you need to create a Windows application as shown in Figure 4-2.

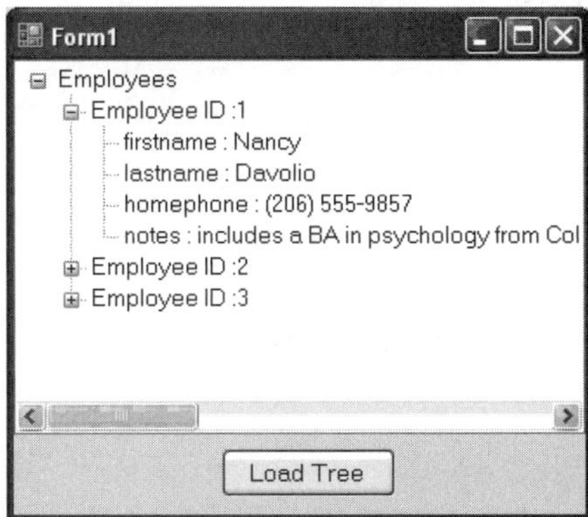

Figure 4-2. *Navigating through XPathNavigator*

The application consists of a TreeView and a button. After you click the Load Tree button, the TreeView is populated with employee information from the `Employees.xml` file. The `Click` event handler of the Load Tree button contains the code shown in Listing 4-2.

Listing 4-2. *Navigating by Using XPathNavigator*

```
private void button1_Click(object sender, EventArgs e)
{
  XPathDocument doc =
    new XPathDocument(Application.StartupPath + @"\employees.xml");
  XPathNavigator navigator = doc.CreateNavigator();
  navigator.MoveToRoot();
  navigator.MoveToFirstChild();

  TreeNode root = treeView1.Nodes.Add("Employees");

  while (navigator.MoveToNext())
  {
    if (navigator.HasChildren)
    {
      navigator.MoveToFirstChild();
      do
      {
        string id = navigator.GetAttribute("employeeid", "");
        TreeNode empnode = new TreeNode("Employee ID :" + id);
        root.Nodes.Add(empnode);
        navigator.MoveToFirstChild();

        do
        {
          string name = navigator.Name;
          TreeNode node = new TreeNode(name + " : " + navigator.Value);
          empnode.Nodes.Add(node);
        }       while (navigator.MoveToNext());

        navigator.MoveToParent();
      }
      while (navigator.MoveToNext());
    }
  }
}
```

The code begins by creating an instance of the XPathDocument class by passing the path of the XML file to its constructor. It then creates an XPathNavigator by calling the CreateNavigator() method of the XPathDocument class. We need to iterate through the document from the root and hence we call the MoveToRoot() method of XPathNavigator. This method moves the cursor of the XPathNavigator to the root of the document. Note that here the root of the document is the node that contains the entire tree of nodes. Because we want to start the iteration from the <employees> node, we call the MoveToFirstChild() method. Calling this method will place the navigator cursor at the <employees> node. A root node of the TreeView is then added.

Next there are three loops. The outermost loop iterates through all the child nodes of the root node. In our case, this loop will be executed just once, because there is only one <employees> node. The second loop iterates through all the <employee> nodes, whereas the innermost loop iterates through the child nodes of the <employee> node, that is, the <firstname>, <lastname>, <homephone>, and <notes> nodes.

The outermost loop uses the MoveToNext() method of the XPathNavigator class to advance the cursor onto the next node. It then decides whether there are any <employee> nodes using the HasChildren property. The HasChildren property returns true if there are child nodes to the current node; otherwise, it returns false. If there are <employee> nodes, the cursor is moved to the first <employee> node by calling the MoveToFirstChild() method, which moves the navigator cursor to the first child node.

Now the code starts iterating through all the <employee> nodes. With each iteration, the value of the employee attribute is retrieved by using the GetAttribute() method. This method accepts two parameters: the name of the attribute to retrieve and the attribute namespace. Because our document does not contain any namespaces, an empty string is passed as the second parameter. A TreeView node is added for that employee ID. The cursor is then moved to the first child node of the <employee> node by using the MoveToFirstChild() method we discussed earlier. After this call, the cursor will be on the <firstname> node.

Now the innermost loop starts. With each iteration, the name of the node is retrieved by using the Name property, and the value of the node is retrieved by using the Value property. The same process is carried out for all the child nodes, that is, <firstname>, <lastname>, <homephone>, and <notes>.

After the innermost loop is finished, the navigator cursor is moved back to the parent <employee> node. This is done with the help of the MoveToParent() method, which moves the cursor pointer to the parent node of the current node. The same process is repeated for the remaining <employee> nodes.

Selecting Nodes

This chapter began with a brief overview of XPath and its vocabulary, including terms such as *axis*, *node test*, *predicate*, and *function*. You might be wondering where they come into the picture. It's time now to see those features in action.

To test various XPath expressions, we will create a simple application that looks like the one shown in Figure 4-3.

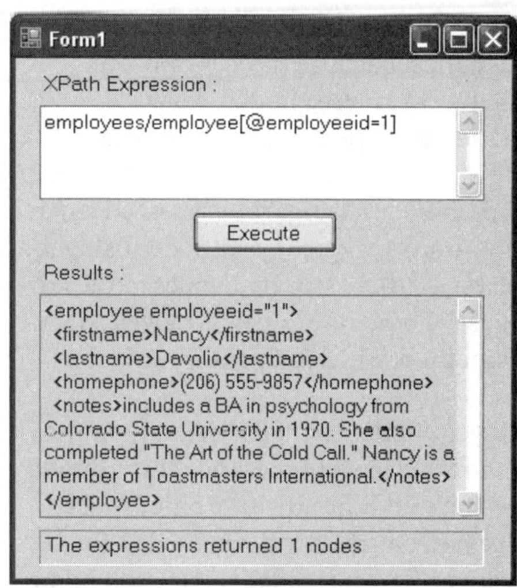

Figure 4-3. *Executing XPath expressions*

The application consists of a text box positioned at the top to enter XPath expressions. After you click the Execute button, the given expression is executed and its results are displayed in another text box at the bottom. The label at the bottom displays the total number of rows returned by the expression. Listing 4-3 shows the `Click` event handler of the Execute button.

Listing 4-3. *Using the Select() Method*

```
private void button1_Click(object sender, EventArgs e)
{
  XPathDocument doc =
    new XPathDocument(Application.StartupPath + @"\employees.xml");
  XPathNavigator navigator = doc.CreateNavigator();
  XPathNodeIterator iterator = navigator.Select(textBox1.Text);
  try
  {
    label3.Text = "The expressions returned " + iterator.Count + " nodes";
    if (iterator.Count > 0)
    {
      while (iterator.MoveNext())
```

```
        {
          textBox2.Text = iterator.Current.OuterXml;
        }
      }
      else
      {
        textBox2.Text = "No results";
      }
    }
    catch (Exception ex)
    {
      MessageBox.Show(ex.Message);
    }
}
```

The code creates an instance of `XPathDocument` by passing the path of the `Employees.xml` file. Then an `XPathNavigator` is obtained by using the `CreateNavigator()` method of `XPathDocument`. The code then calls the `Select()` method of `XPathNavigator`, which accepts an XPath expression and returns an instance of `XPathNodeIterator`.

The `XPathNodeIterator` class allows you to iterate through the returned nodes and has a number of properties and methods to assist you. To start with, the `Count` property tells you how many nodes were selected by the `Select()` method. After you are satisfied that there were some results, you can iterate through the selected nodes by using the `MoveNext()` method. On each node, you then use the `Current` property to give you a reference to the `XPathNavigator` that is positioned at the current node. You can then call any of the methods and properties of `XPathNavigator`.

In our example, we simply display the `OuterXml` property of the underlying `XPathNavigator` in a text box. Though not used in our example, the `CurrentPosition` property of `XPathNodeIterator` returns the current index of the node being accessed.

Now let's try some XPath expressions by using our application. Some XPath expressions relevant to our XML document (`Employees.xml`) are given in Table 4-6.

Table 4-6. *Examples of XPath Expressions*

Purpose	Expression
To select an employee whose employee ID is 1	`employees/employee[@employeeid=1]`
To select the employee whose first name is Andrew	`employees/employee[firstname/text()='Andrew']`
To select the last employee from the document	`employees/employee[last()]`
To select the employee whose index is 2	`employees/employee[position()=2]`
To select an employee whose name contains *Nancy*	`employees/employee[contains(firstname,'Nancy')]`
To select the name of the first employee	`employees/employee/firstname[text()]`

Selecting Single Nodes

The `Select()` method returns all the nodes that are obtained after evaluating the XPath expression. There is a method called `SelectSingleNode()` that executes the supplied XPath expression and returns an `XPathNavigator` object (and not an `XPathNodeIterator`) that contains the first matching node for the specified expression. You can then use the `XPathNavigator` object to navigate through the nodes. `SelectSingleNode()` comes in handy when you know that your XPath expression is going to return just one node. For example, in our document we can use `SelectSingleNode()` to extract an employee matching a specific employee ID.

To illustrate the use of `SelectSingleNode()`, you need to develop an application as shown in Figure 4-4.

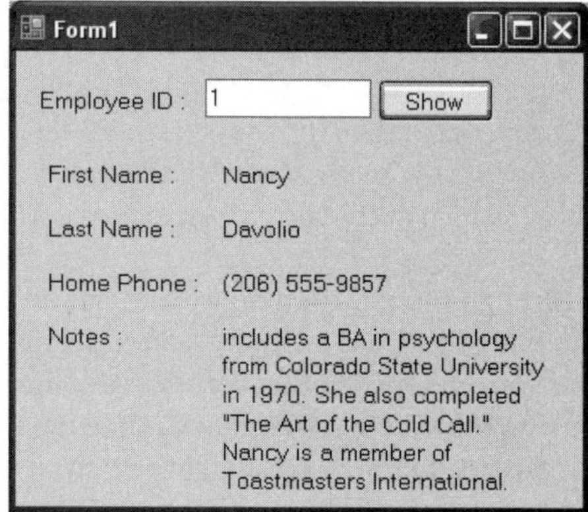

Figure 4-4. *Using the SelectSingleNode() method*

The application contains a text box to accept an employee ID and nine labels. Clicking the Show button displays details of an employee, and because the employee ID is unique in `Employees.xml`, we can safely use `SelectSingleNode()` here. Listing 4-4 shows the relevant code.

Listing 4-4. *Calling the SelectSingleNode() Method*

```
private void button1_Click(object sender, EventArgs e)
{
  XPathDocument doc =
    new XPathDocument(Application.StartupPath + @"\employees.xml");
  XPathNavigator navigator = doc.CreateNavigator();
  XPathNavigator result =
    navigator.SelectSingleNode(@"employees/employee[@employeeid=" +
      textBox1.Text + "]");
  result.MoveToFirstChild();
```

```
  do
  {
    switch (result.Name)
    {
      case "firstname":
        label6.Text=result.Value;
        break;
      case "lastname":
        label7.Text=result.Value;
        break;
      case "homephone":
        label8.Text=result.Value;
        break;
      case "notes":
        label9.Text=result.Value;
        break;
    }
  }
  while (result.MoveToNext());
}
```

The code obtains an XPathNavigator object from an XPathDocument class. To retrieve the <employee> node with the specified employee ID, we use SelectSingleNode(), by supplying the appropriate XPath expression. It in turn returns another XPathNavigator object containing the returned node.

The code then iterates through all the child nodes (<firstname>, <lastname>, <homephone>, and <notes>) of the returned <employee> node. With each iteration, the corresponding values are extracted by using the Value property of XPathNavigator.

Selecting Children, Ancestors, and Descendants

In addition to Select() and SelectSingleNode(), you can also use three specialized methods:

- The SelectChildren() method accepts the name of the child node and returns an XPathNodeIterator containing all the child nodes of the current node matching the supplied name.

- The SelectAncestors() method accepts the name of the ancestor nodes to select and returns an XPathNodeIterator containing all the ancestor nodes of the current node.

- The SelectDescendants() method accepts a node name and returns an XPathNodeIterator containing all the descendant nodes of the current node matching the supplied name.

These methods are optimized for performance and hence are faster than the equivalent XPath expressions.

Compiling XPath Expressions

If you are using the same XPath expression again and again, you can improve the performance of your code by using the `Compile()` method of the `XPathNavigator` class. This method accepts an XPath expression as a string, compiles it, and returns an instance of the `XPathExpression` class. This instance can then be supplied to the `Select()` and `SelectSingleNode()` methods.

To see the `Compile()` method in action, you need to modify the example that we developed for selecting nodes (see the "Selecting Nodes" section). The modified code is given in Listing 4-5.

Listing 4-5. *Using XPathExpression and the Compile() Method*

```
private void button1_Click(object sender, EventArgs e)
{
  XPathDocument doc =
    new XPathDocument(Application.StartupPath + @"\employees.xml");
  XPathNavigator navigator = doc.CreateNavigator();
  XPathExpression expression = navigator.Compile(textBox1.Text);
  XPathNodeIterator iterator = navigator.Select(expression);
  try
  {
    ...
```

Note the lines marked in bold. The code creates an instance of the `XPathExpression` class by calling the `Compile()` method of `XPathNavigator`. This `XPathExpression` instance is then passed to the `Select()` method. The rest of the code of the application remains unchanged. You can pass the same `XPathExpression` instance to any number of `Select()` or `SelectSingleNode()` calls.

Navigating Between Attributes

Previously we accessed the attribute value by using the `GetAttribute()` method of the `XPathNavigator` class. However, there is an alternate technique that allows you to move through the available attributes by using three methods of `XPathNavigator`: `MoveToAttribute()`, `MoveToFirstAttribute()`, and `MoveToNextAttribute()`. These methods allow you to move to a specific attribute, the first attribute, and the next attribute, respectively.

The previous example can be modified as shown in Listing 4-6.

Listing 4-6. *Accessing Attributes by Using the MoveTo . . . Methods*

```
navigator.MoveToAttribute("employeeid", "");
string id = navigator.Value;
navigator.MoveToParent();
```

As you can see, the code now calls the `MoveToAttribute()` method instead of `GetAttribute()`. The `MoveToAttribute()` method takes the same two parameters as `GetAttribute()`, that is, the name of the attribute and the attribute namespace. To access the attribute's value this time, we use the `Value` property of `XPathNavigator`. Because the cursor has been moved to the `employeeid` attribute, the `Value` property returns its value. Before continuing, the cursor is positioned back to the `<employee>` node by calling the `MoveToParent()` method.

Retrieving Inner and Outer XML

In the previous sections, we used the `Value` property of `XPathNavigator` to access the text of various attributes and nodes. There are two more properties—`InnerXml` and `OuterXml`—that return the contents of the `XPathNavigator` as a string. The `InnerXml` property returns the complete markup of all the child nodes (excluding any markup of the current node), whereas the `OuterXml` property returns the complete markup of the node and all the child nodes.

To see how these properties are used, you need to develop an application as shown in Figure 4-5.

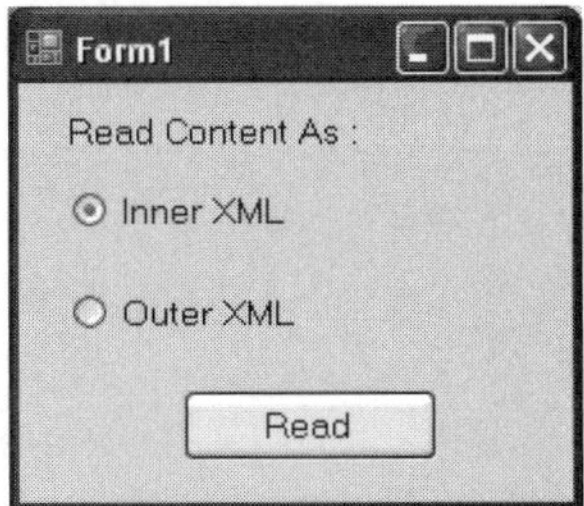

Figure 4-5. *Inner and outer XML*

The application contains two radio buttons to indicate inner or outer XML options. The Read button reads the `Employees.xml` file and displays the content as per the selection made. Listing 4-7 shows the `Click` event handler of the Read button containing the relevant code.

Listing 4-7. *Using InnerXml and OuterXml Propertiess*

```
private void button1_Click(object sender, EventArgs e)
{
  XPathDocument doc=new XPathDocument(Application.StartupPath + @"\employees.xml");
  XPathNavigator navigator = doc.CreateNavigator();
  navigator.MoveToRoot();
  navigator.MoveToFirstChild();

  while (navigator.MoveToNext())
  {
    if (radioButton1.Checked)
    {
      MessageBox.Show(navigator.InnerXml);
    }
    else
    {
      MessageBox.Show(navigator.OuterXml);
    }
  }
}
```

The code creates an instance of `XPathDocument` as before. The `XPathNavigator` is then obtained by using the `CreateNavigator()` method of the `XPathDocument` class. As you learned in the previous examples, the cursor is positioned at the `<employees>` node. Finally, the entire content of the `<employees>` node is retrieved by using the `InnerXml` and `OuterXml` properties of the `XPathNavigator` class. The resultant message boxes for `InnerXml` and `OuterXml` are shown in Figures 4-6 and 4-7.

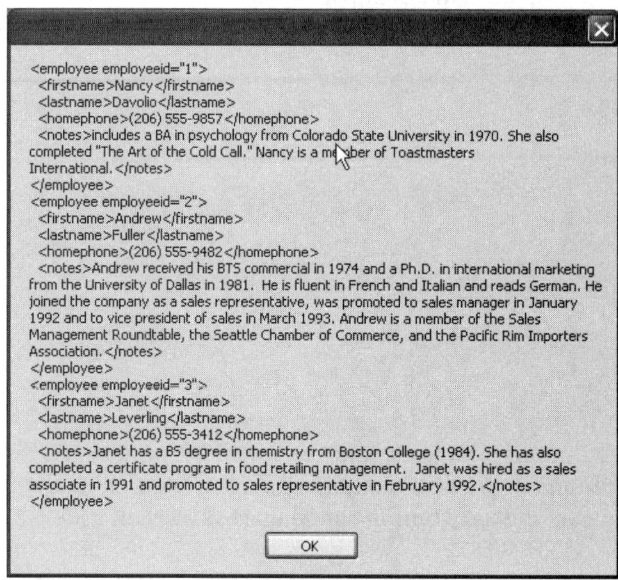

Figure 4-6. *Output of the InnerXml property*

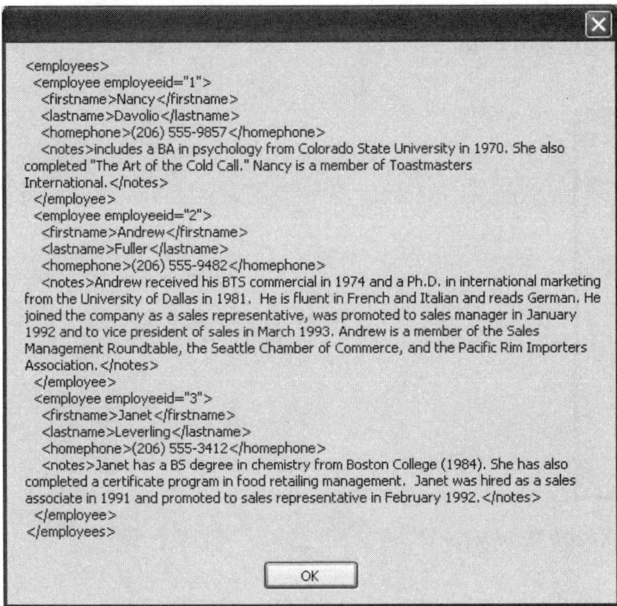

```
<employees>
  <employee employeeid="1">
    <firstname>Nancy</firstname>
    <lastname>Davolio</lastname>
    <homephone>(206) 555-9857</homephone>
    <notes>includes a BA in psychology from Colorado State University in 1970. She also
completed "The Art of the Cold Call." Nancy is a member of Toastmasters
International.</notes>
  </employee>
  <employee employeeid="2">
    <firstname>Andrew</firstname>
    <lastname>Fuller</lastname>
    <homephone>(206) 555-9482</homephone>
    <notes>Andrew received his BTS commercial in 1974 and a Ph.D. in international marketing
from the University of Dallas in 1981.  He is fluent in French and Italian and reads German. He
joined the company as a sales representative, was promoted to sales manager in January
1992 and to vice president of sales in March 1993. Andrew is a member of the Sales
Management Roundtable, the Seattle Chamber of Commerce, and the Pacific Rim Importers
Association.</notes>
  </employee>
  <employee employeeid="3">
    <firstname>Janet</firstname>
    <lastname>Leverling</lastname>
    <homephone>(206) 555-3412</homephone>
    <notes>Janet has a BS degree in chemistry from Boston College (1984). She has also
completed a certificate program in food retailing management.  Janet was hired as a sales
associate in 1991 and promoted to sales representative in February 1992.</notes>
  </employee>
</employees>

OK
```

Figure 4-7. *Output of the OuterXml property*

Note how `OuterXml` returns markup of the `<employees>` node, whereas `InnerXml` doesn't.

Getting an XmlReader from XPathNavigator

Though `XPathNavigator` allows you to read the XML document, at times you may want to pass a set of nodes from `XPathNavigator` to an `XmlReader`. The `XmlReader` can then read the returned nodes further. This is accomplished by using the `ReadSubTree()` method of `XPathNavigator`.

To demonstrate how an XmlReader can be obtained from an XPathNavigator, you need to build a Windows application as shown in Figure 4-8.

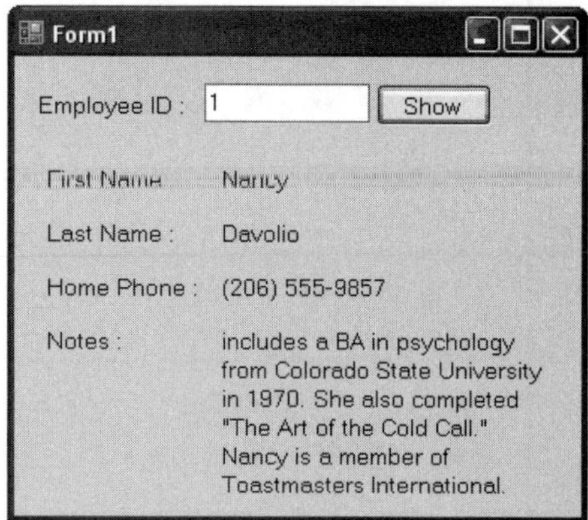

Figure 4-8. *Obtaining XmlReader from XPathNavigator*

The application consists of a text box for entering the employee ID, a button, and nine labels. Upon clicking the Show button, the form displays the employee details on the form.

Listing 4-8 shows the Click event handler of the Show button.

Listing 4-8. *Calling the ReadSubtree() Method*

```
private void button1_Click(object sender, EventArgs e)
{
  XPathDocument doc=new XPathDocument(Application.StartupPath + @"\employees.xml");
  XPathNavigator navigator = doc.CreateNavigator();
  navigator.MoveToRoot();
  navigator.MoveToFirstChild();

  while (navigator.MoveToNext())
  {
    navigator.MoveToFirstChild();

    do
    {
      string id = navigator.GetAttribute("employeeid", "");
      if (id == textBox1.Text)
      {
        XmlReader reader=navigator.ReadSubtree();
        DisplayDetails(reader);
      }
    }
    while (navigator.MoveToNext());
  }
}
```

The code begins by creating an instance of XPathDocument. An XPathNavigator is then obtained by calling CreateNavigator(). Then the code iterates through the document. The navigation logic should be familiar to you because we used it in previous examples. With each iteration, the employeeid attribute is checked against the value supplied from the text box. If they match, the ReadSubtree() method of XPathNavigator is called. In this case, this returns an instance of XmlReader that contains one <employee> node and all its child nodes. The returned XmlReader is passed to a helper function called DisplayDetails(), shown in Listing 4-9.

Listing 4-9. *DisplayDetails() Helper Function*

```
private void DisplayDetails(XmlReader reader)
{
  while (reader.Read())
  {
    if (reader.NodeType == XmlNodeType.Element)
    {
      switch (reader.Name)
      {
        case "firstname":
          label6.Text = reader.ReadString();
          break;
        case "lastname":
          label7.Text = reader.ReadString();
          break;
        case "homephone":
          label8.Text = reader.ReadString();
          break;
        case "notes":
          label9.Text = reader.ReadString();
          break;
      }
    }
  }
  reader.Close();
}
```

The DisplayDetails() function iterates through the supplied XmlReader object calling its Read() method. With each iteration, the values of the <firstname>, <lastname>, <homephone>, and <notes> nodes are retrieved by using the ReadString() method of the XmlReader class and assigned to the labels. Finally, the reader is closed by calling its Close() method.

Note The position of XPathNavigator remains unaffected even after calling the ReadSubtree() method.

Getting an XmlWriter from XPathNavigator

Just as you can create an `XmlReader` from `XPathNavigator`, you can also create an `XmlWriter` from it. This is useful in situations where you want to write selected nodes from `XPathNavigator` to a file or stream. `XPathNavigator` provides a method called `WriteSubtree()` that accepts an `XmlWriter` and writes the current node to it.

To illustrate the use of this technique, you need to develop an application as shown in Figure 4-9.

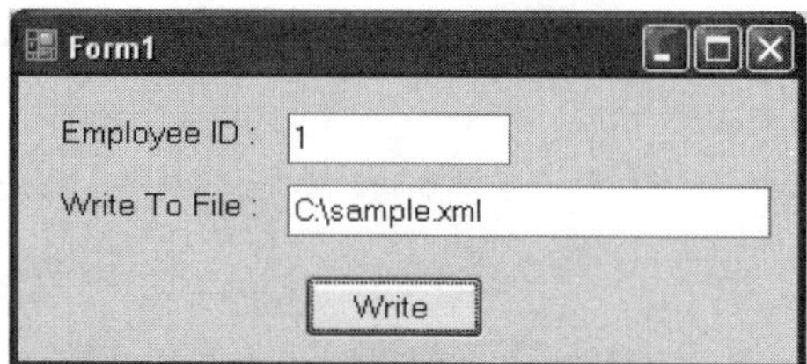

Figure 4-9. *Obtaining an XmlWriter from XPathNavigator*

The application consists of two text boxes: one to accept the employee ID to be extracted, and the other to specify a file path where the extracted employee details are stored.

Listing 4-10 shows the `Click` event handler of the Write button.

Listing 4-10. *Calling the WriteSubtree() Method*

```
private void button1_Click(object sender, EventArgs e)
{
  XPathDocument doc =
    new XPathDocument(Application.StartupPath + @"\employees.xml");
  XPathNavigator navigator = doc.CreateNavigator();
  navigator.MoveToRoot();
  navigator.MoveToFirstChild();

  while (navigator.MoveToNext())
  {
    navigator.MoveToFirstChild();

    do
    {
      string id = navigator.GetAttribute("employeeid", "");
      if (id == textBox1.Text)
```

```
        {
          XmlTextWriter writer = new XmlTextWriter(textBox2.Text, null);
          navigator.WriteSubtree(writer);
          writer.Close();
          if (MessageBox.Show("Do you want to see the file?",
                              "Question",
                              MessageBoxButtons.YesNo) == DialogResult.Yes)
          {
            System.Diagnostics.Process.Start(textBox2.Text);
          }
        }
      }
      while (navigator.MoveToNext());
    }
  }
```

The code creates an instance of XPathDocument and XPathNavigator as before. It then starts navigating the document and finds the matching <employee> node. After the matching employee is found, the code creates an instance of XmlTextWriter (recollect that XmlTextWriter inherits from the XmlWriter abstract class), supplying the file path entered in the text box to the constructor. Though our example writes the data to a disk file, any writable stream can be used.

To write the matching employee to XmlTextWriter, the code calls the WriteSubtree() method of XPathNavigator. The WriteSubtree() method accepts any class derived from the XmlWriter base class and writes the contents of the current node to it. In our example, it will be the <employee> node and its child nodes. After the writing is over, the XmlTextWriter is closed by calling its Close() method. The code then asks the user whether they want to open the resultant file, as shown in Figure 4-10.

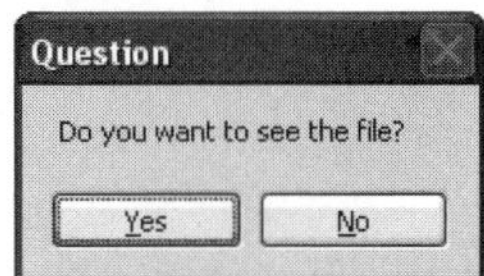

Figure 4-10. *Prompting the user to open the resultant file*

If the user clicks Yes, the resultant XML file is opened in the browser. Note the use of the Process class from the System.Diagnostics namespace. The Start() method of this class accepts a filename and opens it in its associated application. Figure 4-11 shows a sample output document with the <employee> subtree extracted.

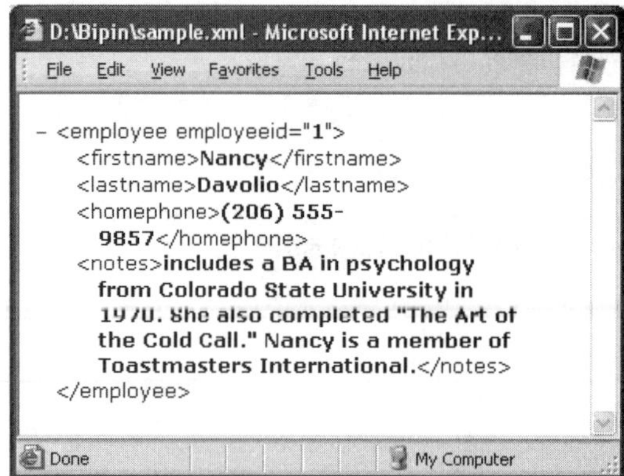

Figure 4-11. *Resultant XML document*

Editing XML Documents with the XPathNavigator Class

Up until now, we have used `XPathNavigator` to navigate and read values from the underlying XML document. However, it is possible to modify the underlying document also, though the `XPathNavigator` must be obtained from the `XmlDocument` class to do so. `XPathNavigator` instances obtained from `XPathDocument` are read-only and hence cannot be used for editing. You can check whether an instance of `XPathNavigator` is editable by using its `CanEdit` property, which returns `true` if the instance is editable, and `false` otherwise.

To see how an XML document can be modified with the help of `XPathNavigator`, you need to develop an application as shown in Figure 4-12.

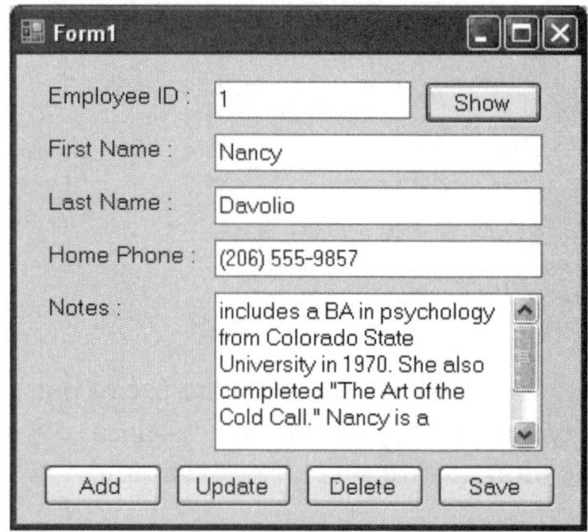

Figure 4-12. *Modifying an XML document by using XPathNavigator*

The application consists of text boxes to supply values for employee ID, first name, last name, home phone, and notes. There are four buttons for adding a new employee, modifying an existing employee, deleting an existing employee, and saving the changed document, respectively. When you enter an employee ID and click the Show button, the details of that employee are displayed in the remaining text boxes. You can change the details as per your requirements and click the Add, Update, or Delete buttons to add, update, or delete an employee, respectively. To save the modified document, you need to click the Save button.

In the source code of the application, you will find two form variables declared as shown Listing 4-11.

Listing 4-11. *Declaring XmlDocument and XPathNavigator*

```
XmlDocument doc = new XmlDocument();
XPathNavigator navigator = null;
```

The `Employees.xml` file is loaded into this `XmlDocument`, and an `XPathNavigator` is obtained from it. This code goes in the `Load` event of the form and is shown in Listing 4-12.

Listing 4-12. *Creating XPathNavigator*

```
private void Form1_Load(object sender, EventArgs e)
{
  doc.Load(Application.StartupPath + @"\employees.xml");
  navigator = doc.CreateNavigator();
}
```

When the user enters an employee ID and clicks the Show button, the details of that employee need to be displayed in the remaining text boxes. The `Click` event handler of the Show button does this job, as shown in Listing 4-13.

Listing 4-13. *Retrieving Details of an Employee*

```
private void button1_Click(object sender, EventArgs e)
{
  navigator.MoveToRoot();
  navigator.MoveToFirstChild();

  while (navigator.MoveToNext())
  {
    navigator.MoveToFirstChild();

    do
    {
      string id = navigator.GetAttribute("employeeid", "");
      if (id == textBox1.Text)
      {
        navigator.MoveToFirstChild();
```

```
          do
          {
            switch (navigator.Name)
            {
              case "firstname":
                textBox2.Text = navigator.Value;
                break;
              case "lastname":
                textBox3.Text = navigator.Value;
                break;
              case "homephone":
                textBox4.Text = navigator.Value;
                break;
              case "notes":
                textBox5.Text = navigator.Value;
                break;
            }
          }
          while (navigator.MoveToNext());

          navigator.MoveToParent();
        }
      }
      while (navigator.MoveToNext());
    }
}
```

The code should be familiar to you, because we used something similar in previous examples. The code loops through all the <employee> nodes and finds the one that matches the supplied employee ID. The values of various child nodes such as <firstname>, <lastname>, <homephone>, and <notes> are displayed in the respective text boxes by using the Value property of XPathNavigator.

Adding Nodes

To add new nodes to the document, the XPathNavigator class provides a method called AppendChild(). The AppendChild() method returns an instance of XmlWriter, and by using this XmlWriter you can write additional nodes to the document. The newly written nodes are added as child nodes of the current node. Listing 4-14 shows how this is accomplished.

Listing 4-14. *Appending New Nodes*

```
private void button2_Click(object sender, EventArgs e)
{
  navigator.MoveToRoot();
  navigator.MoveToFirstChild();

  while (navigator.MoveToNext())
  {
    XmlWriter writer = navigator.AppendChild();
    writer.WriteStartElement("employee");
    writer.WriteAttributeString("employeeid", textBox1.Text);
    writer.WriteElementString("firstname", textBox2.Text);
    writer.WriteElementString("lastname", textBox3.Text);
    writer.WriteElementString("homephone", textBox4.Text);
    writer.WriteElementString("notes", textBox5.Text);
    writer.WriteEndElement();
    writer.Close();
  }
}
```

The code first navigates to the `<employees>` node. This is where we want to add a new `<employee>` child node. Then it calls the `AppendChild()` method of the `XPathNavigator`. The returned `XmlWriter` is used to add a new `<employee>` node with an `employeeid` attribute. The child nodes of the `<employee>` node (`<firstname>`, `<lastname>`, `<homephone>`, and `<notes>`) are also added. The methods such as `WriteStartElement()`and `WriteEndElement()` should already be familiar to you from Chapter 3.

■ **Note** There are a few other overloads of the `AppendChild()` method. For example, one overloaded method accepts the complete XML markup fragment for the new node and appends it to the current node. However, the one that we used is more flexible.

Modifying Nodes

To modify contents of any of the nodes, the `XPathNavigator` class provides a method called `SetValue()`, which accepts the new value and assigns it to the current node. Listing 4-15 shows how this method can be used.

Listing 4-15. *Modifying Content*

```
private void button3_Click(object sender, EventArgs e)
{
  navigator.MoveToRoot();
  navigator.MoveToFirstChild();

  while (navigator.MoveToNext())
  {
    navigator.MoveToFirstChild();

    do
    {
      string id = navigator.GetAttribute("employeeid", "");
      if (id == textBox1.Text)
      {
        navigator.MoveToFirstChild();

        do
        {
          switch (navigator.Name)
          {
            case "firstname":
              navigator.SetValue(textBox2.Text);
              break;
            case "lastname":
              navigator.SetValue(textBox3.Text);
              break;
            case "homephone":
              navigator.SetValue(textBox4.Text);
              break;
            case "notes":
              navigator.SetValue(textBox5.Text);
              break;
          }
        }
        while (navigator.MoveToNext());

        navigator.MoveToParent();
      }
    }
    while (navigator.MoveToNext());
  }
}
```

As before, the code finds out the <employee> node that is to be updated. The switch statement checks the Name property of XPathNavigator for the required node names (firstname, lastname, homephone, and notes). Inside each case, the SetValue() method is called on the navigator by passing the new value from the appropriate text box.

Deleting Nodes

Deleting a node is fairly simple. The DeleteSelf() method of XPathNavigator deletes the current node. After the node is successfully deleted, the cursor is moved to the parent node of the deleted node. Listing 4-16 shows the usage of DeleteSelf().

Listing 4-16. *Deleting a Node*

```
private void button4_Click(object sender, EventArgs e)
{
  navigator.MoveToRoot();
  navigator.MoveToFirstChild();

  while (navigator.MoveToNext())
  {
    navigator.MoveToFirstChild();

    do
    {
      string id = navigator.GetAttribute("employeeid", "");
      if (id == textBox1.Text)
      {
        navigator.DeleteSelf();
      }
    }
    while (navigator.MoveToNext());
  }
}
```

As in the previous case, the code looks for a specific <employee> node. After it finds the node, it calls the DeleteSelf() method on the navigator.

Saving Changes

It is important to remember that while making any modifications via XPathNavigator, the changes are not saved automatically to disk. The changes affect only the DOM tree loaded in memory, so you need to save the underlying document by calling the Save() method of the XmlDocument class. This is illustrated in Listing 4-17.

Listing 4-17. *Saving the Document*

```
private void button5_Click(object sender, EventArgs e)
{
  doc.Save(Application.StartupPath + @"\employees.xml");
}
```

Summary

In this chapter, you learned what XPath is and how to use XPath expressions in the .NET Framework. We covered in detail the `XPathNavigator` class, which represents the XPath data model of the .NET Framework. The `XPathNavigator` class can be constructed from either of the `XPathDocument` or `XmlDocument` classes. The `XPathNavigator` returned from `XPathDocument` is read-only, whereas that returned from `XmlDocument` is editable. You also learned how to select nodes from the XML document by using XPath expressions in string form as well as in compiled form.

CHAPTER 5

■ ■ ■

Validating XML Documents

In Chapters 2, 3, and 4, you learned how to read and write XML documents, though we always assumed that the XML structure (tag names, attribute names, nesting, and so on) contained in the source XML document was correct. However, in many real-world cases this assumption may not be true. For example, a purchase order application might be accepting orders from various customers in XML format. What is the guarantee that each submitted order adheres to the agreed-upon XML structure? What if somebody deviates from the agreed-upon structure? This is where XML schemas come into the picture.

XML schemas describe the structure of an XML document; to use an analogy, they serve the same purpose as database schemas. With the help of schemas, you can do two important things:

- You can create XML documents based on the schema.
- You can validate XML documents against the schema.

In this chapter, you are going to learn about the following:

- Various ways to define the structure of an XML document
- What XML schemas are
- How to create schemas
- How to validate XML documents against schemas
- How to create schemas programmatically by using the Schema Object Model (SOM)

Providing Structure for XML Documents

As mentioned previously, XML schemas define the structure of XML documents. In other words, they provide a template for creating and validating XML documents. However, a schema is not the only way to provide structure for an XML document. The .NET Framework supports three ways of defining XML structure:

- Document Type Definitions (DTDs)
- XML Data Reduced schemas (XDR schemas)
- XML Schema Definition Language schemas (XSD schemas)

Document Type Definitions (DTDs)

DTDs are an older way of representing XML structure but they are still in use. They are a W3C standard, and a considerable number of XML documents depend on them for validation. A DTD defines the overall structure of an XML document in terms of acceptable tag names, acceptable attribute names, and so on. An XML document author uses the DTD while creating a document. The same DTD can be used while validating the document also. Though DTDs are one of the common ways to define XML structure, they suffer from many disadvantages:

- They use non-XML syntax.
- They are difficult to create as well as to understand.
- You need to specifically learn the DTD syntax.
- They are not extensible.
- They do not support data types.
- They do not support namespaces.

XML Data Reduced Schemas (XDR Schemas)

While the XSD Schema proposal was under consideration, Microsoft went ahead and created its implementation, called the XML Data Reduced, or XDR, Schema specification. The XDR Schema specification closely matches the XSD Schema specification. For the sake of backward compatibility, Microsoft retained support for XDR schemas in the .NET Framework. If you are creating a new schema for your XML documents, you should use the XSD Schema specification instead of XDR.

XML Schema Definition Language Schemas (XSD Schemas)

XSD schemas represent the most recent effort to provide standardization for defining XML structures. The XSD Schema specification is a W3C recommendation. One of the key benefits of XSD schemas is that they support data types. They are XML documents themselves and overcome most of the limitations of DTDs. If you are building new schemas for your XML documents, you should create them by using XSD instead of the DTD or XDR standards.

Creating Structure for an XML Document

Now that you know the possible ways to define XML structure, let's put each of the ways to use. In this section, you will create a formal structure for the same `Employees.xml` document by using the DTD and XSD standards. Because XDR and XSD are closely matching standards and XSD supersedes XDR, I will not cover XDR here.

The Structure of Employees.xml

You already know how our Employees.xml file looks. Our aim is to define the structure of the document by using the DTD and XSD standards so that you can validate the document later. The structure of Employees.xml is as follows:

- The root element must be <employees>.
- The root element can contain zero or more <employee> elements.
- The <employee> element must have an attribute called employeeid.
- The <employee> element must contain <firstname>, <lastname>, <homephone>, and <notes> sub-elements.
- The <firstname>, <lastname>, and <homephone> elements contain plain-text values.
- The <notes> element contains character data (CDATA).
- The <firstname>, <lastname>, <homephone>, and <notes> sub-elements must appear in the same order.

Keeping the preceding requirements in mind, let's create the DTD first followed by the XSD schema.

Creating the DTD

In this section, you will learn how to create a DTD for representing the structure of the Employees.xml file. Listing 5-1 shows the complete DTD for the document.

Listing 5-1. *DTD for Employees.xml*

```
<!ELEMENT employees (employee*)>
<!ELEMENT employee (firstname,lastname,homephone,notes)>
<!ELEMENT firstname (#PCDATA)>
<!ELEMENT lastname (#PCDATA)>
<!ELEMENT homephone (#PCDATA)>
<!ELEMENT notes (#PCDATA)>
<!ATTLIST employee employeeid CDATA #REQUIRED>
```

The DTD defines the root element of the XML document to be <employees>. This is done by using the <!ELEMENT> declaration, which specifies the name of the element (employees in our case) and content that can go inside it. In our case, the <employees> element can take zero or more <employee> elements and not any other element or text. This constraint is enforced by placing the acceptable element names (employee in our case) in the brackets. The asterisk (*) indicates that zero or more <employee> elements can be placed inside an <employees> element. Similar to *, you can also use the plus sign (+) and question mark (?). The + operator indicates that you can have one or more occurrences of the element, whereas ? indicates that the element is optional.

Next we define the <employee> element by using the same <!ELEMENT> declaration. Because the <employee> element must contain <firstname>, <lastname>, <homephone>, and <notes> sub-elements, they are specified as a comma-separated list. A comma-separated list of elements must appear in the order specified. If you want to allow the elements to appear in any order, you can use the pipe (|) character instead of the comma.

The document then defines each of the sub-elements of the <employee> element. To indicate that the elements contain plain-character data and no other sub-elements, we use #PCDATA, which stands for *plain-character data*. Thus the DTD enforces that the <firstname>, <lastname>, <homephone>, and <notes> elements can contain only plain-character data and no markup or sub-elements. If our elements contained character data and sub-elements, we could have used ANY instead of #PCDATA. On the same lines, if our elements are empty (that is, they contain neither character data nor sub-elements), we could have used EMPTY.

Finally, the DTD defines the employeeid attribute for the <employee> element by using the <!ATTLIST> declaration. The <!ATTLIST> declaration takes the element whose attributes are being defined, followed by a list of attributes. The CDATA in the markup indicates that the attribute value contains character data. You can mark the attribute as a unique identifier by specifying its type as ID. The #REQUIRED in the declaration indicates that this attribute is mandatory and must be provided in the document.

Note Recollect that in Chapter 2 we used the GetElementById() method of the XmlDocument class. This method requires that the element to search should have an attribute of type ID.

To create the DTD, you can use the Visual Studio IDE: add a new text file, but name it Employees.dtd, key in the entire markup shown in Listing 5-1, and save the file. Open Employees.xml in the Visual Studio IDE and add a DOCTYPE declaration to it at the top, as shown in Listing 5-2.

Listing 5-2. *Attaching the DTD to an XML Document*

```
<?xml version="1.0" encoding="utf-8" ?>
<!DOCTYPE employees SYSTEM "employees.dtd">
<employees>
  <employee employeeid="1">
    <firstname>Nancy</firstname>
    ...
```

As you can see, at the top of the XML file we have put the <!DOCTYPE> declaration. The <!DOCTYPE> declaration is used to attach a DTD to an XML file. The <!DOCTYPE> declaration is immediately followed by <employees>—the root element of the document. The SYSTEM declaration specifies the URL of the DTD file that is providing structure to this XML document. In our case, it is employees.dtd.

You might be wondering why we created the DTD in Visual Studio. Apart from providing some IntelliSense, it is not helping much, is it? But wait a moment before you conclude anything, because it has something more to offer. Now add a new XML file in your project and add the <!DOCTYPE> declaration to it as shown in Listing 5-2. When you start creating the document, you will observe that the IDE shows various elements and attributes in IntelliSense. Figure 5-1 shows how this IntelliSense looks.

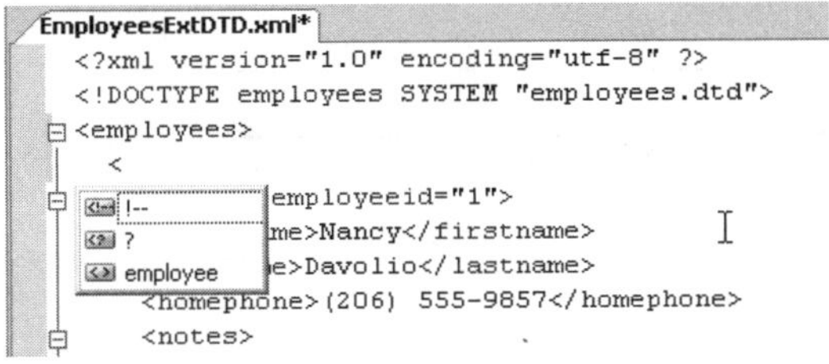

Figure 5-1. *Visual Studio IntelliSense for DTDs*

The IDE also validates your document as you key in. It displays error messages if you enter markup or attributes that violate the DTD rules.

Creating the XSD Schema

In this section, you will learn how to create XSD schemas in various ways, including the following:

- Creating the XSD schema manually
- Creating the XSD schema by using the Visual Studio XML Designer
- Creating the XSD schema from a database table
- Creating the XSD schema by using the `xsd.exe` command-line tool (often called the XML Schema Definition tool)

An XSD schema is typically stored in a file with the extension `.xsd`. A schema consists of various parts, some of which are listed in Table 5-1.

Table 5-1. *Parts of an XSD Schema*

Part Name	Description
Element	Represents a single element.
Attribute	Represents a single attribute of an element.
Attribute group	Represents a group of attributes that can be used further in a complex type.
Simple type	A simple type consists of only text values and no sub-elements—for example, string, numbers, date, and so on. Elements as well as attributes can be of the simple type.
Complex type	A complex type consists of one or more simple types. Only elements can be of the complex type.

One of the key advantages of XSD schemas over DTDs is that they support data types. These data types have been mapped with the .NET Framework's data types; thus XSD data types can be represented by their equivalent data types in .NET. Table 5-2 lists some of the common XSD data types and their .NET counterparts.

Table 5-2. *XSD Data Types*

XSD Data Type	.NET Data Type	Description
`Boolean`	`System.Boolean`	Represents Boolean values (`true` or `false`)
`Byte`	`System.SByte`	Represents an 8-bit signed integer (byte)
`dateTime`	`System.DateTime`	Represents the date and time
`decimal`	`System.Decimal`	Represents a decimal number
`Double`	`System.Double`	Represents a double precision number
`Float`	`System.Single`	Represents a single precision floating number
`Int`	`System.Int32`	Represents a 4-byte signed integer
`Long`	`System.Int64`	Represents an 8-byte signed integer
`String`	`System.String`	Represents string data

Now that you have a brief idea about XSD schemas, their parts, and data types, we will proceed to create XSD schemas by using the various ways described.

Creating an XSD Schema Manually

To create any XSD schema, you first need to think about the simple types, complex types, elements, and attributes going into it. Let's do this exercise for the `Employees.xml` file.

We will create three simple types for `Employees.xml`:

`NameSimpleType`: This simple type represents names used in our XML document (first name and last name). It puts restrictions on the names: the minimum length must be three and the maximum length must be less than 255.

`PhoneSimpleType`: This simple type represents phone numbers (the `<homephone>` element of our XML document). It restricts the phone numbers to no more than 20 characters.

`NotesSimpleType`: This simple type represents notes (the `<notes>` element of our document). It restricts the notes entered to no greater than 500 characters in length.

These three simple types will make a complex type called `EmployeeType`. The `EmployeeType` complex type consists of the following:

- An element called `<firstname>`, which is of simple type `NameSimpleType`
- An element called `<lastname>`, which is of simple type `NameSimpleType`
- An element called `<homephone>`, which is of simple type `PhoneSimpleType`
- An element called `<notes>`, which is of simple type `NotesSimpleType`
- A required attribute called `employeeid`, which is of type `int`

Finally, we will have an element called `<employees>` that will contain zero or more sub-elements named `<employee>`. The `<employee>` sub-elements will be of complex type `EmployeeType`.

Listing 5-3 shows the complete XSD schema containing all the preceding types, elements, and attributes.

Listing 5-3. *XSD Schema for Employees.xml*

```
<?xml version="1.0" encoding="utf-8"?>
<xs:schema attributeFormDefault="unqualified" elementFormDefault="qualified"
           xmlns:xs="http://www.w3.org/2001/XMLSchema">
  <xs:element name="employees">
    <xs:complexType>
      <xs:sequence>
        <xs:element name="employee" type="EmployeeType" minOccurs="0"
                    maxOccurs="unbounded" />
      </xs:sequence>
    </xs:complexType>
  </xs:element>
  <xs:complexType name="EmployeeType">
    <xs:all>
      <xs:element name="firstname" type="NameSimpleType" />
      <xs:element name="notes" type="NotesSimpleType" />
      <xs:element name="lastname" type="NameSimpleType" />
      <xs:element name="homephone" type="PhoneSimpleType" />
    </xs:all>
    <xs:attribute name="employeeid" type="xs:int" use="required" />
  </xs:complexType>
  <xs:simpleType name="NameSimpleType">
    <xs:restriction base="xs:string">
      <xs:minLength value="3" />
      <xs:maxLength value="255" />
    </xs:restriction>
  </xs:simpleType>
  <xs:simpleType name="PhoneSimpleType">
    <xs:restriction base="xs:string">
      <xs:maxLength value="20" />
    </xs:restriction>
  </xs:simpleType>
  <xs:simpleType name="NotesSimpleType">
    <xs:restriction base="xs:string">
      <xs:maxLength value="500" />
    </xs:restriction>
  </xs:simpleType>
</xs:schema>
```

The schema declaration starts with the `<schema>` tag. The XML namespace `http://www.w3.org/2001/XMLSchema` is required and indicates that this is an XSD schema. The xmlns attribute specifies that the namespace prefix for all the tags of this schema will be xs.

Then the schema declares the <employees> element by using the <element> tag. The <employees> element contains sub-elements named <employee>, which are of complex type EmployeeType. The complex type is indicated by the <complexType> element. There can be zero or more occurrences of <employee> sub-elements as defined by the minOccurs and maxOccurs attributes, respectively. Note the use of the unbounded keyword to indicate that any number of the element can exist.

Next the schema defines a complex type called EmployeeType by using the <complexType> element. The name attribute of <complexType> indicates the name of the complex type being defined. The EmployeeType complex type consists of four sub-elements and one attribute. The elements are declared by using the <element> tag and its two attributes, name and type. The name attribute specifies the name of the element, whereas the type attribute indicates the data type of the element.

The attributes are declared by using the <attribute> tag. The name attribute of the <attribute> element specifies the name of the attribute, and the type attribute indicates the data type of the attribute. In our case, the employeeid attribute is of type int and is required, as indicated by the use attribute.

Then the schema defines the NameSimpleType simple type by using the <simpleType> element. Because we want the data type of NameSimpleType to be string, we indicated this in the <restriction> element. The minimum and maximum length of the element is decided by the minLength and maxLength attributes, respectively. In our case, the names must be more than 3 characters in length and should not exceed 255 characters.

The PhoneSimpleType simple type is defined next. It is a string not exceeding 20 characters.

Finally, the NotesSimpleType simple type is defined. It is also a string, but it must not exceed 500 characters.

That's it! After you key in the preceding markup in a plain-text editor, you can save the file as Employees.xsd. You will learn about attaching an XSD schema to an XML document in later sections.

Creating the XSD Schema in Visual Studio Designer

Creating an XSD schema in Visual Studio is easy because the IDE provides visual tools to create elements, simple types, and complex types. To create a new XSD schema, you need to add one to your project by using the Add New Item dialog box. Name the new schema file Employees.xsd. Figure 5-2 shows the Add New Item dialog box with the relevant selection.

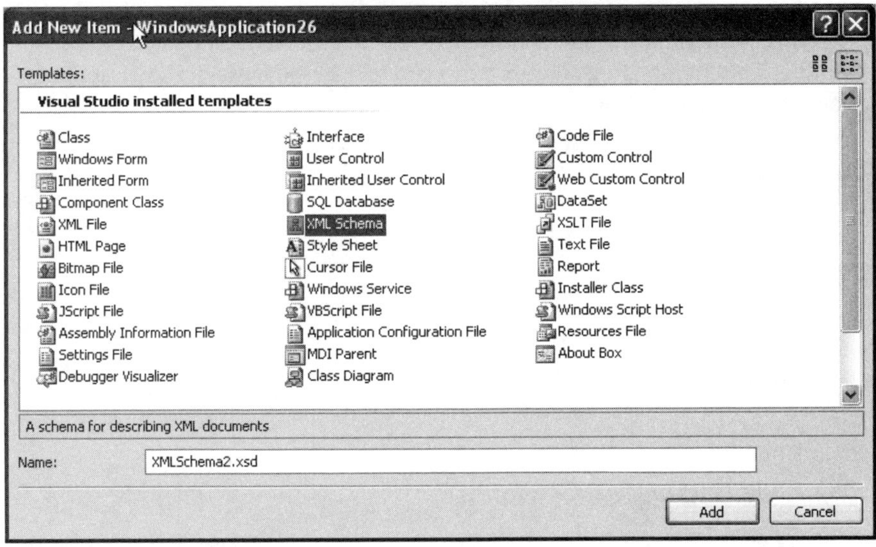

Figure 5-2. *Adding a new XSD schema to your project*

After you have added an XML schema, you will be presented with a canvas on which you can visually design the schema. The toolbox of Visual Studio will now show a node titled XML Schema, as shown in Figure 5-3.

Figure 5-3. *The XML Schema toolbox of Visual Studio*

As you can see in Figure 5-3, many of the schema parts that we discussed previously (simple type, complex type, element, attribute, and so on) are available in the toolbox.

To begin creating the schema, drag and drop three `simpleTypes` to the designer and set their properties as shown in Figure 5-4.

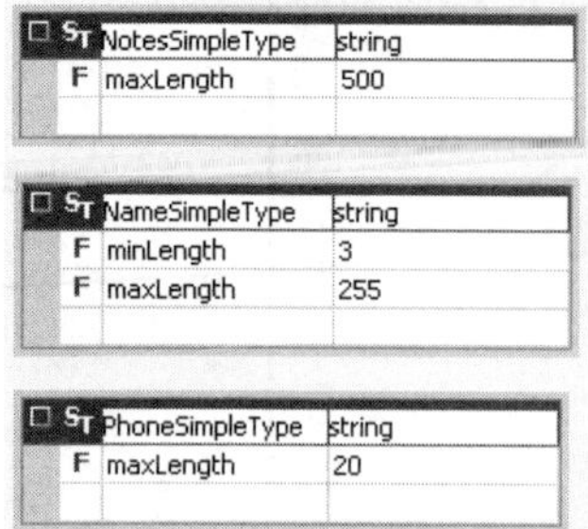

Figure 5-4. *Creating simple types in Visual Studio*

For each simple type, you need to specify its name and data type. You can then right-click on the individual simple type and choose Add ➤ New Facet. For `NameSimpleType` the facets are `minLength` and `maxLength` and have values of 3 and 255, respectively. The `PhoneSimpleType` simple type contains just one facet, `maxLength`, which is set to 20. Finally, `NotesSimpleType` contains the `maxLength` facet `maxLength`, which is set to 500. You can also open the properties window by selecting each simple type and set the values there.

Now drag and drop a `complexType` onto the designer. You need to design it as shown in Figure 5-5.

CT	EmployeeType	
E	firstname	NameSimpleType
E	notes	NotesSimpleType
E	lastname	NameSimpleType
E	homephone	PhoneSimpleType
A	employeeid	int

Figure 5-5. *Creating a complex type in Visual Studio*

Enter `EmployeeType` as the name for the complex type. Using the properties window, set the Order property of the `EmployeeType` element to `All`. This indicates that the sub-elements can appear in any order. Right-click on the `EmployeeType` complex type and add four new elements. Name the newly added elements `firstname`, `lastname`, `homephone`, and `notes`, respectively. Set the type of `firstname` and `lastname` to `NameSimpleType`, and `homephone` to `PhoneSimpleType`. Similarly, set the type of notes to `NotesSimpleType`. Now add a new attribute and name it `employeeid`. Specify its data type as `int`. Using the properties window, set its `use` property to `required`. This completes the `EmployeeType` complex type.

Now drag and drop an element on to the designer and name it `employees`. Using the shortcut menu, add a new element to it. Select the type of the element as `EmployeeType`. The employees element should now resemble Figure 5-6.

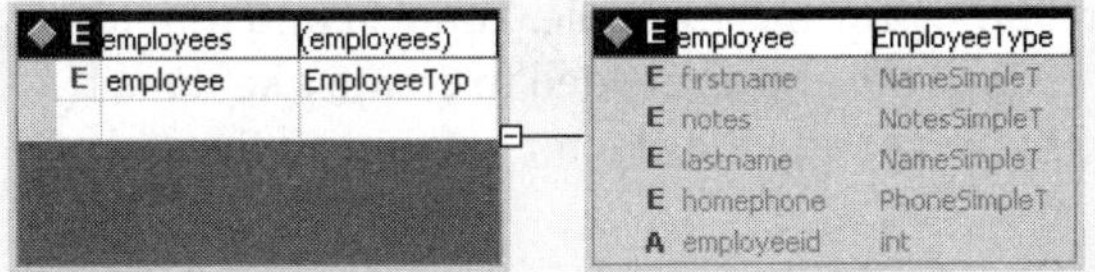

Figure 5-6. *Creating the <employee> element in Visual Studio*

This completes the creation of `Employees.xsd`. The completed schema is shown in Figure 5-7.

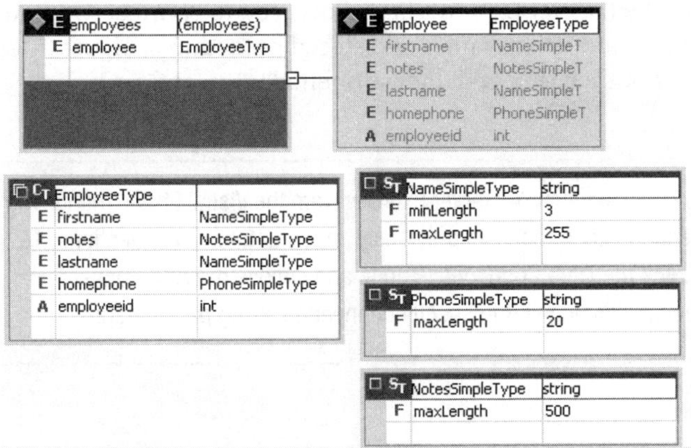

Figure 5-7. *The completed Employees.xsd in Visual Studio*

If you wish to see the generated schema markup, right-click on the schema designer and select View Code. You should see something similar to that shown in Figure 5-8.

```
Employees.xsd*   Employees.xsd*   EmployeesExtDTD.xml*
<?xml version="1.0" encoding="utf-8"?>
<xs:schema attributeFormDefault="unqualified" elementFormDefault="qual
  <xs:element name="employees">
    <xs:complexType>
      <xs:sequence>
        <xs:element name="employee" type="EmployeeType" minOccurs="0" 
      </xs:sequence>
    </xs:complexType>
  </xs:element>
  <xs:complexType name="EmployeeType">
    <xs:all>
      <xs:element name="firstname" type="NameSimpleType" />
      <xs:element name="notes" type="NotesSimpleType" />
      <xs:element name="lastname" type="NameSimpleType" />
      <xs:element name="homephone" type="PhoneSimpleType" />
    </xs:all>
    <xs:attribute name="employeeid" type="xs:int" use="required" />
  </xs:complexType>
  <xs:simpleType name="NotesSimpleType">
```

Figure 5-8. *Viewing the generated source*

Compare the source to what we created in the previous example. You will find that it matches. Thus Visual Studio can effectively reduce the efforts needed to create a schema by offering a visual and friendly environment. This is a compelling factor for using it instead of manually creating the schema.

Creating the Schema from a Database Table

In many situations, the data contained in an XML document goes in and out of a database table. In such cases, the schema of your XML document can be derived from the underlying database table structure. You can of course create the schema manually as described previously, but there is a yet another way.

Visual Studio has a built-in tool called Server Explorer that allows you to connect with the databases and manipulate database objects such as tables and stored procedures. Figure 5-9 shows the Server Explorer with the famous `Northwind` database opened.

Note You can open Server Explorer by choosing View ➤ Server Explorer from the Visual Studio menu. The Server Explorer window has a Data Connections node that lists previously added database connections. To add a new connection, you need to right-click the Data Connections node and choose the Add Connection option. The Add Connection dialog box opens, allowing you to specify connection string parameters.

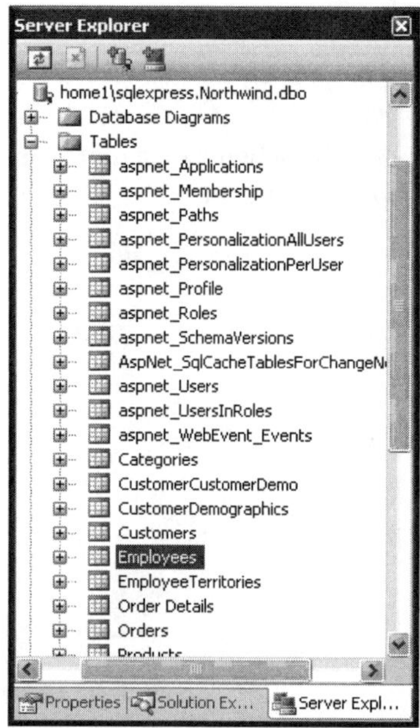

Figure 5-9. *Server Explorer of Visual Studio*

As you can see in Figure 5-9, Server Explorer has displayed a list of all the tables, such as `Employees` and `Customers`. Now suppose that you want to represent data from the `Employees` table as an XML file. It would be helpful in such a case if you could create an XSD schema that maps closely to the underlying table structure. This way, synchronizing the XML file with the database at a later stage will be easy.

To see how an XSD schema can be created from a database table, add a new XML schema to your project. Then open Server Explorer and locate the desired table. If Server Explorer is not opened by default, you can open it by choosing View ➤ Server Explorer from the menu. Finally, drag and drop the table from Server Explorer onto the XML schema. That's it! The Visual Studio IDE is clever enough to create an equivalent XML schema. Figure 5-10 shows an XML schema generated by dragging and dropping the `Employees` table of the `Northwind` database onto the schema designer.

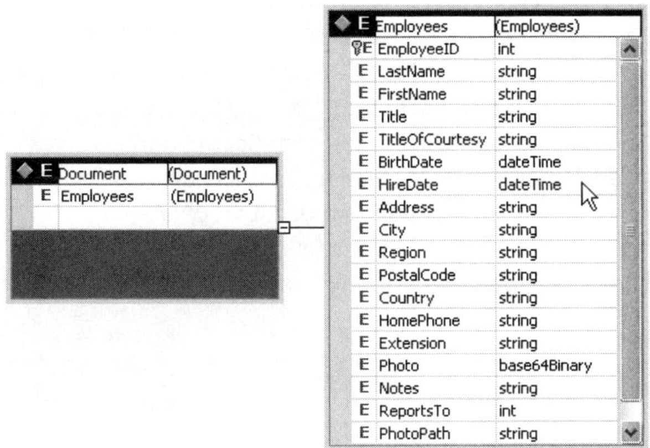

Figure 5-10. *XML schema generated from a database table*

As you can see in Figure 5-10, the designer has created an element called `<Employees>` that has sub-elements matching the columns in the database table. There is also another element called `<Document>` that has a single element called `<Employees>`, which is of type `<Employees>` as defined in this schema. If you right-click on the schema designer and select the View Code menu option, you should see markup as shown in Listing 5-4.

Listing 5-4. *The Auto-generated Schema Markup*

```
<?xml version="1.0" encoding="utf-8"?>
<xs:schema id="XMLSchema1" targetNamespace="http://tempuri.org/XMLSchema1.xsd"
elementFormDefault="qualified" xmlns="http://tempuri.org/XMLSchema1.xsd"
xmlns:mstns="http://tempuri.org/XMLSchema1.xsd"
xmlns:xs="http://www.w3.org/2001/XMLSchema"
xmlns:msdata="urn:schemas-microsoft-com:xml-msdata">
  <xs:element name="Document">
    <xs:complexType>
```

```
      <xs:choice minOccurs="0" maxOccurs="unbounded">
        <xs:element name="Employees">
          <xs:complexType>
            <xs:sequence>
              <xs:element name="EmployeeID" type="xs:int" />
              <xs:element name="LastName" type="xs:string" />
              <xs:element name="FirstName" type="xs:string" />
              <xs:element name="Title" type="xs:string" minOccurs="0" />
              <xs:element name="TitleOfCourtesy" type="xs:string" minOccurs="0" />
              <xs:element name="BirthDate" type="xs:dateTime" minOccurs="0" />
              <xs:element name="HireDate" type="xs:dateTime" minOccurs="0" />
              <xs:element name="Address" type="xs:string" minOccurs="0" />
              <xs:element name="City" type="xs:string" minOccurs="0" />
              <xs:element name="Region" type="xs:string" minOccurs="0" />
              <xs:element name="PostalCode" type="xs:string" minOccurs="0" />
              <xs:element name="Country" type="xs:string" minOccurs="0" />
              <xs:element name="HomePhone" type="xs:string" minOccurs="0" />
              <xs:element name="Extension" type="xs:string" minOccurs="0" />
              <xs:element name="Photo" type="xs:base64Binary" minOccurs="0" />
              <xs:element name="Notes" type="xs:string" minOccurs="0" />
              <xs:element name="ReportsTo" type="xs:int" minOccurs="0" />
              <xs:element name="PhotoPath" type="xs:string" minOccurs="0" />
            </xs:sequence>
          </xs:complexType>
        </xs:element>
      </xs:choice>
    </xs:complexType>
    <xs:unique name="DocumentKey1">
      <xs:selector xpath=".//mstns:Employees" />
      <xs:field xpath="mstns:EmployeeID" />
    </xs:unique>
  </xs:element>
</xs:schema>
```

There are a few things that you may find worth noting. The root element is `<Document>`. Within the `<Document>` element, you can have an `<Employees>` element, which takes its name from the database table name. The SQL Server data types are mapped to the equivalent XSD data types. Thus the `<EmployeeID>` element has a data type of `int`, whereas the `<BirthDate>` element has a data type of `dateTime`. The `EmployeeID` column is a primary key column in the table and it has been added as a primary key in the resultant schema also. (Notice the key icon in the designer or the `<unique>` tag at the bottom in the markup.)

Though the schema is readily created for us, there are some limitations. First of all, the auto-generated schema does not create any simple types. Thus constraints such as minimum length and maximum length cannot be effectively enforced. Also, all the table columns appear as elements, which might be undesirable. For example, you may need the employee ID as an attribute rather than an element. You can of course modify the auto-generated schema to suit your needs.

■ **Note** You can also generate XML schemas from views and stored procedures. In any case, the procedure remains the same. All you need to do is drag and drop the object onto the schema designer.

Creating the Schema by Using the XML Schema Definition Tool

The schema designer and Server Explorer together allow you to create a schema for a database table. Along the same lines, the XML Schema Definition tool allows you to create XSD schemas from the following:

- An existing XML document
- An existing XDR schema
- Types defined in an assembly (.EXE or .DLL)

The XML Schema Definition tool is provided as `xsd.exe` and can be invoked from the Visual Studio command prompt. In the following sections, you will learn how to use this tool to create schemas from XML documents and assemblies.

Creating the Schema from an XML Document

Let's assume that you have the `Employees.xml` file with you and wish to create an XSD schema for it by using the `xsd.exe` command-line tool. To do so, first open the Visual Studio command prompt from the Visual Studio program group. Then enter the following command at the command prompt:

```
xsd.exe "C:\Bipin\Pro XML\Employees.xml" /outputdir:"C:\Bipin\Pro XML"
```

The first parameter is the path and filename of the XML file for which the schema is to be generated. The `/outputdir` switch specifies the folder where the resultant schema file should be created.

After you invoke the command, you will find an .XSD file in the specified folder. By default the name of the schema file is the same as the XML filename. Listing 5-5 shows the schema generated by the tool.

Listing 5-5. *Schema Generated by the xsd.exe Tool*

```
<?xml version="1.0" encoding="utf-8"?>
<xs:schema id="employees" xmlns="" xmlns:xs="http://www.w3.org/2001/XMLSchema" ➥
xmlns:msdata="urn:schemas-microsoft-com:xml-msdata">
  <xs:element name="employees" msdata:IsDataSet="true" ➥
msdata:UseCurrentLocale="true">
    <xs:complexType>
      <xs:choice minOccurs="0" maxOccurs="unbounded">
        <xs:element name="employee">
          <xs:complexType>
            <xs:sequence>
              <xs:element name="firstname" type="xs:string" minOccurs="0" ➥
msdata:Ordinal="0" />
              <xs:element name="lastname" type="xs:string" minOccurs="0" ➥
msdata:Ordinal="1" />
              <xs:element name="homephone" type="xs:string" minOccurs="0" ➥
msdata:Ordinal="2" />
              <xs:element name="notes" type="xs:string" minOccurs="0" ➥
msdata:Ordinal="3" />
            </xs:sequence>
            <xs:attribute name="employeeid" type="xs:string" />
          </xs:complexType>
        </xs:element>
      </xs:choice>
    </xs:complexType>
  </xs:element>
</xs:schema>
```

As you can see, the resultant schema defines a root element called `<employees>`. The `<employees>` element can have zero or more occurrences of the `<employee>` element. The `<employee>` element is defined as a complex type and contains four sub-elements: `<firstname>`, `<lastname>`, `<homephone>`, and `<notes>`. The schema also states that the elements must occur in the same sequence (as indicated by the `<sequence>` tag). The `employeeid` attribute is also defined. You can customize the generated schema to suit your needs.

■ **Note** You can also invoke the `xsd.exe` tool at a standard command prompt. However, you need to specify the complete path of the `xsd.exe` tool while invoking it. Alternatively, you can first navigate to the installation folder of .NET where the tool is located and then invoke it. You can even add it to the `PATH` variable.

Creating the Schema from an Assembly

You might be wondering why we'd need to create a schema from an assembly. This facility, however, comes in handy during XML serialization, during which you often serialize your classes on the wire by using XML format. Thus the XSD schema extracted from the assembly represents the structure of this serialized XML data.

Note You will learn more about XML serialization in Chapter 8.

To see how the `xsd.exe` tool can generate a schema from an assembly, we will create a class library project. The class library will have a single class called `Employee`. The source code of the `Employee` class is shown in Listing 5-6.

Listing 5-6. *The Employee Class*

```
namespace ClassLibrary1
{
    public class Employee
    {
        private int intEmployeeID;
        private string strFirstName;
        private string strLastName;
        private string strHomePhone;
        private string strNotes;

        public int EmployeeID
        {
            get
            {
                return intEmployeeID;
            }
            set
            {
                intEmployeeID = value;
            }
        }
```

```
public string FirstName
{
    get
    {
        return strFirstName;
    }
    set
    {
        strFirstName = value;
    }
}

public string LastName
{
    get
    {
        return strLastName;
    }
    set
    {
        strLastName = value;
    }
}

public string HomePhone
{
    get
    {
        return strHomePhone;
    }
    set
    {
        strHomePhone = value;
    }
}

public string Notes
{
    get
```

```
            {
                return strNotes;
            }
            set
            {
                strNotes = value;
            }
        }
    }
}
```

The class declares five member variables to store the employee ID, first name, last name, home phone, and notes, respectively. The class also contains five public properties—EmployeeID, FirstName, LastName, HomePhone, and Notes—that read and write values to the respective private variables.

After you create the class, make sure to compile it so that its assembly will be called ClassLibrary1.dll. Now invoke the xsd.exe tool as shown here:

```
xsd.exe "C:\Bipin\Pro XML\ClassLibrary1\bin\Debug\classlibrary1.dll"
/outputdir:"C:\Bipin\Pro XML"
```

The first parameter to xsd.exe specifies the path and filename of the assembly, whereas the /outputdir switch specifies the target folder where the schema should be created. Listing 5-7 shows the schema that is based on our Employee class.

Listing 5-7. *Schema Generated for the Employees Class*

```
<?xml version="1.0" encoding="utf-8"?>
<xs:schema elementFormDefault="qualified" ➥
xmlns:xs="http://www.w3.org/2001/XMLSchema">
  <xs:element name="Employee" nillable="true" type="Employee" />
  <xs:complexType name="Employee">
    <xs:sequence>
      <xs:element minOccurs="1" maxOccurs="1" name="EmployeeID" type="xs:int" />
      <xs:element minOccurs="0" maxOccurs="1" name="FirstName" type="xs:string" />
      <xs:element minOccurs="0" maxOccurs="1" name="LastName" type="xs:string" />
      <xs:element minOccurs="0" maxOccurs="1" name="HomePhone" type="xs:string" />
      <xs:element minOccurs="0" maxOccurs="1" name="Notes" type="xs:string" />
    </xs:sequence>
  </xs:complexType>
</xs:schema>
```

As you can see in Listing 5-7, the schema defines an element named `<Employee>` that is of complex type `Employee`. The complex type `Employee` contains five sub-elements: `<EmployeeID>`, `<FirstName>`, `<LastName>`, `<HomePhone>`, and `<Notes>`. As you must have guessed, the names of these elements are extracted from the names of the class properties. These elements must occur in sequence, as indicated by the `<sequence>` tag. As in the previous case, you can customize this schema to suit your needs.

■ **Note** When you use the preceding command, the tool generates a schema for all the classes in the assembly. You can specify only certain classes by using the `/type` switch.

Creating Schemas by Using the Schema Object Model (SOM)

Up until now, we have created schemas by using a variety of techniques, all of which were design-time techniques. That means we ourselves created the schemas by using a text editor, Visual Studio, or the `xsd.exe` tool. However, there is more to the show than this. The .NET Framework also allows you to create schemas programmatically.

You can load existing schemas or create a new one from the ground up. You can then manipulate the schema by adding or removing various parts such as elements, attributes, simple types, and complex types. After you manipulate the schema as per your requirements, you can then compile it. Compiling a schema ensures that there are no errors in the schema structure.

To perform schema manipulation, the .NET Framework provides a set of classes called the Schema Object Model, or SOM for short. The SOM classes reside in the `System.Xml.Schema` namespace. The SOM is for schemas what DOM is for XML documents: the SOM classes represent various parts of a schema. For example, to represent a simple type, the SOM provides a class called `XmlSchemaSimpleType`, and to represent an element, the SOM provides a class called `XmlSchemaElement`. There are many other classes that represent attributes, facets, groups, complex types, and so on.

In the following section, you will learn about some of the core SOM classes. Note that the SOM is very extensive and I will not be discussing every available class here.

The Core SOM Classes

Figure 5-11 shows the object hierarchy of the core SOM classes. As you can see, all the SOM classes inherit from an abstract base class called `XmlSchemaObject`. This class provides common base functionality to all the child classes.

The `XmlSchemaAnnotated` class represents a base class for any element that can contain annotation elements. Classes such as `XmlSchema`, `XmlSchemaType`, `XmlSchemaAttribute`, `XmlSchemaParticle`, and `XmlSchemaFacet` inherit from the `XmlSchemaAnnotated` class.

Note You can use annotation elements to provide information about the XML schema. Annotations can appear anywhere in a schema to explain any element, attribute, or type definition.

The `XmlSchema` class represents an in-memory representation of an XSD schema. This class allows you to read, write, and compile XSD schemas.

The `XmlSchemaType` represents a type in an XSD schema and acts as a base class for all simple and complex types. The `XmlSchemaSimpleType` and `XmlSchemaComplexType` classes inherit from this class and allow you to define new simple and complex types, respectively.

The `XmlSchemaAttribute` represents an attribute of an element. Finally, the `XmlSchemaParticle` class provides base functionality to all particle types such as `XmlSchemaElement`.

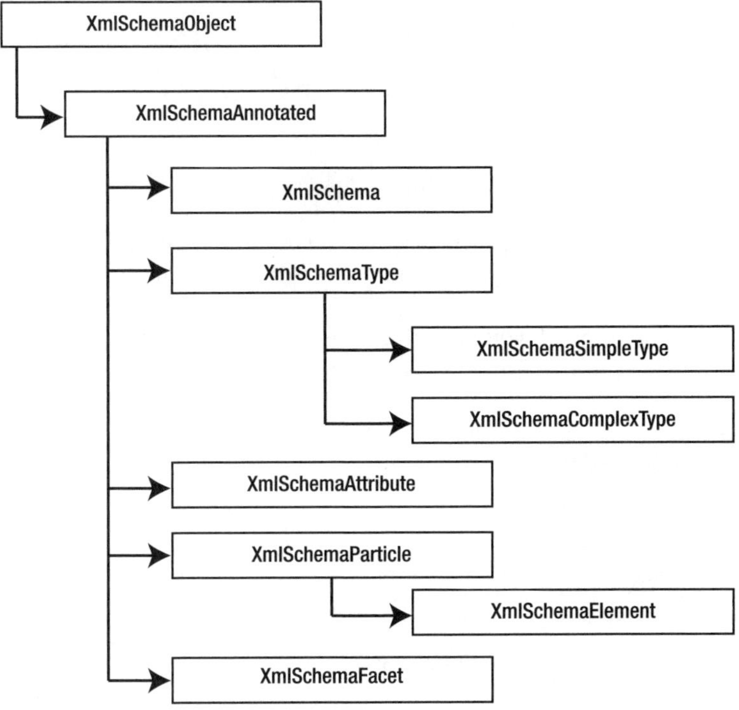

Figure 5-11. *The SOM object hierarchy*

Creating an XSD Schema by Using the SOM

Now that you know what the SOM is, let's put it to use to create a schema for our `Employees.xml` file. The schema will have three simple types:

Simple type for `name`: This simple type represents names used in our XML document (first name and last name). It restricts the name length; the minimum length is 3, and the maximum length is less than 255.

Simple type for `phone`: This simple type represents phone numbers (the `<homephone>` element of our XML document). It enforces a restriction requiring phone numbers to be no longer than 20 characters.

Simple type for `notes`: This simple type represents notes (the `<notes>` element of our document). It enforces a restriction requiring the notes entered to be no longer than 500 characters.

These three simple types will make a complex type that represents an employee. The complex type consists of the following:

- An element called `<firstname>`, which is a name simple type
- An element called `<lastname>`, which is a name simple type
- An element called `<homephone>`, which is a phone simple type
- An element called `<notes>`, which is a notes simple type
- A required attribute called `employeeid`, which is of type `int`

Finally, we will have an element called `<employees>` that will contain zero or more sub-elements named `<employee>`. The `<employee>` sub-elements will be of the complex type I just mentioned.

To create the schema by using the SOM, you need to create a Windows application as shown in Figure 5-12.

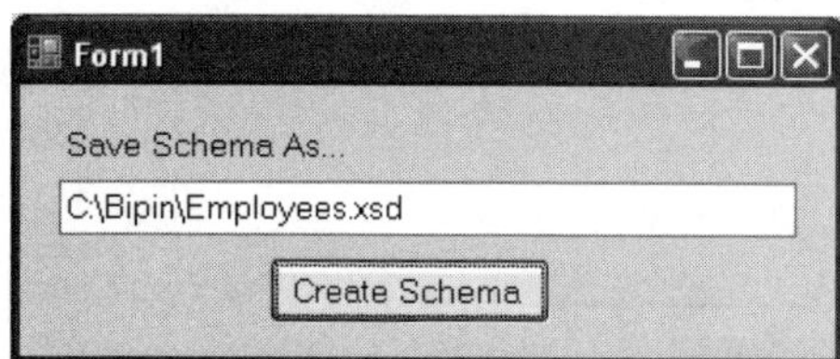

Figure 5-12. *Application for creating a schema by using the SOM*

The application consists of a text box wherein you can specify the full path and name of the destination schema file. Clicking the Create Schema button generates, compiles, and saves the schema to the specified location.

The `Click` event handler of the Create Schema button is shown in Listing 5-8.

Listing 5-8. *Creating a Schema by Using the SOM*

```
private void button1_Click(object sender, EventArgs e)
{
  XmlSchema schema = new XmlSchema();

  //define NameSimpleType
  XmlSchemaSimpleType nametype = new XmlSchemaSimpleType();
  XmlSchemaSimpleTypeRestriction nameRes = new XmlSchemaSimpleTypeRestriction();
  nameRes.BaseTypeName =
    new XmlQualifiedName("string", "http://www.w3.org/2001/XMLSchema");
  XmlSchemaMinLengthFacet nameFacet1 = new XmlSchemaMinLengthFacet();
  nameFacet1.Value = "3";
  XmlSchemaMaxLengthFacet nameFacet2 = new XmlSchemaMaxLengthFacet();
  nameFacet2.Value = "255";
  nameRes.Facets.Add(nameFacet1);
  nameRes.Facets.Add(nameFacet2);
  nametype.Content = nameRes;

  //define PhoneSimpleType
  XmlSchemaSimpleType phonetype = new XmlSchemaSimpleType();
  XmlSchemaSimpleTypeRestriction phoneRes = new XmlSchemaSimpleTypeRestriction();
  phoneRes.BaseTypeName =
    new XmlQualifiedName("string", "http://www.w3.org/2001/XMLSchema");
  XmlSchemaMaxLengthFacet phoneFacet1 = new XmlSchemaMaxLengthFacet();
  phoneFacet1.Value = "20";
  phoneRes.Facets.Add(phoneFacet1);
  phonetype.Content = phoneRes;

  //define NotesSimpleType
  XmlSchemaSimpleType notestype = new XmlSchemaSimpleType();
  XmlSchemaSimpleTypeRestriction notesRes = new XmlSchemaSimpleTypeRestriction();
  notesRes.BaseTypeName =
    new XmlQualifiedName("string", "http://www.w3.org/2001/XMLSchema");
  XmlSchemaMaxLengthFacet notesFacet1 = new XmlSchemaMaxLengthFacet();
  notesFacet1.Value = "500";
  notesRes.Facets.Add(notesFacet1);
  notestype.Content = notesRes;
```

```
//define EmployeeType complex type
XmlSchemaComplexType employeetype = new XmlSchemaComplexType();
XmlSchemaSequence sequence = new XmlSchemaSequence();
XmlSchemaElement firstname = new XmlSchemaElement();
firstname.Name = "firstname";
firstname.SchemaType = nametype;
XmlSchemaElement lastname = new XmlSchemaElement();
lastname.Name = "lastname";
lastname.SchemaType = nametype;
XmlSchemaElement homephone = new XmlSchemaElement();
homephone.Name = "homephone";
homephone.SchemaType = phonetype;
XmlSchemaElement notes = new XmlSchemaElement();
notes.Name = "notes";
notes.SchemaType = notestype;

sequence.Items.Add(firstname);
sequence.Items.Add(lastname);
sequence.Items.Add(homephone);
sequence.Items.Add(notes);
employeetype.Particle = sequence;

//define employeeid attribute
XmlSchemaAttribute employeeid = new XmlSchemaAttribute();
employeeid.Name = "employeeid";
employeeid.SchemaTypeName =
  new XmlQualifiedName("int", "http://www.w3.org/2001/XMLSchema");
employeeid.Use = XmlSchemaUse.Required;
employeetype.Attributes.Add(employeeid);

//define top complex type
XmlSchemaComplexType complextype = new XmlSchemaComplexType();
XmlSchemaSequence sq = new XmlSchemaSequence();
XmlSchemaElement employee = new XmlSchemaElement();
employee.Name = "employee";
employee.SchemaType = employeetype;
employee.MinOccurs = 0;
employee.MaxOccursString = "unbounded";
sq.Items.Add(employee);
complextype.Particle = sq;

//define <employees> element
XmlSchemaElement employees = new XmlSchemaElement();
employees.Name = "employees";
employees.SchemaType = complextype;
```

```
    schema.Items.Add(employees);
    //compile the schema
    XmlSchemaSet set = new XmlSchemaSet();
    set.Add(schema);
    set.Compile();
    //save the schema
    XmlTextWriter writer = new XmlTextWriter(textBox1.Text,null);
    schema.Write(writer);
    writer.Close();
    MessageBox.Show("Schema Created Successfully!");
}
```

The code is a bit lengthy and hence we will dissect it in pieces.

Creating the Schema

An in-memory schema is represented by the XmlSchema class. The code declares an instance of XmlSchema at the top:

```
XmlSchema schema = new XmlSchema();
```

Creating a Simple Type for Names

The schema needs to define a simple type for names. This is defined next:

```
XmlSchemaSimpleType nametype = new XmlSchemaSimpleType();
XmlSchemaSimpleTypeRestriction nameRes = new XmlSchemaSimpleTypeRestriction();
nameRes.BaseTypeName =
  new XmlQualifiedName("string", "http://www.w3.org/2001/XMLSchema");
XmlSchemaMinLengthFacet nameFacet1 = new XmlSchemaMinLengthFacet();
nameFacet1.Value = "3";
XmlSchemaMaxLengthFacet nameFacet2 = new XmlSchemaMaxLengthFacet();
nameFacet2.Value = "255";
nameRes.Facets.Add(nameFacet1);
nameRes.Facets.Add(nameFacet2);
nametype.Content = nameRes;
```

A simple type is represented by the XmlSchemaSimpleType class. The simple type for names has certain restrictions:

- The data type must be a string.
- The minimum length must be 3.
- The maximum length must not exceed 255.

To represent these restrictions, an instance of the XmlSchemaSimpleTypeRestriction class is created. The XmlSchemaSimpleTypeRestriction class's BaseTypeName property, which is of type XmlQualifiedName, specifies the base data type used by this restriction. The XmlQualifiedName class can be used to represent built-in XSD data types such as string and int. In our example, we need string and hence we pass it as the first parameter of the constructor. The second parameter indicates the namespace to which the data type belongs. The minimum and maximum length restrictions can be enforced by facet classes.

The two facet classes we need are XmlSchemaMinLengthFacet and XmlSchemaMaxLengthFacet. These facet classes inherit from the XmlSchemaFacet base class and represent the minimum length and maximum length of the simple type, respectively, indicated by the Value property of each class. The facets are then added to the XmlSchemaSimpleTypeRestriction instance by using its Add() method. Finally, the Content property of the XmlSchemaSimpleType object is set to the restriction we created.

Creating a Simple Type for Phone Numbers

Creating a simple type for phone numbers follows the same procedure as discussed earlier. However, the restriction requirements are slightly different. The relevant code is shown here:

```
XmlSchemaSimpleType phonetype = new XmlSchemaSimpleType();
XmlSchemaSimpleTypeRestriction phoneRes = new XmlSchemaSimpleTypeRestriction();
phoneRes.BaseTypeName =
  new XmlQualifiedName("string", "http://www.w3.org/2001/XMLSchema");
XmlSchemaMaxLengthFacet phoneFacet1 = new XmlSchemaMaxLengthFacet();
phoneFacet1.Value = "20";
phoneRes.Facets.Add(phoneFacet1);
phonetype.Content = phoneRes;
```

As before, instances of XmlSchemaSimpleType and XmlSchemaSimpleTypeRestriction are created. This time we need only one facet for specifying the maximum length of the phone number. Thus the code declares an instance of the XmlSchemaMaxLengthFacet class and sets its Value property to 20. As before, the facet is added to the restriction, and the Content property of the XmlSchemaSimpleType instance is set to the phone number restriction.

Creating a Simple Type for Notes

Creating a simple type for notes is the same as I discussed earlier. The only change is in the maximum length value. The relevant code is shown here:

```
XmlSchemaMaxLengthFacet notesFacet1 = new XmlSchemaMaxLengthFacet();
notesFacet1.Value = "500";
```

Creating a Complex Type That Represents an Employee

A complex type is represented by the XmlSchemaComplexType class. In our example, the four sub-elements (<firstname>, <lastname>, <homephone>, and <notes>) must appear in the same sequence, which is defined by the XmlSchemaSequence class. The code that defines the complex type is shown here:

```
XmlSchemaComplexType employeetype = new XmlSchemaComplexType();
XmlSchemaSequence sequence = new XmlSchemaSequence();
XmlSchemaElement firstname = new XmlSchemaElement();
firstname.Name = "firstname";
firstname.SchemaType = nametype;
XmlSchemaElement lastname = new XmlSchemaElement();
lastname.Name = "lastname";
lastname.SchemaType = nametype;
XmlSchemaElement homephone = new XmlSchemaElement();
homephone.Name = "homephone";
homephone.SchemaType = phonetype;
XmlSchemaElement notes = new XmlSchemaElement();
notes.Name = "notes";
notes.SchemaType = notestype;

sequence.Items.Add(firstname);
sequence.Items.Add(lastname);
sequence.Items.Add(homephone);
sequence.Items.Add(notes);
employeetype.Particle = sequence;

//define employeeid attribute
XmlSchemaAttribute employeeid = new XmlSchemaAttribute();
employeeid.Name = "employeeid";
employeeid.SchemaTypeName =
  new XmlQualifiedName("int", "http://www.w3.org/2001/XMLSchema");
employeeid.Use = XmlSchemaUse.Required;
employeetype.Attributes.Add(employeeid);
```

This section of the code starts by declaring instances of the XmlSchemaComplexType and XmlSchemaSequence classes. Next we need four elements. Each is defined by an XmlSchemaElement class and should assume one of the simple types defined earlier. The Name property of the XmlSchemaElement class specifies the name of the element; the SchemaType property specifies the data type of the element and can be set to a simple type or a complex type. After all four elements are defined, they are added to the XmlSchemaSequence object by using its Add() method.

After the sequence instance is ready, you need to set the Particle property of the XmlSchemaComplexType object to it. The Particle property specifies the compositor type of the complex type, and an attribute of a complex type is represented by the XmlSchemaAttribute class. The Name property of XmlSchemaAttribute specifies the name of the attribute. The data type of the attribute is specified by using the SchemaTypeName property, which is of type XmlQualifiedName. In our case, the employeeid attribute is an integer and hence the XmlQualifiedName uses int as the data type. The Use property of the XmlSchemaAttribute class indicates how the attribute is used in the XML document. This property is an enumeration of type XmlSchemaUse. In our case, the employeeid attribute is mandatory and hence we set the Use property to Required.

Creating a Top-Level Complex Type

The root element of our XML document needs to have zero or more instances of the <employee> element, which is of the complex type we defined in the previous section. To represent the <employee> element, we define it as another complex type, as shown here:

```
XmlSchemaComplexType complextype = new XmlSchemaComplexType();
XmlSchemaSequence sq = new XmlSchemaSequence();
XmlSchemaElement employee = new XmlSchemaElement();
employee.Name = "employee";
employee.SchemaType = employeetype;
employee.MinOccurs = 0;
employee.MaxOccursString = "unbounded";
sq.Items.Add(employee);
complextype.Particle = sq;
```

The code creates an instance of the XmlSchemaComplexType and XmlSchemaSequence classes as before. This time it creates a single XmlSchemaElement to represent an <employee> element. This element is of type employeetype (the complex type we defined in the previous section). The MinOccurs property of the XmlSchemaElement class indicates the minimum number of times the element must appear in the document. Along the same lines, the MaxOccursString property indicates the maximum permissible instances of the element. Note that this property accepts numbers as a string. If there is no restriction on the number, you can set it to unbounded. After the element is created, it is added to the sequence, and the sequence is assigned to the Particle property of the XmlSchemaComplexType class.

Creating the Root Element

The schema needs to have the `<employees>` root element that can contain one or more `<employee>` elements. The root element is defined as follows:

```
//define <employees> element
XmlSchemaElement employees = new XmlSchemaElement();
employees.Name = "employees";
employees.SchemaType = complextype;
```

As before, an instance of `XmlSchemaElement` is created. Its `Name` property is set to `employees`, and its `SchemaType` property is set to the top-level complex type we created in the previous section.

Compiling the Schema

Now we have completed all the simple types, complex types, and attributes. We can now add the root element to the schema. This is done by using the `Add()` method of the `Items` collection of the `XmlSchema` class:

```
schema.Items.Add(employees);
```

After the schema is ready, you can compile it. Compiling the schema ensures that the schema is syntactically correct and well formed. The `XmlSchemaSet` class represents a set of schemas and allows you to compile them. The relevant code is given here:

```
//compile the schema
try
{
  XmlSchemaSet set = new XmlSchemaSet();
  set.Add(schema);
  set.Compile();
}
catch (Exception ex)
{
  MessageBox.Show("Schema compilation failed");
  return;
}
```

The `Add()` method of the `XmlSchemaSet` class accepts the `XmlSchema` objects that are to be added to the schema set. The `Compile()` method of the `XmlSchemaSet` class compiles all the schemas in the given set.

Saving the Schema

Now that we have created and compiled the schema, it is ready to be written to disk:

```
XmlTextWriter writer = new XmlTextWriter(textBox1.Text,null);
schema.Write(writer);
writer.Close();
```

The Write() method of the XmlSchema class writes the schema to a stream and has many overloads. We used one that accepts an XmlWriter pointing to the desired file. After the writing operation is over, the XmlWriter is closed.

That's it! You just created a complete schema using the SOM. You can run the application and see how the schema is generated. Figure 5-13 shows the resultant schema.

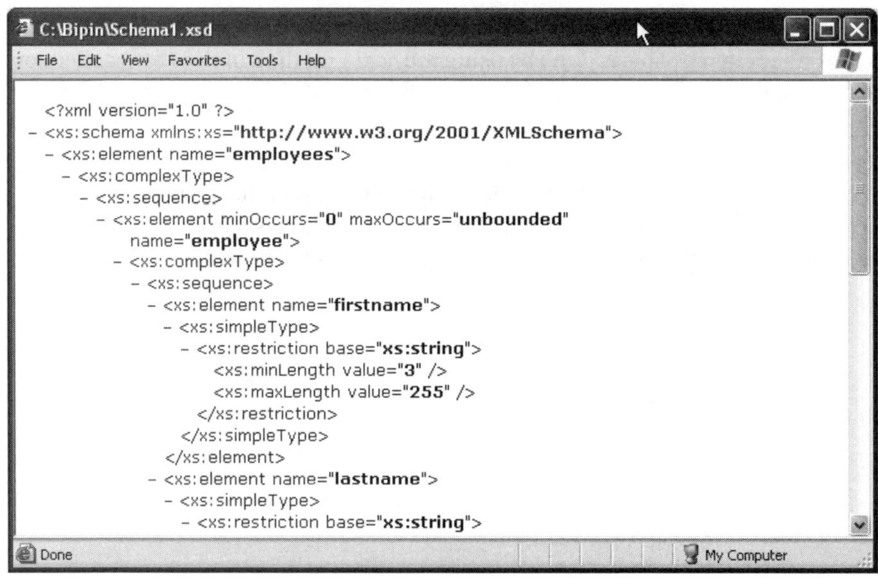

Figure 5-13. *Schema generated by using the SOM*

Validating XML Documents Against DTDs and XSD Schemas

Up until this point, you have learned what DTDs and XSD schemas are. You've also learned how to create DTDs and XSD schemas. Now it's time to learn how to validate XML documents against DTDs and XSD schemas.

Before you can validate an XML document, you must attach a DTD or schema to it. The DTD or schema can be attached via two techniques:

In-line DTD or schema: In this technique, the DTD or schema is specified at the top of the XML document.

External DTD or schema: In this technique, the DTD or schema resides in its own file—that is, it is external to the XML document. The DTD or schema is then attached to the XML document.

Inline DTD

To specify a DTD in inline fashion, you need to add a `<!DOCTYPE>` declaration at the top of the XML document. Listing 5-9 shows how this is done for `Employees.xml`.

Listing 5-9. *Inline DTD*

```
<?xml version="1.0" encoding="utf-8" ?>
<!DOCTYPE employees [
<!ELEMENT employees (employee*)>
<!ELEMENT employee (firstname,lastname,homephone,notes)>
<!ELEMENT firstname (#PCDATA)>
<!ELEMENT lastname (#PCDATA)>
<!ELEMENT homephone (#PCDATA)>
<!ELEMENT notes (#PCDATA)>
<!ATTLIST employee employeeid CDATA #REQUIRED>
]>

<employees>
  <employee employeeid="1">
    <firstname>Nancy</firstname>
    <lastname>Davolio</lastname>
...
```

Notice the markup in bold: it is the same DTD that we created previously. However, this time it is placed inline with the XML document inside the `<!DOCTYPE>` declaration. Note that the `<!DOCTYPE>` declaration must precede the root element of the XML markup. Using inline DTDs comes in handy when your XML documents are small and you don't want to maintain separate DTD files.

External DTD

External DTDs are stored in separate files, usually with the `.dtd` extension. The DTD is then linked to the XML document by using a `<!DOCTYPE>` declaration. Listing 5-10 shows how this is done.

Listing 5-10. *External DTD*

```
<?xml version="1.0" encoding="utf-8" ?>
<!DOCTYPE employees SYSTEM "employees.dtd">
<employees>
  <employee employeeid="1">
    <firstname>Nancy</firstname>
    <lastname>Davolio</lastname>
...
```

When attaching an external DTD, the `<!DOCTYPE>` declaration is immediately followed by the name of the root element of the XML document (`employees` in our case). The `SYSTEM` declaration is followed by the URL of the DTD file. In the preceding example, it is assumed that the DTD resides in a file named `employees.dtd`.

Inline Schema

A schema can be specified inline by embedding it within the XML markup itself. As shown in Listing 5-11, the complete schema (starting from `<xs:schema>` to `<xs:/schema>`) is placed immediately inside the root element `<employees>`. The schema must be placed here because an XML document cannot have two root elements.

Listing 5-11. *Inline Schema*

```
<?xml version="1.0" encoding="utf-8" ?>
<employees>
  <xs:schema attributeFormDefault="unqualified" elementFormDefault="qualified"
           xmlns:xs="http://www.w3.org/2001/XMLSchema">
    <xs:element name="employees">
      <xs:complexType>
...
```

Though the XML editor of Visual Studio supports inline schemas, as a programming recommendation you should avoid using them. W3C recommendations allow inline schemas but they are not a mandatory feature. That means all vendors may not provide support for them. Further, because they are included within the XML document, they consume more network bandwidth because they must be transferred across the wire every time.

External Schema

External schemas reside in a physical file, usually with the `.xsd` extension. To attach an external schema to an XML document, you need to modify the root element of the XML document as shown in Listing 5-12.

Listing 5-12. *External Schema*

```
<?xml version="1.0" encoding="utf-8" ?>
<employees xmlns:xsi="http://www.w3.org/2001/XMLSchema-instance"
           xsi:noNamespaceSchemaLocation="employees.xsd">
  <employee employeeid="1">
    <firstname>Nancy</firstname>
    <lastname>Davolio</lastname>
...
```

As you can see, the `<employees>` root element now has an `xmlns:xsi` attribute that specifies the W3C namespace for XML documents, which are referred to as *XML schema instances*. The `xsi:noNamespaceSchemaLocation` attribute specifies the URL of the schema file (`employees.xsd` in our case).

In the preceding example, our XML document doesn't use a namespace. If it did, we would have to make two changes to our schema and XML documents:

- Add the `targetNamespace` attribute to the schema declaration.
- Use the `xsi:schemaLocation` attribute instead of the `xsi:noNamespaceSchemaLocation` attribute.

Listing 5-13 shows the modified schema, and Listing 5-14 shows the modified XML document.

Listing 5-13. *Schema with Target Namespace*

```
<xs:schema
  attributeFormDefault="qualified"
  elementFormDefault="qualified"
  xmlns:xs="http://www.w3.org/2001/XMLSchema"
  targetNamespace="myns"
  xmlns="myns">
...
```

As you can see, the schema now has a `targetNamespace` attribute that specifies the target namespace as `myns`. The XML document must use this namespace, as illustrated in Listing 5-14.

Listing 5-14. *XML Document with Namespace*

```
<myns:employees
  xmlns:myns="myns"
  xmlns:xsi="http://www.w3.org/2001/XMLSchema-instance"
  xsi:schemaLocation="myns employeesns.xsd">
<myns:employee myns:employeeid="1">
<myns:firstname>Nancy</myns:firstname>
...
```

Note the markup in bold. The root element now declares a namespace called `myns`, and instead of `xsi:noNamespaceSchemaLocation` it now uses an `xsi:schemaLocation` attribute. Observe carefully how the attribute value is specified: it must contain the namespace name, a space, and then the URL of the XSD file.

Using the XmlReader Class to Validate XML Documents

The `XmlReader` class provides you with a way to validate XML documents by using its `Create()` method, which accepts the URL of the XML document and an instance of the `XmlReaderSettings` class. The `XmlReaderSettings` class configures the `XmlReader` class and can be used to indicate your intention of validating XML documents. You can also wire up an event handler to receive notification about validation errors. The `XmlReader` instance returned by the `Create()` method can be used to read the XML document in the same way as you learned in Chapter 3.

To illustrate how to use `XmlReader` to validate XML documents, you will develop an application as shown in Figure 5-14.

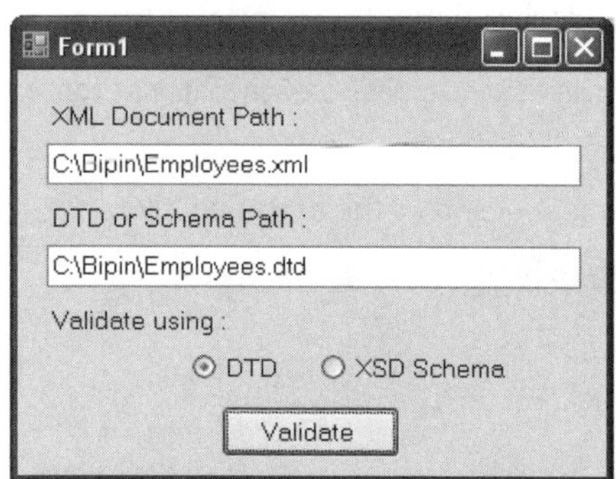

Figure 5-14. *Application for validating an XML document by using the XmlReader class*

The application consists of two text boxes for accepting the XML document filename and the DTD or schema filename, respectively. The radio buttons indicate whether you are validating against a DTD or schema. Clicking the Validate button validates the document. Any errors encountered during the validation process are indicated via a message box. Listing 5-15 shows the complete code of the application.

Listing 5-15. *Validating an XML Document by Using XmlReader*

```
private void button1_Click(object sender, EventArgs e)
{
  XmlReaderSettings settings = new XmlReaderSettings();

  if(radioButton1.Checked)
  {
    settings.ProhibitDtd = false;
    settings.ValidationType = ValidationType.DTD;
  }
  else
  {
    settings.Schemas.Add("", textBox2.Text);
    settings.ValidationType=ValidationType.Schema;
  }

  settings.ValidationEventHandler += new ValidationEventHandler(OnValidationError);
  XmlReader reader = XmlReader.Create(textBox1.Text, settings);

  while (reader.Read())
  {
    //you can put code here
    //that reads and processes
    //the document
  }

  reader.Close();
  MessageBox.Show("Validation over");
}
```

If the XML document is to be validated against a DTD (as indicated by the radio buttons), the `ProhibitDtd` property of the `XmlReaderSettings` class is set to `false`. The `ProhibitDtd` property decides whether validation against a DTD is allowed. By default this property is `true`. If the document is to be validated against an XSD schema, the schema is added to the `Schemas` collection, which can accept an in-memory schema in the form of an `XmlSchema` class or a file path. The `Add()` method of the schemas collection used by our code accepts the target namespace and schema file path.

The ValidationType property indicates whether the XmlReader should perform validation and whether to use a DTD or a schema. The ValidationType property is an enumeration of type ValidationType and has five possible values, as listed in Table 5-3.

Table 5-3. *Possible Values of ValidationType*

Value	Description
None	No validation will be performed. This is the default.
Auto	Automatically decides whether to validate against a DTD or schema by observing the XML document.
DTD	Validation will be performed against a DTD.
Schema	Validation will be performed against an XSD schema.
XDR	Validation will be performed against an XDR schema.

To trap the validation errors, the XmlReaderSettings class raises a ValidationEventHandler event. This event is raised only when the ValidationType property is other than None. The signature of the event-handler function (OnValidationError()in our example) must match the one shown here:

```
void OnValidationError(object sender, ValidationEventArgs e)
{
  MessageBox.Show(e.Message);
}
```

The event handler receives a ValidationEventArgs object as an event argument, which allows you to examine the underlying exception. You can get the descriptive error message by using the Message property as we do in our example. In this case, we simply display a message box with the validation error message.

The code from Listing 5-15 then creates an instance of the XmlReader class by calling its Create() static method. The URL of the XML document and the instance of XmlReaderSettings are the arguments. A while loop then reads the XML document. If any validation error is detected during this reading operation, the ValidationEventHandler event is raised. We could have placed code to read the element and attribute values inside the while loop if required (refer to Chapter 3 for information about reading XML documents by using the XmlReader class). Finally, the reader is closed.

To test the preceding code, you need to run the application and supply the full path and filenames of an XML document and a DTD or schema. You can use the same Employees.xml file that we have used throughout this chapter. We also created a DTD and an XSD schema for Employees.xml previously. After you click the Validate button, the XmlReader will attempt to validate the XML document and notify you of any validation errors. Figure 5-15 shows a message box generated after deliberately removing the required attribute employeeid.

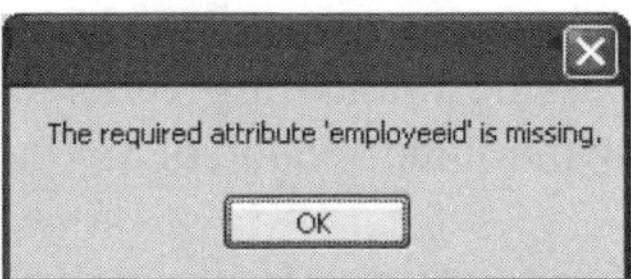

Figure 5-15. *Detecting a validation error*

Using XmlDocument to Validate XML Documents Being Loaded

You are not limited to the `XmlReader` approach to validate your XML documents; you can also use `XmlDocument` to validate them. This is useful when you are modifying documents and want to ensure that the new data is consistent with the underlying schema or DTD. The `XmlDocument` class allows you to validate XML documents in two ways:

- You can validate the document while it is being loaded by the `XmlDocument` class.
- You can validate the document explicitly when you perform any modification on it such as adding or removing nodes.

In the following example, you will learn how both of the preceding approaches can be used. We will modify the same example that we developed in the "Modifying XML Documents" section of Chapter 2. Figure 5-16 shows the user interface of the application.

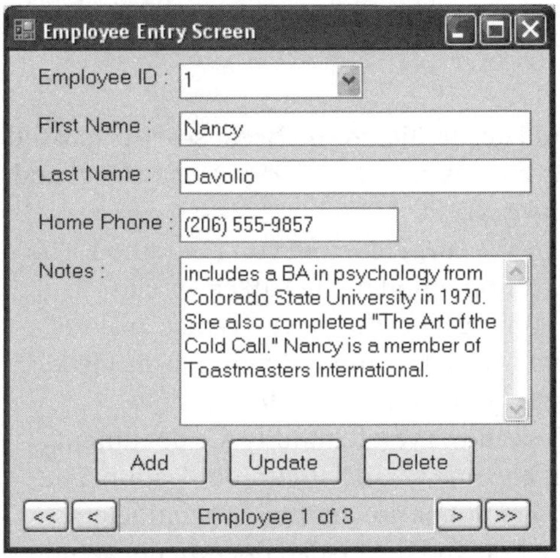

Figure 5-16. *Application for validating XML documents by using XmlDocument*

Because we have already dissected the complete code in Chapter 2, I will not discuss it again here. I will discuss only the modifications that are necessary to validate XML documents.

Previously in this section it was mentioned that XmlDocument allows you to validate XML documents when they are being loaded. This is accomplished by passing a validating reader to the Load() method of the XmlDocument class. Listing 5-16 shows the modified version of the Form_Load event handler.

Listing 5-16. *Validating an XML Document When It Is Being Loaded*

```
private void Form1_Load(object sender, EventArgs e)
{
  XmlReaderSettings settings = new XmlReaderSettings();
  settings.ValidationType = ValidationType.Schema;
  settings.Schemas.Add("", Application.StartupPath + @"\employees.xsd");
  settings.ValidationEventHandler += new
          ValidationEventHandler(OnValidationError);
  XmlReader reader =
    XmlReader.Create(Application.StartupPath + @"\employees.xml", settings);
  doc.Load(reader);
  reader.Close();

  foreach (XmlNode node in doc.DocumentElement.ChildNodes)
  {
    comboBox1.Items.Add(node.Attributes["employeeid"].Value);
  }
  FillControls();
}
```

Notice the code marked in bold. This code should be familiar to you because we discussed it in the earlier sections of this chapter: it essentially creates an XmlReaderSettings object and configures it to validate Employees.xml against Employees.xsd.

The ValidationEventHandler event is handled by the OnValidationError() method. The XmlReaderSettings object is then passed to the Create() method of the XmlReader class to get an XmlReader object. The Load() method of XmlDocument accepts the newly created XmlReader object as a parameter, internally iterates through the XmlReader, and validation takes place. If there are any validation errors, the OnValidationError() method gets called.

Now comes the tricky part. The XmlDocument class allows you to modify the document. Thus a document can be valid when loaded but can become invalid after modification. For example, as per our schema, the telephone number cannot be greater than 20 characters. The user of the form can, however, ignore this restriction and the loaded document can now have invalid data. This makes it necessary to revalidate the changes made to the document. Fortunately, the XmlDocument class provides a method called Validate() that does the job. Listing 5-17 shows the use of Validate() during the update operation.

Listing 5-17. *Validating a Node Explicitly*

```
private void button2_Click(object sender, EventArgs e)
{
  XmlNode node =
    doc.SelectSingleNode("//employee[@employeeid='" +
                         comboBox1.SelectedItem + "']");
  if (node != null)
  {
    node.ChildNodes[0].InnerText = textBox1.Text;
    node.ChildNodes[1].InnerText = textBox2.Text;
    node.ChildNodes[2].InnerText = textBox3.Text;
    XmlCDataSection notes = doc.CreateCDataSection(textBox4.Text);
    node.ChildNodes[3].ReplaceChild(notes, node.ChildNodes[3].ChildNodes[0]);
  }

  doc.Validate(OnValidationError,node);

  if (!isError)
  {
    doc.Save(Application.StartupPath + "/employees.xml");
  }
}
```

Note the code marked in bold. The `Validate()` method of `XmlDocument` can validate the entire document or just a node against a previously specified schema or DTD. The `Validate()` method accepts two parameters: the name of a function that matches the `ValidationEventHandler` delegate signature, and the `XmlNode` to validate. There is one more overload of `Validate()` that takes just a function matching the `ValidationEventHandler` delegate signature and validates the entire document. The `OnValidationError` function is shown in Listing 5-18.

Listing 5-18. *The OnValidationError Function*

```
void OnValidationError(object sender, ValidationEventArgs e)
{
  MessageBox.Show(e.Message);
  isError = true;
}
```

The function simply shows the error message in a message box and sets a class-level Boolean variable—`isError`—to true. This variable is checked to decide whether to save the document. To test the application, modify the phone number of any employee to more than 20 characters and click the Update button. You should see a message box similar to Figure 5-17.

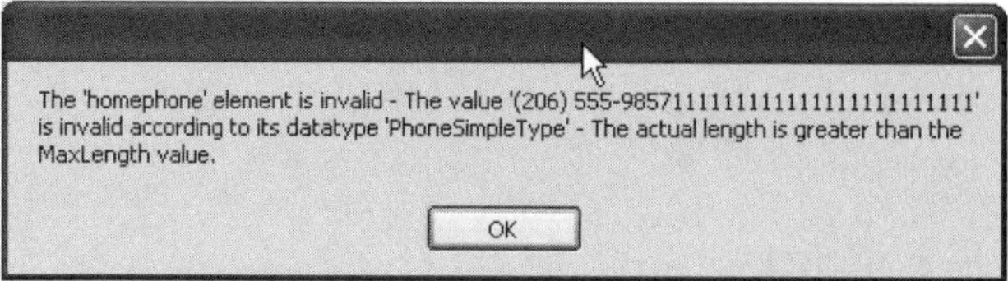

Figure 5-17. *Validation error during saving changes*

Using XPath Navigator to Validate XML Documents

You might be using XPathNavigator to read XML documents and may wish to perform validation on those documents. Recollect from Chapter 4 that XPathNavigator can be obtained by using the XmlDocument or XPathDocument classes. The XPathNavigator obtained by using XmlDocument is editable, whereas that obtained by using XPathDocument is read-only. The XPathNavigator class by itself does not allow you to validate data, but you can use the underlying XmlDocument or XPathDocument classes to perform the validation.

We have already seen the validation performed by using XmlDocument, but just like XmlDocument, the XPathDocument class allows you to validate XML documents against a schema or DTD during loading. In this case, the constructor of XPathDocument can accept a validating XmlReader to perform the validation. Because the XPathNavigator obtained by using XPathDocument is read-only, there is no way to revalidate the XML document after it has been loaded. Listing 5-19 shows how the XPathNavigator obtained by using XPathDocument can perform the validation.

Listing 5-19. *Validating by Using XPathNavigator*

```
XmlReaderSettings settings = new XmlReaderSettings();
settings.ValidationType = ValidationType.Schema;
settings.Schemas.Add("", "C:\Bipin\employees.xsd");
settings.ValidationEventHandler += new ValidationEventHandler(OnValidationError);
XmlReader reader = XmlReader.Create("C:\Bipin\employees.xml", settings);
XPathDocument doc = new XPathDocument(reader);
XPathNavigator navigator = doc.CreateNavigator();
```

The code creates an XmlReaderSettings object as before and adds a schema to use for validation. The Create() method of XmlReader accepts this XmlReaderSettings object and returns an XmlReader instance. The XmlReader instance is then supplied to the constructor of the XPathDocument class. The CreateNavigator() method of XPathDocument finally creates the XPathNavigator that can be used to navigate through the XML document.

Summary

This chapter introduced you to DTDs and schemas. You learned how to create a DTD and a schema. You also learned to use Visual Studio tools for creating XSD schemas. The .NET Framework's Schema Object Model (SOM) is an extensive collection of objects that allows you to create XSD schemas programmatically. You learned some of the important and commonly used classes from the SOM hierarchy.

Creating a schema or DTD is just half of the story. The other half involves actually validating your XML documents against the specified schema or DTD. To validate an XML document against a schema or DTD, you can use several approaches—that is, with the `XmlReader`, `XmlDocument`, and `XPathNavigator` classes. All the approaches essentially rely on two classes: `XmlReaderSettings` and `XmlReader`. The former class configures the `XmlReader` to perform validation. It also attaches an event handler for handling validation events. The latter actually reads the document and notifies you of validation errors.

CHAPTER 6

Transforming XML with XSLT

In the previous chapters, we dealt with XML documents and their manipulation. Our interaction with XML documents was limited to reading, writing, querying, and validating them with the help of .NET Framework classes. No doubt these operations are widely needed in real-world XML applications. However, often you also need to transform XML data from one representation to another. For example, you may need to convert XML data into HTML so that it can be displayed in the browser. So, how do we accomplish such a transformation? This is where Extensible Stylesheet Language Transformations (XSLT) comes into the picture.

This chapter covers details of XSLT processing via .NET Framework classes. Specifically, you will learn the following:

- What XSLT is
- The `XslCompiledTransform` class that is the .NET Framework's XSLT processor
- How to transform XML documents by using `XslCompiledTransform`
- How to use XSLT extension objects
- How to pass parameters to XSLT style sheets
- How to emit script in XSLT style sheets

Overview of XSLT

XML markup often needs to be transformed before it can be put to any use. To cater to this requirement, the W3C introduced Extensible Stylesheet Language (XSL)—a standard for representing style sheets for XML documents. XSL was intended to act along the same lines as Cascading Style Sheets (CSS), which are used to style HTML pages. However, over a period of time the W3C realized the complexity involved in transforming XML documents, and the overall XSL standards were separated into XSLT, XPath, and XSL-FO. Out of these three main subdivisions, XSLT is intended for transforming XML documents.

Note The XPath standard allows you to query and navigate XML documents. Chapter 4 covered XPath. XSL Formatting Objects (XSL-FO) is intended to format XML documents. XSL-FO is beyond the scope of this book.

XSLT consists of elements and functions that together allow you to transform XML documents. To understand how XSLT elements and functions are used, you will use a simple example.

Suppose that you have an XML document as shown in Listing 6-1. As you can see, it is the same `Employees.xml` file that we have been using for all of our examples.

Listing 6-1. *Sample XML Document (Employees.xml)*

```
<?xml version="1.0" encoding="utf-8" ?>
<!-- This is list of employees -->
<employees>
  <employee employeeid="1">
    <firstname>Nancy</firstname>
    <lastname>Davolio</lastname>
    <homephone>(206) 555-9857</homephone>
    <notes>
<![CDATA[includes a BA in psychology from Colorado State University in 1970.
She also completed "The Art of the Cold Call." Nancy is a member of Toastmasters
International.]]>
    </notes>
  </employee>
  <employee employeeid="2">
    <firstname>Andrew</firstname>
    <lastname>Fuller</lastname>
    <homephone>(206) 555-9482</homephone>
    <notes>
<![CDATA[Andrew received his BTS commercial in 1974 and a Ph.D. in international
marketing from the University of Dallas in 1981.  He is fluent in French and Italian
and reads German. He joined the company as a sales representative, was promoted
 to sales manager in January 1992 and to vice president of sales in March 1993.
Andrew is a member of the Sales Management Roundtable, the Seattle Chamber of
Commerce, and the Pacific Rim Importers Association.]]>
    </notes>
  </employee>
  <employee employeeid="3">
    <firstname>Janet</firstname>
    <lastname>Leverling</lastname>
    <homephone>(206) 555-3412</homephone>
    <notes>
<![CDATA[Janet has a BS degree in chemistry from Boston College (1984).
She has also completed a certificate program in food retailing management.
Janet was hired as a sales associate in 1991 and promoted to sales representative
 in February 1992.]]>
    </notes>
  </employee>
</employees>
```

Now further assume that you wish to display this XML file in a web browser, as shown in Figure 6-1.

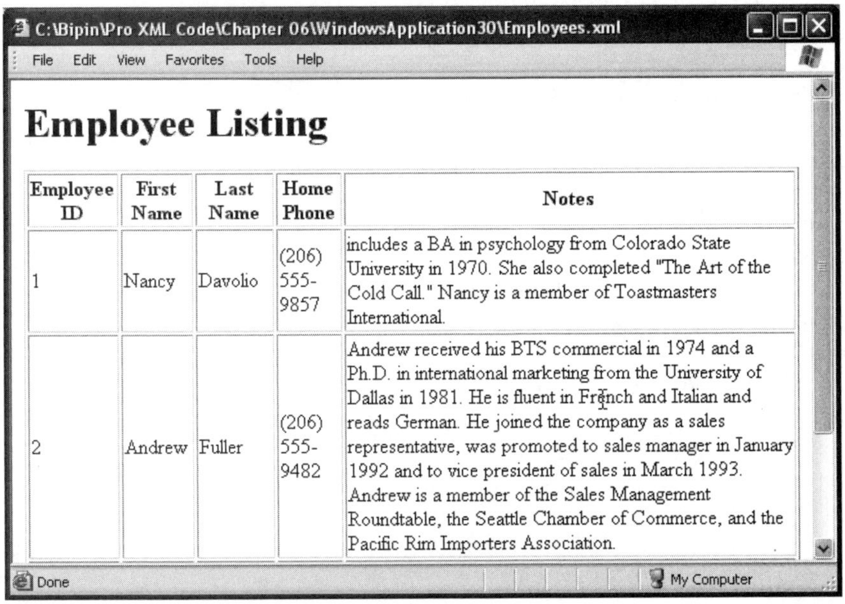

Figure 6-1. *XML document converted to an HTML table*

This means you wish to convert XML markup into HTML markup (XHTML, to be more specific). This transformation is achieved by XSLT. Let's see how.

Listing 6-2 shows `Employees.xslt`—an XSLT style sheet that will be applied to `Employees.xml`.

Listing 6-2. *XSLT for Transforming Employees.xml into an HTML Table*

```
<?xml version="1.0" encoding="UTF-8" ?>
<xsl:stylesheet version="1.0" xmlns:xsl="http://www.w3.org/1999/XSL/Transform">
  <xsl:template match="/">
    <html>
      <body>
        <h1>Employee Listing</h1>
        <table border="1">
          <tr>
            <th>Employee ID</th>
            <th>First Name</th>
            <th>Last Name</th>
            <th>Home Phone</th>
            <th>Notes</th>
          </tr>
```

```
          <xsl:for-each select="employees/employee">
            <tr>
              <td>
                <xsl:value-of select="@employeeid"/>
              </td>
              <td>
                <xsl:value-of select="firstname"/>
              </td>
              <td>
                <xsl:value-of select="lastname"/>
              </td>
              <td>
                <xsl:value-of select="homephone"/>
              </td>
              <td>
                <xsl:value-of select="notes"/>
              </td>
            </tr>
          </xsl:for-each>
        </table>
      </body>
    </html>
  </xsl:template>
</xsl:stylesheet>
```

An XSLT file is an XML document in itself as indicated by the XML processing instruction at the top. The root element of any XSLT style sheet must be `<xsl:stylesheet>`. An XSLT style sheet consists of one or more templates, which are marked with the `<xsl:template>` element. Each template works on one or more elements from the XML file as indicated by the `match` attribute. The forward slash (`/`) indicates the root element. The `match` attribute can take any valid XPath expression.

Inside the outermost `<xsl:template>` element, the markup outputs an HTML table with four columns: employee ID, first name, last name, and notes. We wish to pick up every `<employee>` element from the document and extract its attribute and sub-element values. The `<xsl:for-each>` element works like a `for each` loop in any programming language and selects a node set based on the criteria specified in the `select` attribute. In our example, because we wish to work with `<employee>` elements, the `select` attribute is set to `employees/employee`. The `select` attribute of `<xsl:for-each>` can take any valid XPath expression.

Inside the `<xsl:for-each>` construct, the values of attributes and elements are retrieved by using the `<xsl:value-of>` element. The `select` attribute of `<xsl:value-of>` must be any valid XPath expression that returns the value to be outputted. Note the use of `@employeeid` to retrieve the value of the `employeeid` attribute. Thus the `employeeid` attribute and the values of the four sub-elements (`<firstname>`, `<lastname>`, `<homephone>`, and `<notes>`) are outputted in the cells of the HTML table.

The same process is repeated for all the employees in the `Employees.xml` file.

Now that you are familiar with the XSLT style sheet, it's time to attach the style sheet to the XML document. To do so, you must add the markup shown in Listing 6-3 to the `Employees.xml` file.

Listing 6-3. *Attaching an XSLT Style Sheet to an XML Document*

```
<?xml version="1.0" encoding="utf-8" ?>
<?xml-stylesheet type="text/xsl" href="Employees.xslt"?>
<!-- This is list of employees -->
<employees>
  <employee employeeid="1">
    <firstname>Nancy</firstname>
...
```

Notice the use of the `<?xml-stylesheet?>` processing instruction. This processing instruction indicates that the type of style sheet being applied is XSL, and it is located at the URL specified by the `href` attribute. After you attach the style sheet to the XML document, you can view the XML file in the browser and you should see output similar to Figure 6-1.

In the following sections, you will learn a few more constructs of XSLT.

Applying Templates by Using <xsl:apply-templates>

The `<xsl:apply-templates>` element applies templates to the elements specified by its `select` attribute. To illustrate the use of `<xsl:apply-templates>`, we will create an XSLT style sheet that renders the XML markup from `Employees.xml`, as shown in Figure 6-2.

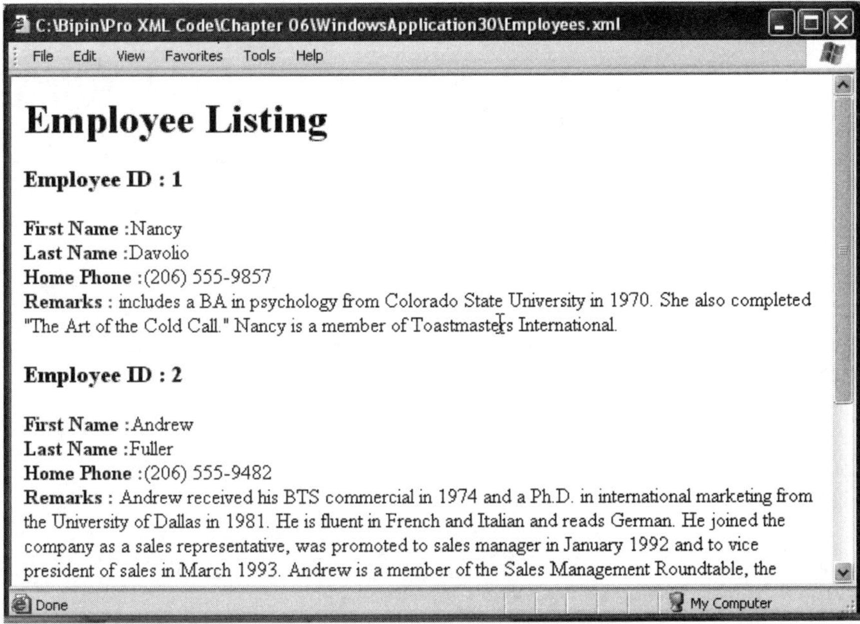

Figure 6-2. *Rendering Employees.xml by applying templates*

The corresponding style sheet is shown in Listing 6-4.

Listing 6-4. *Using <xsl:apply-templates>*

```
<?xml version="1.0" encoding="UTF-8" ?>
<xsl:stylesheet version="1.0" xmlns:xsl="http://www.w3.org/1999/XSL/Transform">
  <xsl:template match="/">
    <html>
      <body>
        <h1>Employee Listing</h1>
        <xsl:apply-templates/>
      </body>
    </html>
  </xsl:template>

  <xsl:template match="employee">
    <div>
      <h3>Employee ID :
      <xsl:value-of select="@employeeid"/>
      </h3>
      <xsl:apply-templates select="firstname"/>
      <xsl:apply-templates select="lastname"/>
      <xsl:apply-templates select="homephone"/>
      <xsl:apply-templates select="notes"/>
    </div>
  </xsl:template>

  <xsl:template match="firstname">
    <b>First Name :</b><xsl:value-of select="."/>
    <br />
  </xsl:template>

  <xsl:template match="lastname">
    <b>Last Name :</b>
    <xsl:value-of select="."/>
    <br />
  </xsl:template>

  <xsl:template match="homephone">
    <b>Home Phone :</b>
    <xsl:value-of select="."/>
    <br />
  </xsl:template>
```

```
  <xsl:template match="notes">
    <b>Remarks :</b>
    <xsl:value-of select="."/>
    <br />
  </xsl:template>

</xsl:stylesheet>
```

This time the topmost `<xsl:template>` element includes an `<xsl:apply-templates>` element. If the `<xsl:apply-templates>` element is used without the `select` attribute, `<xsl:apply-templates>` applies matching templates to all sub-elements. Then the XSLT declares five templates for the `<employee>`, `<firstname>`, `<lastname>`, `<homephone>`, and `<notes>` elements, respectively. The template for the `<employee>` element actually decides the order in which the remaining templates will be applied. This is done by specifying the `select` attribute in the `<xsl:apply-templates>` element. The `select` attribute can contain any valid XPath expression.

Branching by Using <xsl:if>

The XSLT standard provides the `<xsl:if>` element that is equivalent to the `if` statement provided by many programming languages. Suppose that you wish to display details only where the first name is *Nancy*. You can achieve this by using `<xsl:if>` as shown in Listing 6-5.

Listing 6-5. *Using <xsl:if>*

```
<?xml version="1.0" encoding="UTF-8" ?>
<xsl:stylesheet version="1.0" xmlns:xsl="http://www.w3.org/1999/XSL/Transform">
  <xsl:template match="/">
    <html>
      <body>
        <h1>Employee Listing</h1>
        <table border="1">
          <tr>
            <th>Employee ID</th>
            <th>First Name</th>
            <th>Last Name</th>
            <th>Home Phone</th>
            <th>Notes</th>
          </tr>
          <xsl:for-each select="employees/employee">
            <xsl:if test="firstname[text()='Nancy']">
              <tr>
                <td>
                  <xsl:value-of select="@employeeid"/>
                </td>
```

```
                <td>
                  <xsl:value-of select="firstname"/>
                </td>
                <td>
                  <xsl:value-of select="lastname"/>
                </td>
                <td>
                  <xsl:value-of select="homephone"/>
                </td>
                <td>
                  <xsl:value-of select="notes"/>
                </td>
              </tr>
            </xsl:if>
          </xsl:for-each>
        </table>
      </body>
    </html>
  </xsl:template>
</xsl:stylesheet>
```

This is the same style sheet that we used in our first example, but this time it includes the `<xsl:if>` construct. The `test` attribute of `<xsl:if>` tests for a specific condition. The condition in our example checks whether the value of the `<firstname>` element (`text()`) is `Nancy`. If it is `Nancy`, the details are outputted in the resultant HTML table. Figure 6-3 shows a sample view of the `Employees.xml` file after applying the preceding style sheet.

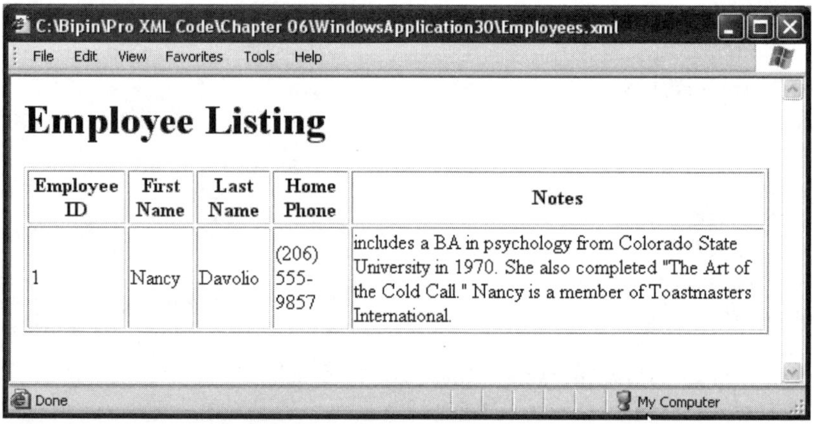

C:\Bipin\Pro XML Code\Chapter 06\WindowsApplication30\Employees.xml

File Edit View Favorites Tools Help

Employee Listing

Employee ID	First Name	Last Name	Home Phone	Notes
1	Nancy	Davolio	(206) 555-9857	includes a BA in psychology from Colorado State University in 1970. She also completed "The Art of the Cold Call." Nancy is a member of Toastmasters International.

Done My Computer

Figure 6-3. *Output after using <xsl:if>*

Branching by Using <xsl:choose> and <xsl:when>

The `<xsl:choose>` and `<xsl:when>` elements are equivalent to the `switch` statement used by programming languages. Using our example file, suppose that you wish to display an additional column called Qualification in the resultant HTML table. You wish to search the notes about an employee for certain qualifications and accordingly want to display them in this additional column. Listing 6-6 shows the style sheet that accomplishes this task.

Listing 6-6. *Using <xsl:choose> and <xsl:when>*

```
<?xml version="1.0" encoding="UTF-8" ?>
<xsl:stylesheet version="1.0" xmlns:xsl="http://www.w3.org/1999/XSL/Transform">
  <xsl:template match="/">
    <html>
      <body>
        <h1>Employee Listing</h1>
        <table border="1">
          <tr>
            <th>Employee ID</th>
            <th>First Name</th>
            <th>Last Name</th>
            <th>Home Phone</th>
            <th>Notes</th>
            <th>Qualification</th>
          </tr>
          <xsl:for-each select="employees/employee">
            <tr>
              <td>
                <xsl:value-of select="@employeeid"/>
              </td>
              <td>
                <xsl:value-of select="firstname"/>
              </td>
              <td>
                <xsl:value-of select="lastname"/>
              </td>
              <td>
                <xsl:value-of select="homephone"/>
              </td>
              <td>
                <xsl:value-of select="notes"/>
              </td>
```

```
                <td>
                <xsl:choose>
                  <xsl:when test="notes[contains(.,'BA')]">
                    BA (Arts)
                  </xsl:when>
                  <xsl:when test="notes[contains(.,'BS')]">
                    BS (Science)
                  </xsl:when>
                  <xsl:when test="notes[contains(.,'BTS')]">
                    BTS (Other)
                  </xsl:when>
                  <xsl:otherwise>
                    Unknown
                  </xsl:otherwise>
                </xsl:choose>
                </td>
              </tr>
            </xsl:for-each>
          </table>
        </body>
      </html>
  </xsl:template>
</xsl:stylesheet>
```

Notice the markup in bold. The <xsl:choose> element starts the switch statement. Each individual <xsl:when> element tests a specific condition. In our example, we check whether the <notes> element contains BA, BS, or BTS, and accordingly emit the qualification of the employee. If the test fails, the markup from <xsl:otherwise> is emitted. Figure 6-4 shows the table with the Qualification column added.

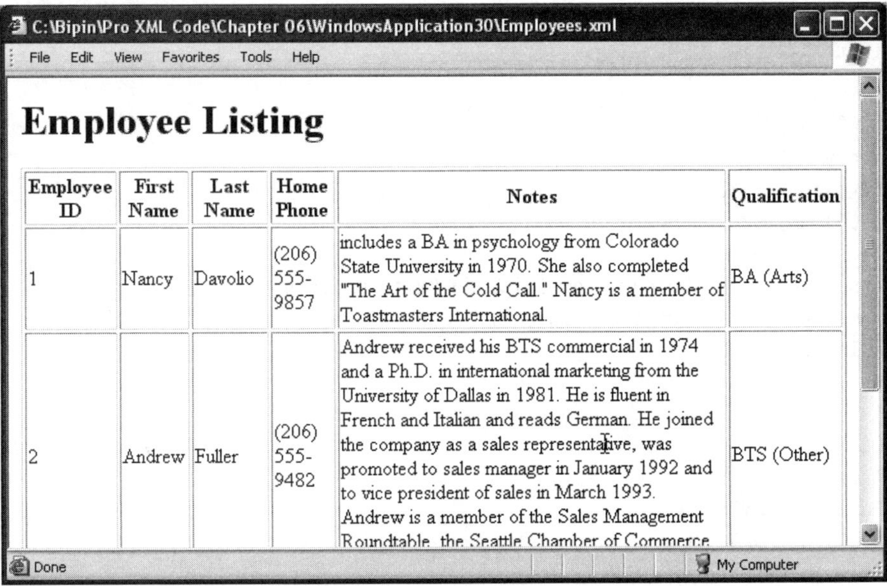

Employee ID	First Name	Last Name	Home Phone	Notes	Qualification
1	Nancy	Davolio	(206) 555-9857	includes a BA in psychology from Colorado State University in 1970. She also completed "The Art of the Cold Call." Nancy is a member of Toastmasters International.	BA (Arts)
2	Andrew	Fuller	(206) 555-9482	Andrew received his BTS commercial in 1974 and a Ph.D. in international marketing from the University of Dallas in 1981. He is fluent in French and Italian and reads German. He joined the company as a sales representative, was promoted to sales manager in January 1992 and to vice president of sales in March 1993. Andrew is a member of the Sales Management Roundtable, the Seattle Chamber of Commerce	BTS (Other)

Figure 6-4. *Qualification column added by using <xsl:choose> and <xsl:when>*

Transforming Elements and Attributes

Up until now, we have transformed XML data into HTML. However, often you may need to transform XML data into another XML representation. For example, a B2B application might be receiving orders electronically in XML format. While receiving such orders, you must ensure that the source XML markup and expected XML markup match. If they do not match, you can apply XSLT transformations to generate the desired markup.

To illustrate how XSLT transformations can convert one XML representation into another, we will transform `Employees.xml` into another XML representation, as shown in Listing 6-7.

Listing 6-7. *Required XML Markup from Employees.xml*

```
<?xml version="1.0" encoding="utf-8"?>
<EMPLOYEES>
  <E1 EMPCODE="1">
    <FNAME>Nancy</FNAME>
    <LNAME>Davolio</LNAME>
    <PHONE>(206) 555-9857</PHONE>
    <REMARKS>
      includes a BA in psychology from Colorado State University in 1970.
She also completed "The Art of the Cold Call." Nancy is a member of
Toastmasters International.
    </REMARKS>
  </E1>
  <E2 EMPCODE="2">
    <FNAME>Andrew</FNAME>
    <LNAME>Fuller</LNAME>
    <PHONE>(206) 555-9482</PHONE>
    <REMARKS>
      Andrew received his BTS commercial in 1974 and a Ph.D. in international
marketing from the University of Dallas in 1981.  He is fluent in French and
Italian and reads German. He joined the company as a sales representative,
was promoted to sales manager in January 1992 and to vice president of sales
 in March 1993. Andrew is a member of the Sales Management Roundtable,
the Seattle Chamber of Commerce, and the Pacific Rim Importers Association.
    </REMARKS>
  </E2>
  <E3 EMPCODE="3">
    <FNAME>Janet</FNAME>
    <LNAME>Leverling</LNAME>
    <PHONE>(206) 555-3412</PHONE>
    <REMARKS>
      Janet has a BS degree in chemistry from Boston College (1984).
She has also completed a certificate program in food retailing management.
Janet was hired as a sales associate in 1991 and promoted to sales representative
 in February 1992.
    </REMARKS>
  </E3>
</EMPLOYEES>
```

Notice the several changes made to the XML markup:

- The root node is now <EMPLOYEES> and not <employees>.
- Each <employee> element is replaced with an element of the form E<employeeid>—that is, <E1>, <E2>, and <E3>. That means the element name consists of a constant part (E) followed by the employee ID.
- The employeeid attribute has now become the EMPCODE attribute.
- The <firstname>, <lastname>, <homephone>, and <notes> elements have now become <FNAME>, <LNAME>, <PHONE>, and <REMARKS>, respectively.

The XSLT style sheet that brings about this transformation is shown in Listing 6-8.

Listing 6-8. *Transforming Employees.xml*

```
<?xml version="1.0" encoding="UTF-8" ?>
<xsl:stylesheet version="1.0" xmlns:xsl="http://www.w3.org/1999/XSL/Transform">
  <xsl:template match="/">
    <EMPLOYEES>
      <xsl:apply-templates/>
    </EMPLOYEES>
  </xsl:template>

  <xsl:template match="employee">
    <xsl:element name="E{@employeeid}">
      <xsl:attribute name="EMPCODE">
        <xsl:value-of select="@employeeid"/>
      </xsl:attribute>
      <xsl:apply-templates select="firstname"/>
      <xsl:apply-templates select="lastname"/>
      <xsl:apply-templates select="homephone"/>
      <xsl:apply-templates select="notes"/>
    </xsl:element>
  </xsl:template>

  <xsl:template match="firstname">
    <FNAME>
      <xsl:value-of select="."/>
    </FNAME>
  </xsl:template>
```

```
  <xsl:template match="lastname">
    <LNAME>
      <xsl:value-of select="."/>
    </LNAME>
  </xsl:template>

  <xsl:template match="homephone">
    <PHONE>
      <xsl:value-of select="."/>
    </PHONE>
  </xsl:template>

  <xsl:template match="notes">
    <REMARKS>
      <xsl:value-of select="."/>
    </REMARKS>
  </xsl:template>
</xsl:stylesheet>
```

Notice the code marked in bold. The topmost `<xsl:template>` element now contains the `<EMPLOYEES>` element. The template that matches the `<employee>` element does an interesting job: the `<xsl:element>` element is used to define new elements in the resultant output. You might be wondering why we need this element; after all, you can directly specify new element names (as we do for `<FNAME>`, `<LNAME>`, `<PHONE>`, and `<REMARKS>` later on). Note that we need to create an element name that is `E` followed by the employee ID. Something like this can be accomplished only by using the `<xsl:element>` element. Observe carefully how the element name has been formed by specifying the dynamic part (employee ID) in curly brackets. Next, the `<xsl:attribute>` element defines the `EMPCODE` attribute. The templates for `<firstname>`, `<lastname>`, `<homephone>`, and `<notes>` are then applied. In each of these templates, the new markup tag is emitted along with the value of the element.

If you open this file in a web browser, you may not see the desired markup because the output is not HTML this time. The Visual Studio IDE provides an easy way to see the resultant output. Open the XML document (`Employees.xml`) in the IDE, and apply the latest style sheet to it by using the `xml-stylesheet` processing instruction. Then choose XML ➤ Show XSLT Output from the menu. Visual Studio will apply the style sheet to the XML document and display the resultant output.

The XslCompiledTransform Class

Up until now, we have attached XSLT style sheets to XML documents at design time. However, in many real-world cases you may need to apply them programmatically. For example, you might be generating the XML data at run time and wish to transform it by using XSLT. The `XslCompiledTransform` class is intended for just such a situation. The `XslCompiledTransform` class resides in the `System.Xml.Xsl` namespace and represents the .NET Framework's XSLT processor. It compiles the XSLT style sheets and performs XSLT transformations.

The `XslCompiledTransform` class can accept XML data to transform it in several forms. Similarly, the output generated by `XslCompiledTransform` can be in various forms. To be specific, the source of transformation can be as follows:

- An object that implements `IXPathNavigator` (for example, `XmlNode` or `XPathDocument`)
- An `XmlReader`
- A URL or path of the XML file

The output of the transformation can be in the form of the following:

- An `XmlWriter` class
- A physical disk file
- A stream (for example, `MemoryStream` or `FileStream`)
- A class inheriting from the `TextWriter` abstract class (for example, `StringWriter` or `StreamWriter`)

Performing Transformations by Using XslCompiledTransform

In this section, you will learn to use the `XslCompiledTransform` class. You will develop an application as shown in Figure 6-5.

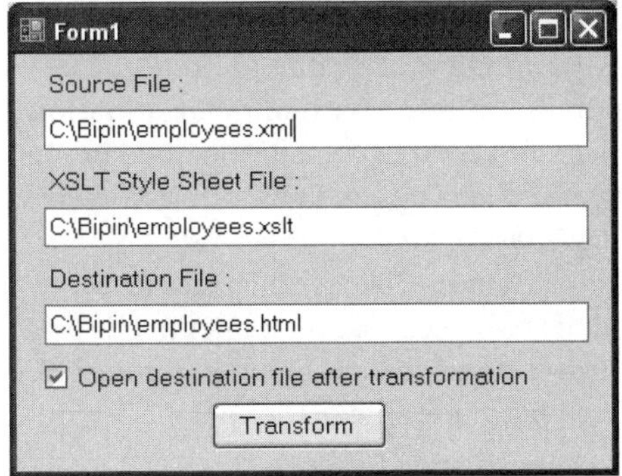

Figure 6-5. *Application to apply XSLT transformations*

As shown in Figure 6-5, the application consists of three text boxes to accept the source XML filename, the XSLT style sheet filename, and the destination filename, respectively. Clicking the Transform button performs the transformation, and the output of the transformation is stored in a file specified by the destination file text box. You can also open the destination file after a successful transformation by selecting the check box. Listing 6-9 shows the `Click` event handler of the Transform button.

Listing 6-9. *Using the XslCompiledTransform Class*

```
private void button1_Click(object sender, EventArgs e)
{
  if(Path.GetExtension(textBox3.Text)!=".htm" &&
       Path.GetExtension(textBox3.Text)!=".html")
   {
     MessageBox.Show("File extention must be .htm or .html");
     return;
   }
  XslCompiledTransform xslt = new XslCompiledTransform();
  xslt.Load(textBox2.Text);
  xslt.Transform(textBox1.Text, textBox3.Text);
  if (checkBox1.Checked)
  {
    System.Diagnostics.Process.Start(textBox3.Text);
  }
}
```

Make sure to import the `System.Xml.Xsl` namespace because the `XslCompiledTransform` class resides in it. Notice the code marked in bold. To start with, the code creates an instance of the `XslCompiledTransform` class. The `Load()` method of `XslCompiledTransform` accepts the path of the XSLT style sheet to be applied and loads it for transformation. However, it is the `Transform()` method that actually performs the transformation by applying the style sheet loaded by using the `Load()` method. There are several overloads of the `Transform()` method: the one that we have used accepts two string parameters. The first parameter is the path of the source XML document, and the second parameter is the path of the destination document. After the transformation, the resultant output is saved in the file specified by the second parameter of the `Transform()` method. Finally, the file is opened with the associated application by using the `Start()` method of the `Process` class.

To test the application, you can use the `Employees.xml` and `Employees.xslt` files (see Listing 6-2) that we used earlier in this chapter. Note that `Employees.xml` no longer needs to have the `xml-stylesheet` processing instruction. When you supply all the filenames and click the Transform button, you should see the `Employees.html` file generated in the specified folder. The `Employees.html` file will have HTML markup as shown in Listing 6-10.

Listing 6-10. *Output After Applying the Style Sheet*

```
<html>
  <body>
    <h1>Employee Listing</h1>
    <table border="1">
      <tr>
        <th>Employee ID</th>
        <th>First Name</th>
        <th>Last Name</th>
        <th>Home Phone</th>
        <th>Notes</th>
      </tr>
      <tr>
        <td>1</td>
        <td>Nancy</td>
        <td>Davolio</td>
        <td>(206) 555-9857</td>
        <td>
          includes a BA in psychology from Colorado State University in 1970.
          She also completed "The Art of the Cold Call." Nancy is a member
          of Toastmasters International.
        </td>
      </tr>
      <tr>
        <td>2</td>
        <td>Andrew</td>
        <td>Fuller</td>
        <td>(206) 555-9482</td>
        <td>
          Andrew received his BTS commercial in 1974 and a Ph.D. in international
          marketing from the University of Dallas in 1981.  He is fluent in French
          and Italian and reads German. He joined the company as a sales
          representative, was promoted to sales manager in January 1992 and to vice
          president of sales in March 1993. Andrew is a member of the Sales
          Management Roundtable, the Seattle Chamber of Commerce, and the Pacific
          Rim Importers Association.
        </td>
      </tr>
```

```
      <tr>
        <td>3</td>
        <td>Janet</td>
        <td>Leverling</td>
        <td>(206) 555-3412</td>
        <td>
          Janet has a BS degree in chemistry from Boston College (1984).
          She has also completed a certificate program in food retailing management.
          Janet was hired as a sales associate in 1991 and promoted to sales
          representative in February 1992.
        </td>
      </tr>
    </table>
  </body>
</html>
```

As you can see, the source XML markup is transformed into HTML markup as specified in the style sheet.

Note In our example, we converted XML markup into HTML markup. However, you can easily use the `XslCompiledTransform` class to transform source XML into another XML representation.

Passing Arguments to a Transformation

In Listing 6-5, you created a style sheet that transforms details of a single employee, Nancy, by using the `<xsl:if>` element. The problem with our XSLT is that we hard-coded the name *Nancy* in the style sheet. In real-world cases, this name will probably come from a user interface element. Thus it becomes necessary that the employee's first name be accepted as a parameter in the XSLT rather than a fixed value.

Fortunately, XSLT allows you to declare parameters in your style sheet. These parameters can then be supplied at run time from your application. A collection of these parameters is represented by the `XsltArgumentList` class, and you can add individual parameters to this collection. To illustrate the use of `XsltArgumentList`, we will develop an application as shown in Figure 6-6.

Figure 6-6. *Application for passing parameters to the XSLT style sheet*

The application consists of a single text box for accepting the first name of the employee. Clicking the Transform button applies the style sheet and stores the resultant output in an HTML file. Our XML file remains the same (`Employees.xml`). However, you need to modify the style sheet from Listing 6-5 as shown in Listing 6-11.

Listing 6-11. *XSLT Style Sheet with Parameter*

```
<?xml version="1.0" encoding="UTF-8" ?>
<xsl:stylesheet version="1.0" xmlns:xsl="http://www.w3.org/1999/XSL/Transform">
  <xsl:param name="firstname"/>
  <xsl:template match="/">
    <html>
      <body>
        <h1>Employee Listing</h1>
        <table border="1">
          <tr>
            <th>Employee ID</th>
            <th>First Name</th>
            <th>Last Name</th>
            <th>Home Phone</th>
            <th>Notes</th>
          </tr>
          <xsl:for-each select="employees/employee">
            <xsl:if test="firstname[text()=$firstname]">
            <tr>
              <td>
                <xsl:value-of select="@employeeid"/>
              </td>
```

```
              <td>
                <xsl:value-of select="firstname"/>
              </td>
              <td>
                <xsl:value-of select="lastname"/>
              </td>
              <td>
                <xsl:value-of select="homephone"/>
              </td>
              <td>
                <xsl:value-of select="notes"/>
              </td>
            </tr>
            </xsl:if>
          </xsl:for-each>
        </table>
      </body>
    </html>
  </xsl:template>
</xsl:stylesheet>
```

Notice the style sheet markup displayed in bold. At the top of the style sheet, we have declared a parameter by using the `<xsl:param>` element. The `name` attribute of the `<xsl:param>` element indicates the name of the parameter (`firstname` in our example). To use this parameter further in the XSLT, you prefix it with the dollar ($) symbol. Notice the `firstname` parameter of the `<xsl:if>` element. Listing 6-12 shows the code that passes this parameter value at the time of actual transformation.

Listing 6-12. *Using the XsltArgumentList Class to Pass XSLT Parameters*

```
private void button1_Click(object sender, EventArgs e)
{
  string sourcefile=Application.StartupPath + @"\employees.xml";
  string xsltfile=Application.StartupPath + @"\employees.xslt";
  string destinationfile=Application.StartupPath + @"\employees.html";

  FileStream stream = new FileStream(destinationfile, FileMode.Create);

  XslCompiledTransform xslt = new XslCompiledTransform();
  xslt.Load(xsltfile);
  XsltArgumentList arguments = new XsltArgumentList();
  arguments.AddParam("firstname", "", textBox1.Text);
  xslt.Transform(sourcefile, arguments, stream);
  stream.Close();
  if (checkBox1.Checked)
```

```
    {
      System.Diagnostics.Process.Start(destinationfile);
    }
}
```

The code declares three string variables to store the paths of the source XML file, the XSLT style sheet file, and the destination HTML file, respectively. Then the code creates a `FileStream` object for writing to the destination HTML file. This `FileStream` object will be passed to the `Transform()` method later.

A new instance of the `XslCompiledTransform` class is then created and the `Load()` method loads the XSLT style sheet. Then comes the important part. The code creates an instance of the `XsltArgumentList` class and adds a parameter to it by using its `AddParam()` method, which takes three parameters: the name of the parameter, the namespace if any, and the parameter value. Then the `Transform()` method of `XslCompiledTransform` is called by passing the `XsltArgumentList` object that we just created. This time we pass the source filename, the parameter list, and a stream to which the resultant output will be written. In our case, this stream points to the `Employees.html` file. After the transformation is over, the stream is closed and the newly generated HTML file is shown to the user.

If you run the application and supply `Nancy` as the parameter value, the resultant HTML file will look like Listing 6-13.

Listing 6-13. *Output After Passing the Parameter*

```
<html>
  <body>
    <h1>Employee Listing</h1>
    <table border="1">
      <tr>
        <th>Employee ID</th>
        <th>First Name</th>
        <th>Last Name</th>
        <th>Home Phone</th>
        <th>Notes</th>
      </tr>
      <tr>
        <td>1</td>
        <td>Nancy</td>
        <td>Davolio</td>
        <td>(206) 555-9857</td>
        <td>
          includes a BA in psychology from Colorado State University in 1970.
          She also completed "The Art of the Cold Call." Nancy is a member of
          Toastmasters International.
        </td>
      </tr>
    </table>
  </body>
</html>
```

As you can see, only one record is transformed, indicating that the output was indeed filtered based on the parameter value.

Using Script Blocks in an XSLT Style Sheet

Though XSLT offers a few programming constructions and built-in functions, it is not a fully fledged programming language in itself. Sometimes you may need to perform an operation that is beyond the capabilities of XSLT. For example, you may want to connect with a SQL Server database and fetch some data that is used further by the style sheet or you may need to perform disk IO. To cater to such needs, `XslCompiledTransform` allows you to embed scripts within your XSLT style sheets. After the style sheet is loaded, the embedded code is compiled into Microsoft Intermediate Language (MSIL) and executed at run time.

Our `Employees.xml` file stores a subset of information from the `Employees` table of the `Northwind` database; it represents only four fields of the actual table: `firstname`, `lastname`, `homephone`, and `notes`. Let's assume that for some reason you also need the extract the date of birth of each employee at run time. That means we need to write some ADO.NET code to retrieve the `BirthDate` column value from the database table. We will do this by embedding a script block in the style sheet. Listing 6-14 shows the complete style sheet.

Listing 6-14. *Embedded Script Blocks in the XSLT Style Sheet*

```
<?xml version="1.0" encoding="UTF-8" ?>
<xsl:stylesheet version="1.0" xmlns:xsl="http://www.w3.org/1999/XSL/Transform"
xmlns:msxsl="urn:schemas-microsoft-com:xslt"
xmlns:myscripts="urn:myscripts">
<msxsl:script language="C#" implements-prefix="myscripts">
  <msxsl:assembly name="System.Data" />
  <msxsl:using namespace="System.Data" />
  <msxsl:using namespace="System.Data.SqlClient" />
  <![CDATA[
  public string GetBirthDate(int employeeid)
  {
    SqlConnection cnn = new SqlConnection(@"data source=.\sqlexpress;initial ➥
catalog=northwind;integrated security=true");
    SqlCommand cmd = new SqlCommand();
    cmd.Connection = cnn;
    cmd.CommandText = "SELECT birthdate FROM employees WHERE employeeid=@id";
    SqlParameter pDOB = new SqlParameter("@id",employeeid);
    cmd.Parameters.Add(pDOB);
    cnn.Open();
    object obj = cmd.ExecuteScalar();
    cnn.Close();
    DateTime dob = DateTime.Parse(obj.ToString());
    return dob.ToString("MM/dd/yyyy");
  }
  ]]>
</msxsl:script>
```

```
<xsl:template match="/">
    <html>
      <body>
        <h1>Employee Listing</h1>
        <table border="1">
          <tr>
            <th>Employee ID</th>
            <th>First Name</th>
            <th>Last Name</th>
            <th>Home Phone</th>
            <th>Birth Date</th>
            <th>Notes</th>
          </tr>
          <xsl:for-each select="employees/employee">
            <tr>
              <td>
                <xsl:value-of select="@employeeid"/>
              </td>
              <td>
                <xsl:value-of select="firstname"/>
              </td>
              <td>
                <xsl:value-of select="lastname"/>
              </td>
              <td>
                <xsl:value-of select="homephone"/>
              </td>
              <td>
                <xsl:value-of select="myscripts:GetBirthDate(@employeeid)"/>
              </td>
              <td>
                <xsl:value-of select="notes"/>
              </td>
            </tr>
          </xsl:for-each>
        </table>
      </body>
    </html>
  </xsl:template>
</xsl:stylesheet>
```

Notice the markup in bold. The `<xsl:stylesheet>` element now has two more attributes. The `xmlns:msxsl` attribute defines the `msxml` prefix for the `urn:schemas-microsoft-com:xslt` namespace. Similarly, the `xmlns:myscripts` attribute defines a `myscripts` prefix.

The `<msxml:script>` block defines one or more functions that are used in the style sheet. The `language` attribute of the script block indicates the coding language (C# in our example). Your code may need to add a reference to external assemblies, which is done by using the `<msxsl:assembly>` element. The `name` attribute of this tag specifies the name of the assembly excluding the extension. Similarly, the `<msxml:using>` tag specifies the namespaces to be imported.

The actual function is placed in a `CDATA` section. In our example, we defined a function called `GetBirthDate()` that accepts the ID of the employee whose date of birth is to be retrieved and returns the birth date in MM/dd/yyyy format. The code of the function connects with the `Northwind` database, fires a `SELECT` query against the `employees` table, and retrieves the birth date.

■ **Note** Make sure to change the database connection string to suit your development environment.

The `GetBirthDate()` function is called later in the style sheet by using the `namespaceprefix:function_name(parameter list)` syntax. The `GetBirthDate()` function expects the employee ID, which is passed by using the `employeeid` attribute (`@employeeid`) as a parameter.

To test our new style sheet, we will develop an application as shown in Figure 6-7.

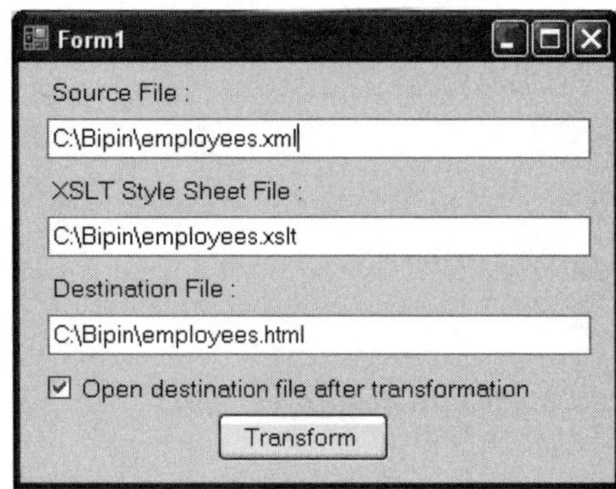

Figure 6-7. *Application for testing our embedded function*

The application user interface is the same as I discussed earlier (see Figure 6-5). However, the code inside the Transform button is slightly different. Listing 6-15 highlights these differences.

Listing 6-15. *Enabling Scripting*

```
private void button1_Click(object sender, EventArgs e)
{
  XsltSettings settings = new XsltSettings();
  settings.EnableScript = true;
  XslCompiledTransform xslt = new XslCompiledTransform();
  xslt.Load(textBox2.Text,settings,null);
  xslt.Transform(textBox1.Text, textBox3.Text);
  if (checkBox1.Checked)
  {
    System.Diagnostics.Process.Start(textBox3.Text);
  }
}
```

The `XsltSettings` class specifies the features to support during the transformation. The `EnableScript` property indicates whether to enable embedded script blocks. The `Load()` method of the `XslCompiledTransform` class accepts the `XsltSettings` object as one of its parameters. If you run the application and specify the three paths, you will get output as shown in Figure 6-8.

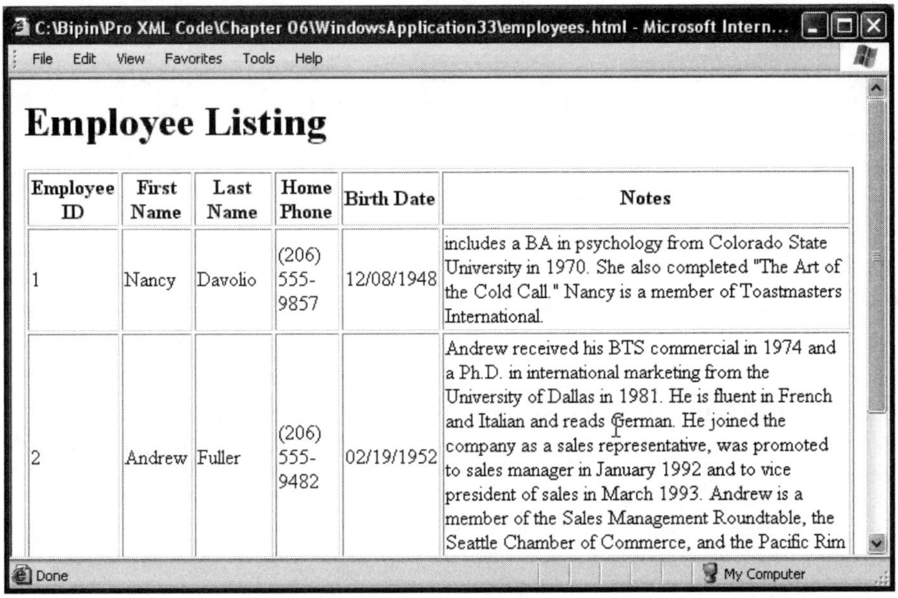

C:\Bipin\Pro XML Code\Chapter 06\WindowsApplication33\employees.html - Microsoft Intern...

File Edit View Favorites Tools Help

Employee Listing

Employee ID	First Name	Last Name	Home Phone	Birth Date	Notes
1	Nancy	Davolio	(206) 555-9857	12/08/1948	includes a BA in psychology from Colorado State University in 1970. She also completed "The Art of the Cold Call." Nancy is a member of Toastmasters International.
2	Andrew	Fuller	(206) 555-9482	02/19/1952	Andrew received his BTS commercial in 1974 and a Ph.D. in international marketing from the University of Dallas in 1981. He is fluent in French and Italian and reads German. He joined the company as a sales representative, was promoted to sales manager in January 1992 and to vice president of sales in March 1993. Andrew is a member of the Sales Management Roundtable, the Seattle Chamber of Commerce, and the Pacific Rim

Done My Computer

Figure 6-8. *Output with the Birth Date column added*

Using Extension Objects

Embedding scripts in the style sheet does indeed provide a handy way to perform operations that are beyond the capabilities of XSLT. However, it doesn't provide a good mechanism for reusing your code. What if you wish to use the same function elsewhere in the application or in other style sheets? This is where extension objects come into the picture. Simply put, extension objects are objects external to the style sheet that provide some functionality to the style sheet. Extension objects promote greater code reuse and are more flexible and maintainable than embedded script blocks.

To illustrate the use of extension objects, we will modify our previous example. First, we will put the `GetBirthDate()` function in a separate class called `Employee` rather than embedding it in the style sheet. The newly created `Employee` class should look similar to Listing 6-16.

Listing 6-16. *Placing the GetBirthDate() Function in a Class*

```
class Employee
{
  public string GetBirthDate(int employeeid)
  {
    SqlConnection cnn = new SqlConnection(@"data source=.\sqlexpress;initial ➥
catalog=northwind;integrated security=true");
    SqlCommand cmd = new SqlCommand();
    cmd.Connection = cnn;
    cmd.CommandText = "SELECT birthdate FROM employees WHERE employeeid=@id";
    SqlParameter pDOB = new SqlParameter("@id", employeeid);
    cmd.Parameters.Add(pDOB);
    cnn.Open();
    object obj = cmd.ExecuteScalar();
    cnn.Close();
    DateTime dob = DateTime.Parse(obj.ToString());
    return dob.ToString("MM/dd/yyyy");
  }
}
```

The function by itself is the same that we used before but it has been encapsulated in the `Employee` class. Next you need to modify the `Click` event handler of the Transform button to resemble Listing 6-17.

Listing 6-17. *Using Extension Objects*

```
private void button1_Click(object sender, EventArgs e)
{
  XsltSettings settings = new XsltSettings();
  settings.EnableScript = true;
  XslCompiledTransform xslt = new XslCompiledTransform();
  xslt.Load(textBox2.Text,settings,null);

  XsltArgumentList arguments = new XsltArgumentList();
  Employee employee = new Employee();
  arguments.AddExtensionObject("urn:myscripts", employee);

  FileStream stream = new FileStream(textBox3.Text, FileMode.Create);
  xslt.Transform(textBox1.Text, arguments,stream);
  stream.Close();
  if (checkBox1.Checked)
  {
    System.Diagnostics.Process.Start(textBox3.Text);
  }
}
```

Notice the code marked in bold. After loading the style sheet by using the `Load()` method as before, it creates an instance of the `XsltArgumentList` class, which we used when passing parameters to the style sheet. This time, however, the code uses the `AddExtensionObject()` method of the `XsltArgumentList` class. This method accepts the namespace URI and an instance of the extension object. In our case, the `Employee` class instance acts as an extension object. While calling the `Transform()` method of `XslCompiledTransform`, the `XsltArgumentList` object is passed to it. If you run the application now, you should get a result identical to the previous example.

Summary

This chapter gave you a detailed understanding of XSLT processing in .NET. By using XSLT style sheets, XML data can be transformed from one form to another. The `XslCompiledTransform` class represents the .NET Framework's XSLT processor. It allows you to load the style sheets and apply them to source XML. You can also pass parameters while transformation is being carried out, by using the `XsltArgumentList` class. The `XslCompiledTransform` class also allows you to embed script blocks. A better way to use your code is to create extension objects, which are more flexible and maintainable than embedded script blocks.

CHAPTER 7

XML in ADO.NET

ADO.NET is a technology for accessing and manipulating databases. Disconnected data access and XML integration are the key features of ADO.NET. In this chapter, you are going to see how ADO.NET has harnessed the power of XML in data representation. Specifically, this chapter covers the following:

- An overview of XML integration in ADO.NET
- Working with `SqlDataReader` and XML
- `DataSet` architecture and disconnected data access
- XML integration in `DataSet`
- The `XmlDataDocument` class

Overview of ADO.NET Architecture

ADO.NET provides two ways of working with your data:

- Connected data access
- Disconnected data access

Connected Data Access

In *connected data access*, you establish a connection with the database. Then, as long as you are working with the data, you maintain this live connection. The following are the steps that you typically take when using connected data access:

1. Establish a connection with the database.
2. Fetch a set of records in a cursor.
3. Work with the fetched data (perform read, modify, and delete operations or even calculations).
4. Update the database, if there are any changes.
5. Close the database connection.

The advantage of this model is that you can see changes in the database in real time. However, this approach is not recommended for scalable applications because it can hamper the overall performance and scalability of the system. Also, even though ADO.NET provides cursor-oriented connected data access, it is strictly read-only and forward-only. This incurs fewer overheads and improves performance as compared to updatable cursors.

You will typically use connected data access in the following situations:

- You are developing applications that are online all the time. For example, in a ticket reservation application it is necessary that you work with the latest data from the database. In such cases, connected data access becomes necessary.
- You want to avoid the overhead of using offline data. When you use queries directly against a database, naturally they bypass any of the intermediate layers that are involved in disconnected data-access techniques. For example, suppose that you wish to display a simple employee listing to the end user. This task does not involve any processing as such. Using connected data access in such cases will of course give the best performance.
- You need a cursor model for some reason.

The `Connection`, `Command`, and `DataReader` classes are used for such connected data access. You will learn about these classes in later sections.

Disconnected Data Access

Many modern systems need to be distributed and scalable. Consider an example of a distributed application that performs some database-intensive tasks. A typical programming approach is to open a live connection with the database and maintain it as long as the database-related tasks are in progress. This is fine if the number of users is small, but as the user base grows, the available database connections become precious. In such heavily loaded systems, a live connection approach is not recommended. The alternative is to have offline or disconnected access to the data. *Disconnected data access* involves the following steps:

1. Establish a connection with the database.
2. Fetch the data that you require and store it in some offline medium.
3. Close the database connection.
4. Work with the fetched data (perform read, modify, and delete operations or even calculations).
5. Again, open a database connection if you wish to update the changes made to the data back to the database.
6. Update the database, if there are any changes.
7. Close the database connection.

As you can see, the database connection is opened only when required. You will typically use disconnected data access in the following situations:

- Your application data can be updated in batches.
- Your application does not need up-to-the minute data from the database.
- You want to pass data across multiple layers of your system.
- You want to pass data from your application to another application.
- Your application data is generated programmatically and is not coming from any data source.

This disconnected data access is provided by a `DataAdapter` and a `DataSet` class. You will learn more about these classes in upcoming sections.

ADO.NET Data Providers

To communicate with the data source, you need some kind of layer that will facilitate this communication for you. In the early days, Open Database Connectivity (ODBC) drivers provided such a layer. With the introduction of Object Linking and Embedding Database (OLEDB), OLEDB providers did the same job. Now, with ADO.NET it is data providers that do it for you by providing managed access to the underlying data source. The data source can be a relational database management system (RDBMS) such as SQL Server or it can be some nonrelational entity such as XML documents.

Four data providers are available out of the box with ADO.NET:

- SQL Server data provider
- OLEDB data provider
- Oracle data provider
- ODBC data provider

You can also build your own data provider.

Each ADO.NET data provider implements a certain set of interfaces. This makes the overall object model look almost the same, irrespective of the data provider used. The following sections will give you a brief introduction to the various data providers available.

SQL Server Data Provider

The SQL Server data provider is specifically designed for SQL Server 7 and later versions. It is optimized for SQL Server and uses SQL Server's native data format—tabular data stream (TDS) for communication. As this data provider talks with SQL Server via its native format, there are none of the overheads associated with the OLEDB layer.

OLEDB Data Provider

As the name suggests, the OLEDB data provider is used to communicate with any OLEDB-compliant databases such as SQL Server and Oracle. The OLEDB data provider is actually a wrapper over the corresponding OLEDB service provider and thus introduces a small performance overhead. If your database is OLEDB compliant but does not have its own ADO.NET data provider, this is the data provider for you.

Oracle Data Provider

Microsoft has developed a data provider for Oracle databases.

ODBC Data Provider

If you are working with an RDBMS that does not have an OLEDB provider or ADO.NET data provider (say, dBASE), this is the data provider available to you.

The Assemblies and Namespaces Involved

Now that you have a brief idea about ADO.NET data providers, let's see the related namespaces. We will focus our attention on only the SQL Server data provider and the OLEDB data provider because they are very commonly used in many business applications. All the data-access classes of these two providers reside in the assembly `System.Data.dll`. There are five major namespaces pertaining to the preceding data providers:

- The `System.Data` namespace provides classes and interfaces that are common to all data providers. For example, the `DataSet` class is the same irrespective of whether it is populated with data from SQL Server or another OLEDB database. This namespace also contains interfaces that are implemented by all the data providers.
- The `System.Data.Common` namespace contains classes shared by all the .NET data providers.
- The `System.Data.OleDb` namespace contains all the classes pertaining to the OLEDB data provider. For example, there are classes such as `OleDbConnection`, `OleDbCommand`, and `OleDbParameter`.
- The `System.Data.SqlClient` namespace contains all the classes related to the SQL Server data provider. For example, there are classes such as `SqlConnection`, `SqlCommand`, and `SqlParameter`. As you will see, the `OleDb` and `SqlClient` namespaces contain closely matching classes.
- The `System.Data.SqlTypes` namespace provides classes for native data types within SQL Server. For example, the `SqlInt32` class represents the SQL Server integer data type. These classes help in preventing loss of precision while converting decimal or numeric data types. They also help in optimizing type conversion between .NET data types and SQL Server data types.

Basic ADO.NET Classes

Now it's time to become familiar with the common classes that play a vital role in database access. This section will give you a basic introduction to the classes so that you can perform common data-access tasks. Note that in the following section when I specify `Connection`, it is shorthand for the `SqlConnection` and `OleDbConnection` classes. The same convention applies to other classes as well.

Connection (SqlConnection and OleDbConnection)

As the name suggests, the `Connection` classes represent a connection with a database. The use of the ADO.NET `Connection` object is similar to its ADO counterpart. For example, in order to establish a connection with a SQL Server database, you will need to specify the connection string and then call the `Open()` method of the `SqlConnection` object. Note that after you finish working with the `Connection` object, you should explicitly close it by using the `Close()` method. Otherwise, the object will maintain a live connection with the database.

Command (SqlCommand and OleDbCommand)

ADO.NET `Command` objects are similar to ADO `Command` objects in that they are used to execute SQL queries and stored procedures. You specify the SQL query or stored procedure name by using the `CommandText` property. You can also specify the type of command (SQL statement or stored procedure) by using the `CommandType` property. If your query has some parameters, you can add them to the `Parameters` collection. Before executing the command, you should set its `Connection` property to an open connection object. `Command` objects can return only read-only and forward-only result sets in the form of a `DataReader`.

Parameter (SqlParameter and OleDbParameter)

Often your queries and stored procedures are parameterized. Using parameters allows you to pass external values to your queries and also avoids the risk of SQL injection attack. Parameters are also better in terms of performance because they avoid frequent parsing of queries. The `Parameter` class represents a parameter of your query or stored procedure.

DataReader (SqlDataReader and OleDbDataReader)

As I have mentioned, the `Command` object can return only read-only and forward-only cursors. The results are collected in an object called the `DataReader`, which is a firehose cursor that provides an optimized way to loop through your results.

Note Read-only and forward-only cursors are often called *fire-hose cursors*. They are one of the most efficient ways of transferring data from the server to the client.

To loop through the results, you can use its Read() method that advances the record pointer to the next row.

Note that DataReader does not have MoveXxxx()-style methods as ADO has. This helps to avoid the common programming mistake of forgetting to call MoveNext() in Do...While loops. Also, note that for DataReader only one row remains in memory at a time, so DataReader can improve the performance and memory footprint of your application significantly as compared to traditional dynamic cursors.

DataAdapter (SqlDataAdapter and OleDbDataAdapter)

In the section about disconnected data access, you learned that ADO.NET offers a way to work with disconnected data via the DataSet class. The DataSet needs to be populated from the data residing in the data source. Similarly, after you are finished with the data modifications, the data needs to be updated in the underlying data source, and the DataAdapter class is designed just for that. Note that the DataSet class is the same for any kind of data provider (SQL or OLEDB), but DataAdapter has separate implementations (SqlDataAdapter and OleDbDataAdapter). This is because, unlike DataSet, which is totally unaware of the underlying data source, DataAdapter needs to communicate with the underlying data source.

DataSet

The DataSet object is at the heart of ADO.NET disconnected architecture. DataSet is somewhat analogous to the Recordset object of ADO, but, unlike Recordset, DataSet always works in a disconnected fashion. Also, DataSet can have more than one set of data.

A DataSet is represented as an XML document over the network, which makes it a great choice for passing data from one component layer to another. It can also be used to integrate heterogeneous systems.

A DataSet can be considered an in-memory representation of a database. Just as a database consists of one or more tables, a DataSet consists of one or more DataTable objects. Each DataTable is a set of DataRow objects. Just like a database, DataTable objects can have relations and constraints. Also, they need not always be populated from the database but can be created and populated programmatically also.

XML and Connected Data Access

In the preceding sections, you saw that the SqlCommand object is used to execute SQL commands and stored procedures against a database. To execute SELECT queries and retrieve the results as XML data, you need to use the ExecuteXmlReader() method of the SqlCommand object. This method executes the SELECT query or stored procedure and returns the results in the form of an XmlReader object. You can then navigate through and access values from the XmlReader, as you learned in Chapter 3.

Using the ExecuteXmlReader() Method

When you use the ExecuteXmlReader() method of SqlCommand, the SELECT query must have the FOR XML clause specified in it. You will learn about the FOR XML clause in detail in Chapter 10. For now it is sufficient to know that this clause ensures that an XML representation of the result set is returned and it must be present.

To see how `ExecuteXmlReader()` works, you will develop an application as shown in Figure 7-1.

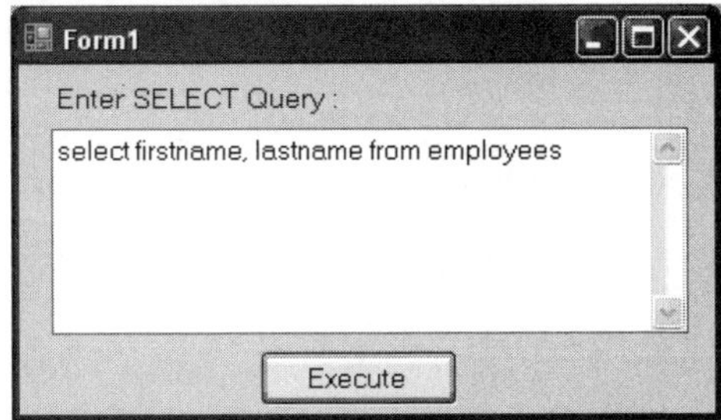

Figure 7-1. *Application for retrieving SQL Server data in XML format*

As you can see, the application consists of a text box for entering `SELECT` queries. The Execute button allows you to execute the query. The XML results returned from the query are displayed in a browser window.

Before you write the code for the `Click` event handler of the Execute button, make sure to including the namespaces as shown in Listing 7-1.

Listing 7-1. *Importing Relevant Namespaces*

```
using System.Data;
using System.Data.SqlClient;
using System.Xml;
using System.IO;
using System.Diagnostics;
```

The `Click` event handler of the Execute button contains the code shown in Listing 7-2.

Listing 7-2. *Using the ExecuteXmlReader() Method*

```
private void button1_Click(object sender, EventArgs e)
{
  SqlConnection cnn = new SqlConnection(@"data source=.\sqlexpress;initial ➥
catalog=northwind;integrated security=true");

  SqlCommand cmd = new SqlCommand();
  cmd.Connection = cnn;
  cmd.CommandType = CommandType.Text;
  cmd.CommandText = textBox1.Text + " FOR XML AUTO";
  cnn.Open();
```

```
  XmlReader reader=cmd.ExecuteXmlReader();
  StreamWriter writer= File.CreateText(Application.StartupPath + @"\temp.xml");
  writer.Write("<root>");

  while (reader.Read())
  {
    writer.Write(reader.ReadOuterXml());
  }

  writer.Write("</root>");
  writer.Close();
  reader.Close();
  cnn.Close();
  Process.Start(Application.StartupPath + @"\temp.xml");
}
```

The code creates an instance of the SqlConnection class by passing the database connection string in the constructor.

■ **Note** Throughout this chapter, it is assumed that you have SQL Server 2005 Express Edition installed on your machine. It is also assumed that you have the Northwind database installed. If you are using some other version of SQL Server, you need to change the database connection string accordingly. Also, note that SQL Server 2005 Express Edition does not include the Northwind database by default. You can, however, download the necessary scripts from Microsoft's website.

Then the code creates a SqlCommand object and sets three important properties: Connection, CommandType, and CommandText. The Connection property specifies the SqlConnection instance that is to be used for firing queries. The CommandType property is an enumeration of type CommandType and indicates the type of command being executed. In our example, it is a plain SQL statement and hence set to CommandType.Text. The CommandText property specifies the SQL query or name of the stored procedure to be executed. In our example, the query is being supplied via the text box. While assigning the CommandText property, the FOR XML AUTO clause is appended to the original query. This clause indicates that the results are returned as a sequence of elements, where the element name is the same as the table name, attribute names are the same as column names, and attribute values are the same as column values. The connection is then established by using the Open() method of the SqlConnection class.

The query is executed against the database by using the ExecuteXmlReader() method, which, as you saw, returns an instance of XmlReader that points to the result set. In our example, the code creates a physical disk file named temp.xml, iterates through the XmlReader by using its Read() method, and writes the XML data to the file. Notice the use of the ReadOuterXml() method to retrieve the XML data. Also, note that the XML data returned by ExecuteXmlReader() is in the form of elements and doesn't have a root node as such, so the code adds a <root> element to enclose all the returned data.

After the writing of XML data is done, the `StreamWriter`, `XmlReader`, and `SqlConnection` are closed by using the `Close()` method of the respective classes. The `Process` class (residing in the `System.Diagnostics` namespace) opens the `temp.xml` file in a new browser window.

If you run the application and supply a `SELECT` query, you should see the output shown in Figure 7-2.

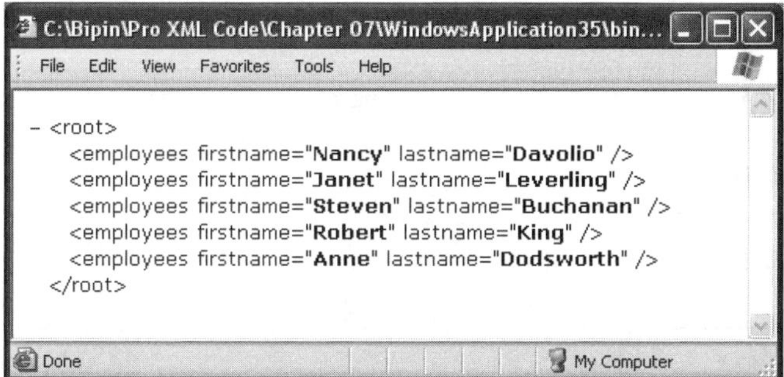

Figure 7-2. *XML data returned by the ExecuteXmlReader() method*

Figure 7-2 shows the output for the following query:

```
SELECT firstname, lastname FROM employees
```

As you can see, the element name is the same as the table name, and columns appear as attributes.

XML and Disconnected Data Access

In the preceding section, you learned the connected way of working by using ADO.NET and `XmlReader`. However, for building scalable applications, connected data access poses problems of its own. In such circumstances, disconnected data access is strongly preferred. In fact, disconnected data access is the core feature of ADO.NET.

Two classes—`DataSet` and `SqlDataAdapter`—together provide a way to work with database data in disconnected mode. The `DataSet` object is a totally disconnected one and can even be created manually. The `SqlDataAdapter` class fills the `DataSet` with data from a database and later propagates the changes made to the `DataSet` back to the database. In the next sections, you will learn the architecture of `DataSet` and `DataAdapter`, and how to work with them.

Understanding DataSet

`DataSet` is an object for storing results of your queries offline for further processing and can be viewed as an in-memory representation of a database. `DataSet` consists of one or more `DataTable` objects, which in turn consist of a collection of `DataRow` objects. Figure 7-3 gives you a complete picture of the internals of `DataSet`.

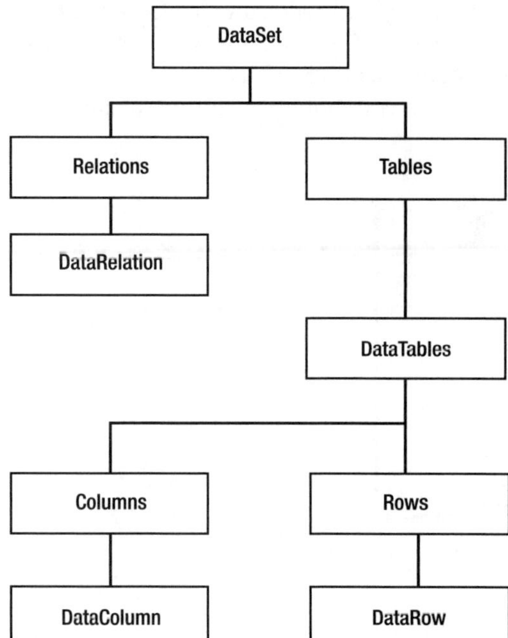

Figure 7-3. *DataSet architecture*

As you can see, DataSet has two primary collections:

- The Tables collection is exposed by the Tables property and consists of a DataTableCollection object that can have zero or more DataTable objects. Each DataTable represents a set of data from the underlying data source.
- The Relations collection is exposed as the Relations property and consists of a DataRelationCollection object. The DataRelationCollection object in turn contains zero or more DataRelation objects. Each DataRelation object represents the parent-child relationship between two DataTable objects.

As stated earlier, DataTable is a set of data and consists of rows and columns. The DataTable class has the following three important collections:

- The Columns collection is exposed as the Columns property and is an instance of the DataColumnCollection class. It contains zero or more DataColumn objects. Each DataColumn object represents a column or field of the DataTable, just like a database column. These columns define the structure of a DataTable.
- The Rows collection is exposed as the Rows property and is an instance of the DataRowCollection class. It contains zero or more DataRow objects. Each DataRow is similar to a database record and contains the actual data of the DataTable.
- Just like a database table, a DataTable can also have constraints, such as unique key constraints and foreign key constraints. The Constraints collection is exposed as the Constraints property and is an instance of the ConstraintCollection class. It can contain zero or more instances of the UniqueConstraint or ForeignKeyConstraint classes.

In addition to the preceding classes, there is a special object called DataView that is based on a DataTable. As the name suggests, DataView is used to present different views of data by sorting and filtering data from the DataTable. Note that DataView does not have independent existence and is always based on a DataTable.

Generally, you will populate your DataSet with the data from a data source such as SQL Server. However, DataSet is fully disconnected. Most of the objects of DataSet explained earlier can be created independently without any interaction with any data source. This means you can programmatically create your DataSet without even connecting with any data source. For example, you may wish to import a comma-separated list of string data into a database table. In such cases, you can create DataSet and DataTable objects programmatically and populate the data. Later you can save this data to a database table.

Understanding DataAdapter

DataAdapter is a bridge between the underlying data source and the DataSet. DataAdapter comes into the picture when you want to perform any of the following:

- Populate the DataSet from database data
- Update the data source after modifying the DataSet by adding, deleting, or updating DataRow objects

Before seeing an example of how to populate a DataSet and update the data source, you need to understand the architecture of DataAdapter. Take a look at Figure 7-4.

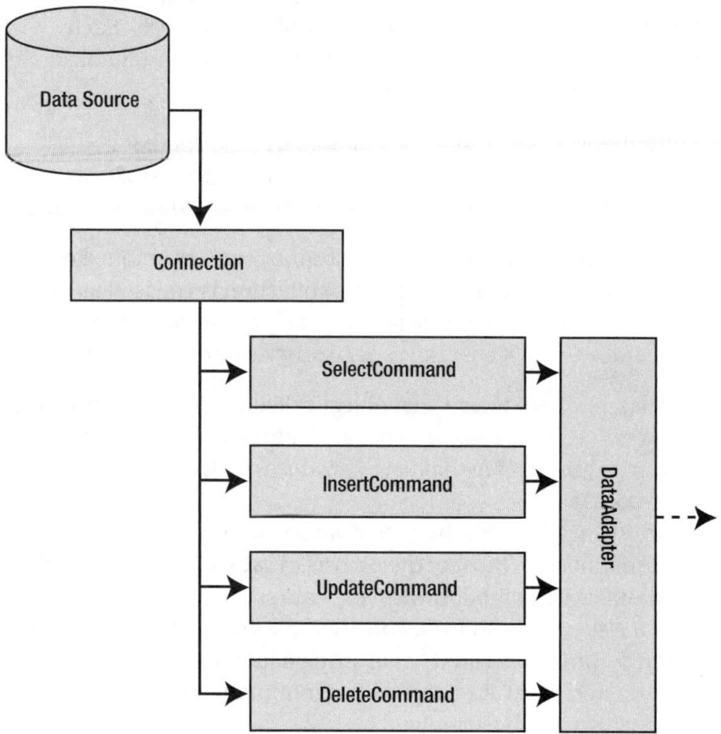

Figure 7-4. *DataAdapter architecture*

As shown in Figure 7-4, DataAdapter uses four Command objects for executing SELECT, INSERT, UPDATE, and DELETE queries. Each command is represented by the SelectCommand, InsertCommand, UpdateCommand, and DeleteCommand properties of the DataAdapter, respectively. Note that these Command objects are the same as you saw in connected data access. However, each one is assigned a specific task of selecting, inserting, updating, and deleting records from the data source. As with standard Command objects, the CommandText property of these command objects can be any valid SQL query or stored procedure.

DataAdapter provides the Fill() method that uses the Command object specified by the SelectCommand property and populates the DataSet. If you change the DataSet populated by the preceding method and want to propagate the changes back to the underlying data source, you need to set other properties (InsertCommand, UpdateCommand, and so forth) of valid Command instances. DataAdapter provides another method called Update() that uses the Command objects specified by the InsertCommand, UpdateCommand, and DeleteCommand properties and takes the changes from a DataSet back to the underlying data source.

Working with DataSet and DataAdapter

To understand how DataSet and DataAdapter can be used to manipulate data, you will create an application as shown in Figure 7-5.

Figure 7-5. *Application to illustrate DataSet functionality*

The application is a typical data-entry screen. The combo box shows a list of all employee IDs. After you select an employee ID, the details of that employee (first name, last name, home phone, and notes) are displayed in the text boxes. The Insert, Update, and Delete buttons perform the respective operations. All the operations—INSERT, UPDATE, and DELETE—are performed on the DataSet and not against the actual database table. After all the operations are completed, you can click the Save button to make all the changes in the actual database. The application uses the Employees table of the famous Northwind database.

Now let's dissect the application step by step and see how DataSet and DataAdapter have been put to use.

Filling a DataSet

If you see the source code of the preceding application, you will find a few variables declared at the form level. The declaration is shown in Listing 7-3.

Listing 7-3. *Form-Level Variables*

```
string strConn = @"data source=.\sqlexpress;initial catalog=northwind; ➥
integrated security=true";
DataSet ds = new DataSet();
SqlDataAdapter da = new SqlDataAdapter();
SqlConnection cnn;
```

The strConn string variable stores the database connection string, which uses a local installation of SQL Server Express as indicated by the data source attribute. Then variables of type DataSet, SqlDataAdapter, and SqlConnection are declared. You must ensure that you have imported the System.Data and System.Data.SqlClient namespaces before you declare these variables.

The Form_Load event handler of the form contains the code shown in Listing 7-4.

Listing 7-4. *Filling a DataSet*

```
private void Form1_Load(object sender, EventArgs e)
{
  cnn = new SqlConnection(strConn);
  SqlCommand cmdEmployees = new SqlCommand();
  cmdEmployees.CommandText = "SELECT * FROM employees";
  cmdEmployees.Connection = cnn;
  da.SelectCommand = cmdEmployees;
  da.Fill(ds, "Employees");
  FillEmployees();
}
```

The code creates a SqlCommand object and sets its CommandText property to fetch all the records from the Employees table. The Connection property is set to the SqlConnection object created earlier. The SqlCommand object just created is assigned to the SelectCommand property of the SqlDataAdapter instance. The SelectCommand property determines the records to be populated in the DataSet later.

Next, the Fill() method of the SqlDataAdapter is called. It takes two parameters: the DataSet to be filled and the name of the resultant DataTable. Notice that the code neither opens the connection nor closes it. This is so because the SqlDataAdapter class does that internally for us. Finally, a helper method, FillEmployees(), is called and fills the combo box with the list of employee IDs. The FillEmployees() method is discussed later.

■ **Note** The SqlDataAdapter class closes the connection automatically for us only if opened by SqlDataAdapter itself. If the connection is opened prior to calling the Fill() method, SqlDataAdapter will not close it automatically.

Accessing Data from DataSet

When you select an employee ID from the combo box, the employee details should be displayed in the other text boxes. The relevant code is written in the SelectedIndexChanged event of the combo box and is shown in Listing 7-5.

Listing 7-5. *Accessing Data from a DataSet*

```
private void comboBox1_SelectedIndexChanged(object sender, EventArgs e)
{
  string id = comboBox1.SelectedItem.ToString();
  DataRow[] rows = ds.Tables["Employees"].Select("EmployeeID=" + id);
  textBox1.Text = rows[0]["firstname"].ToString();
  textBox2.Text = rows[0]["lastname"].ToString();
  textBox3.Text = rows[0]["homephone"].ToString();
  textBox4.Text = rows[0]["notes"].ToString();
}
```

The code first stores the selected employee ID in a string variable. To find the corresponding employee record from the DataSet, we use the Select() method of DataTable, which accepts the selection criteria and returns an array of DataRow objects matching those criteria. In our example, we need to select the employee whose EmployeeID column value matches the one selected in the combo box. EmployeeID is the primary column for the Employees table and hence we know that it will return only one DataRow. The DataRow can be accessed by using typical array notation. Notice how the column names are used to access the individual column values. Instead of column names, you could have used column indexes. The various column values are displayed in the respective text boxes.

Adding New Rows

After you enter details of a new employee to be added and click the Insert button, a new row is added to the underlying DataTable. The code that makes it possible is shown in Listing 7-6.

Listing 7-6. *Adding a New DataRow*

```
private void button2_Click(object sender, EventArgs e)
{
  DataRow row = ds.Tables["Employees"].NewRow();
  row["employeeid"] = comboBox1.Text;
  row["firstname"] = textBox1.Text;
  row["lastname"] = textBox2.Text;
  row["homephone"] = textBox3.Text;
  row["notes"] = textBox4.Text;
  ds.Tables["Employees"].Rows.Add(row);
  FillEmployees();
}
```

The code creates a new DataRow by calling the NewRow() method on the Employees DataTable. The NewRow() method creates a new stand-alone row in memory, matching the schema of the underlying DataTable. Then various column values of the DataRow are assigned. The newly created row is not yet part of the DataTable, so to add it to the DataTable, the Add() method of the Rows collection is called. Finally, the combo box is repopulated so as to display the newly added employee ID.

Updating an Existing Row

To update an existing row, you must find it first and then update the column values. To find a specific row, you can use the same Select() method that we used earlier. This is shown in Listing 7-7.

Listing 7-7. *Updating a DataRow*

```
private void button1_Click(object sender, EventArgs e)
{
  if (comboBox1.SelectedItem == null)
  {
    MessageBox.Show("Please select Employee ID!");
    return;
  }  string id = comboBox1.SelectedItem.ToString();
  DataRow[] rows = ds.Tables["Employees"].Select("EmployeeID=" + id);
  rows[0].BeginEdit();
  rows[0]["firstname"] = textBox1.Text;
  rows[0]["lastname"] = textBox2.Text;
  rows[0]["homephone"] = textBox3.Text;
  rows[0]["notes"] = textBox4.Text;
  rows[0].EndEdit();
}
```

The code selects the employee record that is to be updated by using the Select() method of the DataTable. The BeginEdit() method of the DataRow class takes the row in edit mode. The column values are then assigned. Finally, the EndEdit() method of the DataRow class is called. This saves the changes to the underlying DataTable.

Deleting a Row

To delete a row, you must locate it first and then call the Delete() method on it. This is illustrated in Listing 7-8.

Listing 7-8. *Deleting a DataRow*

```
private void button3_Click(object sender, EventArgs e)
{
  if (comboBox1.SelectedItem == null)
  {
    MessageBox.Show("Please select Employee ID!");
    return;
  }
  string id = comboBox1.SelectedItem.ToString();
  DataRow[] rows = ds.Tables["Employees"].Select("EmployeeID=" + id);
  rows[0].Delete();
  FillEmployees();
}
```

The code retrieves the row to be deleted by using the `Select()` method of the `DataTable` class. The `Delete()` method of the `DataRow` class marks the underlying row for deletion. Finally, the combo box is repopulated so that the deleted employee ID doesn't show up.

Using DataRow States

In the preceding sections, you inserted, updated, and deleted `DataRow` objects from a `DataTable`. Whenever you perform any of these operations (insert, update, or delete) on a `DataRow`, its `RowState` property is affected automatically. The `RowState` property is an enumeration of type `DataRowState` and indicates the state of the `DataRow`. Table 7-1 shows various possible values of the `DataRowState` enumeration.

Table 7-1. *DataRowState Enumeration*

RowState Setting	Description
`Unchanged`	The row is unchanged since it was placed in the `DataSet`.
`Added`	The row is newly added to the `DataTable`.
`Modified`	The row is changed.
`Deleted`	The row is deleted from the `DataTable`.
`Detached`	The row is created but not yet attached to the `DataTable`.

The `RowState` property is used by the helper function `FillEmployees()` as shown in Listing 7-9.

Listing 7-9. *Using the RowState Property*

```
private void FillEmployees()
{
  comboBox1.Items.Clear();
  foreach (DataRow row in ds.Tables["Employees"].Rows)
  {
    if (row.RowState != DataRowState.Deleted)
    {
      comboBox1.Items.Add(row["EmployeeID"].ToString());
    }
  }
}
```

The `FillEmployees()` method simply iterates through each `DataRow` from the `Employees` `DataTable` and adds the `EmployeeID` to the combo box. Notice the code marked in bold. Before adding any value in the combo box, the code checks whether the `RowState` of the row is `Deleted`. Only those rows whose `RowState` is not `Deleted` are added to the combo box.

Saving the Changes to the Database

Up until now, all the changes that we made are saved in the DataSet only; they are yet to be committed back to the database. You can test this by making some changes to the records and then closing the application without clicking the Save button. You will observe that the changes are lost. The Click event handler of the Save button contains code that propagates changes from the DataSet back to the database. Listing 7-10 shows this code.

Listing 7-10. *Saving the DataSet Changes to the Database*

```
private void button4_Click(object sender, EventArgs e)
{
  SqlCommand cmdInsert = new SqlCommand();
  SqlCommand cmdUpdate = new SqlCommand();
  SqlCommand cmdDelete = new SqlCommand();
  cmdInsert.Connection = cnn;
  cmdUpdate.Connection = cnn;
  cmdDelete.Connection = cnn;
  cmdInsert.CommandText =
    "INSERT INTO employees(firstname,lastname,homephone,notes)
     VALUES(@fname,@lname,@phone,@notes)";
  cmdUpdate.CommandText =
    "UPDATE employees SET firstname=@fname,lastname=@lname,homephone=@phone
     WHERE employeeid=@empid";
  cmdDelete.CommandText = "DELETE FROM employees WHERE employeeid=@empid";

  SqlParameter[] pInsert = new SqlParameter[4];
  pInsert[0] = new SqlParameter("@fname", SqlDbType.VarChar);
  pInsert[0].SourceColumn = "firstname";
  pInsert[1] = new SqlParameter("@lname", SqlDbType.VarChar);
  pInsert[1].SourceColumn = "lastname";
  pInsert[2] = new SqlParameter("@phone", SqlDbType.VarChar);
  pInsert[2].SourceColumn = "homephone";
  pInsert[3] = new SqlParameter("@notes", SqlDbType.VarChar);
  pInsert[3].SourceColumn = "notes";
  foreach (SqlParameter p in pInsert)
  {
    cmdInsert.Parameters.Add(p);
  }
```

```
  SqlParameter[] pUpdate = new SqlParameter[5];
  pUpdate[0] = new SqlParameter("@fname", SqlDbType.VarChar);
  pUpdate[0].SourceColumn = "firstname";
  pUpdate[1] = new SqlParameter("@lname", SqlDbType.VarChar);
  pUpdate[1].SourceColumn = "lastname";
  pUpdate[2] = new SqlParameter("@phone", SqlDbType.VarChar);
  pUpdate[2].SourceColumn = "homephone";
  pUpdate[3] = new SqlParameter("@notes", SqlDbType.VarChar);
  pUpdate[3].SourceColumn = "notes";
  pUpdate[4] = new SqlParameter("@empid", SqlDbType.VarChar);
  pUpdate[4].SourceColumn = "employeeid";
  foreach (SqlParameter p in pUpdate)
  {
    cmdUpdate.Parameters.Add(p);
  }

  SqlParameter[] pDelete = new SqlParameter[1];
  pDelete[0] = new SqlParameter("@empid", SqlDbType.VarChar);
  pDelete[0].SourceColumn = "employeeid";
  foreach (SqlParameter p in pDelete)
  {
    cmdDelete.Parameters.Add(p);
  }

  da.InsertCommand = cmdInsert;
  da.UpdateCommand = cmdUpdate;
  da.DeleteCommand = cmdDelete;
  da.Update(ds,"Employees");
  ds.AcceptChanges();
}
```

The code creates three `SqlCommand` objects for `INSERT`, `UPDATE`, and `DELETE` operations, respectively. The `Connection` property of these `SqlCommand` objects is set to the same `SqlConnection` object that we declared at the top initially. The `CommandText` property of each `SqlCommand` is set to the corresponding SQL statement. Note the use of the `@` character to represent parameters. For each of these parameter placeholders, a `SqlParameter` object needs to be created. This is done by declaring three arrays of the `SqlParameter` class: `pInsert`, `pUpdate`, and `pDelete`.

Then each array element is instantiated as a SqlParameter object by passing the parameter name and parameter data type in the constructor of the SqlParameter class. The SourceColumn property of SqlParameter specifies the name of the DataColumn that will be supplying the value for the parameter. All the parameters from the corresponding arrays are added to the Parameters collection of the respective SqlCommand object. These three SqlCommand objects are assigned to the InsertCommand, UpdateCommand, and DeleteCommand properties of the SqlDataAdapter instance that we declared at the top.

The Update() method of the SqlDataAdapter class is then called and takes all the changes—inserts, updates, and deletes—from the DataSet back to the database. The Update() method takes two parameters: the DataSet to be updated, and the name of the DataTable from the DataSet that is to be updated. After the changes are saved to the underlying database, the RowState properties of all the DataRow objects must become Unchanged. This is done by calling the AcceptChanges() method of the DataSet class.

That's it! You can now run the application and test it for the expected functionality.

Saving DataSet Contents As XML

One of the powerful features of the DataSet class is that you can serialize it in XML format, which means that relational data can be saved in XML format. This feature comes in handy while working in offline mode and transporting data to heterogeneous systems.

The WriteXml() method of the DataSet class writes the contents of the DataSet to a stream or physical file in XML format. Optionally, you can also add schema information. To illustrate the use of WriteXml(), you need to create an application as shown in Figure 7-6.

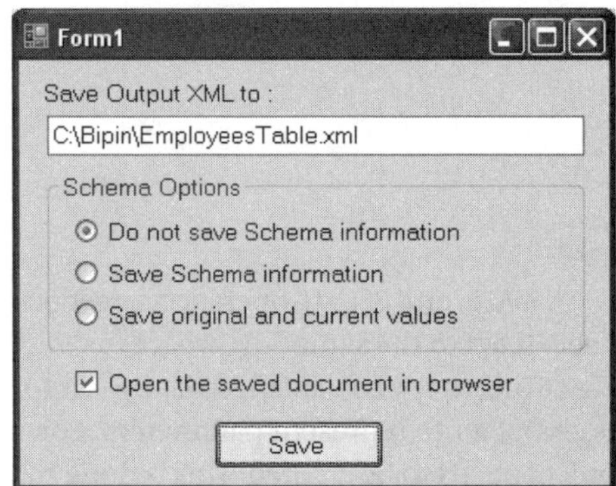

Figure 7-6. *Application that writes DataSet contents as an XML file*

The application consists of a text box for specifying the path of the output XML file. The first two radio buttons specify whether schema information is to be included. The last radio button specifies whether you wish to write the original as well as current values to the file. If you select this radio button, the DiffGram of the original and current values is written in the file.

■ **Note** *DiffGram* is a special XML format that stores original as well as current row values. SQL Server 2000 introduced capabilities to update the database via UpdateGrams. DiffGram is a subset of UpdateGram and can be used to update a SQL Server database over the Web.

If selected, the check box opens the saved XML file in a browser. The Save button actually writes the `DataSet` to the specified file. The `Click` event handler of the Save button contains the code shown in Listing 7-11.

Listing 7-11. *Using the WriteXml() Method*

```
private void button1_Click(object sender, EventArgs e)
{
  DataSet ds = new DataSet();
  SqlDataAdapter da =
    new SqlDataAdapter("SELECT employeeid,firstname,lastname,homephone,notes
                       FROM employees",
                       @"data source=.\sqlexpress;initial catalog=northwind;
                         integrated security=true");
  da.Fill(ds, "employees");
  if (radioButton1.Checked)
  {
    ds.WriteXml(textBox1.Text, XmlWriteMode.IgnoreSchema);
  }
  if (radioButton2.Checked)
  {
    ds.WriteXml(textBox1.Text, XmlWriteMode.WriteSchema);
  }
  if (radioButton3.Checked)
  {
    foreach (DataRow row in ds.Tables[0].Rows)
    {
      row.SetModified();
    }
    ds.WriteXml(textBox1.Text, XmlWriteMode.DiffGram);
  }
  if (checkBox1.Checked)
  {
    Process.Start(textBox1.Text);
  }
}
```

The code creates a new DataSet and a SqlDataAdapter. One of the overloads of the SqlDataAdapter constructors accepts the SELECT query and database connection string, and it is this overload that we use. The DataSet is then filled by using the Fill() method of the DataAdapter. The name of the DataTable is specified as employees.

Then a series of if conditions check the status of the radio buttons. In each of the if conditions, the WriteXml() method of the DataSet class is called, which writes the contents of the DataSet to the specified stream or disk file. Notice that although each of the if conditions calls WriteXml(), the second parameter—XmlWriteMode—is different in each case.

The XmlWriteMode enumeration governs two things. First, it specifies whether schema information is to be written along with the XML contents. Second, it decides whether the output XML data will contain just the current values or both the original and current values. As you saw in the preceding example, the latter format is called DiffGram. The three possible values of the XmlWriteMode enumeration are shown in Table 7-2.

Table 7-2. *XmlWriteMode Values*

Value	Description
IgnoreSchema	Writes the contents of the DataSet as XML data. No XSD schema information is written.
WriteSchema	Writes the contents of the DataSet as XML data. Also, writes XSD schema information along with the data.
DiffGram	Writes the contents of the DataSet as DiffGram XML markup. The DiffGram stores the current as well as original column values.

Notice the if condition for radioButton3. Because we have not made any changes to the DataSet as such, the code deliberately marks each row as modified. This is done by using the SetModified() method of the DataRow class. This way, we will be able to see how the DiffGram format stores old and new values. Finally, the saved XML file is opened in a browser by using the Start() method of the Process class. Figure 7-7 shows a sample run of the application without saving any schema information. Similarly, Figures 7-8 and 7-9 show the output XML file with schema information and DiffGram, respectively.

Notice how the schema information is emitted in Figure 7-8. Also, examine Figure 7-9 carefully. This XML output is in DiffGram format. See how the <diffgr:before> section stores the original values of the DataRows, whereas the current values are displayed at the top.

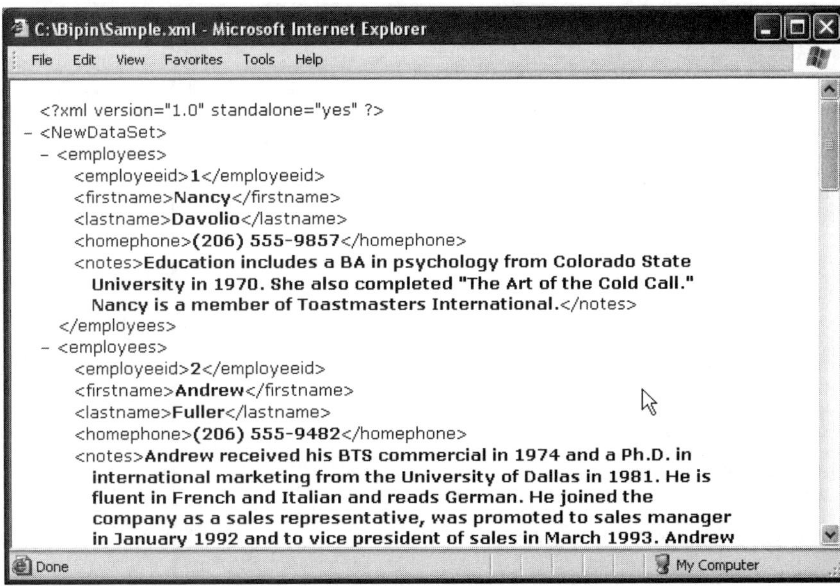

Figure 7-7. *Writing DataSet as XML without schema information*

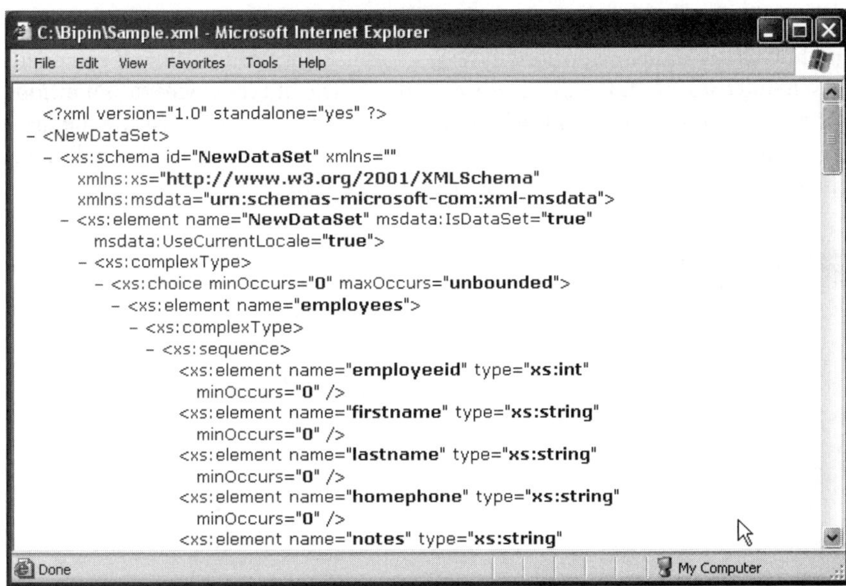

Figure 7-8. *Writing DataSet as XML with schema information*

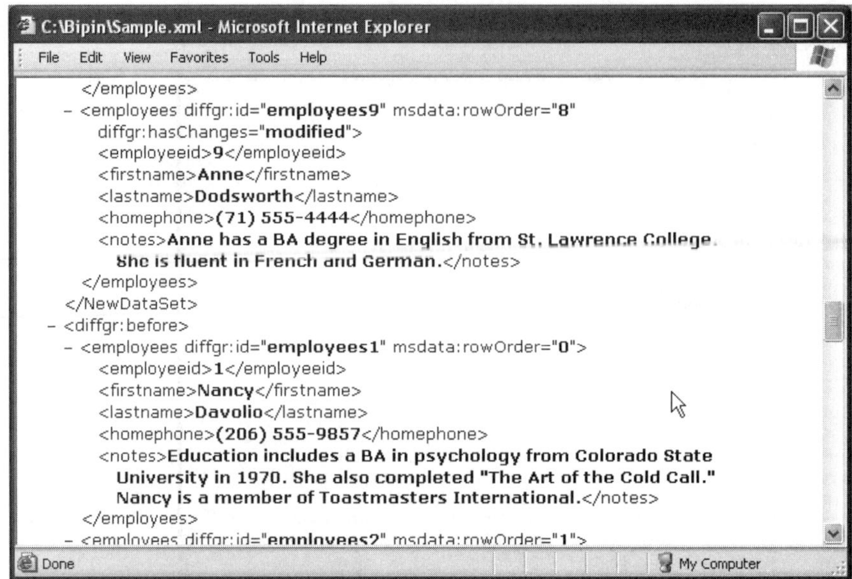

Figure 7-9. *Writing DataSet as XML in DiffGram format*

Saving Only the Schema

The `WriteXml()` method writes data and optionally XSD schema information. What if you need to extract only the schema information and not the data itself? The `WriteXmlSchema()` method does that job by writing only the schema of the `DataSet` and not the data. To illustrate the use of `WriteXmlSchema()`, you can modify the preceding application to include an additional radio button. The new interface of the application is shown in Figure 7-10.

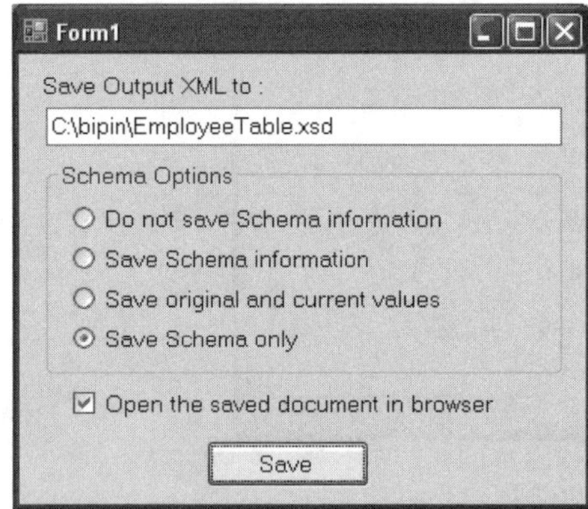

Figure 7-10. *Application for illustrating the WriteXmlSchema() method*

If you select the newly added radio button titled Save Schema, only the schema of the DataSet will be saved. Listing 7-12 shows the modified version of the code.

Listing 7-12. *Using the WriteXmlSchema() Method*

```
private void button1_Click(object sender, EventArgs e)
{
  DataSet ds = new DataSet();
  SqlDataAdapter da =
    new SqlDataAdapter("SELECT employeeid,firstname,lastname,homephone,notes
                        FROM employees",
                       @"data source=.\sqlexpress;initial catalog=northwind;
                        integrated security=true");
  da.Fill(ds, "employees");
  if (radioButton1.Checked)
  {
    ds.WriteXml(textBox1.Text, XmlWriteMode.IgnoreSchema);
  }
  if (radioButton2.Checked)
  {
    ds.WriteXml(textBox1.Text, XmlWriteMode.WriteSchema);
  }
  if (radioButton3.Checked)
  {
    foreach (DataRow row in ds.Tables[0].Rows)
    {
      row.SetModified();
    }
    ds.WriteXml(textBox1.Text, XmlWriteMode.DiffGram);
  }
  if (radioButton4.Checked)
  {
    ds.WriteXmlSchema(textBox1.Text);
  }
  if (checkBox1.Checked)
  {
    Process.Start(textBox1.Text);
  }
}
```

Notice the code marked in bold. The code calls the WriteXmlSchema() method by passing the file in which the schema information will be stored. You will observe that the schema obtained by this method is the same as that obtained by the WriteXml() method with XmlWriteMode.WriteSchema. However, no data is written to the file.

Extracting DataSet Contents As an XML String

The WriteXml()and WriteXmlSchema() methods write XML data and schema to a stream or file, respectively. Sometimes you may wish to get the XML data and schema as a string rather than writing to a file. This is accomplished with two methods:

- The GetXml() method returns just the contents of the DataSet in XML format as a string. No schema information is returned.
- Similarly, the GetXmlSchema()method returns the XSD schema information of the DataSet as a string. Because these methods return strings, they incur more overhead than corresponding WriteXxx() methods.

Reading XML Data into DataSet

In the preceding sections, you learned to serialize DataSet contents as XML data. There might be cases when you would like to do the opposite—that is, you may need to read XML data into a DataSet and process it further. The ReadXml() method of the DataSet class is the counterpart of the WriteXml() method that we discussed already and allows you to read XML data into a DataSet.

Note In the following examples, you will frequently need XML files containing a schema and data. It is recommended that you run the preceding example (Figure 7-10) and save the resultant XML files on your disk for later use.

To illustrate the use of ReadXml(), you need to develop an application as shown in Figure 7-11.

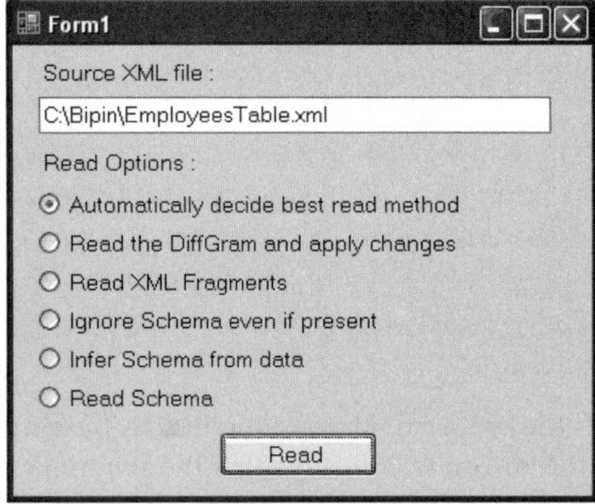

Figure 7-11. *Application that reads XML data into a DataSet*

The application consists of a text box for accepting the source XML file path. There is an array of radio buttons that govern how the XML document will be read by the DataSet. The Read button triggers the read operation. Listing 7-13 shows the complete code that reads the XML data into a DataSet.

Listing 7-13. *Using the ReadXml() Method*

```
private void button1_Click(object sender, EventArgs e)
{
  DataSet ds = new DataSet();
  XmlReadMode mode=XmlReadMode.Auto;
  if (radioButton1.Checked)
  {
    mode = XmlReadMode.Auto;
  }
  if (radioButton2.Checked)
  {
    mode = XmlReadMode.DiffGram;
  }
  if (radioButton3.Checked)
  {
    mode = XmlReadMode.Fragment;
  }
  if (radioButton4.Checked)
  {
    mode = XmlReadMode.IgnoreSchema;
  }
  if (radioButton5.Checked)
  {
    mode = XmlReadMode.InferSchema;
  }
  if (radioButton6.Checked)
  {
    mode = XmlReadMode.ReadSchema;
  }
  ds.ReadXml(textBox1.Text, mode);
  MessageBox.Show("XML file read successfully!");
}
```

The code creates a new DataSet object. It then declares a variable of enumeration type XmlReadMode. This enumeration plays an important role in deciding how the XML data will be loaded into the DataSet. You can see all the possible values of the XmlReadMode enumeration in Table 7-3. Then a series of if conditions check the status of the various radio buttons and set the value of the XmlReadMode variable. Finally, the ReadXml() method of the DataSet class is called.

The ReadXml() method has several overloads. The one that we use accepts the name of the XML file to read and the XmlReadMode value. After ReadXml() has finished, the DataSet has populated DataTable objects depending on the source XML document. For example, if you use the EmployeesTable.xml file that we created previously, your DataSet will contain one DataTable called employees.

Table 7-3. *XmlReadMode Values*

Value	Description
Auto	Is the default value and uses the most appropriate read mode from the remaining values
DiffGram	Loads a DiffGram and applies the changes
Fragment	Loads XML fragments such as the ones created when using the FOR XML clause
IgnoreSchema	Ignores the inline schema present in the source XML document
InferSchema	Infers the schema from the data present and loads the data into the DataSet
ReadSchema	Reads the inline schema present in the XML document

The XmlReadMode options need more explanation because there are a number of possibilities during the read operation. These options are discussed next.

Using the Automatic Read Operation

The Auto option of the XmlReadMode enumeration uses the most appropriate mechanism while loading the XML data. If the data is a DiffGram, it sets XmlReadMode to DiffGram. If the DataSet already has a schema or the XML document contains an inline schema, it sets XmlReadMode to ReadSchema. Finally, if the DataSet does not already have a schema and the XML document does not contain an inline schema, it sets XmlReadMode to InferSchema.

Reading DiffGrams

The DiffGram option of the XmlReadMode enumeration is exclusively used with DiffGrams. Generally, these DiffGrams will be generated by using the WriteXml() method of DataSet. The schema of the DataSet and the DiffGram must match in order to successfully read the data. Because the DiffGram stores the original and current values of DataRows, the changes are applied after the DiffGram is loaded in the DataSet.

Reading XML Fragments

In the earlier sections of this chapter, you learned that SQL Server provides an extension to the normal SELECT statement in the form of the FOR XML clause. You also saw how the FOR XML clause returns XML data in the form of fragments. If you wish to load these XML fragments into a DataSet, you must set XmlReadMode to Fragment.

Ignoring Schema Information

The XML document that you wish to load into a DataSet might contain schema information embedded in it. If you wish to ignore this schema, you must use the IgnoreSchema option of the XmlReadMode enumeration. If the DataSet already has a schema and the XML data being loaded doesn't match this schema, the data is discarded.

Inferring Schema Information

The InferSchema option of XmlReadMode ignores schema information from the source XML data if present and loads the data into a DataSet. If the DataSet already has its schema, that is extended to accommodate the new data. However, if there is any mismatch between the existing schema and the newly inferred schema, an exception is raised.

Reading Schema Information

The ReadSchema option of XmlReadMode reads the inline schema from the source XML document and loads the schema as well as the data into the DataSet. If the DataSet already contains a schema, it is extended as per the new schema. However, any mismatch between the existing schema and the new schema causes an exception to be thrown.

Generating Menus Dynamically Based On an XML File

The ReadXml() method performs many operations behind the scenes to make our lives easier. To get a taste of what it does, you will develop a Windows application that dynamically adds menu items. The application will look like Figure 7-12.

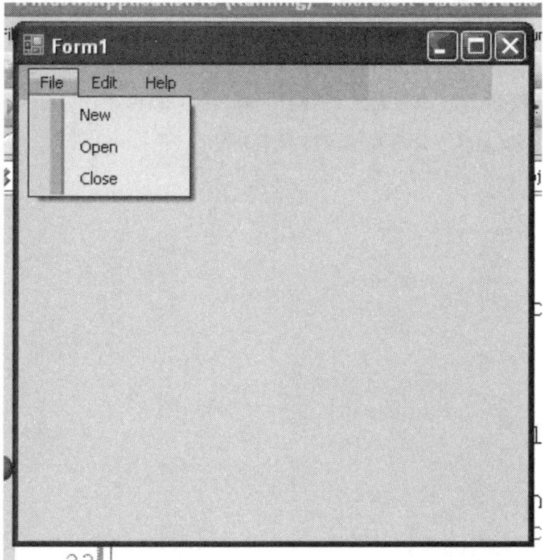

Figure 7-12. *Form showing dynamically loaded menu items*

The form consists of a single MenuStrip control. The menu items are stored in an XML file as shown in Listing 7-14. Save this file as `menus.xml` in your application's `Bin\Debug` folder.

Listing 7-14. *XML File Representing the Menu Structure*

```
<?xml version="1.0" encoding="utf-8" ?>
<menus>
  <topmenu text="File">
    <submenu>New</submenu>
    <submenu>Open</submenu>
    <submenu>Close</submenu>
  </topmenu>
  <topmenu text="Edit">
    <submenu>Cut</submenu>
    <submenu>Copy</submenu>
    <submenu>Paste</submenu>
  </topmenu>
  <topmenu text="Help">
    <submenu>Help</submenu>
    <submenu>Search</submenu>
    <submenu>About</submenu>
  </topmenu>
</menus>
```

The root element of the XML file is `<menus>`. Inside there can be zero or more `<topmenu>` items, which represent the top-level menu items. The `text` attribute of `<topmenu>` indicates the text of that menu. The `<topmenu>` element can contain zero or more `<submenu>` elements, which indicate submenus of the top-level menus. The text of the submenus is specified in the `<submenu>` element's value.

Let's see how this file can be loaded in a `DataSet` and how the data can be accessed. Listing 7-15 shows the `Load` event handler of the form with the required code.

Listing 7-15. *Adding Menu Items Dynamically*

```
private void Form1_Load(object sender, EventArgs e)
{
  DataSet ds = new DataSet();
  ds.ReadXml(Application.StartupPath + @"\menus.xml");

  foreach (DataRow topmenu in ds.Tables[0].Rows)
  {
    ToolStripMenuItem item = new ToolStripMenuItem(topmenu["text"].ToString());
    menuStrip1.Items.Add(item);
    DataRow[] submenus= topmenu.GetChildRows(ds.Relations[0]);
    foreach (DataRow submenu in submenus)
    {
      item.DropDownItems.Add(submenu[0].ToString());
    }
  }
}
```

The code creates a new `DataSet` and reads the `menus.xml` file that we created earlier. While reading this file, the `DataSet` does some interesting things:

1. It observes the nesting of the XML data in the file and creates two `DataTable` objects. The first `DataTable` stores all the top menus, and the second `DataTable` stores all the submenus.

2. It creates `DataRow` objects in the top-menu `DataTable` and adds a `DataColumn` to them. The value contained in these columns is the value of the `text` attribute of the `<topmenu>` element.

3. It does a similar thing for the submenus `DataTable`, but loads the element values of the `<submenu>` items in the column.

4. It sets a `DataRelation` between the two tables by automatically adding an integer column to both of these `DataTable` objects.

The code then iterates through all the rows from the first DataTable (the DataTable storing the top menus) and adds ToolStripMenuItem objects to the MenuStrip. The GetChildRows() method is called on each DataRow of the top-menu DataTable. This method accepts a DataRelation object and returns all the DataRow objects from the child table matching that relationship. In our case, the submenu DataTable is the child DataTable. The return value of GetChildRows() is an array of DataRow objects. The second foreach loop iterates through all the elements of this array and adds sub-items to the DropDownItems collection of the ToolStripMenuItem class.

If you run the application, you should see something similar to Figure 7-12.

Reading Only the Schema Information

The ReadXml() method allows you to read data and optionally schema information. However, at times you may need to extract just the schema information from the XML file and not the data. The DataSet class provides two methods that allow you to extract schema information from the source XML. They are ReadXmlSchema() and InferXmlSchema().

ReadXmlSchema() accepts the XML with an inline schema and reads just the schema part of it. The schema is then loaded into the DataSet. What if your XML document doesn't contain an inline schema? That is where the InferXmlSchema() method comes into the picture. The InferXmlSchema() method observes the XML markup supplied and then creates a matching schema automatically. The schema is then loaded into the DataSet.

To illustrate the use of both of these methods, you need to develop an application as shown in Figure 7-13.

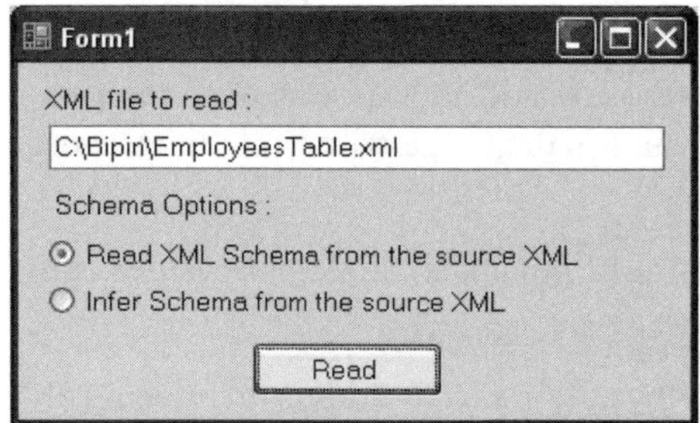

Figure 7-13. *Application that reads schema*

The application consists of a text box for specifying the source XML file. The two radio buttons enable you to decide whether `ReadXmlSchema()` or `InferXmlSchema()` is to be called. The code for the Read button reads the schema into a `DataSet` and displays it in a message box. The code that reads the schema is shown in Listing 7-16.

Listing 7-16. *Using the ReadXmlSchema() and InferXmlSchema() Methods*

```
private void button1_Click(object sender, EventArgs e)
{
  DataSet ds = new DataSet();
  if (radioButton1.Checked)
  {
    ds.ReadXmlSchema(textBox1.Text);
  }
  if (radioButton2.Checked)
  {
    ds.InferXmlSchema(textBox1.Text,null);
  }
  MessageBox.Show(ds.GetXmlSchema());
}
```

The code creates a new `DataSet` object. Depending on the radio button selected, the code calls either `ReadXmlSchema()` or `InferXmlSchema()`. `ReadXmlSchema()` accepts the source XML document as a parameter and loads the inline schema from the document into the `DataSet`. No data is loaded.

The `InferXmlSchema()` method accepts the source XML document and an array of namespaces (null in our example) and infers the schema from the data. Again, no data is loaded. The loaded schema is shown in a message box by calling the `GetXmlSchema()` method of the `DataSet`. Figure 7-14 shows the schema loaded by using `ReadXmlSchema()`, whereas Figure 7-15 shows the schema loaded by using `InferXmlSchema()`.

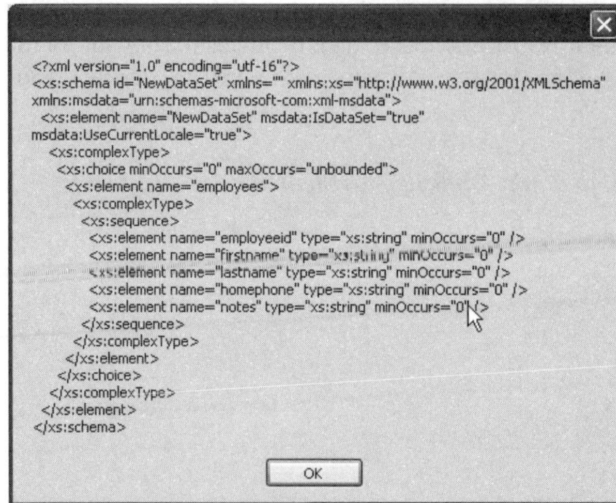
<?xml version="1.0" encoding="utf-16"?>
<xs:schema id="NewDataSet" xmlns="" xmlns:xs="http://www.w3.org/2001/XMLSchema" xmlns:msdata="urn:schemas-microsoft-com:xml-msdata">
<xs:element name="NewDataSet" msdata:IsDataSet="true" msdata:UseCurrentLocale="true">
<xs:complexType>
<xs:choice minOccurs="0" maxOccurs="unbounded">
<xs:element name="employees">
<xs:complexType>
<xs:sequence>
<xs:element name="employeeid" type="xs:string" minOccurs="0" />
<xs:element name="firstname" type="xs:string" minOccurs="0" />
<xs:element name="lastname" type="xs:string" minOccurs="0" />
<xs:element name="homephone" type="xs:string" minOccurs="0" />
<xs:element name="notes" type="xs:string" minOccurs="0" />
</xs:sequence>
</xs:complexType>
</xs:element>
</xs:choice>
</xs:complexType>
</xs:element>
</xs:schema>
OK

Figure 7-14. *Schema extracted by using the ReadXmlSchema() method*

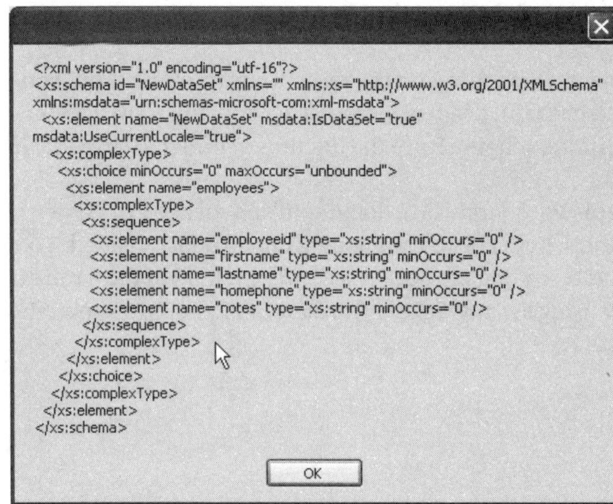
<?xml version="1.0" encoding="utf-16"?>
<xs:schema id="NewDataSet" xmlns="" xmlns:xs="http://www.w3.org/2001/XMLSchema" xmlns:msdata="urn:schemas-microsoft-com:xml-msdata">
<xs:element name="NewDataSet" msdata:IsDataSet="true" msdata:UseCurrentLocale="true">
<xs:complexType>
<xs:choice minOccurs="0" maxOccurs="unbounded">
<xs:element name="employees">
<xs:complexType>
<xs:sequence>
<xs:element name="employeeid" type="xs:string" minOccurs="0" />
<xs:element name="firstname" type="xs:string" minOccurs="0" />
<xs:element name="lastname" type="xs:string" minOccurs="0" />
<xs:element name="homephone" type="xs:string" minOccurs="0" />
<xs:element name="notes" type="xs:string" minOccurs="0" />
</xs:sequence>
</xs:complexType>
</xs:element>
</xs:choice>
</xs:complexType>
</xs:element>
</xs:schema>
OK

Figure 7-15. *Schema extracted by using the InferXmlSchema() method*

As you can see, the schema loaded by both methods is identical in our example.

Creating a Typed DataSet

While discussing `DataSet` and `DataAdapter`, we developed an application that allowed us to perform inserts, updates, and deletes on a `DataSet` and then save those changes back to the database (see Figure 7-6). In that application, we frequently used collections such as `Tables` and `Rows`. We also needed to remember column names while accessing their values from a `DataRow`. Don't you think it is a bit tedious to access data in this fashion? To make things clearer, have a look at Listings 7-17 and 7-18.

Listing 7-17. *Inserting a DataRow by Using an Untyped DataSet*

```
private void button2_Click(object sender, EventArgs e)
{
  DataRow row = ds.Tables["Employees"].NewRow();
  row["employeeid"] = comboBox1.Text;
  row["firstname"] = textBox1.Text;
  row["lastname"] = textBox2.Text;
  row["homephone"] = textBox3.Text;
  row["notes"] = textBox4.Text;
  ds.Tables["Employees"].Rows.Add(row);
  FillEmployees();
}
```

Listing 7-18. *Inserting a DataRow by Using a Typed DataSet*

```
private void button2_Click(object sender, EventArgs e)
{
  EmployeesDataSet.EmployeesRow row = ds.Employees.NewEmployeesRow();
  row.EmployeeID = int.Parse(comboBox1.Text);
  row.FirstName = textBox1.Text;
  row.LastName = textBox2.Text;
  row.HomePhone = textBox3.Text;
  row.Notes = textBox4.Text;
  ds.Employees.AddEmployeesRow(row);
  FillEmployees();
}
```

Both of these listings represent code that inserts a new `DataRow` into a `DataTable`. Compare the listings carefully. In Listing 7-17, we access the `Employees` `DataTable` and its columns by specifying them in double quotes. That means you need to remember these names when you are coding. However, Listing 7-18 looks different. You will notice that it uses the `Employees` property to create a new row. Further, it uses column names such as `FirstName` and `LastName` as if they are properties. Obviously, the second version is far easier to code and is much neater, which demonstrates what typed `DataSet`s are about.

A typed `DataSet` is nothing but a class that internally derives from `DataSet` as a base class. It extends this base class further and adds certain properties and methods that make the developer's life easy. When using a typed `DataSet`, you can access `DataTable` and `DataColumn` objects by using strongly typed names instead of the collection syntax. A typed `DataSet` has an XSD schema attached to it that defines the `DataTable` and `DataColumn` objects of the `DataSet`.

Using Visual Studio to Create a Typed DataSet

Now that you know what a typed `DataSet` is, let's create one for our `Employees` table. To do so, you first need to add a typed `DataSet` to your project. Figure 7-16 shows the Add New Item dialog box of Visual Studio, through which you can add a new typed `DataSet`.

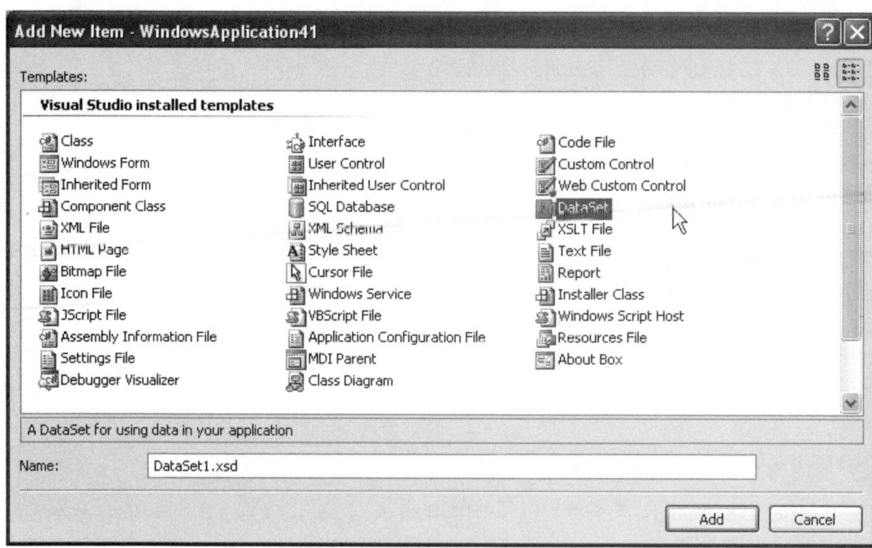

Figure 7-16. *Adding a new typed DataSet to your project*

After you are on the `DataSet` designer, you can see the `DataSet` toolbox, as shown in Figure 7-17.

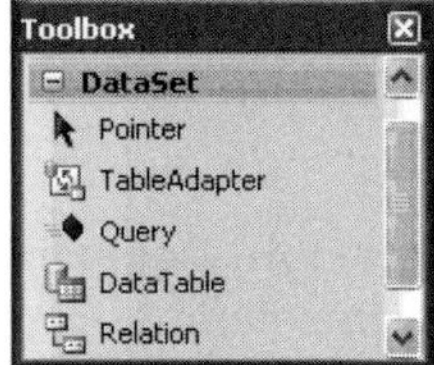

Figure 7-17. *The DataSet toolbox*

As you can see, the toolbox has items such as `DataTable` and `Relation` that you can drag and drop on the `DataSet` designer. For our example, you need to drag and drop a `DataTable` on the `DataSet` designer and set its `Name` property to `Employees`. To add columns to the `DataTable`, you can right-click on it and add the required number of columns. The name and data type of each column can then be set via the properties window. After designing the `Employees DataTable`, it should look like Figure 7-18.

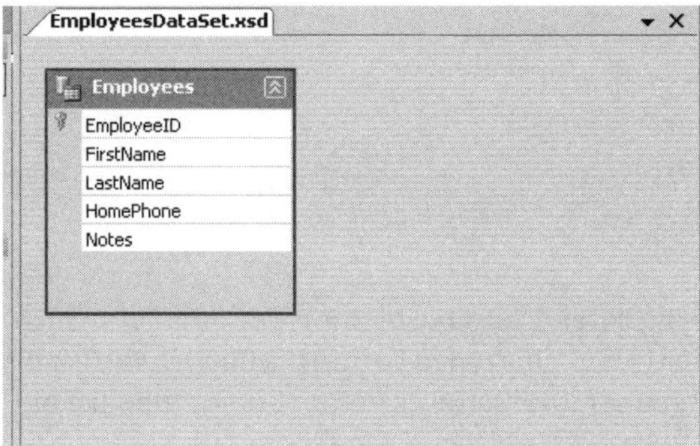

Figure 7-18. *The Employees DataTable in the DataSet designer*

As you are designing the `DataSet` in the designer, Visual Studio creates a class that inherits from `DataSet` as the base class and adds certain properties and methods to it. You can see it in the Solution Explorer.

Next, you need to design the main form of your application as shown in Figure 7-19.

Figure 7-19. *Application that consumes a typed DataSet*

The application behaves exactly the same as the one shown in Figure 7-6 earlier, but this time it uses our typed `DataSet`. Listing 7-19 shows the variable declarations at the form level.

Listing 7-19. *Declaring a Typed DataSet Variable*

```
private string strConn = @"data source=.\sqlexpress;
initial catalog=northwind;integrated security=true";
EmployeesDataSet ds = new EmployeesDataSet();
SqlDataAdapter da = new SqlDataAdapter();
SqlConnection cnn;
```

Notice the line marked in bold. The code declares a variable of our typed DataSet, which bears the same name as the DataSet XSD schema file. This typed DataSet is filled in the Load event of the form. The code in the Load event remains the same as before but for the sake of completeness is given in Listing 7-20.

Listing 7-20. *Filling a Typed DataSet*

```
private void Form1_Load(object sender, EventArgs e)
{
  cnn = new SqlConnection(strConn);
  SqlCommand cmdEmployees = new SqlCommand();
  cmdEmployees.CommandText = "SELECT * FROM employees";
  cmdEmployees.Connection = cnn;
  da.SelectCommand = cmdEmployees;
  da.Fill(ds, "Employees");
  FillEmployees();
}
```

The code uses a SqlDataAdapter and calls its Fill() method to populate the typed DataSet. One thing to note here is that the name of the DataTable specified in the Fill() method must match the name of the DataTable that you created in the typed DataSet. Listing 7-21 shows the modified version of the code responsible for inserting, updating, and deleting DataRow objects.

Listing 7-21. *Inserting, Updating, and Deleting Data from a Typed DataSet*

```
private void button2_Click(object sender, EventArgs e)
{
  EmployeesDataSet.EmployeesRow row = ds.Employees.NewEmployeesRow();
  row.EmployeeID = int.Parse(comboBox1.Text);
  row.FirstName = textBox1.Text;
  row.LastName = textBox2.Text;
  row.HomePhone = textBox3.Text;
  row.Notes = textBox4.Text;
  ds.Employees.AddEmployeesRow(row);
  FillEmployees();
}
```

```
private void button1_Click(object sender, EventArgs e)
{
  string id = comboBox1.SelectedItem.ToString();
  EmployeesDataSet.EmployeesRow[] rows =
    (EmployeesDataSet.EmployeesRow[])ds.Employees.Select("EmployeeID=" + id);
  rows[0].BeginEdit();
  rows[0].FirstName = textBox1.Text;
  rows[0].LastName = textBox2.Text;
  rows[0].HomePhone = textBox3.Text;
  rows[0].Notes = textBox4.Text;
  rows[0].EndEdit();
}

private void button3_Click(object sender, EventArgs e)
{
  string id = comboBox1.SelectedItem.ToString();
  EmployeesDataSet.EmployeesRow[] rows =
    (EmployeesDataSet.EmployeesRow[])ds.Employees.Select("EmployeeID=" + id);
  rows[0].Delete();
  FillEmployees();
}
```

Notice the changes made to the original code. In the `Click` event handler of the Insert button, the new `DataRow` is created by calling `NewEmployeesRow()`. The typed `DataSet` automatically show the available `DataTable` objects as properties, and each `DataTable` provides the `NewEmployeesRow()` method to create a new row. The newly created row is of type `EmployeesRow`, which is a nested class generated by Visual Studio in the `EmployeesDataSet` class. `EmployeesRow` exposes each column of the row as a property, and these properties can then be assigned new values. The newly created row is then added to the `Employees` `DataTable` by using its `AddEmployeesRow()` method. There are similar modifications in the `Click` event handlers of the Update and Delete buttons.

Using the xsd.exe Tool to Create a Typed DataSet

Though Visual Studio provides a visual way to create typed `DataSets`, the .NET Framework also provides a command-line tool called `xsd.exe` that can generate typed `DataSets` for you. The tool accepts an XSD schema and outputs the typed `DataSet` class. Though we will not discuss the `xsd.exe` tool at great length, here is a sample use of it:

```
xsd.exe /d /l:CS Employees.xsd /n:MyTypedDataSets
```

The `/d` switch indicates that the tool should generate a typed `DataSet`. The `/l` switch specifies the language used to create the output typed `DataSet` class. In our example, we specify the language as C# (`CS`). Finally the `/n` switch specifies the namespace in which the typed `DataSet` class will be placed. The output of the preceding command will be a class file named `Employees.cs`. You can compile this class file separately or along with your other classes.

The XmlDataDocument Class

There is no doubt that the DataSet class provides rich XML functionality, but what if you need to do the following in your application?

- Sort, filter, and bind the data effectively in your application
- Apply XSLT transformations and run XPath expressions
- Work with your XML data in a relational manner, still keeping its hierarchical nature intact

All the preceding requirements call for a technique that will bridge the relational model of DataSet and the hierarchical model of XmlDocument, and the XmlDataDocument provides just such a bridge. It allows you to synchronize data from a DataSet and an XML document, and inherits from XmlDocument as the base class. Naturally, it provides all the functionality of DOM.

An XmlDataDocument class can be constructed in two ways depending on your requirement:

- From a DataSet
- From an XML document

Using the XmlDataDocument Class

To see how the XmlDataDocument class can be used, let's consider the following scenario: assume that you wish to develop a data-entry screen for the same Employees.xml file that we used earlier. The data-entry screen should be grid based and should allow the user to export the data as an HTML file. The HTML file can then be published in a web application.

The preceding scenario calls for a DataSet to bind with the grid and it also calls for XSLT processing so that the data can be exported to HTML. In such cases, XmlDataDocument provides an effective solution. Let's see how.

You need to develop a Windows application as shown in Figure 7-20.

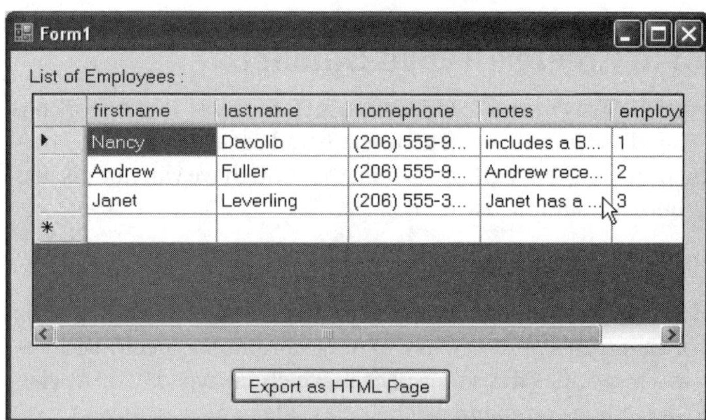

Figure 7-20. *Application for illustrating the use of XmlDataDocument*

The application consists of a DataGridView control that displays the data from the Employees.xml file. You can modify the data and click the Export as HTML Page button to save the data as an HTML file. The Load event of the form is shown in Listing 7-22.

Listing 7-22. *Creating an XmlDataDocument from an XML File*

```
XmlDataDocument doc = null;
private void Form1_Load(object sender, EventArgs e)
{
  DataSet ds = new DataSet();
  ds.ReadXml(Application.StartupPath + @"\employees.xml");
  doc = new XmlDataDocument(ds);
  dataGridView1.DataSource = ds.Tables[0];
}
```

The code declares a class-level variable of type XmlDataDocument. The Load event of the form creates an instance of DataSet and reads the Employees.xml file into it by using ReadXml(). Then a new instance of XmlDataDocument is created by passing the DataSet we just created to its constructor. Thus our example constructs an XmlDataDocument by using a DataSet. The DataTable from the DataSet is then assigned as the DataSource of the DataGridView control. This way, the data from Employees.xml is available for editing. The Click event of the Export as HTML Page button is shown in Listing 7-23.

Listing 7-23. *Applying XSLT Transformations on XmlDataDocument*

```
private void button1_Click(object sender, EventArgs e)
{
  XslCompiledTransform xslt = new XslCompiledTransform();
  xslt.Load(Application.StartupPath + @"\employees.xslt");
  XmlTextWriter writer =
    new XmlTextWriter(Application.StartupPath + @"\employees.html", null);
  xslt.Transform(doc, writer);
  writer.Close();
}
```

The code creates an instance of the XslCompiledTransform class, and the XSLT style sheet is loaded by using its Load() method. Then an instance of XmlTextWriter is created to write the transformed data into an HTML file (Employees.html). The Transform() method of XslCompiledTransform is then called, and the XmlDataDocument and XmlTextWriter objects are passed to it as parameters. The Transform() method accesses the XML data from the XmlDataDocument class, applies the style sheet to it, and writes the transformed data by using XmlTextWriter.

■ **Note** In the preceding example, we use the same XML file and XSLT style sheet that we developed in Chapter 6. See Listing 6-2 for the complete markup of `Employees.xslt`. Also, make sure that you copy these files to the `Bin\Debug` folder of your project before you run the application.

In the preceding example, we created an `XmlDataDocument` by using a `DataSet`, but you can also create an `XmlDataDocument` by using an XML document. In the latter case, you can use the `Load()` method of `XmlDataDocument`. This method works the same way as with the `XmlDocument` class (see Chapter 2). You can then use the loaded XML data in a relational manner with the help of the `DataSet` property of the `XmlDataDocument` class.

Converting Between DataRow and XmlElement

Sometimes you may need to access the XML element belonging to a `DataRow` from the `DataSet`. This can be achieved by using the `GetElementFromRow()` method of `XmlDataDocument`. This method accepts a reference to a `DataRow` instance from the `DataSet` and returns an `XmlElement` corresponding to that row. The working of the `GetElementFromRow()` method will be clear when you develop the application shown in Figure 7-21.

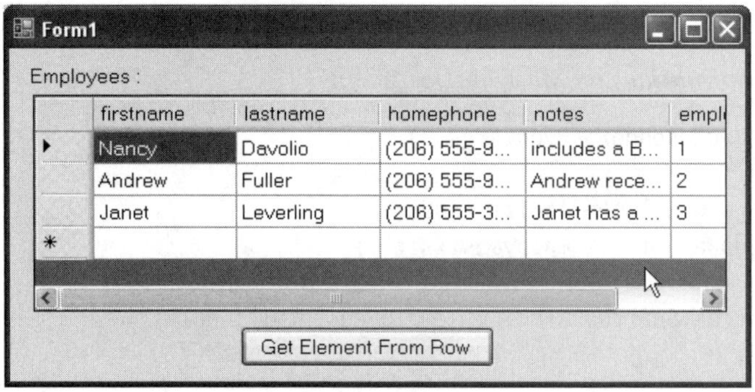

Figure 7-21. *Application using the GetElementFromRow() method*

The application consists of a DataGridView control. The `Employees.xml` file is read into a `DataSet`, and the `DataSet` is bound to the grid. After you click the Get Element From Row button, a message box displays the XML markup of the corresponding element (Figure 7-22).

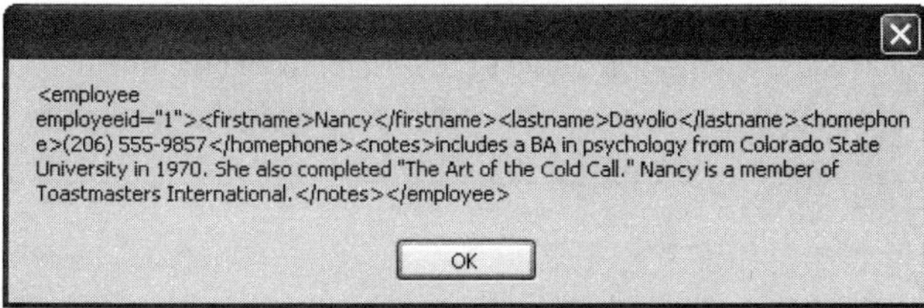

Figure 7-22. *The XmlElement retrieved by using the GetElementFromRow() method*

The `Load` event of the form is shown in Listing 7-24.

Listing 7-24. *Creating XmlDataDocument*

```
XmlDataDocument doc = null;

private void Form1_Load(object sender, EventArgs e)
{
  DataSet ds = new DataSet();
  ds.ReadXml(Application.StartupPath + @"\employees.xml");
  doc = new XmlDataDocument(ds);
  dataGridView1.DataSource = ds.Tables[0];
}
```

The code should be familiar to you, because it is the same code from our previous example. The code simply creates an instance of `XmlDataDocument` on the basis of a `DataSet`. The code from the `Click` event handler of the Get Element From Row button is shown in Listing 7-25.

Listing 7-25. *Using the GetElementFromRow() Method*

```
private void button1_Click(object sender, EventArgs e)
{
  int index=dataGridView1.CurrentCell.RowIndex;
  XmlElement element = doc.GetElementFromRow(doc.DataSet.Tables[0].Rows[index]);
  MessageBox.Show(element.OuterXml);
}
```

The code retrieves the current row index of the DataGridView by using the `CurrentCell` property of the `DataGridView` object. Then the `GetElementFromRow()` method is called by passing the `DataRow` reference. Notice how the `DataSet` is accessed by using the `DataSet` property of the `XmlDataDocument` class. The return value of `GetElementFromRow()` is an `XmlElement` object; the `OuterXml` property of the `XmlElement` is then displayed in a message box.

■Note The `GetRowFromElement()` method is the counterpart of the `GetElementFromRow()` method. `GetRowFromElement()` accepts an `XmlElement` and returns a `DataRow` corresponding to the element.

Summary

ADO.NET is a very important part of the overall .NET Framework. Modern data-driven applications tend to work with relational as well as hierarchical data stores. The ADO.NET object model, though primarily inclined toward RDBMSs, has tight integration with XML.

This chapter gave you a thorough understanding of the XML features of ADO.NET. You learned how to work with XML data in connected and disconnected mode. The `DataSet` class is the cornerstone of the ADO.NET disconnected model and allows you to read and write XML data, and to work with schemas. Further, typed `DataSets` make your development easy by providing typed `DataTable` and `DataColumn` names. The `DataSet` and the underlying XML document class can be used interchangeably. The `XmlDataDocument` class provides a bridge between the relational and hierarchical data models involved in such communication.

CHAPTER 8

XML Serialization

Your .NET applications consist of one or more classes. The objects of these classes are used to store state information. As long as your objects are available in the memory of your application, this state information is readily available. But what if you would like to persist object state across application shutdowns? At first you may think of saving object state in a database. However, databases generally store information in relational format, whereas objects often have a hierarchical structure. Moreover, you would need to create many tables in the database on your own. Storing object data in a database comes with its own overheads. Wouldn't it be nice if the entire object state could be stored to a medium and retrieved later? That is what serialization offers.

Serialization is a process by which object state is persisted to a medium. The medium can be a physical disk file, memory, or even a network stream. The serialized objects can be retrieved later in your application by a process called *deserialization*. The .NET Framework provides extensive support for serialization and uses serialization in many places. Remoting and web services are two main areas where serialization is heavily used. In this chapter, you are going to learn about the following topics:

- Understanding the flavors of serialization
- Using the `XmlSerializer` class to serialize object state in XML format
- Customizing the serialization process with the help of certain attributes
- Using the `SoapFormatter` class to serialize object state in SOAP format
- Customizing the SOAP serialization process with the help of certain attributes

Understanding the Flavors of Serialization

Serialization can be classified based on the format of serialization or on the depth of serialization. The three formats in which you can serialize data in the .NET Framework are as follows:

Binary: This format is generally better in terms of performance than the others. However, in terms of extensibility and cross-application integration, the other formats are better.

XML: Objects serialized in this way are stored as plain XML. If you are talking with multiple heterogeneous systems, this format will prove useful. For example, your .NET applications may serialize objects as XML documents, and a Java application may read these serialized objects by using its standard XML parser and work with the data further.

Simple Object Access Protocol (SOAP): Objects serialized in this way store information as per the SOAP standards. SOAP is the core pillar for web services.

The other way to classify serialization is based on the depth of serialization. The two flavors based on the depth of serialization are as follows:

Deep serialization: This serializes all the public, protected, and private members of your class. Even the nested classes and their public, protected, and private members are serialized.

Shallow serialization: This serializes only the public members of your class.

In the .NET Framework, the classes that serialize objects in binary format use deep serialization, whereas the classes that serialize objects in XML format use shallow serialization.

Classes Involved in the Serialization Process

There are three core classes that are used to perform serialization in binary, XML, and SOAP formats, respectively:

- The `BinaryFormatter` class serializes objects in binary format. It resides in the `System.Runtime.Serialization.Formatters.Binary` namespace.
- The `XmlSerializer` class serializes objects in XML format. It resides in the `System.Xml.Serialization` namespace. The `System.Xml.Serialization` namespace physically resides in the `System.Xml.dll` assembly.
- The `SoapFormatter` class serializes objects in SOAP format. It resides in the `System.Runtime.Serialization.Formatters.Soap` namespace. The `System.Runtime.Serialization.Formatters.Soap` namespace physically resides in the `System.Runtime.Serialization.Formatters.Soap.dll` assembly.

Serializing and Deserializing Objects by Using XML Format

Now that you have a basic understanding of what serialization is, let's delve straight into XML serialization. You will be building an application that illustrates the serialization and deserialization process by using the `XmlSerializer` class. The application user interface is shown in Figure 8-1.

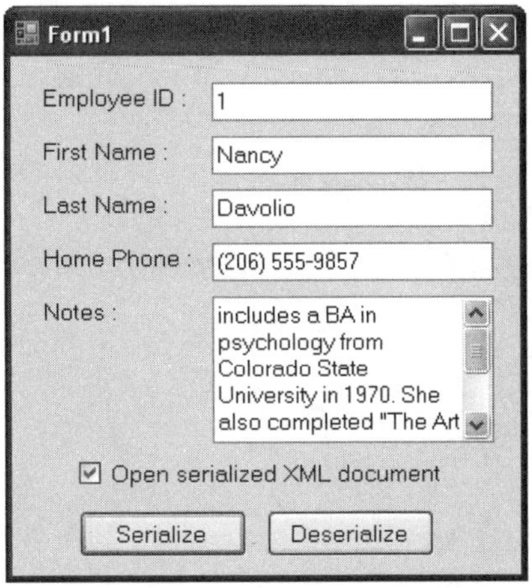

Figure 8-1. *Application for illustrating XML serialization*

The application consists of a class called `Employee` with five public properties: `EmployeeID`, `FirstName`, `LastName`, `HomePhone`, and `Notes`. There are five text boxes that accept values for these properties. The two buttons, Serialize and Deserialize, do the job of serializing and deserializing the `Employee` object, respectively. The check box determines whether the serialized XML document will be opened in a browser for viewing.

Before you can use the `XmlSerializer` class, you should create the `Employee` class as shown in Listing 8-1.

Listing 8-1. *The Employee Class*

```
public class Employee
{
        private int intID;
        private string strFName;
        private string strLName;
        private string strHPhone;
        private string strNotes;
```

```
public int EmployeeID
{
    get
    {
        return intID;
    }
    set
    {
        intID = value;
    }
}

public string FirstName
{
    get
    {
        return strFName;
    }
    set
    {
        strFName = value;
    }
}

public string LastName
{
    get
    {
        return strLName;
    }
    set
    {
        strLName = value;
    }
}

public string HomePhone
{
    get
    {
        return strHPhone;
    }
    set
```

```
            {
                strHPhone = value;
            }
        }

        public string Notes
        {
            get
            {
                return strNotes;
            }
            set
            {
                strNotes = value;
            }
        }
    }
```

The class declares five private variables for storing various pieces of information about an employee. These five private variables are exposed to the external world via five public properties (EmployeeID, FirstName, LastName, HomePhone, and Notes).

The Click event handler of the Serialize button contains the code shown in Listing 8-2.

Listing 8-2. *Serializing Objects in XML Format*

```
private void button1_Click(object sender, EventArgs e)
{
  Employee emp = new Employee();
  emp.EmployeeID = int.Parse(textBox1.Text);
  emp.FirstName = textBox2.Text;
  emp.LastName = textBox3.Text;
  emp.HomePhone = textBox4.Text;
  emp.Notes = textBox5.Text;
  FileStream stream =
    new FileStream(Application.StartupPath + @"\employee.xml", FileMode.Create);
  XmlSerializer serializer = new XmlSerializer(typeof(Employee));
  serializer.Serialize(stream, emp);
  stream.Close();
  if (checkBox1.Checked)
  {
    Process.Start(Application.StartupPath + @"\employee.xml");
  }
}
```

The code creates an instance of the Employee class. It then assigns values from various text boxes to the corresponding properties of the Employee class. A FileStream is then created for writing to a physical disk file (Employee.xml). This stream is used while actually serializing the object. Then the code creates an object of the XmlSerializer class. As mentioned previously, the XmlSerializer class allows you to serialize data in XML format.

There are several overloads of the XmlSerializer constructor, and the code uses the one that accepts the type of class whose objects are to be serialized. The type information about the Employee class is obtained by using the typeof keyword. The Serialize() method of XmlSerializer serializes an object to a specified stream, TextWriter, or XmlWriter.

Because our example uses a FileStream to serialize the Employee object, after serialization is complete, the stream is closed. Finally, the serialized data residing in the XML file is displayed in a browser by using the Start() method of the Process class.

The Click event handler of the Deserialize button contains the code shown in Listing 8-3.

Listing 8-3. *Deserializing by Using the XmlSerializer Class*

```
private void button2_Click(object sender, EventArgs e)
{
  Employee emp;
  FileStream stream =
    new FileStream(Application.StartupPath + @"\employee.xml", FileMode.Open);
  XmlSerializer serializer = new XmlSerializer(typeof(Employee));
  emp=(Employee)serializer.Deserialize(stream);
  stream.Close();
  textBox1.Text = emp.EmployeeID.ToString();
  textBox2.Text = emp.FirstName;
  textBox3.Text = emp.LastName;
  textBox4.Text = emp.HomePhone;
  textBox5.Text = emp.Notes;
}
```

The code declares a variable of type Employee. Then it creates a FileStream pointing to the same file that was created during the serialization process. Note that this time the file is opened in Open mode and not in Create mode. Then an object of XmlSerializer is created as before. The Deserialize() method of the XmlSerializer class accepts a Stream, a TextReader, or an XmlReader from which the object is to be read for deserialization. It then returns the deserialized object. The deserialized data is always returned as a generic-type object and needs to be cast to the Employee type. Then various property values of the deserialized object are assigned to respective text boxes.

To test the application, you run it, enter some values in the text boxes, and click the Serialize button. Figure 8-2 shows a sample XML document obtained by running the preceding application.

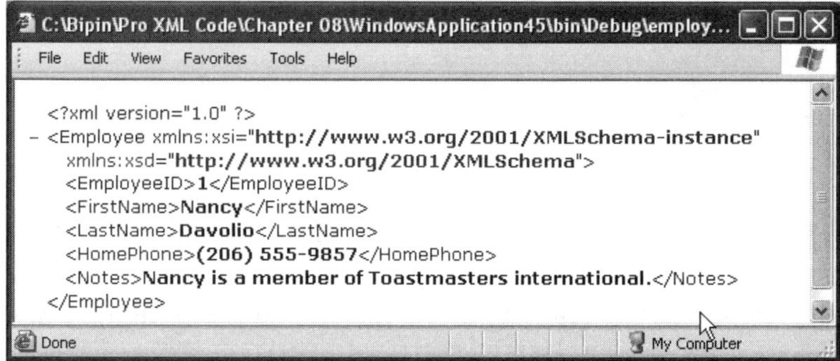

Figure 8-2. *Employee object serialized as an XML document*

Examine the resultant XML markup carefully. The class name (`Employee`) has become the name of the root element. The elements such as `<EmployeeID>`, `<FirstName>`, and `<LastName>` have the same name as the corresponding properties in the `Employee` class. Now close the application and run it again. This time click the Deserialize button. You will find that the text boxes show the property values that you specified during the last run of the application.

Handling Events Raised During Deserialization

Imagine a case where one application is serializing objects and the other is deserializing them. What if the serialized objects contain some extra attributes and elements? The application that is deserializing such objects must have some way to signal this discrepancy. Fortunately, the `XmlSerializer` class comes with certain events to handle such situations. These events are raised during the deserialization process when the structure of the class and the serialized XML don't match. Table 8-1 lists these events.

Table 8-1. *Events of the XmlSerializer Class*

Event Name	Description
`UnknownAttribute`	This event is raised when the data being deserialized contains some unexpected attribute. The event receives an event argument of type `XmlAttributeEventArgs` that supplies more information about the event.
`UnknownElement`	This event is raised when the data being deserialized contains some unexpected element. The event receives an event argument of type `XmlElementEventArgs` that supplies more information about the event.
`UnknownNode`	This event is raised when the data being deserialized contains some unexpected node. The event receives an event argument of type `XmlNodeEventArgs` that supplies more information about the event.
`UnreferencedObject`	This event is raised when the data being deserialized contains some recognized type that is not used or is unreferenced. The event receives an event argument of type `UnreferencedObjectEventArgs` that supplies more information about the event. This event applies only to SOAP-encoded XML.

To illustrate the use of these events, you need to modify the previous application as shown in Listing 8-4.

Listing 8-4. *Events of the XmlSerializer Class*

```
private void button2_Click(object sender, EventArgs e)
{
  Employee emp;
  FileStream stream =
    new FileStream(Application.StartupPath + @"\employee.xml", FileMode.Open);
  XmlSerializer serializer = new XmlSerializer(typeof(Employee));
  serializer.UnknownAttribute +=
    new XmlAttributeEventHandler(serializer_UnknownAttribute);
  serializer.UnknownElement +=
    new XmlElementEventHandler(serializer_UnknownElement);
  serializer.UnknownNode += new XmlNodeEventHandler(serializer_UnknownNode);
  emp = (Employee)serializer.Deserialize(stream);
  stream.Close();
  textBox1.Text = emp.EmployeeID.ToString();
  textBox2.Text = emp.FirstName;
  textBox3.Text = emp.LastName;
  textBox4.Text = emp.HomePhone;
  textBox5.Text = emp.Notes;
}

void serializer_UnknownNode(object sender, XmlNodeEventArgs e)
{
  MessageBox.Show("Unknown Node " + e.Name + " found at Line " + e.LineNumber);
}
void serializer_UnknownElement(object sender, XmlElementEventArgs e)
{
  MessageBox.Show("Unknown Element " + e.Element.Name + " found at Line " +
                  e.LineNumber);
}
void serializer_UnknownAttribute(object sender, XmlAttributeEventArgs e)
{
  MessageBox.Show("Unknown Attribute " + e.Attr.Name + " found at Line " +
                  e.LineNumber);
}
```

Notice the code marked in bold. After declaring the instance of the `XmlSerializer` class, it wires up three event handlers—`UnknownAttribute`, `UnknownElement`, and `UnknownNode`—that simply display a message box showing the name of the attribute, element, or node and the line number at which the attribute, element, or node is encountered. Notice how the event argument parameter is used to extract information about the unexpected content.

To test these events, modify the serialized XML file manually as shown in Listing 8-5.

Listing 8-5. *Modifying the Serialized XML Manually*

```
<?xml version="1.0"?>
<Employee xmlns:xsi="http://www.w3.org/2001/XMLSchema-instance"
 xmlns:xsd="http://www.w3.org/2001/XMLSchema" EmpCode="E001">
  <EmployeeID>1</EmployeeID>
  <FirstName>Nancy</FirstName>
  <LastName>Davolio</LastName>
  <HomePhone>(206) 555-9857</HomePhone>
  <Notes>includes a BA in psychology from Colorado State University in 1970. She
also completed "The Art of the Cold Call." Nancy is a member of Toastmasters
International.</Notes>
  <OfficePhone>(206) 555-1234</OfficePhone>
</Employee>
```

Notice the markup in bold. We have added an `EmpCode` attribute and an `<OfficePhone>` element manually to the XML file. Save the file and run the application. This time when you click the Deserialize button, you will see message boxes informing you of the discrepancies. Figure 8-3 shows one such message box.

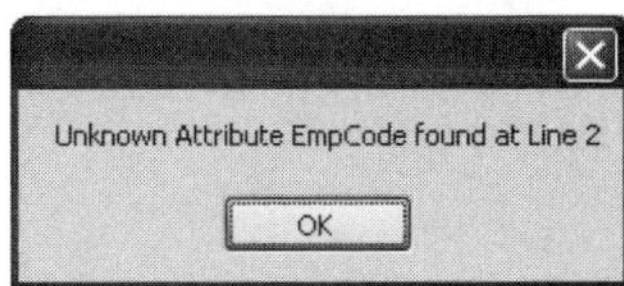

Figure 8-3. *Unexpected content encountered during the deserialization process*

Serializing and Deserializing Complex Types

In the preceding example, we serialized a simple type; the members of the `Employee` class were simple types such as an integer and a string. However, real-world classes are often complex ones. They may contain members that are class types, enumerated types, or even arrays. The `XmlSerializer` class provides support for such complex types, and that is what you are going to see in the next example.

The user interface of the application now changes as shown in Figure 8-4.

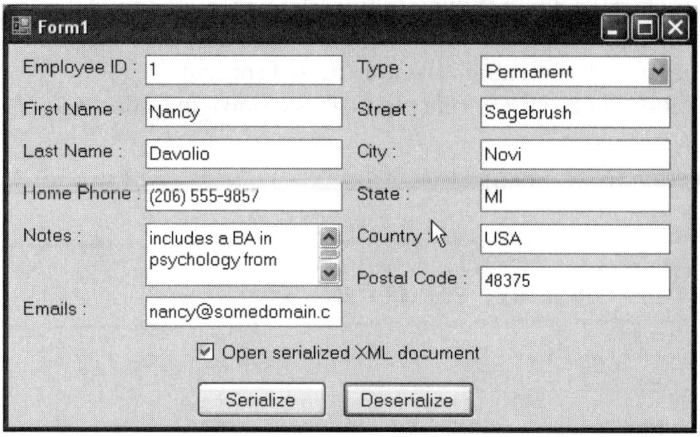

Figure 8-4. *Application for illustrating XML serialization of complex types*

The first five text boxes remain the same as in the previous example. However, six text boxes and one combo box are new. The newly added text boxes capture the email, street, city, state, country, and postal code information of the employee. The combo box captures the employee type (permanent or contract).

To store the address information of employees, you need to add a property called `Address` to the `Employee` class. The `Address` property itself is a class called `Address`, as shown in Listing 8-6.

Listing 8-6. *The Address Class*

```
public class Address
{
        private string strStreet;
        private string strCity;
        private string strState;
        private string strCountry;
        private string strPostalCode;

        public string Street
        {
            get
            {
                return strStreet;
            }
            set
            {
                strStreet = value;
            }
        }
```

```
public string City
{
    get
    {
        return strCity;
    }
    set
    {
        strCity = value;
    }
}

public string State
{
    get
    {
        return strState;
    }
    set
    {
        strState = value;
    }
}

public string Country
{
    get
    {
        return strCountry;
    }
    set
    {
        strCountry = value;
    }
}

public string PostalCode
{
    get
    {
        return strPostalCode;
    }
    set
```

```
            {
                strPostalCode = value;
            }
        }
}
```

This class has five private string variables for storing street address, city, state, country, and postal code, respectively. These private variables are exposed to the external world by wrapping them in corresponding public properties.

To store the employee type, you need to add a property called `Type` to the `Employee` class. The `Type` property will be an enumeration of type `EmployeeType`, which contains two values: `Permanent` and `Contract`. The `EmployeeType` enumeration is shown in Listing 8-7.

Listing 8-7. *The EmployeeType Enumeration*

```
public enum EmployeeType
{
        Permanent, Contract
}
```

The email information is stored in a property called `Emails`. An employee can have more than one email address and hence this property is of the string array type. Listing 8-8 shows the modified version of the `Employee` class.

Listing 8-8. *The Employee Class After Adding Address, Type, and Emails Properties*

```
public class Employee
{
        private int intID;
        private string strFName;
        private string strLName;
        private string strHPhone;
        private string strNotes;
        private string[] strEmails;
        private EmployeeType enumType;
        private Address objAddress=new Address();

        public int EmployeeID
        {
            get
            {
                return intID;
            }
            set
            {
                intID = value;
            }
        }
```

```
public string FirstName
{
    get
    {
        return strFName;
    }
    set
    {
        strFName = value;
    }
}

public string LastName
{
    get
    {
        return strLName;
    }
    set
    {
        strLName = value;
    }
}

public string HomePhone
{
    get
    {
        return strHPhone;
    }
    set
    {
        strHPhone = value;
    }
}

public string Notes
{
    get
    {
        return strNotes;
    }
    set
    {
        strNotes = value;
    }
}
```

```
        public Address Address
        {
            get
            {
                return objAddress;
            }
            set
            {
                objAddress = value;
            }
        }

        public EmployeeType Type
        {
            get
            {
                return enumType;
            }
            set
            {
                enumType = value;
            }
        }

        public string[] Emails
        {
            get
            {
                return strEmails;
            }
            set
            {
                strEmails = value;
            }
        }
    }
```

Notice the property definitions marked in bold. The three public properties `Address`, `Type`, and `Emails` are of type `Address`, `EmployeeType`, and string array, respectively. The code in the `Click` event handler of the Serialize button now changes as shown in Listing 8-9.

Listing 8-9. *Serializing Complex Types*

```
private void button1_Click(object sender, EventArgs e)
{
  Employee emp = new Employee();
  emp.EmployeeID = int.Parse(textBox1.Text);
  emp.FirstName = textBox2.Text;
  emp.LastName = textBox3.Text;
  emp.HomePhone = textBox4.Text;
  emp.Notes = textBox5.Text;
  emp.Type =
    (comboBox1.SelectedIndex == 0 ? EmployeeType.Permanent :
     EmployeeType.Contract);
  emp.Address.Street = textBox6.Text;
  emp.Address.City = textBox7.Text;
  emp.Address.State = textBox8.Text;
  emp.Address.Country = textBox9.Text;
  emp.Address.PostalCode = textBox10.Text;
  emp.Emails = textBox11.Text.Split(',');
  FileStream stream =
    new FileStream(Application.StartupPath + @"\employee.xml", FileMode.Create);
  XmlSerializer serializer = new XmlSerializer(typeof(Employee));
  serializer.Serialize(stream, emp);
  stream.Close();
  if (checkBox1.Checked)
  {
    Process.Start(Application.StartupPath + @"\employee.xml");
  }
}
```

The code is essentially the same as in the preceding examples. However, it sets the newly added properties to corresponding values from the text boxes and combo box. Notice how the complex property `Address` is set. Also, notice how comma-separated emails entered in the email text box are converted into a string array by using the `Split()` method. After the `Employee` object is serialized by calling `Serialize()`, the serialized XML document looks like that in Figure 8-5.

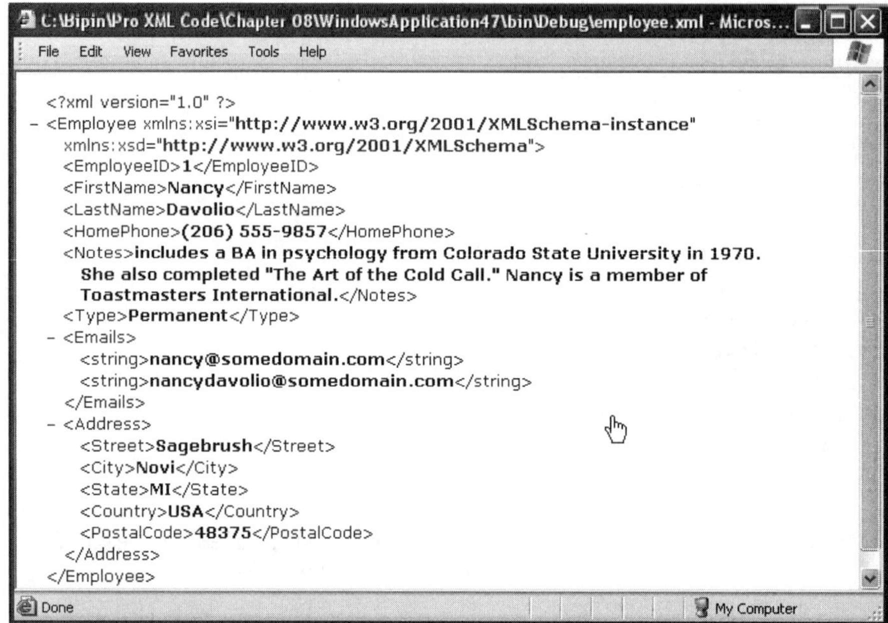

```
<?xml version="1.0" ?>
- <Employee xmlns:xsi="http://www.w3.org/2001/XMLSchema-instance"
    xmlns:xsd="http://www.w3.org/2001/XMLSchema">
    <EmployeeID>1</EmployeeID>
    <FirstName>Nancy</FirstName>
    <LastName>Davolio</LastName>
    <HomePhone>(206) 555-9857</HomePhone>
    <Notes>includes a BA in psychology from Colorado State University in 1970.
      She also completed "The Art of the Cold Call." Nancy is a member of
      Toastmasters International.</Notes>
    <Type>Permanent</Type>
  - <Emails>
      <string>nancy@somedomain.com</string>
      <string>nancydavolio@somedomain.com</string>
    </Emails>
  - <Address>
      <Street>Sagebrush</Street>
      <City>Novi</City>
      <State>MI</State>
      <Country>USA</Country>
      <PostalCode>48375</PostalCode>
    </Address>
</Employee>
```

Figure 8-5. *Serialized XML for complex types*

Examine the serialized XML data carefully. The address is represented by the `<Address>` node, the name of which is derived from the `Address` property of the `Employee` class. The `<Address>` node has five child nodes: `<Street>`, `<City>`, `<State>`, `<Country>`, and `<PostalCode>`. Their names are derived from the respective properties of the `Address` class.

The `<Type>` element represents the `Type` property of the `Employee` class. The enumeration value, `Permanent`, is stored in the XML markup. Finally, the `<Emails>` node represents the `Emails` property, and its child nodes are nothing but individual array elements. Because the emails are stored in a string array, the individual values are enclosed in `<string></string>` elements.

Listing 8-10 shows the code in the `Click` event of the Deserialize button.

Listing 8-10. *Deserializing Complex Types*

```
private void button2_Click(object sender, EventArgs e)
{
 Employee emp;
 FileStream stream = new FileStream(Application.StartupPath +
 @"\employee.xml",   FileMode.Open);
 XmlSerializer serializer = new XmlSerializer(typeof(Employee));
 emp=(Employee)serializer.Deserialize(stream);
 stream.Close();
 textBox1.Text = emp.EmployeeID.ToString();
 textBox2.Text = emp.FirstName;
 textBox3.Text = emp.LastName;
 textBox4.Text = emp.HomePhone;
 textBox5.Text = emp.Notes;
 comboBox1.SelectedIndex = (emp.Type == EmployeeType.Permanent?0:1);
 textBox6.Text=emp.Address.Street;
 textBox7.Text=emp.Address.City;
 textBox8.Text=emp.Address.State;
 textBox9.Text=emp.Address.Country;
 textBox10.Text=emp.Address.PostalCode;
 textBox11.Text = string.Join(",", emp.Emails);
 stream.Close();
}
```

The code is very much the same as in previous examples. It deserializes the previously serialized Employee object by using the XmlSerializer class. The property values are then assigned to various controls on the form. Notice how the Emails property is converted into a comma-separated string by using the Join() method of the string class. The following points are worth noting when serializing complex types:

- To serialize and deserialize enumerated values, the application that serializes the object and the application that deserializes it must define the same enumeration under consideration.
- While serializing object properties, all the public members of the object are serialized. The member names are assigned to the child elements in the resultant XML.
- During the deserialization process, XmlSerializer instantiates the main class (Employee) as well as all the subclasses (Address) and assigns values to the respective properties.
- While serializing arrays, an XML element represents the array. The individual array elements form the child element of this element. The individual array elements are enclosed in an element depending on the data type of the array.
- While deserializing, XmlSerializer creates an array with the same number of elements as the serialized elements. It then assigns the array element values accordingly.

Serialization and Inheritance

Serialization is not limited to simple and complex types. It is equally applicable to inherited classes. Assume that you have a class called Manager that inherits from our Employee class. Now when you serialize Manager, all the public properties of the Employee base class and Manager are serialized. This is also true in the case of a long chain of inheritance.

To demonstrate how inherited classes are serialized, we need to add a class called Manager to our application. The Manager class inherits from the Employee class (see Listing 8-1) and extends it by adding an integer property NoOfSubordinates. The Manager class is shown in Listing 8-11.

Listing 8-11. *The Manager Class*

```
public class Manager:Employee
{
        private int intNoOfSubordinates;

        public int NoOfSubordinates
        {
            get
            {
                return intNoOfSubordinates;
            }
            set
            {
                intNoOfSubordinates = value;
            }
        }
}
```

The code creates a class named Manager that inherits from the Employee class. It then adds a private integer variable to store the number of subordinates of a manager. The variable is exposed to the external world via a public property, NoOfSubordinates. To accommodate the additional property, the user interface of the application changes as shown in Figure 8-6.

The application is almost the same as in Figure 8-1, but there is an extra text box for accepting the number of subordinates of the manager. Listing 8-12 shows the Click event handler of the Serialize button.

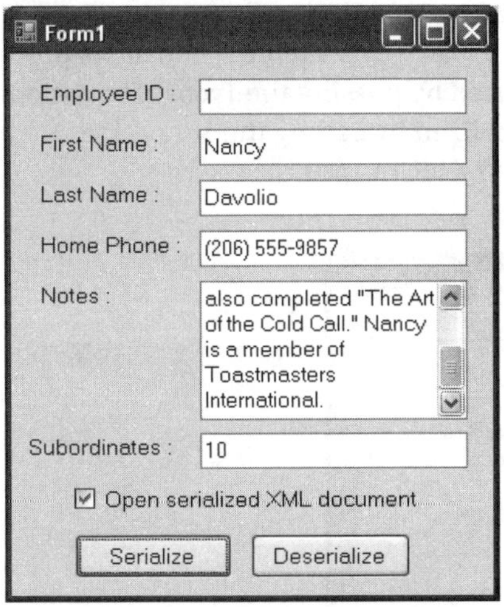

Figure 8-6. *Application to demonstrate serialization of inherited classes*

Listing 8-12. *Serializing the Inherited Manager Class*

```
private void button1_Click(object sender, EventArgs e)
{
  Manager manager = new Manager();
  manager.EmployeeID = int.Parse(textBox1.Text);
  manager.FirstName = textBox2.Text;
  manager.LastName = textBox3.Text;
  manager.HomePhone = textBox4.Text;
  manager.Notes = textBox5.Text;
  manager.NoOfSubordinates = int.Parse(textBox6.Text);
  FileStream stream =
    new FileStream(Application.StartupPath + @"\employee.xml", FileMode.Create);
  XmlSerializer serializer = new XmlSerializer(typeof(Manager));
  serializer.Serialize(stream, manager);
  stream.Close();
  if (checkBox1.Checked)
  {
    Process.Start(Application.StartupPath + @"\employee.xml");
  }
}
```

The code is essentially the same as we have been using up until now but it uses the `Manager` class instead of the `Employee` class. An instance of `Manager` is created, and all its properties are set. Then an instance of `XmlSerializer` is created by passing the `Type` information of the `Manager` class. Finally, the `Manager` instance is serialized by calling the `Serialize()` method of `XmlSerializer`. Figure 8-7 shows the resultant XML output.

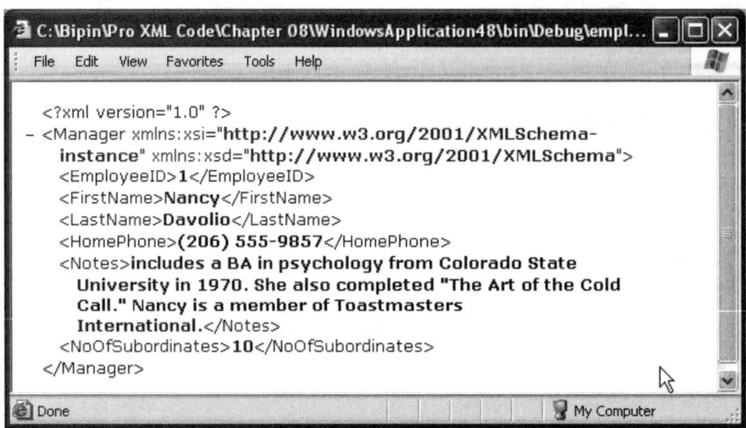

Figure 8-7. *Serialized XML of the Manager class*

Notice how all the public properties from the `Employee` base class as well as the one from `Manager` are serialized. The code to deserialize the `Manager` class is very similar to the one we used previously. Listing 8-13 shows this code.

Listing 8-13. *Deserializing the Manager Class*

```
private void button2_Click(object sender, EventArgs e)
{
  Manager manager;
  FileStream stream =
    new FileStream(Application.StartupPath + @"\employee.xml", FileMode.Open);
  XmlSerializer serializer = new XmlSerializer(typeof(Manager));
  manager = (Manager)serializer.Deserialize(stream);
  stream.Close();
  textBox1.Text = manager.EmployeeID.ToString();
  textBox2.Text = manager.FirstName;
  textBox3.Text = manager.LastName;
  textBox4.Text = manager.HomePhone;
  textBox5.Text = manager.Notes;
  textBox6.Text = manager.NoOfSubordinates.ToString();
}
```

The only difference in this code is that it uses `Manager` in the deserialization process instead of `Employee`.

Customizing the Serialized XML

The `XmlSerializer` class automatically uses the name of the public members as the names for the resultant XML elements. This is what is required in many cases. However, sometimes you may need to customize the serialized XML data to suit your needs. In the previous example illustrating the serialization of complex types, we got the XML document shown in Listing 8-14.

Listing 8-14. *Serialized XML Document Without Any Customization*

```
<?xml version="1.0"?>
<Employee xmlns:xsi="http://www.w3.org/2001/XMLSchema-instance"
xmlns:xsd="http://www.w3.org/2001/XMLSchema">
  <EmployeeID>1</EmployeeID>
  <FirstName>Nancy</FirstName>
  <LastName>Davolio</LastName>
  <HomePhone>(206) 555-9857</HomePhone>
  <Notes>includes a BA in psychology from Colorado State University in 1970. She
also completed "The Art of the Cold Call." Nancy is a member of Toastmasters
International.</Notes>
  <Type>Permanent</Type>
  <Emails>
    <string>nancy@somedomain.com</string>
    <string>nancydavolio@somedomain.com</string>
  </Emails>
  <Address>
    <Street>Sagebrush</Street>
    <City>Novi</City>
    <State>MI </State>
    <Country>USA</Country>
    <PostalCode>48375</PostalCode>
  </Address>
</Employee>
```

However, what if you want the resultant XML structure to resemble Listing 8-15?

Listing 8-15. *Serialized XML After Customization*

```
<?xml version="1.0"?>
<MyEmployee xmlns:xsi="http://www.w3.org/2001/XMLSchema-instance"
xmlns:xsd="http://www.w3.org/2001/XMLSchema" EmployeeCode="1">
  <FName>Nancy</FName>
  <LName>Davolio</LName>
  <Remarks>
  includes a BA in psychology from Colorado State University in 1970. She also
completed "The Art of the Cold Call." Nancy is a member of Toastmasters
International.
</Remarks>
  <EmployeeType>Permanent Employee</EmployeeType>
```

```
  <EmailAddresses>
    <Email>nancy@somedomain.com</Email>
    <Email>nancydavolio@somedomain.com</Email>
  </EmailAddresses>
  <Address>
    <Street>Sagebrush</Street>
    <City>Novi</City>
    <State>MI</State>
    <Country>USA</Country>
    <PostalCode>48375</PostalCode>
  </Address>
</MyEmployee>
```

Observe Listing 8-15 carefully. There are some significant changes:

- The root element of the document is `<MyEmployee>` and not `<Employee>`.
- The element names are totally different from the public property names.
- The employee ID is stored as the `EmployeeCode` attribute.
- The `EmployeeType` enumeration value is different from the actual enumeration item text.
- Email addresses are stored as `<Email>` elements and not as `<string>` elements.
- The `HomePhone` property value is not serialized even if it is a public member of the class.

To achieve such customization, the `System.Xml.Serialization` namespace provides several attributes. You are required to decorate your classes, enumeration, and properties with these attributes to customize the way they are serialized. Listing 8-16 shows the `Employee` class and the `EmployeeType` enumeration after applying many of these attributes.

Listing 8-16. *Customizing Serialization by Using Attributes*

```
[XmlRoot(ElementName="MyEmployee")]
public class Employee
{
        private int intID;
        private string strFName;
        private string strLName;
        private string strHPhone;
        private string strNotes;
        private string[] strEmails;
        private EmployeeType enumType;
        private Address objAddress=new Address();
```

```
[XmlAttribute(AttributeName="EmployeeCode")]
public int EmployeeID
{
    get
    {
        return intID;
    }
    set
    {
        intID = value;
    }
}

[XmlElement(ElementName="FName")]
public string FirstName
{
    get
    {
        return strFName;
    }
    set
    {
        strFName = value;
    }
}

[XmlElement(ElementName = "LName")]
public string LastName
{
    get
    {
        return strLName;
    }
    set
    {
        strLName = value;
    }
}
```

```
[XmlIgnore]
public string HomePhone
{
    get
    {
        return strHPhone;
    }
    set
    {
        strHPhone = value;
    }
}

[XmlElement(ElementName="Remarks")]
public string Notes
{
    get
    {
        return strNotes;
    }
    set
    {
        strNotes = value;
    }
}

[XmlElement(ElementName="EmployeeType")]
public EmployeeType Type
{
    get
    {
        return enumType;
    }
    set
    {
        enumType = value;
    }
}
```

```
        [XmlArray(ElementName="EmailAddresses")]
        [XmlArrayItem(ElementName="Email")]
        public string[] Emails
        {
            get
            {
                return strEmails;
            }
            set
            {
                strEmails = value;
            }
        }

        [XmlElement(IsNullable=true)]
        public Address Address
        {
            get
            {
                return objAddress;
            }
            set
            {
                objAddress = value;
            }
        }
}
public enum EmployeeType
{
        [XmlEnum(Name="Permanent Employee")]
        Permanent,
        [XmlEnum(Name = "Employee on contract")]
        Contract
}
```

Let's dissect the preceding listing step by step and see the significance of each attribute used.

Changing the XML Document Root

By default the XmlSerializer class uses the name of the class as the name of the XML root element. To alter this behavior, you can decorate your class with the [XmlRoot] attribute. The [XmlRoot] attribute has a property called ElementName that indicates the new name of the XML document root element. The [XmlRoot] attribute must be applied to a class definition and hence we've placed it on top of the Employee class.

Changing the Element Names

By default the XmlSerializer class uses the names of the public members to assign to the output XML elements. For example, the FirstName property gets serialized as the <FirstName> element. This default behavior can be altered by using the [XmlElement] attribute. The [XmlElement] attribute has a property called ElementName that specifies the name of the resulting XML element. The [XmlElement] attribute is applied to the public member that will be serialized, and thus the FirstName, LastName, Notes, Type, and Address properties are decorated with the [XmlElement] attribute.

Serializing Members As Attributes

By default all the public members of your class are serialized as XML elements in the output document. The [XmlAttribute] attribute allows you to change this default behavior. The AttributeName property of the [XmlAttribute] attribute indicates the name that will be given to the resultant XML attribute. [XmlAttribute] is applied to the public member that you wish to serialize as an attribute. In our example, we add the [XmlAttribute] attribute to the EmployeeID property.

Ignoring Public Members in the Serialization Process

By default all the public members of a class are serialized, but sometimes this is not what you want. For example, if you are storing credit card information in a public property, you may not want to serialize it for obvious security reasons. A public member can be ignored during the serialization process by decorating it with the [XmlIgnore] attribute. In our example, the HomePhone property is marked with this attribute.

Changing Array and Array Element Names

The Employee class has a property called Emails that is of type string array. Under the default naming scheme, when this property is serialized, an XML node is created with the name Emails. This node further contains child nodes, each containing the array element value. The names of the child elements are the same as the data type of the array (<string> in our example). You can alter this behavior with the help of the [XmlArray] and [XmlArrayElement] attributes. The former marks public members that are array types and specifies the XML element name for the member. The latter attribute governs the name of the XML element assigned to the individual array members. In our example, the `Emails` property will be serialized as `<EmailAddresses>`, and each array element will be enclosed within an `<Email>` element.

Ignoring Null Objects in the Serialization Process

The `Employee` class has an `Address` property that is an object type. If this property is null, `XmlSerializer` still emits an empty XML element for it, but you can use the `[XmlElement]` attribute to change this behavior. The `IsNullable` Boolean property of the `[XmlElement]` attribute indicates whether the empty XML element will be emitted when the member is null. Setting this property to `true` will not emit the empty XML element if the `Address` property is null.

Changing Enumeration Identifiers

The `EmployeeType` enumeration has two values: `Permanent` and `Contract`. By default when a member of the `EmployeeType` type is serialized, the value of these enumeration identifiers is emitted in the serialized XML. The `[XmlEnum]` attribute specifies the alternate value to serialize instead of the actual identifier name, and is applied on enumeration identifiers. The `Name` property of the `[XmlEnum]` attribute specifies the text that will be serialized instead of the identifier name.

Serializing Data in SOAP Format

In the beginning of this chapter, you learned that there are three flavors of serialization based on the format (binary, XML, and SOAP). Serializing objects into binary format is outside the scope of this book, and you have already learned how to serialize objects in XML format. Now it's time to learn how objects can be serialized in SOAP format.

SOAP is an industry standard that forms one of the pillars of web services. Though SOAP is used extensively along with web services, you can use it as an encoding format for object serialization.

When you serialize objects by using the `XmlSerializer` class, you need not do anything special to the classes themselves. However, when you wish to use SOAP as a serialization format, you must mark your classes with the `[Serializable]` attribute. Only then can your classes be serialized.

The `SoapFormatter` class takes care of all the intricacies of serializing your objects in SOAP format. The `SoapFormatter` class resides in the `System.Runtime.Serialization.Formatters.Soap` namespace, which physically resides in the `System.Runtime.Serialization.Formatters.Soap.dll` assembly.

Let's revisit the application that we developed when we began this chapter (see Figure 8-1) and modify it to use `SoapFormatter` instead of `XmlSerializer`. The user interface of the application remains unchanged, but the way we serialize and deserialize the objects differs.

First, you need to mark the `Employee` class with the `[Serializable]` attribute. The modified `Employee` class is shown in Listing 8-17.

Listing 8-17. *Marking a Class with the [Serializable] Attribute*

```
[Serializable]
public class Employee
{
        private int intID;
        private string strFName;
        private string strLName;
        private string strHPhone;
        private string strNotes;

        public int EmployeeID
        {
            get
            {
                return intID;
            }
            set
            {
                intID = value;
            }
        }

        public string FirstName
        {
            get
            {
                return strFName;
            }
            set
            {
                strFName = value;
            }
        }

        public string LastName
        {
            get
            {
                return strLName;
            }
            set
            {
                strLName = value;
            }
        }
```

```
        public string HomePhone
        {
            get
            {
                return strHPhone;
            }
            set
            {
                strHPhone = value;
            }
        }

        public string Notes
        {
            get
            {
                return strNotes;
            }
            set
            {
                strNotes = value;
            }
        }
}
```

As yAou can see, the [Serializable] attribute is a class-level attribute. Hence it is placed at the top of the Employee class and marks it as a serializable class. Listing 8-18 shows the Click event handler of the Serialize button. This time the code uses the SoapFormatter class.

Listing 8-18. *Serializing Objects by Using the SoapFormatterClass*

```
private void button1_Click(object sender, EventArgs e)
{
  Employee emp = new Employee();
  emp.EmployeeID = int.Parse(textBox1.Text);
  emp.FirstName = textBox2.Text;
  emp.LastName = textBox3.Text;
  emp.HomePhone = textBox4.Text;
  emp.Notes = textBox5.Text;
  FileStream stream =
    new FileStream(Application.StartupPath + @"\employee.xml", FileMode.Create);

  SoapFormatter formatter = new SoapFormatter();
  formatter.Serialize(stream, emp);
```

```
  stream.Close();
  if (checkBox1.Checked)
  {
    Process.Start(Application.StartupPath + @"\employee.xml");
  }
}
```

The code creates an instance of the Employee class and sets its properties to the values entered in the text boxes. A FileStream object is then created and creates a file to which the serialized data is to be written. Then a SoapFormatter object is created. The Serialize() method of SoapFormatter accepts two parameters: a stream to which the serialized data is to be written and the object that is to be serialized. The counterpart of this operation is performed in the Click event handler of the Deserialize button and is shown in Listing 8-19.

Listing 8-19. *Deserialization by Using the SoapFormatter Class*

```
private void button2_Click(object sender, EventArgs e)
{
  Employee emp;
  FileStream stream =
    new FileStream(Application.StartupPath + @"\employee.xml", FileMode.Open);
  SoapFormatter formatter = new SoapFormatter();
  emp=(Employee)formatter.Deserialize(stream);
  textBox1.Text = emp.EmployeeID.ToString();
  textBox2.Text = emp.FirstName;
  textBox3.Text = emp.LastName;
  textBox4.Text = emp.HomePhone;
  textBox5.Text = emp.Notes;
  stream.Close();
}
```

The code declares a variable of type Employee. It then opens a stream pointing to the same file to which the object was serialized before. An instance of SoapFormatter is then created. The Deserialize() method of SoapFormatter reads the stream and deserializes the object. The return value of Deserialize() is of type object and hence it is type converted to the Employee class. After the Employee object is retrieved, its property values are assigned to the corresponding text boxes. If you run the application and serialize the Employee object, you should see output similar to Figure 8-8.

As you can see, the XML output is now in SOAP format. There is also mention of some namespaces related to SOAP. There is another important difference: the names given to various elements containing data correspond to private variable names that hold the actual value and not the property names. Unlike XML serialization, which is shallow by nature, SOAP serialization done via the SoapFormatter class is deep serialization. It serializes private, protected, and public data.

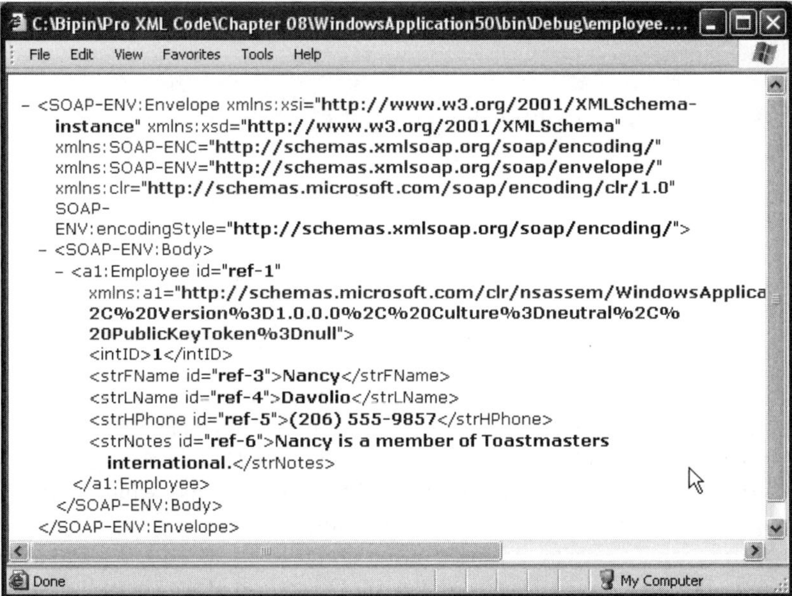

Figure 8-8. *Object serialized in SOAP format*

Customizing SOAP Serialization

Just as we customized the serialization process during XML serialization, we can customize the SAP serialization also. There are two ways to achieve this:

- Implement the `ISerializable` interface.
- Use certain serialization and deserialization attributes.

The first method has been available since .NET Framework 1.*x*. The latter method was introduced in .NET 2.0 and supersedes the first method. In our example, we are going to use the latter method to customize the serialization process.

We will use the same application that we developed in the previous section while illustrating the use of the `SoapFormatter` class. Suppose that you wish to protect the serialized XML data from casual users. You want to implement Base64 encoding to the data that is being serialized so that casual readers cannot easily read the contents. That data needs to be encoded in a Base64 encoding scheme and decoded when deserialized. In such cases, the custom serialization attributes come in handy. Add two helper functions called `Encode()` and `Decode()` to the preceding application as shown in Listing 8-20.

Listing 8-20. *Encoding and Decoding Data by Using Base64 Encoding*

```
private string Encode(string str)
{
  byte[] data = ASCIIEncoding.ASCII.GetBytes(str);
  return Convert.ToBase64String(data);
}

private string Decode(string str)
{
  byte[] data=Convert.FromBase64String(str);
  return ASCIIEncoding.ASCII.GetString(data);
}
```

The `Encode()` function accepts a string that is to be encoded in Base64 format. It then converts the string into a byte array by using the `GetBytes()` method of the `ASCIIEncoding` class. The byte array is then fed to the `ToBase64String()` method of the `Convert` class, which returns a Base64-encoded string representing the supplied array of bytes.

The `Decode()` function accepts a Base64-encoded string that is to be decoded back to a plain string representation. It then calls the `FromBase64String()` method of the `Convert` class and passes the supplied Base64 string to it. The `FromBase64String()` method returns a byte array representing the decoded version of the supplied string. The byte array is converted to a string by using the `GetString()` method of the `ASCIIEncoding` class.

Now we need to add four methods to our class, as shown in Listing 8-21.

Listing 8-21. *Customizing SOAP Serialization and Deserialization*

```
 [OnSerializing]
public void OnSerializing(StreamingContext context)
{
  strFName = Encode(strFName);
  strLName = Encode(strLName);
  strHPhone = Encode(strHPhone);
  strNotes = Encode(strNotes);
}

[OnSerialized]
public void OnSerialized(StreamingContext context)
{
  strFName = Decode(strFName);
  strLName = Decode(strLName);
  strHPhone = Decode(strHPhone);
  strNotes = Decode(strNotes);
}
```

```
[OnDeserializing]
public void OnDeserializing(StreamingContext context)
{
  //no code here
}

[OnDeserialized]
public void OnDeserialized(StreamingContext context)
{
  strFName = Decode(strFName);
  strLName = Decode(strLName);
  strHPhone = Decode(strHPhone);
  strNotes = Decode(strNotes);
}
```

The four methods are marked with the [OnSerializing], [OnSerialized], [OnDeserializing], and [OnDeserialized] attributes. These attributes allow you to customize the serialization and deserialization process by using pre- and post-methods:

- The method marked with [OnSerializing] is automatically called by the serialization framework before the data is serialized.
- The method marked with [OnSerialized] is called when the serialization is complete.
- Similarly, the methods marked with [OnDeserializing] and [OnDeserialized] are called before and after the deserialization operation.

All these methods must accept a parameter of type StreamingContext. The StreamingContext parameter provides additional information about the serialization or deserialization process.

In our example, the OnSerializing() method calls the Encode() helper method that we created earlier to encode the variable values into Base64 format. Thus the data being serialized is not a plain string but a Base64 string. After the serialization is complete, we may still need the same data in plain-string format. That is why the Decode() method is called in the OnSerialized() method.

The OnDeserializing() method doesn't include any code in our example. However, if you wish to execute some code before deserialization takes place, you can add your custom logic in this method. After the previously serialized data is deserialized, it should give us the values in plain-string format and not in Base64 format. Hence the OnDeserialized() method calls Decode() and converts the Base64 values into plain text. Figure 8-9 shows a sample run of the application.

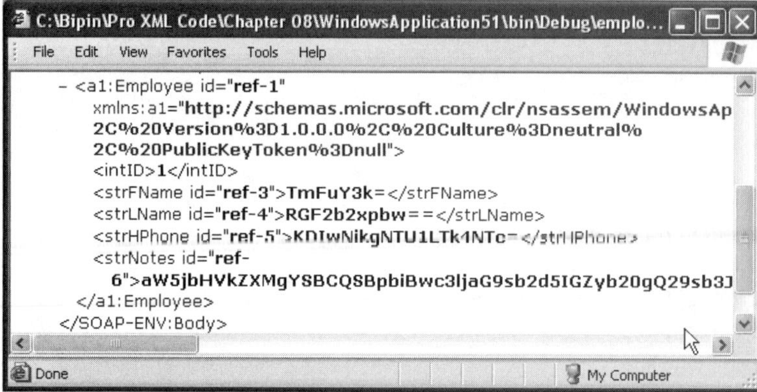

Figure 8-9. *Base64-encoded data after serialization*

Notice how the entire data is serialized in Base64 format.

Summary

In this chapter, we examined the XML serialization process in detail. The .NET Framework itself uses serialization in many places including remoting and web services. There are two flavors of serialization: binary serialization and XML serialization. You can serialize object state in XML format by using the `XmlSerializer` and `SoapFormatter` classes. The former serializes data in plain XML, whereas the latter serializes it in SOAP format. The serialization provided by `XmlSerializer` is shallow, whereas that provided by `SoapFormatter` is deep. The serialization and deserialization process can be customized with the help of various attributes. XML serialization is extensively used in XML web services. Most of the time the web service framework of .NET shields you from manual work, but behind the scenes it makes heavy use of XML serialization. You are going to learn about XML web services in the next chapter.

CHAPTER 9

XML Web Services

The idea of distributed application development is not new. Distributed technologies such as Distributed Component Object Model (DCOM), Remote Method Invocation (RMI), and Common Object Request Broker Architecture (CORBA) have existed for years. Applications based on Microsoft platforms commonly use DCOM, whereas Java-based applications use RMI and CORBA. However, none of these technologies is an unambiguous industry standard. That is where web services step in. *Web services* offer an industry standard for developing distributed and service-oriented applications, which are becoming more and more popular in modern computing.

The .NET Framework provides a powerful and flexible foundation for building web services. Using this foundation, you can quickly develop and consume web services, as we will do in this chapter. In addition, it will acquaint you with the building blocks of web services. Specifically, you will learn about the following topics:

- What web services are
- Creating web services by using the .NET Framework
- Consuming web services in your applications
- Understanding protocols involved in the web service infrastructure
- Calling web services asynchronously

What Are Web Services?

The concept of web services can be best understood with the help of components that you might have built with .NET (or even COM). What is a component? A *component* is a reusable piece of software that provides certain functionality to your application. For example, a component developed for a banking application might be providing services such as loan calculation, interest calculation, and so forth. If you need the same business logic at any other place, such a component will be of great use. Components also isolate your business logic from the rest of the application. Such components do not provide any user interface to your application. They simply provide the required services to you.

Generally, components reside on the same machine as your application. What if they are to be located on a separate server altogether? What if the network involved is not a LAN but the Internet? What if you wish to host the components on a Unix box and consume them from a Windows machine? That is where web services come into the picture.

You can think of web services as components that reside on a web server, while applications consume them over a network. More formally, web services can be defined as a set of programmable APIs that can be called over a network by using XML, SOAP, and HTTP.

Web services are an industry standard, and no single company owns web services. Naturally they are being widely accepted among software vendors and developers. The three standards—XML, SOAP, and HTTP—are the pillars of the web service infrastructure. The following are some points to be remembered about web services:

- Web service standards are platform-independent industry standards.
- Web services do not provide any user interface. They provide only functionality or services to your application.
- Web services use XML, SOAP, and HTTP as the communication protocols.
- Web services use the same request-response model as used by web applications.
- All communication between a web service and its consumer happens in a plain-text format.
- Web services can reside on any web server as long as the consumer has network connectivity with that server.
- A web service and its client can be developed by using totally different platforms. For example, you may develop a web service by using the .NET Framework and consume it in a Java application.

Creating and Consuming Web Services

Building web services requires three essential steps:

- Creating the web service
- Creating a proxy for the web service
- Creating the client or consumer application of the web service

All the modern software development platforms introduce the concept of a proxy while performing remote communication. A *proxy* is an entity that stands in for some other entity and pretends to your client application that the proxy itself is the actual web service. In doing so, the proxy shields you from low-level network programming details (such as socket programming, underlying protocols, communication formats, and security). Your client application never talks with the web service directly. All the communication (request as well as response) is passed through the proxy.

If the proxy wants to pretend that the proxy itself is the web service, it must look like the web service. To help the proxy look like the web service, the web service standards provide a format called Web Services Description Language (WSDL). WSDL is an XML dialect that describes the web service, listing details such as the functions exposed by the web service, their parameters, data types, and return values. The proxy constructs itself by using this WSDL document of a web service.

The file extension used by .NET web services is `.asmx`. The web services are developed as classes and can have code behind them just like ASP.NET web forms.

Creating a Web Service

To create a web service by using Visual Studio, you need to create a new website and choose ASP.NET Web Service as the project type. Figure 9-1 shows the New Web Site dialog box of Visual Studio.

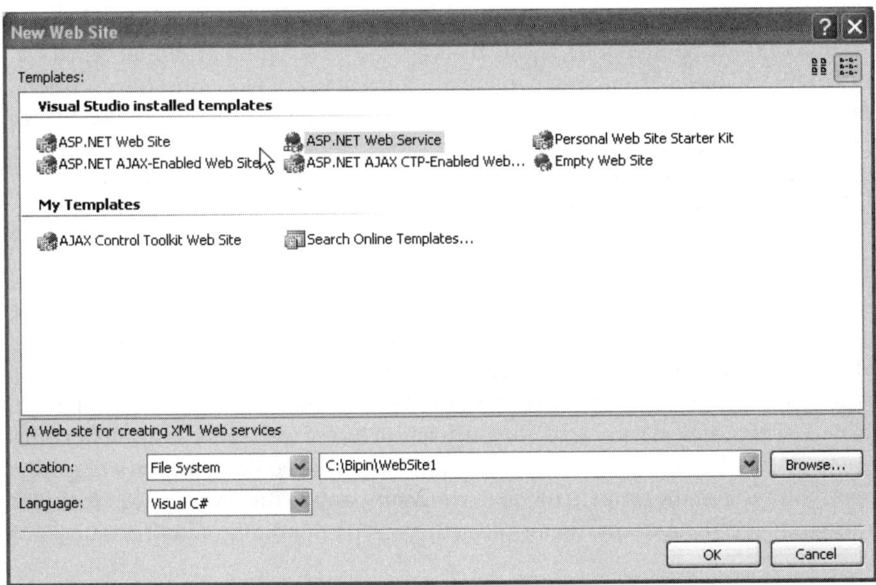

Figure 9-1. *Creating a new web service*

After you create the project, you should see a file called `Service.asmx`. This file contains the markup shown in Listing 9-1.

Listing 9-1. *@WebService Directive*

```
<%@ WebService Language="C#" CodeBehind="~/App_Code/Service.cs" Class="Service" %>
```

The `@WebService` directive specifies that this is a web service. Note that the `CodeBehind` attribute points to a file located in the `App_Code` folder (`Service.cs`). The `Class` attribute specifies the class from the `CodeBehind` file that contains web service functionality. If you open the `Service.cs` file, you should see something similar to Listing 9-2.

Listing 9-2. *The Web Service Class*

```
[WebService(Namespace = "http://tempuri.org/")]
public class Service : System.Web.Services.WebService
{
    [WebMethod]
    public string HelloWorld()
    {
        return "Hello World";
    }
}
```

Here we have a class called `Service` that inherits from the `System.Web.Services.WebService` class. Actually, inheriting from the `WebService` class is not mandatory, but doing so will give you added facilities such as state maintenance. Inside this class we have a public method called `HelloWorld()`. The method by itself does not contain anything special—you must have written many such methods in your own applications. What makes it special, however, is the `WebMethod` attribute, which makes the method web callable—that is, the client application can call this method over a network. Your class can contain any number of public or private methods. However, only the methods that are public and decorated with the `WebMethod` attribute are web callable.

Notice that the `Service` class is decorated with the `[WebService]` attribute. The `[WebService]` attribute is used to specify some additional information about the web service such as its description and namespace. The `Namespace` property indicates the default XML namespace to use for the XML web service. The XML namespaces allow you to uniquely identify elements and attributes from an XML document. Every web service needs to have a unique XML namespace to identify itself so that client applications can distinguish it from other web services. By default this namespace is set to `http://tempuri.org/` but it is recommended that you change it to some other URI. For example, you can use the domain name of your company as the namespace. Note that although many times the XML namespaces are URLs, they need not point to actual resources on the Web.

Run the application and you should see something similar to Figure 9-2.

You might be wondering why our web service is showing this user interface when we know that web services do not have a user interface. Actually, this is not a user interface for the web service. This interface is called a *web service help page* and allows you to test your web services. Because web services by themselves do not have a user interface, how will you or your clients test them to see whether they function correctly? To help you in such cases, ASP.NET generates these help pages automatically. At the top of the help page you will see a link titled Service Description. Just click on it and you will be presented with the WSDL of your web service (Figure 9-3).

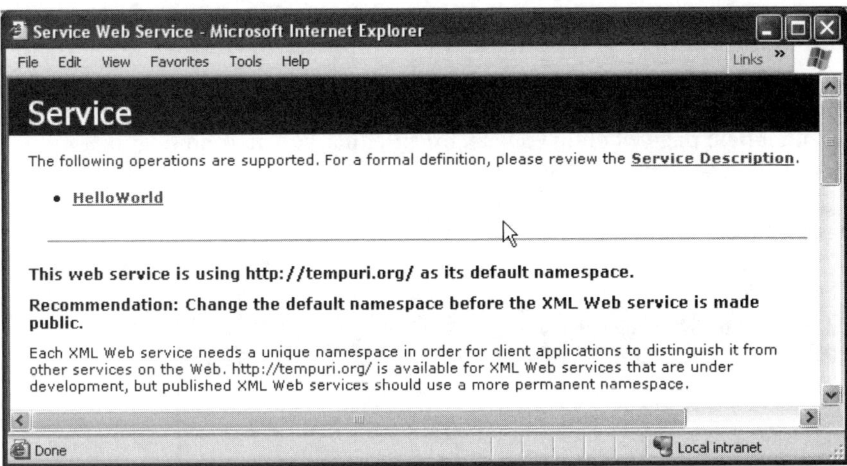

Figure 9-2. *Web Service help page*

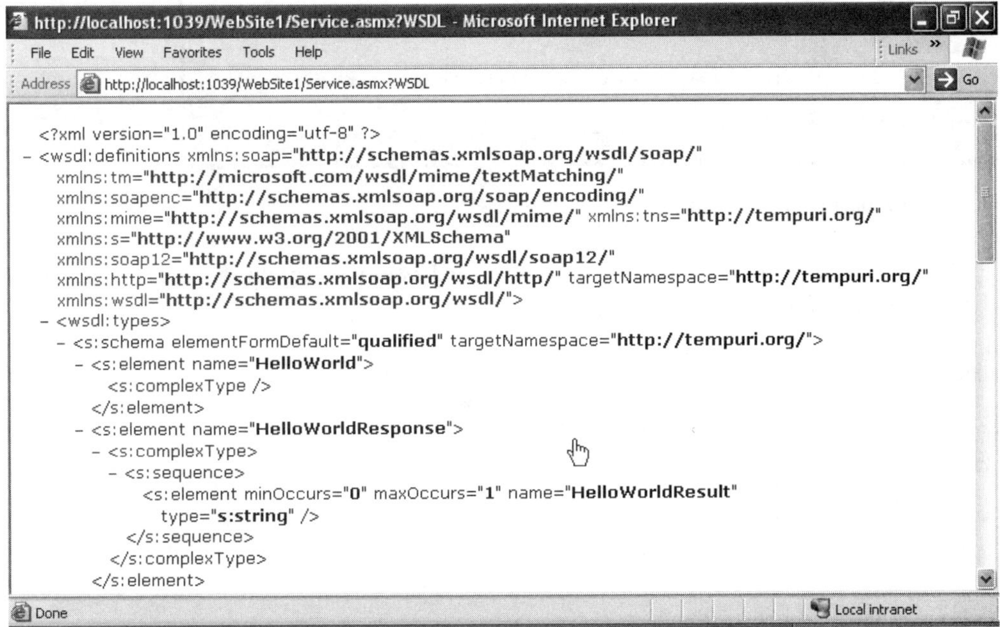

Figure 9-3. *WSDL of a web service*

Have a look in the address bar. Do you see the `WSDL` in the query string? This is how you can manually retrieve the WSDL of any ASP.NET web service. Simply attach *WSDL* at the end of the web service URL and you get the WSDL. Click the Back button to return to the previous page. You will notice the list of web methods (operations). Click on the HelloWorld web method. You will be taken to another help page wherein you can execute this web method (Figure 9-4).

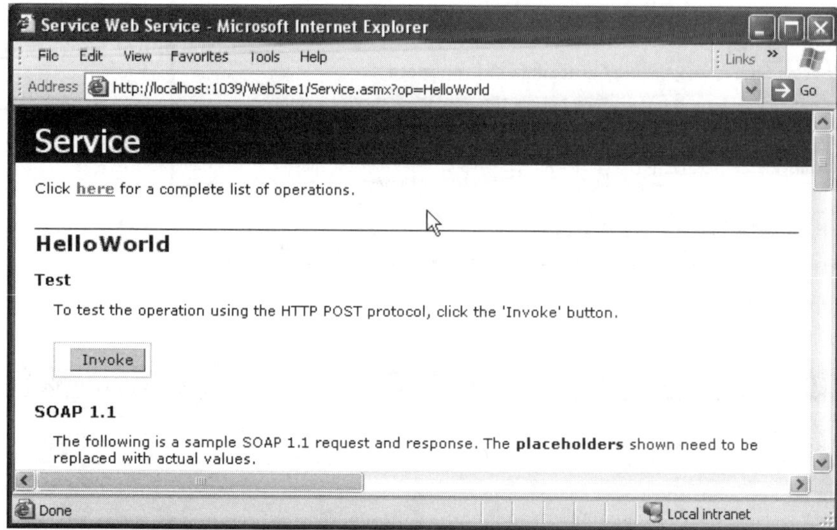

Figure 9-4. *Invoking a web method*

Before you click the Invoke button, have a look below it. You should see markup as shown in Listings 9-3 and 9-4.

Listing 9-3. *SOAP Request*

```
POST /WebServiceDemos/Service.asmx HTTP/1.1
Host: localhost
Content-Type: text/xml; charset=utf-8
Content-Length: length
SOAPAction: "http://tempuri.org/HelloWorld"

<?xml version="1.0" encoding="utf-8"?>
<soap:Envelope xmlns:xsi="http://www.w3.org/2001/XMLSchema-instance"
xmlns:xsd="http://www.w3.org/2001/XMLSchema"
xmlns:soap="http://schemas.xmlsoap.org/soap/envelope/">
  <soap:Body>
    <HelloWorld xmlns="http://tempuri.org/" />
  </soap:Body>
</soap:Envelope>
```

Listing 9-4. *SOAP Response*

```
HTTP/1.1 200 OK
Content-Type: text/xml; charset=utf-8
Content-Length: length

<?xml version="1.0" encoding="utf-8"?>
<soap:Envelope xmlns:xsi="http://www.w3.org/2001/XMLSchema-instance"
xmlns:xsd="http://www.w3.org/2001/XMLSchema"
xmlns:soap="http://schemas.xmlsoap.org/soap/envelope/">
  <soap:Body>
    <HelloWorldResponse xmlns="http://tempuri.org/">
      <HelloWorldResult>string</HelloWorldResult>
    </HelloWorldResponse>
  </soap:Body>
</soap:Envelope>
```

These two blocks represent the SOAP request being sent to the web service and the SOAP response being received from the web service. As you can see, the SOAP request and response consist of a tag called `<soap:Envelope>`. Inside there is a mandatory tag called `<soap:Body>`. The `Body` tag contains the XML data being passed or returned. There can be an optional tag, `<soap:Header>`, inside the `<soap:Envelope>` tag that can be used to pass arbitrary data to the web service.

Now click the Invoke button. The help page will execute the web method and open another window to show the web method response (Figure 9-5).

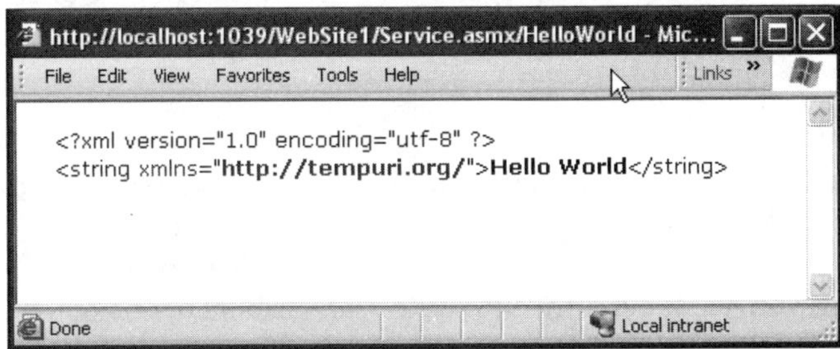

Figure 9-5. *Hello World response*

Now, close the browser and return to Visual Studio 2005. Modify the `HelloWorld()` method as shown in Listing 9-5.

Listing 9-5. *Web Method with a String Parameter*

```
[WebMethod]
public string HelloWorld(string name)
{
  return "Hello " + name;
}
```

Here we have added one string parameter to the HelloWorld() method. The method now returns Hello concatenated with the name supplied. Run the web service again. This time you should see a help page as shown in Figure 9-6 for invoking the web method.

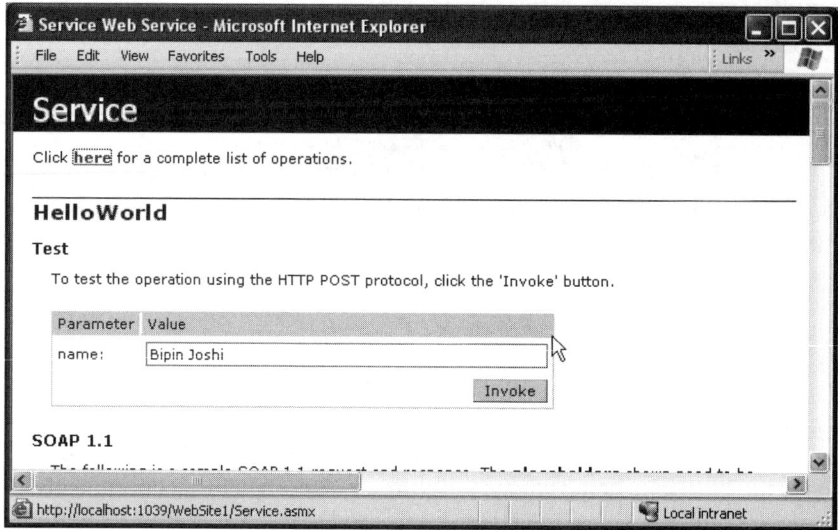

Figure 9-6. *Invoking a web method with a string parameter*

ASP.NET automatically generates a text box for you to enter the parameter. Of course this works only for primitive data types such as strings and integers. ASP.NET will not be able to do so for array, object, or collection parameters.

Creating Overloaded Web Methods

Just as you create an overloaded method for a standard class, you can also create an overloaded web method. However, this requires a bit of work on your part. If you simply create two web methods with the same name but different parameters and run the web service, you will receive an error. To rectify the error, you need to modify the WebMethod attribute of one of the web methods as shown in Listing 9-6.

Listing 9-6. *Overloading Web Methods*

```
[WebMethod]
public string HelloWorld()
{
  return "Hello World";
}
```

```
[WebMethod(MessageName="HelloWorldAgain")]
public string HelloWorld(string name)
{
  return "Hello " + name;
}
```

The code modifies the WebMethod attribute of the second method and sets the MessageName property to an alternate name (or alias) for that version of the web method. In the XML markup that is generated internally during the request and response, this alternate name is used instead of the actual method name. However, as you will see later, the proxy is intelligent enough to provide overloaded versions of web methods in the client application. Figure 9-7 shows what the overloaded web methods look like in the help page.

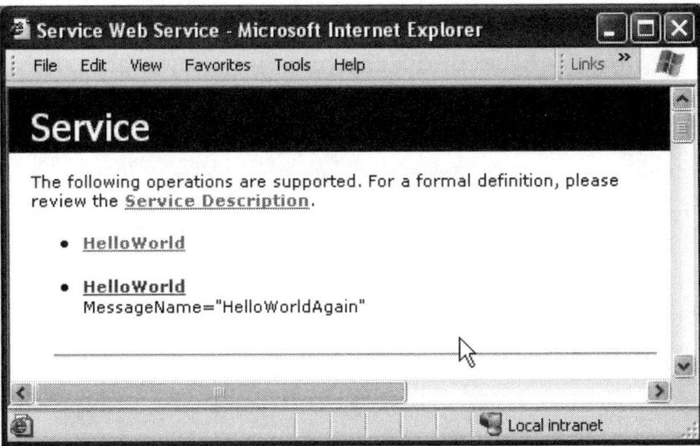

Figure 9-7. *The web method after setting the MessageName property*

Buffering the Web Method Response

You can decide whether the web method should start emitting the response back to the client immediately or buffer it until the entire serialization is over by using a property called BufferResponse. Setting this property to true buffers the response until serialization is complete and then sends all the serialized data at once to the client. Setting this property to false will return the data to the client as it is serialized. The web service's performance will be better with BufferResponse set to true because buffering the response reduces the frequent serialization calls. If your web method is returning only a small amount of data in the response stream, buffering the response will improve the performance. On the other hand, if your web method is returning a large amount of data, you may consider turning buffering off so as to avoid large memory consumption on the server.

Listing 9-7 illustrates the use of this property.

Listing 9-7. *Using the BufferResponse Property*

```
[WebMethod(BufferResponse = true)]
public string BufferMyResponse()
{
  return "Hello World";
}
```

Caching the Output of Web Methods

Caching refers to preserving the output of a web method on the web server in order to improve the performance. With caching implemented, the web service remembers what response it gave to method calls, so that when the same method calls are made again, the results are readily returned without executing the method again and again. This naturally improves the performance. To implement caching for a web method, you need to set the `CacheDuration` property of the `WebMethod` attribute to the number of seconds for which the return value of the web method is to be cached. By default the web method response is not cached. Listing 9-8 illustrates the use of this property.

Listing 9-8. *Using the CacheDuration Property*

```
[WebMethod(CacheDuration = 30)]
public string CacheMe(string name)
{
  return "Hello " + name;
}
```

Enabling Session State for Web Methods

The ASP.NET session-management feature allows you to persist user-specific data while users are using your website. You can also use the `Session` object in web services. To store data in the `Session` object, the web service class must inherit from the `System.Web.Services.WebService` base class, and the `EnableSession` property of the `WebMethod` attribute must be set to `true`. Listing 9-9 shows the use of this property.

Listing 9-9. *Using the EnableSession Property*

```
[WebMethod(EnableSession=true)]
public void PutNameInSession(string name)
{
  Session["myname"] = name;
}

[WebMethod(EnableSession = true)]
public string GetNameFromSession()
{
  return Session["myname"].ToString();
}
```

Each client session is uniquely identified by a cookie issued by the web service. In order for the web service to maintain session state for a client application, the client must save this cookie somewhere. Clients can receive the cookie by creating a new instance of a class called `CookieContainer` and assigning that to the `CookieContainer` property of the proxy class before calling the web method. This technique will be illustrated when we create the client application for our web service.

Enabling Transactions for Web Methods

In real-world financial applications, it is often necessary that certain operations be executed as a single unit or transaction. You can mark your web method to execute in a transaction by using the `TransactionOption` property of the `WebMethod` attribute. This property is an enumeration of type `System.EnterpriseServices.TransactionOption`. All the possible values of the `TransactionOption` enumeration and their effects on the web method are listed in Table 9-1.

Table 9-1. *Values of the TransactionOption Enumeration and Their Effects on the Web Method*

Value	Effect on the Web Method
`Disabled`	When a request is processed, the web service method is executed without a transaction.
`NotSupported`	When a request is processed, the web service method is executed without a transaction.
`Supported`	When a request is processed, the web method is executed without a transaction.
`Required`	When a request is processed, a new transaction will be created for the web service method.
`RequiresNew`	When a request is processed, a new transaction will be created for the web service method.

As you might have guessed, the last two options are most commonly used. If the web method throws an exception, the transaction is automatically aborted. Otherwise, the transaction is automatically committed. The code in Listing 9-10 illustrates the use of this property.

Listing 9-10. *Using the TransactionOption Property*

```
[WebMethod(TransactionOption = TransactionOption.Required)]
public string SomeMethod()
{
   //code here
}
```

Setting a Description for a Web Method

You can set a description for a web method by using the `Description` property of the `WebMethod` attribute. This description will be displayed on the help page. The code in Listing 9-11 illustrates its use.

Listing 9-11. *Using the Description Property*

```
[WebMethod(Description = "This is description for web method")]
public string DescribeMe()
{
  return "Hello World";
}
```

Returning a DataSet from a Web Method

Up until now, we have simply returned strings from our web methods. You can also return complex data types such as a DataSet from your web methods. The code in Listing 9-12 illustrates how to return a DataSet from a web method.

Listing 9-12. *Returning a DataSet from a Web Method*

```
[WebMethod]
public DataSet GetEmployees()
{
  DataSet ds = new DataSet();
  SqlDataAdapter da = new SqlDataAdapter("SELECT * FROM employees", "data ➥
source=.\\sqlexpress;initial catalog=northwind;Integrated Security=True");
  da.Fill(ds, "myemployees");
  return ds;
}
```

The code creates an instance of DataSet and SqlDataAdapter. The code then calls the Fill() method of SqlDataAdapter, which accepts two parameters: the DataSet to fill and the name of the DataTable to be created. The code then returns the DataSet to the caller. If you run this web method by using the help page, you should see something similar to Figure 9-8.

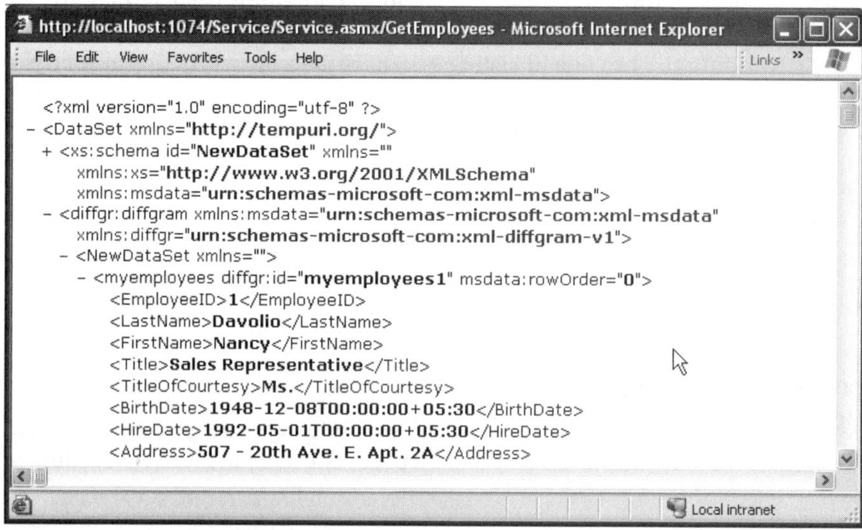

Figure 9-8. *Web method returning a DataSet*

As you can see, the entire DataSet is serialized as XML data.

Returning Custom Objects from a Web Method

In the previous examples, you saw how to return primitive data types such as a string and built-in class types such as DataSet. In this example, you will see how to return custom objects from a web method. First, you need to create a new class inside the web service project. To do so, right-click on the App_Code folder and choose Add New Item. From the dialog box that opens, select Class and call it Employee. Add the property definitions as shown in Listing 9-13 to the Employee class.

Listing 9-13. *Creating the Employee Class*

```
public class Employee
{
    private int intID;
    private string strFName;
    private string strLName;
    private string strHPhone;
    private string strNotes;

    public int EmployeeID
    {
        get
        {
            return intID;
        }
        set
        {
            intID = value;
        }
    }

    public string FirstName
    {
        get
        {
            return strFName;
        }
        set
        {
            strFName = value;
        }
    }
```

```
    public string LastName
    {
        get
        {
            return strLName;
        }
        set
        {
            strLName = value;
        }
    }

    public string HomePhone
    {
        get
        {
            return strHPhone;
        }
        set
        {
            strHPhone = value;
        }
    }

    public string Notes
    {
        get
        {
            return strNotes;
        }
        set
        {
            strNotes = value;
        }
    }
}
```

The code creates a class named `Employee` with five public properties: `EmployeeID`, `FirstName`, `LastName`, `HomePhone`, and `Notes`. Note that when an instance of any class is serialized as a return value of a web method, only the public members are serialized. Next, we will create a web method called `GetEmployee()` that creates an instance of the `Employee` class, sets its properties, and returns it back to the client. Listing 9-14 shows the `GetEmployee()` method.

Listing 9-14. *Returning an Object from a Web Method*

```
[WebMethod]
public Employee GetEmployee()
{
        Employee emp = new Employee();
        emp.EmployeeID = 1;
        emp.FirstName = "Nancy";
        emp.LastName = "Davolio";
        emp.HomePhone = "(206) 555-9857";
        emp.Notes = "Notes go here";
        return emp;
    }
```

If you invoke the web method via the help page, you should see something similar to Figure 9-9.

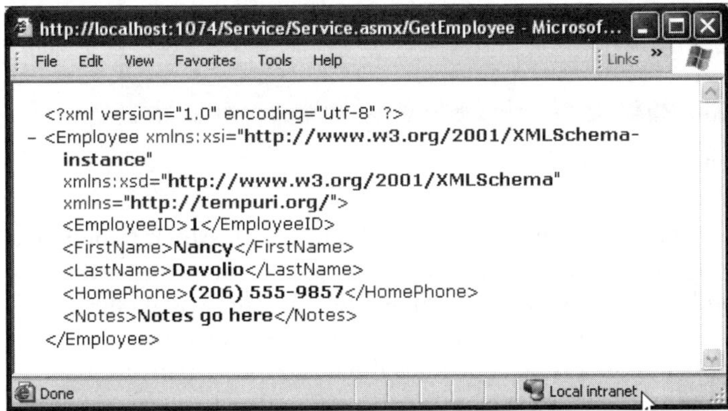

Figure 9-9. *Returning a custom object from web methods*

You will find that the output is very similar to the one generated during XML serialization in Chapter 8.

Creating a Proxy for a Web Service

To create a proxy for the web service by using Visual Studio, you must first create the client application because the proxy always resides there. Though any type of application can act as a client to the web service, as an example we will create a Windows application that consumes the web service.

Create a new Windows application in Visual Studio. Right-click on the project in Solution Explorer and choose Add Web Reference. The Add Web Reference dialog box will be displayed, as shown in Figure 9-10.

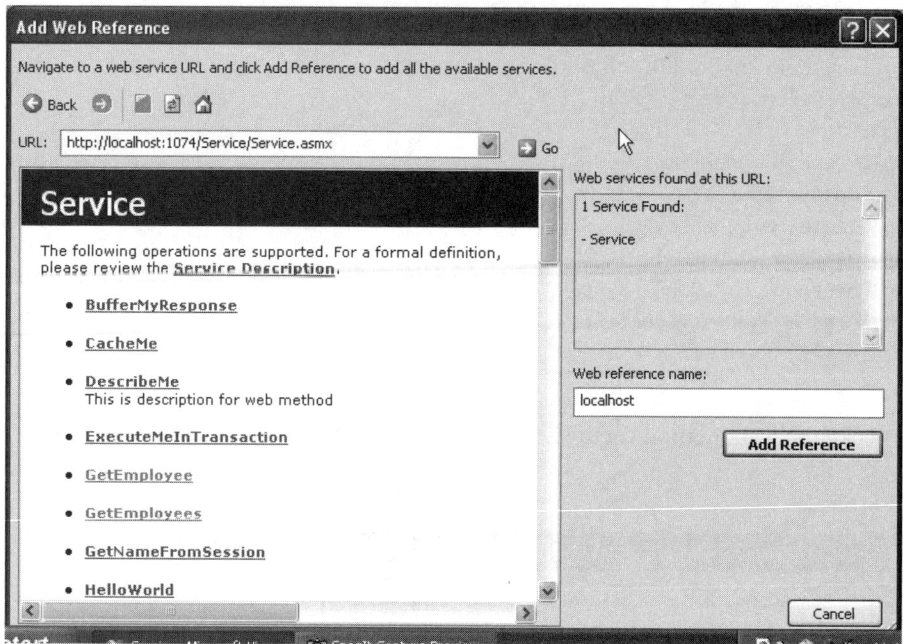

Figure 9-10. *The Add Web Reference dialog box*

A *web reference* is nothing but a proxy class that allows you to use classes and methods exposed by a web service in your client application. In this dialog box, enter the complete URL of the `Service.asmx` file and click the Go button. You will see the same help page as before. In the Web Reference Name text box, key in a name for the web reference or leave it unchanged. Whatever you supply in this text box becomes the namespace name for the proxy class being created. Click the Add Reference button. Your Solution Explorer should now look like Figure 9-11.

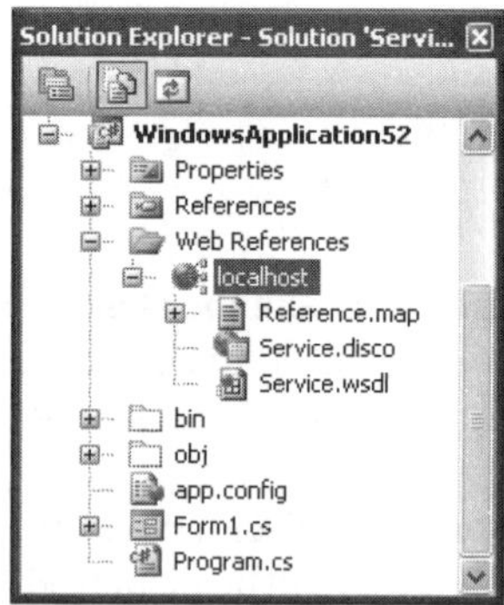

Figure 9-11. *Web References folder*

Note how a new folder called `Web References` has been added with a subfolder called `localhost`. The `localhost` folder further contains a WSDL file. There will also be a file called `Reference.cs`. This file contains the source code of the web service proxy class. If you change the web service after adding the proxy, you need to update the web reference again. You can do so by right-clicking on the web reference and selecting the Update Web Reference option.

Creating a Form That Consumes a Web Method

To demonstrate how to call web methods, you will need to create a form that will display the records from the `Employees` table. The form should look like Figure 9-12.

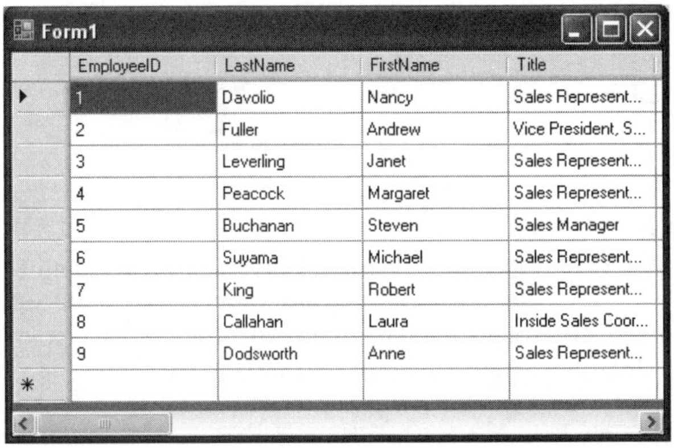

Form1

EmployeeID	LastName	FirstName	Title
1	Davolio	Nancy	Sales Represent...
2	Fuller	Andrew	Vice President, S...
3	Leverling	Janet	Sales Represent...
4	Peacock	Margaret	Sales Represent...
5	Buchanan	Steven	Sales Manager
6	Suyama	Michael	Sales Represent...
7	King	Robert	Sales Represent...
8	Callahan	Laura	Inside Sales Coor...
9	Dodsworth	Anne	Sales Represent...

Figure 9-12. *Application that calls the GetEmployees() web method*

The application consists of a DataGridView control that displays all the records from the `Employees` table of the `Northwind` database. Import the `localhost` namespace in your project (recollect that we have specified the web reference name as `localhost`). In the `Load` event of the form, write the code shown in Listing 9-15.

Listing 9-15. *Calling a Web Method*

```
private void Form1_Load(object sender, EventArgs e)
{
  Service proxy = new Service();
  DataSet ds = proxy.GetEmployees();
  dataGridView1.DataSource = ds.Tables["myemployees"].DefaultView;
}
```

The code creates an instance of the proxy class. Note that `Service` is the proxy class, not the web service class itself. We then call the `GetEmployees()` method of the proxy, which in turn will call the actual `GetEmployees()` web method of the web service. Remember that the return value of `GetEmployees()` is a `DataSet` populated with records from the `Employees` table. The code then binds the `DataSet` to the DataGridView. If you run the application, you should see the DataGridView populated with records from the `Employees` table.

Storing Values in a Web Service Session

Recollect that earlier we created two web methods—`PutNameInSession()` and `GetNameFromSession()`—that deal with session storage. Let's see how you can call these methods in the client application. To see how this works, you need to create an application as shown in Figure 9-13.

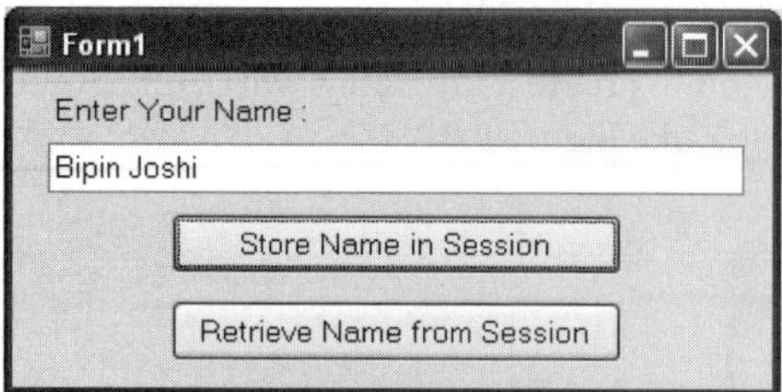

Figure 9-13. *Storing session values*

The application consists of a text box and two buttons. The text box accepts a name that is to be stored in a session variable. The Store Name in Session button calls the `PutNameInSession()` web method and stores the name in a session variable. The Retrieve Name from Session button calls the `GetNameFromSession()` web method and displays the returned name in a message box. Listing 9-16 shows the code that is responsible for storing the name in a session variable.

Listing 9-16. *Storing a Value in a Session Variable*

```
CookieContainer cookiecontainer = new CookieContainer();
private void button1_Click(object sender, EventArgs e)
{
  Service proxy = new Service();
  proxy.CookieContainer = cookiecontainer;
  proxy.PutNameInSession(textBox1.Text);
}
```

The code creates a form-level variable of type `CookieContainer`, which resides in the `System.Net` namespace and acts as storage for cookies. You might be wondering why we need this class. By default the session management of web services depends on a cookie, and the web service needs to identify each and every session with the help of a unique identifier. This identifier is passed to and fro with the help of a cookie.

The code then creates an instance of the web service proxy class. It sets its `CookieContainer` property to the `CookieContainer` object we just created. The `CookieContainer` property of the proxy class specifies the storage for the cookies created during the web service communication. Finally, the code calls the `PutNameInSession()` method of the proxy by passing the name entered in the text box. The `Click` event handler of the Retrieve Name from Session button contains the code shown in Listing 9-17.

Listing 9-17. *Retrieving a Value Stored in a Session Variable*

```
private void button2_Click(object sender, EventArgs e)
{
  Service proxy = new Service();
  proxy.CookieContainer = cookiecontainer;
  MessageBox.Show(proxy.GetNameFromSession());
}
```

The code creates an instance of the proxy class as before. It then sets the `CookieContainer` property of the proxy to the `CookieContainer` object we created previously. This way, the previously issued session identifier can be passed back to the web service. Finally, the `GetNameFromSession()` method is called. The value returned by the `GetNameFromSession()` method is displayed in a message box.

Changing a Web Service URL at Run Time

While developing clients for a web service, you add a web reference to the web service by specifying the URL of the .ASMX file, and it is this URL that Visual Studio uses when generating the required proxy object. However, after adding a web reference, the web service could be moved to some other location. In such cases, the easiest way out is to re-create the proxy object. But what if this happens after you deploy your web service client? It would be nice if you could change the URL programmatically so that even if the original web service is moved, your clients need not be recompiled. The `Url` property of the web service proxy class allows you to do just that. Listing 9-18 shows the relevant code.

Listing 9-18. *Changing the Web Service URL at Run Time*

```
Service proxy=new Service();
proxy.Url="http://localhost/newlocation/Service.asmx";
```

Calling a Web Method Asynchronously

Up until now, we have called web methods synchronously. That means that unless the web method is not finished, our form processing is blocked. Synchronous calls are what you need in most applications, but at times you may need to call web methods in asynchronous fashion.

Imagine that you are developing a portal by using ASP.NET 2.0. As a part of the feature set, you want to provide a facility whereby users can get a comparative price list of computer books. The users will specify a book title whose price list is to be generated. To obtain the cost of the book, you consume web services exposed by various book suppliers. That means for a book title you call many web methods that return the cost of the title by individual suppliers. You then collectively display the costs to the user. If you call the web methods in synchronous fashion, the total time taken will be the summation of the processing time taken by the individual web methods. On the other hand, if you call the web methods in asynchronous fashion, the time taken will be reduced to the processing time taken by the lengthiest web method (Figure 9-14).

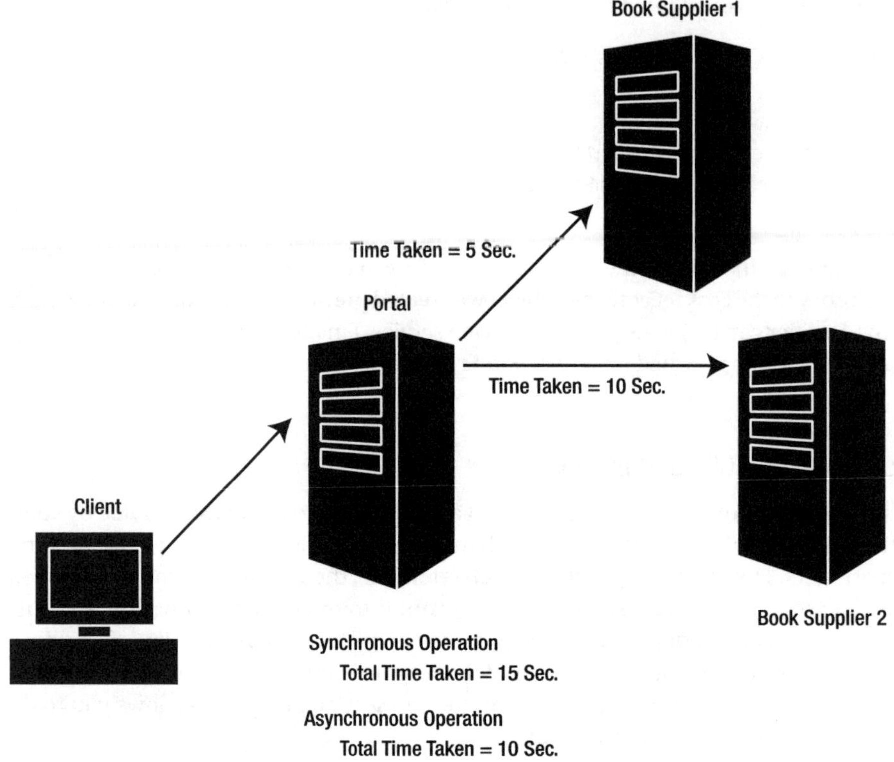

Figure 9-14. *Asynchronous web method calls*

In a traditional approach, you might have created threads manually and then executed each individual web method call on a separate thread. Fortunately, the web service proxy automatically provides the entire infrastructure needed to call web methods asynchronously. The proxy automatically creates methods of the form `XXXXAsync()`, where `XXXX` is the name of your web method. For example, if your web method name is `HelloWorld()`, there will be a method called `HelloWorldAsync()`. Calling this method invokes the web method in asynchronous fashion.

After the web method has completed its processing, the proxy raises an event of the form `XXXXComplete`, where `XXXX` is the name of your web method. Taking the preceding example further, you will have the `HelloWorldComplete` event for your proxy. The automatically generated events are based on an automatically generated delegate. The delegate will be of the form `XXXXEventHandler`, where `XXXX` is the name of the event. You can use this event to trap the return value of the web method.

To see how a web method can be called asynchronously, we will modify the example shown previously in Figure 9-12. The modified code is shown in Listing 9-19.

Listing 9-19. *Calling a Web Method Asynchronously*

```
private void Form1_Load(object sender, EventArgs e)
{
  Service proxy = new Service();
  proxy.GetEmployeesCompleted +=
    new GetEmployeesCompletedEventHandler(proxy_GetEmployeesCompleted);
  proxy.GetEmployeesAsync();
}

void proxy_GetEmployeesCompleted(object sender, GetEmployeesCompletedEventArgs e)
{
  DataSet ds = e.Result;
  dataGridView1.DataSource = ds.Tables["myemployees"].DefaultView;
}
```

The code creates an instance of the web service proxy class in the `Load` event handler of the form. Notice how the proxy automatically contains the `GetEmployeesCompleted` event and the `GetEmployeesCompletedEventHandler` delegate. The code then wires this event to its event handler function, `proxy_GetEmployeesCompleted()`. Finally, the `GetEmployeesAsync()` method of the proxy is called to start executing the web method in asynchronous fashion.

After the execution is done, the proxy will raise the `GetEmployeesCompleted` event handler, which receives a parameter of type `GetEmployeesCompletedEventArgs`. This event argument parameter has a property called `Result` that gives you the actual return value of the web method. In our case, the return value is a `DataSet` and hence the code collects it in a `DataSet` variable. The DataGridView control is then bound with this returned `DataSet`.

Understanding SOAP

In the previous section, you learned that SOAP is a lightweight XML-based protocol that forms one of the building blocks of the web service infrastructure. You also learned how web service requests and responses are encoded in SOAP format. Now it's time to peek inside SOAP in a bit of detail. Have a look at Listing 9-20.

Listing 9-20. *SOAP Request*

```
POST /WebServiceDemos/Service.asmx HTTP/1.1
Host: localhost
Content-Type: text/xml; charset=utf-8
Content-Length: length
SOAPAction: "http://tempuri.org/HelloWorld"
```

```
<?xml version="1.0" encoding="utf-8"?>
<soap:Envelope xmlns:xsi="http://www.w3.org/2001/XMLSchema-instance"
xmlns:xsd="http://www.w3.org/2001/XMLSchema"
xmlns:soap="http://schemas.xmlsoap.org/soap/envelope/">
  <soap:Body>
    <HelloWorld xmlns="http://tempuri.org/" />
  </soap:Body>
</soap:Envelope>
```

As you might have guessed, Listing 9-20 represents a SOAP request. If you observe this markup carefully, you will find that the request consists of an envelope (`<soap:Envelope>`) and body (`<soap:Body>`). In fact, a SOAP request or response can contain four possible parts. Each of these parts is described in Table 9-2.

Table 9-2. *Parts of a SOAP Message*

Part	Description
Envelope	The SOAP envelope wraps the SOAP request or response. It is the root element of the SOAP message and is represented by the `<soap:Envelope>` markup tag. All SOAP messages must have an envelope.
Header	SOAP headers are an optional part of a SOAP message. They are used to pass arbitrary data to and from the web service and its client. For example, you can use them to pass authentication information to the web service. A SOAP header is represented by the `<soap:Header>` markup tag.
Body	The SOAP body is a mandatory part of a SOAP message. It includes the actual request or response data in XML format. The SOAP body is represented by the `<soap:Body>` markup tag.
Fault	A SOAP fault is an optional part of a SOAP message. It comes into the picture whenever there is a runtime exception in the web service. The exception details are enclosed in the `<soap:Fault>` tag and sent back to the client application.

Using SOAP Headers

In this section, you will develop an application that illustrates the use of SOAP headers for user authentication purposes. The application passes user credentials to the web service via a custom SOAP header. The web service tries to authenticate the user on the basis of these credentials and returns the requested data if authentication is successful.

To begin developing the application, you need to create a new web service by using Visual Studio. Then add a class called `User` in the `App_Code` folder. This class represents a user of the web service and contains two public properties: `UserID` and `Password`. Listing 9-21 shows the completed `User` class.

Listing 9-21. *Creating a Custom Class That Inherits from the SoapHeader Class*

```
public class User:SoapHeader
{
    private string strUid;
    private string strPwd;

    public string UserID
    {
        get
        {
            return strUid;
        }
        set
        {
            strUid=value;
        }
    }

    public string Password
    {
        get
        {
            return strPwd;
        }
        set
        {
            strPwd = value;
        }
    }
}
```

Notice that the `User` class inherits from the `SoapHeader` base class, which resides in the `System.Web.Services.Protocols` namespace and represents a basic SOAP header. All the custom SOAP header classes must inherit directly or indirectly from the `SoapHeader` class. Make sure that you have imported the `System.Web.Services.Protocols` namespace before creating the `User` class.

The `User` class simply contains two public properties: `UserID` and `Password`. After you create the `User` class, you can create the web service as shown in Listing 9-22.

Listing 9-22. *Using a SOAP Header*

```
public class Service : System.Web.Services.WebService
{
  public User CurrentUser;

 [WebMethod]
 [SoapHeader("CurrentUser",Direction=SoapHeaderDirection.In,Required=true)]
  public DataSet GetEmployees()
  {
    if (CurrentUser == null)
    {
      throw new SoapHeaderException("Authentication details not found!",
                                    SoapException.ClientFaultCode);
    }
    if (CurrentUser.UserID == "Admin" && CurrentUser.Password == "password")
    {
      DataSet ds = new DataSet();
      SqlDataAdapter da =
        new SqlDataAdapter("SELECT * FROM employees", ➥
  "data source=.\\sqlexpress;initial catalog=northwind;Integrated Security=True");
      da.Fill(ds, "myemployees");
      return ds;
    }
    else
    {
      throw new SoapException("Authentication failed!",
                              SoapException.ClientFaultCode);
    }
  }
}
```

Examine the web service class carefully. At the top it declares a variable of type `User`. The `GetEmployees()` web method fills a `DataSet` with all the records from the `Employees` table and returns the `DataSet` back to the caller. The important thing to note about the `GetEmployees()` web method is that it is decorated with the `SoapHeader` attribute. This is how you inform the web method that a SOAP header is to be processed.

The `SoapHeader` attribute specifies one parameter and two properties. The first parameter specifies the instance name of the SOAP header class that we wish to use. In our example, the name of the `User` variable is `CurrentUser` and hence that is what we pass to the web method. This instance variable must be available publicly in the web service class. The `Direction` property indicates the direction of the SoapHeader and is of enumeration type SoapHeaderDirection. The possible values of the SoapHeaderDirection enumeration are as follows:

> In: The direction of In indicates that the SOAP header is passed from the client to the web service.
>
> Out: The direction of Out indicates that the SOAP header is passed from the web service to the client.
>
> InOut: The direction of InOut indicates that the SOAP header is passed to and from the web service and its client.

The Required property indicates that the presence of the SOAP header is mandatory.

Inside the GetEmployees() web method, we check whether the SOAP header is null. If so, this indicates that the authentication details were not sent and hence the code raises a SoapHeaderException. The SoapHeaderException class is used to represent an error in the SOAP header. The first parameter of the SoapHeaderException constructor is the error message, and the second parameter is the SOAP fault code for the client call. The code then checks the user credentials. If the credentials are correct, a DataSet is created and filled with all the records from the Employees table. Otherwise, a SoapException is raised. The SoapException class is used to represent an error with the SOAP request processing. The constructor of SoapException takes the same two parameters as the SoapHeaderException class.

To consume the web service you just created, you need to develop a client application as shown in Figure 9-15.

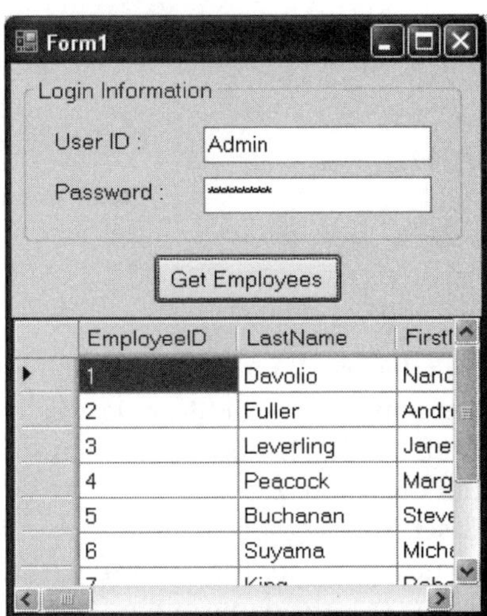

Figure 9-15. *Application that uses SOAP headers*

The application consists of two text boxes for specifying the user ID and password. The Get Employees button calls the GetEmployees() web method and displays the results in a DataGridView control. After you create the user interface of the application, add a web reference to the web service. Then write the code as shown in Listing 9-23 in the Click event of the Get Employees button.

Listing 9-23. *Passing a SOAP Header from the Client to the Web Service*

```
private void button1_Click(object sender, EventArgs e)
{
  Service proxy = new Service();
  if (textBox1.Text != "" && textBox2.Text != "")
  {
    User currentuser = new User();
    currentuser.UserID = textBox1.Text;
    currentuser.Password = textBox2.Text;
    proxy.UserValue = currentuser;
  }
  try
  {
    DataSet ds = proxy.GetEmployees();
    dataGridView1.DataSource = ds.Tables["myemployees"].DefaultView;
  }
  catch (SoapHeaderException ex2)
  {
    MessageBox.Show(ex2.Message + "[" + ex2.Code + "]");
  }
  catch (SoapException ex1)
  {
    MessageBox.Show(ex1.Message + "[" + ex1.Code + "]");
  }
}
```

Notice the code marked in bold. The code checks whether the user ID and password have been entered. If so, it creates an instance of the User class. Remember that this User class is created when you add a web reference to the web service. Then the UserID and Password properties of the User class are set with corresponding values from the text boxes.

Next, the UserValue property of the web service proxy is set. You might be wondering where this UserValue property has come from. When you create a proxy for the web service, it automatically creates a property of the form XXXXValue, where XXXX is the name of the SOAP header class. The type of the XXXXValue property is the same as the class XXXX. After this property has been set, the GetEmployees() web method is called and the DataSet returned is bound to the DataGridView control.

The code also has some exception-handling code. The try...catch block checks for two types of exceptions: SoapHeaderException and SoapException. Remember that these are the same exceptions that we raise from the web service if there is an authentication error. The

Message property of both of these exception classes gives you the detailed error message, and the Code property gives the SOAP fault code details.

To test the application, run it and click the Get Employees button without specifying any credentials. You should get a message box as shown in Figure 9-16 that informs you about the SoapHeaderException.

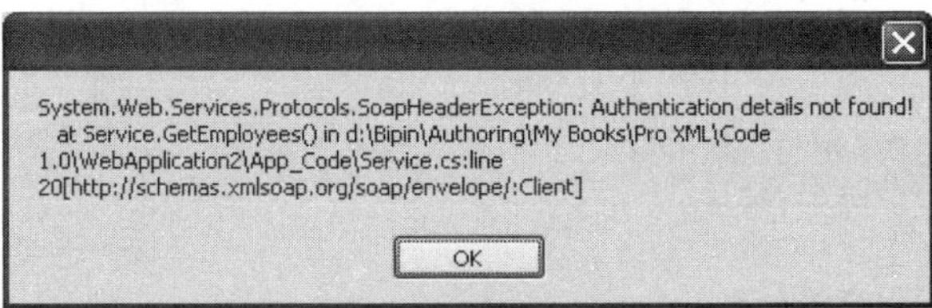

Figure 9-16. *Catching a SoapHeaderException*

Similarly, enter some invalid credentials and click the Get Employees button again. This time the message box should resemble Figure 9-17.

Figure 9-17. *Catching SoapException*

Finally, if you supply valid credentials and then click the Get Employees button, your form should resemble Figure 9-15.

Understanding the WSDL Document

While developing your first web service in this chapter, you learned that WSDL is an XML vocabulary that describes the web service in terms of web methods exposed, their parameters, data types, and return values. Though you will rarely modify or construct WSDL yourself (at least when you are using Visual Studio), it is helpful to understand the internal structure of the WSDL document. This way, your understanding of the web service metadata will broaden. You will also find the knowledge of WSDL useful while learning Windows Communication Foundation services, which are covered in Chapter 12.

Let's see the WSDL of a simple Hello World web service that we created initially in this chapter. We will be using this web service only as a sample. The discussion that follows is applicable to any other WSDL document also. The WSDL of the preceding web service is shown in Listing 9-24.

Listing 9-24. *A Sample WSDL Document*

```
<?xml version="1.0" encoding="utf-8"?>
<wsdl:definitions xmlns:soap="http://schemas.xmlsoap.org/wsdl/soap/"
xmlns:tm="http://microsoft.com/wsdl/mime/textMatching/"
xmlns:soapenc="http://schemas.xmlsoap.org/soap/encoding/"
xmlns:mime="http://schemas.xmlsoap.org/wsdl/mime/"
xmlns:tns="http://tempuri.org/"
xmlns:s="http://www.w3.org/2001/XMLSchema"
xmlns:soap12="http://schemas.xmlsoap.org/wsdl/soap12/"
xmlns:http="http://schemas.xmlsoap.org/wsdl/http/"
targetNamespace="http://tempuri.org/"
xmlns:wsdl="http://schemas.xmlsoap.org/wsdl/">
  <wsdl:types>
    <s:schema elementFormDefault="qualified" targetNamespace="http://tempuri.org/">
      <s:element name="HelloWorld">
        <s:complexType />
      </s:element>
      <s:element name="HelloWorldResponse">
        <s:complexType>
          <s:sequence>
            <s:element minOccurs="0" maxOccurs="1" name="HelloWorldResult"
                       type="s:string" />
          </s:sequence>
        </s:complexType>
      </s:element>
    </s:schema>
  </wsdl:types>
  <wsdl:message name="HelloWorldSoapIn">
    <wsdl:part name="parameters" element="tns:HelloWorld" />
  </wsdl:message>
  <wsdl:message name="HelloWorldSoapOut">
    <wsdl:part name="parameters" element="tns:HelloWorldResponse" />
  </wsdl:message>
  <wsdl:portType name="ServiceSoap">
    <wsdl:operation name="HelloWorld">
      <wsdl:input message="tns:HelloWorldSoapIn" />
      <wsdl:output message="tns:HelloWorldSoapOut" />
    </wsdl:operation>
  </wsdl:portType>
```

```
  <wsdl:binding name="ServiceSoap" type="tns:ServiceSoap">
    <soap:binding transport="http://schemas.xmlsoap.org/soap/http" />
    <wsdl:operation name="HelloWorld">
      <soap:operation soapAction="http://tempuri.org/HelloWorld" style="document" />
      <wsdl:input>
        <soap:body use="literal" />
      </wsdl:input>
      <wsdl:output>
        <soap:body use="literal" />
      </wsdl:output>
    </wsdl:operation>
  </wsdl:binding>
  <wsdl:binding name="ServiceSoap12" type="tns:ServiceSoap">
    <soap12:binding transport="http://schemas.xmlsoap.org/soap/http" />
    <wsdl:operation name="HelloWorld">
      <soap12:operation soapAction="http://tempuri.org/HelloWorld"
                        style="document" />
      <wsdl:input>
        <soap12:body use="literal" />
      </wsdl:input>
      <wsdl:output>
        <soap12:body use="literal" />
      </wsdl:output>
    </wsdl:operation>
  </wsdl:binding>
  <wsdl:service name="Service">
    <wsdl:port name="ServiceSoap" binding="tns:ServiceSoap">
      <soap:address location="http://localhost:2230/WebApplication3/Service.asmx" />
    </wsdl:port>
    <wsdl:port name="ServiceSoap12" binding="tns:ServiceSoap12">
      <soap12:address
          location="http://localhost:2230/WebApplication3/Service.asmx" />
    </wsdl:port>
  </wsdl:service>
</wsdl:definitions>
```

If you observe the WSDL markup in Listing 9-24, you can identify six parts of the document. These six parts are the core elements of any WSDL document and are listed in Table 9-3.

Table 9-3. *Parts of WSDL*

Part	Description
types	The <wsdl:types> element encloses all the type definitions from the web service.
message	A message is the XML data that is being carried between the web service and its client. The <wsdl:message> element represents this message.
portType	The <wsdl:portType> section contains a list of operations (web methods) exposed by the web service.
binding	A binding is the protocol and format used by the port. It is represented by the <wsdl:binding> markup tag.
port	A port is an end point of web service communication. It is represented by the <wsdl:port> markup tag.
service	A service is the collection of one or more ports. It is represented by the <wsdl:service> markup tag.

Let's look at each of these parts in more detail.

The Messages

You learned previously that web service communication works on the basis of a request and response model. A web service request as well as response consists of SOAP data. This SOAP data is called a *SOAP message*. Each web method has a message that represents a request for the web method and a message that represents the response from that web method. Thus our HelloWorld() web method will have two messages:

- The name of the request message is of the form XXXXSoapIn, where XXXX is the name of the web method.
- Similarly, the name of the response message is of the form XXXXSoapOut, where XXXX is the name of the web method.

The WSDL message elements provide a consolidated list of all the messages exposed by the web service. The message names provided by this list are used everywhere else in the WSDL document.

The Type Definitions

Each message in a web service has a specific structure, or schema. This schema is specified by the types element of the WSDL document. If you observe the types section in the WSDL mentioned earlier, you will find that it specifies a schema of two messages: HelloWorld and HelloWorldResponse. You will also notice that the data type of the return value is specified here. This schema closely matches the XSD schema you saw in earlier chapters.

The Port Types

A web service consists of one or more operations. In simple terms, an *operation* is analogous to a function or method. Each operation has an input message (request) and an output message (response). All the operations of a web service are listed under the `portType` section. The port name is of the form `XXXXSoap`, where `XXXX` is the name of the web service class. Thus our sample web service has one operation called `HelloWorld`. The `HelloWorld` operation consists of two messages. The input message name is `HelloWorldSoapIn`, and the output message name is `HelloWorldSoapOut`. Recollect that these message names were defined earlier in the message section.

The Binding

A *binding* specifies the message format and protocol for each port type. For example, in our web service there is a binding defined for the `ServiceSoap` port type. The linking between a binding and port type is the `type` attribute of the `<wsdl:binding>` element. The binding name is of the form `XXXXSoap`, where `XXXX` is the name of the web service class. Thus our WSDL has a binding defined named `ServiceSoap` that is for a port type `ServiceSoap`.

The Service

A *service* is a set of ports and bindings. A web service port is a logical end point for a web service. A service has the same name as the web service class. In our example, the `service` element defines a port called `ServiceSoap` and links it with the `ServiceSoap` binding.

A Summary of WSDL

To summarize what we have discussed:

- Every web service consists of one or more operations.
- Each operation typically has a request message and a response message.
- Each message is listed in the `message` section of the WSDL.
- The schema of all the messages are defined by the `types` section of the WSDL.
- All the operations exposed by a web service are listed under the `portType` section of the WSDL.
- For each port type, a transport format and protocol needs to be specified. This is referred to as *binding*.
- The binding for a port type is specified by the `binding` section of the WSDL.
- The `service` section of the WSDL defines an end point for the web service called a *port*.
- A port has a specific binding associated with it.

Summary

In this chapter, you learned one of the powerful features of the .NET Framework: web services. Web services are a programmable set of APIs that can be called over a network by using industry standards such as XML, SOAP, and HTTP. Web services can prove to be very beneficial in areas such as application integration, cross-platform communication, and distributed communication over the Internet.

You learned to create web services, a proxy for the web service, and a client that consumes the web service. You also learned many features that can be implemented on your web methods such as caching, response buffering, and transactions. Finally, you peeked into the internal structure of SOAP and WSDL.

CHAPTER 10

XML in SQL Server 2005

Most business applications store data in some kind of data store, which is usually a relational database. To that end, SQL Server is one of Microsoft's flagship products. With the increasing use of XML in business applications, Microsoft found it necessary to incorporate strong support for XML in their database engine also, with SQL Server 2000 being possibly the first version where this XML integration was clearly visible.

Since then, Microsoft has added many other features to SQL Server 2005. Because SQL Server is such a popular database, it is worth learning its XML features. Moreover, it would be interesting to see how these features can be consumed from the applications built on top of the .NET Framework. In this chapter, you will learn about the following:

- Using XML extensions to the `SELECT` statement of SQL Server 2005
- Using SQLXML managed classes
- Working with the new `XML` data type
- Creating web services native to SQL Server 2005

You should note, however, that an extensive examination of all the XML features of SQL Server 2005 is out of scope of this book. The intention here is to make you familiar with the XML capabilities of SQL Server 2005.

Using XML Extensions to the SELECT Statement

As of SQL Server 2000, you can execute `SELECT` statements that return the results in XML format. In Chapter 7, you got a taste of this feature while using the `ExecuteXmlReader()` method of the `SqlCommand` class. Now it's time to look at these extensions in detail.

The FOR XML Clause

To fetch `FOR XML` clause SQL Server data in XML format, you need to use the `FOR XML` clause with the `SELECT` statement. The `FOR XML` clause has four modes that allow you to return the XML results in different formats. The modes of the `FOR XML` clause are listed in Table 10-1.

Table 10-1. *Modes of the FOR XML Clause*

Mode	Description
AUTO	The AUTO mode returns the results of the SELECT query as XML fragments. By default it returns the data as XML elements. The name of the XML element is the same as the table name, and column values are returned as XML attributes. You have the option to return all the columns as elements instead of attributes.
RAW	The RAW mode returns the results as a <row> element. The column values are returned as XML attributes.
PATH	The PATH mode allows you to define the nesting of the returned XML by using simple XPath syntax.
EXPLICIT	The EXPLICIT mode defines a schema for the returned results explicitly in the SELECT query.

To test these modes of the FOR XML clause, you will execute some SELECT queries against the famous Northwind database by using the SQL Server 2005 Management Studio, shown in Figure 10-1.

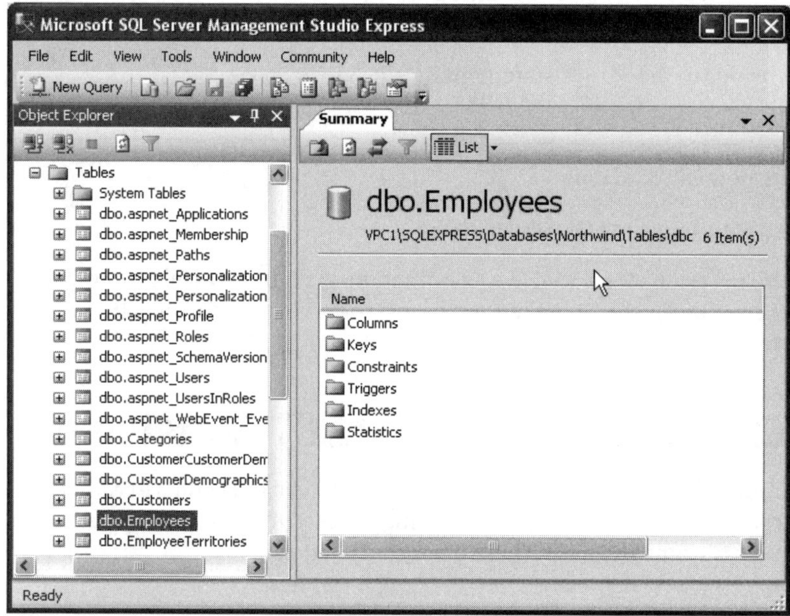

Figure 10-1. *The SQL Server 2005 Management Studio*

■ **Note** To work with the examples discussed in this chapter, you need to have SQL Server 2005 or SQL Server 2005 Express Edition, SQL Server 2005 Management Studio, and SQLXML managed classes installed on your machine.

The AUTO Mode

Open SQL Server 2005 Management Studio and issue the SELECT statement shown in Listing 10-1.

Listing 10-1. *Using the AUTO Mode of the FOR XML Clause*

```
SELECT EMPLOYEEID,FIRSTNAME,LASTNAME FROM EMPLOYEES FOR XML AUTO
```

```
<EMPLOYEES EMPLOYEEID="1" FIRSTNAME="Nancy" LASTNAME="Davolio"/>
<EMPLOYEES EMPLOYEEID="2" FIRSTNAME="Andrew" LASTNAME="Fuller"/>
<EMPLOYEES EMPLOYEEID="3" FIRSTNAME="Janet" LASTNAME="Leverling"/>
....
```

The SELECT statement from Listing 10-1 selects three columns—EmployeeID, FirstName, and LastName—from the Employees table. Listing 10-1 also shows the returned data in XML format. Notice how the table name is used for the XML element names (<EMPLOYEES>), and column names are used for attribute names.

Have you noticed something about the character casing of the returned XML? It depends totally on the table name and columns used in the SELECT statement. For example, if you specify column names in uppercase, the XML attributes will be in uppercase. You may need to keep this in mind while parsing the XML data in your application. By default the AUTO mode returns all the column values as XML attributes. If you wish, you can return them as elements instead. This is achieved by using the ELEMENTS clause with the AUTO mode. Listing 10-2 shows how the ELEMENTS clause works.

Listing 10-2. *Using the ELEMENTS Clause of the AUTO Mode*

```
SELECT EMPLOYEEID,FIRSTNAME,LASTNAME FROM EMPLOYEES FOR XML AUTO,ELEMENTS
```

```
<EMPLOYEES>
<EMPLOYEEID>1</EMPLOYEEID>
<FIRSTNAME>Nancy</FIRSTNAME>
<LASTNAME>Davolio</LASTNAME>
</EMPLOYEES>
....
```

As you can see, we specify the ELEMENTS clause after the AUTO mode. Notice how the column values are returned as elements this time. The names of the elements are the same as the column names.

Note The XML data returned by the FOR XML clause in the preceding code is not well formed by default. It doesn't include the root element. However, as you will see later, you can specify the root element yourself.

The RAW Mode

The RAW mode of the FOR XML clause returns the XML data as zero or more XML elements. By default the name of the elements is <row>. You can change this default behavior by specifying an element name yourself. The column values are returned as XML attributes. Listing 10-3 shows the use of RAW mode.

Listing 10-3. *Using the RAW Mode of the FOR XML Clause*

```
SELECT EmployeeID,FirstName,LastName FROM Employees FOR XML RAW
```

```
<row EmployeeID="1" FirstName="Nancy" LastName="Davolio"/>
<row EmployeeID="2" FirstName="Andrew" LastName="Fuller"/>
<row EmployeeID="3" FirstName="Janet" LastName="Leverling"/>
<row EmployeeID="4" FirstName="Margaret" LastName="Peacock"/>
....
```

As you can see, the FOR XML clause is followed by the RAW mode. The returned XML contains <row> elements with attributes holding the column values. If you wish to change the default element name, you can specify your own element name as shown in Listing 10-4.

Listing 10-4. *Assigning a Custom Element Name to the Output of RAW Mode*

```
SELECT EmployeeID,FirstName,LastName FROM Employees FOR XML RAW ('Employee')
```

```
<Employee EmployeeID="1" FirstName="Nancy" LastName="Davolio"/>
<Employee EmployeeID="2" FirstName="Andrew" LastName="Fuller"/>
<Employee EmployeeID="3" FirstName="Janet" LastName="Leverling"/>
<Employee EmployeeID="4" FirstName="Margaret" LastName="Peacock"/>
....
```

As you can see, we've now specified Employee as the element name in parentheses. This element name is given to all the returned rows.

Returning the Schema of the XML

The XMLSCHEMA clause of the FOR XML clause allows you to return the XSD schema of the XML data being returned. You may use this schema to validate your data further in your application. Listing 10-5 shows how the XMLSCHEMA clause is used.

Listing 10-5. *Returning an XSD Schema*

```
SELECT EmployeeID,FirstName,LastName FROM Employees FOR XML AUTO, XMLSCHEMA
```

```
<xsd:schema targetNamespace="urn:schemas-microsoft-com:sql:SqlRowSet1"
xmlns:schema="urn:schemas-microsoft-com:sql:SqlRowSet1"
xmlns:xsd="http://www.w3.org/2001/XMLSchema"
xmlns:sqltypes="http://schemas.microsoft.com/sqlserver/2004/sqltypes"
elementFormDefault="qualified">
<xsd:import namespace="http://schemas.microsoft.com/sqlserver/2004/sqltypes"
schemaLocation="http://schemas.microsoft.com/sqlserver/2004/sqltypes/sqltypes.xsd"/>
<xsd:element name="Employees">
<xsd:complexType>
<xsd:attribute name="EmployeeID" type="sqltypes:int" use="required"/>
<xsd:attribute name="FirstName" use="required">
<xsd:simpleType><xsd:restriction base="sqltypes:nvarchar" sqltypes:localeId="1033"
sqltypes:sqlCompareOptions="IgnoreCase IgnoreKanaType IgnoreWidth"
sqltypes:sqlSortId="52">
<xsd:maxLength value="10"/>
</xsd:restriction>
</xsd:simpleType>
</xsd:attribute>
<xsd:attribute name="LastName" use="required">
<xsd:simpleType>
<xsd:restriction base="sqltypes:nvarchar" sqltypes:localeId="1033"
sqltypes:sqlCompareOptions="IgnoreCase IgnoreKanaType IgnoreWidth"
sqltypes:sqlSortId="52">
<xsd:maxLength value="20"/>
</xsd:restriction>
</xsd:simpleType>
</xsd:attribute>
</xsd:complexType>
</xsd:element>
</xsd:schema>
<Employees xmlns="urn:schemas-microsoft-com:sql:SqlRowSet1" EmployeeID="1"
FirstName="Nancy" LastName="Davolio"/>
<Employees xmlns="urn:schemas-microsoft-com:sql:SqlRowSet1" EmployeeID="2"
FirstName="Andrew" LastName="Fuller"/>
....
```

As you can see, the XMLSCHEMA clause returns the XSD schema along with the data.

The PATH Mode

Though the AUTO and RAW modes return data in XML format, you have very little control over the nesting and naming conventions of the returned data. The PATH mode, on the other hand, allows you to specify the nesting structure as well as element and attribute names by using simple XPath syntax. Suppose you wish to retrieve records from the Employee table in the format shown in Listing 10-6.

Listing 10-6. *Custom Nesting and Naming*

```
<Employee ID="1">
<Name>
<FirstName>Nancy</FirstName>
<LastName>Davolio</LastName>
</Name>
</Employee>
```

Each record is to be returned as an <Employee> element. The EmployeeID column value is to be returned as the ID attribute of the <Employee> element. There should be an element named <Name> with two further sub-elements: <FirstName> and <LastName>. The <FirstName> and <LastName> elements should contain data from the FirstName and LastName columns, respectively. To retrieve XML data in this format, you can use the PATH mode as shown in Listing 10-7.

Listing 10-7. *Using the PATH Mode of the FOR XML Clause*

```
SELECT EmployeeID "@ID",FirstName "Name/FirstName",LastName "Name/LastName"
FROM Employees FOR XML PATH ('Employee')
```

As you can see, the SELECT query now specifies certain extra pieces of information along with the column names. We wish to return the EmployeeID column value as the ID attribute and hence the query adds @ID after the EmployeeID column. Similarly, the FirstName and the LastName columns are followed by the desired nesting and element names, that is, Name/FirstName and Name/LastName, respectively. The name of the element generated is specified after the PATH mode in parentheses. Notice how the XPath syntax (@, /) is used to specify the attributes and element nesting.

The EXPLICIT Mode

The EXPLICIT mode is possibly the most confusing mode of the FOR XML clause. On one hand it increases the complexity of the SELECT statement, but on the other it gives much more fine-grained control on the resultant output.

■ **Note** I will discuss the EXPLICIT mode only to the extent of giving a feeling of how it renders the XML output. In no way does this book try to teach you the EXPLICIT mode apart from the basics. If you wish to learn about the EXPLICIT mode in detail, you may consider *Pro SQL Server 2005* by Thomas Rizzo and others (Apress, 2005).

Suppose that you wish to return the XML content as shown in Listing 10-8.

Listing 10-8. *Customized XML Output Using EXPLICIT Mode*

```
<Employee EmpID="1">
<FirstName>Nancy</FirstName>
<LastName>Davolio</LastName>
</Employee>
```

You can identity two levels in this markup. Level 1 consists of the <Employee> element, and level 2 consists of the <FirstName> and <LastName> elements. The EmployeeID column is outputted as the EmpID attribute of the <Employee> element and hence belongs to level 1.

When using EXPLICIT mode to generate this XML output, we will need to write two SELECT queries:

- The first query will outline the structure, nesting, and element names of the various columns involved.
- The second query will actually fetch the data. The results of the two queries will be merged with a UNION clause.

Let's look at the first SELECT query (see Listing 10-9).

Listing 10-9. *Defining the Structure of the XML Output*

```
SELECT
1 AS Tag,
NULL AS Parent,
EmployeeID AS [Employee!1!EmpID],
FirstName AS [Employee!1!FirstName!element],
LastName AS [Employee!1!LastName!element]
FROM Employees
```

The query selects five columns: `1`, `NULL`, `EmployeeID`, `FirstName`, and `LastName`. The last three columns are obvious, but what are `1` and `NULL`? The `Tag` and `Parent` columns are implicit columns in the resultant table that are created by SQL Server internally:

- The `Tag` column specifies the nesting level of the current element. A `Tag` value of `1` indicates that this query is defining the structure for level 1 of the XML output.
- The `Parent` column specifies the parent level of the current tag. A `Parent` value of `NULL` indicates that this is the top-level element.

Each column specified after the `Parent` column has some metadata specifications enclosed in square brackets. Multiple pieces of metadata are separated by an exclamation character (`!`):

- The first part indicates the name of the parent element of the current element or attribute.
- The second part indicates the tag number of the element.
- The third part indicates the name of the current element or attribute.
- If you specify only these three parts, the column value will be outputted as an attribute. To specify that it should be outputted as an element, you must specify the fourth part. The fourth part is a predefined keyword called `element`.

In our example, the top-level element is `<Employee>`. This top-level element name is decided by the first real column in the `SELECT` list (in our case, `EmployeeID`). The top-level element name is picked up from the first piece of metadata information specified after the `EmployeeID` column. We want to output the `EmployeeID` column value as an attribute named `EmpID`. Thus the parent level of the `EmpID` attribute is tag 1. Finally, the third piece of metadata information specifies that the attribute name is `EmpID`.

The metadata for the `FirstName` and `LastName` columns specifies that their parent is the level 1 element and they are to be outputted as `<FirstName>` and `<LastName>` elements, respectively.

The second `SELECT` query is shown in Listing 10-10.

Listing 10-10. *Fetching the Data for the Structure Defined in the Previous Query*

```
SELECT
1,
NULL,
EmployeeID,
FirstName,
LastName
FROM Employees
ORDER BY
[Employee!1!EmpID],
[Employee!1!FirstName!element],
[Employee!1!LastName!element]
FOR XML EXPLICIT
```

The query selects data for tag 1 and selects the EmployeeID, FirstName, and LastName columns. The ORDER BY clause indicates the sequence in which the elements will appear in the resultant XML. Finally, the query adds a FOR XML EXPLICIT clause.

Now that you understand both queries, you can use the UNION ALL clause as shown in Listing 10-11.

Listing 10-11. *Using the UNION ALL Clause*

```
SELECT
1 AS Tag,
NULL AS Parent,
EmployeeID AS [Employee!1!EmpID],
FirstName AS [Employee!1!FirstName!element],
LastName AS [Employee!1!LastName!element]
FROM Employees
UNION All
SELECT
1,NULL,
EmployeeID,
FirstName,
LastName
FROM Employees
ORDER BY [Employee!1!EmpID],
[Employee!1!FirstName!element],
[Employee!1!LastName!element]
FOR XML EXPLICIT
```

The UNION ALL clause combines the results of both of these queries, and you get XML output as shown in Listing 10-8. Let's go a bit further and assume that you wish to retrieve XML in the format shown in Listing 10-12.

Listing 10-12. *XML Output with Deeper Nesting*

```
<Employee empid="1">
<Name>
<FName>Nancy</FName>
<LName>Davolio</LName>
</Name>
</Employee>
```

The XML output has one more level of nesting. The <FName> and <LName> elements are enclosed in the <Name> element, which in turn is enclosed in the <Employee> element. The EmployeeID column is outputted as an empid attribute. The SELECT queries required to generate this output are given in Listing 10-13.

Listing 10-13. *SELECT Queries for Generating Output as Shown in Listing 10-12*

```
SELECT
1 AS Tag,
NULL AS Parent,
EmployeeID AS [employee!1!empid],
FirstName AS [Name!2!FName!element],
LastName AS [Name!2!LName!element]
FROM Employees

UNION ALL

SELECT 2 AS Tag,
1 AS Parent,
EmployeeID,
FirstName,
LastName
FROM Employees
ORDER BY
[Employee!1!empid],
[Name!2!FName!element],
[Name!2!LName!element]
FOR XML EXPLICIT
```

The first SELECT statement defines the structure of the resultant XML output. Notice that this time, the FirstName and LastName columns define their parent element as <Name> and have a tag level of 2. They also define element names for the FirstName and LastName columns as <FName> and <LName>, respectively. The second query defines tag 2. It specifies that the parent of tag 2 is tag 1 via the Parent column. It orders the result set by using the ORDER BY clause as before. If you run this script in Management Studio, you should see the XML output shown in Listing 10-12.

Specifying the Root Element Name

In all the preceding queries, you obtained XML markup for an individual table row but there was no root element specified for the markup. If you wish, you can specify the root element by adding the ROOT clause, as shown in Listing 10-14.

Listing 10-14. *Using the ROOT Clause*

```
SELECT EmployeeID,FirstName,LastName FROM Employees FOR XML AUTO, ROOT('MyRoot')
```

```
<MyRoot>
<Employees EmployeeID="1" FirstName="Nancy" LastName="Davolio"/>
<Employees EmployeeID="2" FirstName="Andrew" LastName="Fuller"/>
....
</MyRoot>
```

As you can see, the ROOT clause is appended at the end of the query with the name of the root element in parentheses. The returned XML is now wrapped inside this root element.

Using OPENXML

As you've seen, the FOR XML clause of SQL Server 2005 allows you to retrieve relational data in XML format. However, there is another way to do it—the OPENXML function, which allows you to read XML data in a relational fashion. Suppose that you have XML markup that contains a list of employees and your aim is to import this list into your Employees table. In the absence of something like OPENXML, accomplishing this task would be tedious. As you will soon see, the OPENXML function makes your job much easier. Listing 10-15 shows the source XML markup containing the employee listing.

Listing 10-15. *The Source XML Markup*

```
<Employees>
<Employee EmployeeID="10" FirstName="John" LastName="Moore" />
<Employee EmployeeID="11" FirstName="Bill" LastName="Short" />
</Employees>
```

As you can see, the root element of the markup is <Employees>. Further, it contains <Employee> elements representing an employee record. The EmployeeID, FirstName, and LastName appear as attributes of the <Employee> element. To read any XML markup by using the OPENXML function, you need to perform the following steps:

1. Prepare and load the XML document for processing.
2. Call the OPENXML function as per your need.
3. Remove the loaded XML document from memory.

These three steps are illustrated in Listing 10-16.

Listing 10-16. *Using the OPENXML Function*

```
SET IDENTITY_INSERT Employees ON
DECLARE @hDoc INT
DECLARE @xml VARCHAR(1000)

SET @xml=
'<Employees>
<Employee EmployeeID="10" FirstName="John" LastName="Gates" />
<Employee EmployeeID="11" FirstName="Bill" LastName="Short" />
</Employees>'

EXEC sp_xml_preparedocument @hDoc OUTPUT, @xml

INSERT INTO EMPLOYEES (EMPLOYEEID,FIRSTNAME,LASTNAME)
(
SELECT * FROM
OPENXML(@hDoc,'Employees/Employee',0)
WITH (EmployeeID int,FirstName varchar(50),LastName varchar(50))
)

EXEC sp_xml_removedocument @hDoc
```

The script in Listing 10-16 declares two variables named hDoc and xml. The integer variable hDoc is used later for storing a handle to the loaded XML document. The VARCHAR variable xml is used to store the XML markup shown in Listing 10-15 as a string. The SET statement assigns the XML markup to the xml variable. Then we call the sp_xml_preparedocument system stored procedure, which parses and loads the supplied XML markup in memory. It returns a handle to the loaded document in the form of an integer.

Next, this handle is collected in the hDoc variable that we declared earlier. Then an INSERT statement is executed, making use of the OPENXML function. Observe the call to OPENXML carefully. The OPENXML function is used in a SELECT statement as if it were a table. It accepts three parameters:

- The first parameter is a handle to the XML data loaded by using sp_xml_preparedocument.
- The second parameter is an XPath pattern pointing to the node of the XML data that is to be treated as a row. In our example, this base path is Employees/Employee.
- The third parameter is a flag indicating the mapping between the XML data and the relational rowset. The third parameter can take values as shown in Table 10-2.

Table 10-2. *Mapping Between XML Data and a Relational Rowset*

Flag Value	Description
0	Specifies that attributes of the XML elements are supplying column values for the relational rowset. This is the default.
1	Specifies that attributes of the XML elements are supplying column values for the relational rowset. When combined with a flag value of 2, attributes are picked up as column values and then element values are assigned to the remaining columns.
2	Specifies that elements of the source XML are supplying column values for the relational rowset.
8	This flag can be combined with 1 or 2 and indicates that the consumed data should not be copied to the overflow property @mp:xmltext.

Further, the WITH clause of OPENXML specifies the structure of the resultant rowset. The structure can be specified as a comma-separated list of column names and their data types. In our example, we have three columns: EmployeeID, FirstName, and LastName. Note that these column names are the same as the attribute names in the source XML markup.

Thus the rowset returned from the SELECT statement and OPENXML is fed to the INSERT statement. The INSERT statement then adds the data to the Employees table. In our example, it will add two rows.

After the INSERT operation is done, the XML document is removed from memory by using another system stored procedure: sp_xml_removedocument. This accepts the handle of an XML document loaded previously by using sp_xml_preparedocument and cleans up the memory consumed by the document. Calling sp_xml_removedocument is very important because failing to do so can waste valuable memory of your application.

■ **Note** A thorough discussion of the OPENXML clause is outside the scope of this book. The aim here is to give you a reasonable understanding of the XML functionality of SQL Server 2005.

Using SQLXML Features

Modern applications are becoming more and more Internet centric. In Chapter 9, you learned that web services offer an industry standard for communicating over HTTP. Web services are, however, generic programmable APIs and do not associate themselves to any database as such. However, SQL Server 2005 allows you to expose your data over the Internet in XML format. The underlying channel is, of course, HTTP. By using this feature, you can query your database over the Internet and retrieve the returned results as an XML document in your client applications. This feature of SQL Server 2005 is referred to as *SQLXML*.

Note If you wish to use SQLXML on SQL Server 2000, you need to download the SQLXML installable separately and install it on your machine.

SQLXML also provides you with a set of managed classes, which you can use in your .NET applications to query the SQL Server database and read the returned results in XML format. You can also send updates from the client application in special XML formats, and SQL Server 2005 can update the database.

Note The version of SQLXML that ships with SQL Server 2005 is 4.0. If you have SQL Server 2000, you can download SQLXML 3.0. Though the overall concepts that you learn in this chapter are applicable to SQL Server 2000, there are some differences between these two versions. In this book, I focus solely on SQL Sever 2005.

The SQLXML Managed Classes

SQLXML provides you with a set of managed classes that can be used to execute queries against the database and return results in XML form. The classes provided by SQLXML physically reside in an assembly, `Microsoft.Data.SqlXml`. The three core classes exposed by SQLXML are listed in Table 10-3.

Table 10-3. *SQLXML Managed Classes*

Class Name	Description
`SqlXmlCommand`	`SqlXmlCommand` allows you to execute queries as well as non-queries against the database. This class exposes methods such as `ExecuteNonQuery()`, `ExecuteStream()`, and `ExecuteXmlReader()`. This class is analogous to the ADO.NET `SqlCommand` class.
`SqlXmlParameter`	`SqlXmlParameter` represents parameters to the queries executed by using the `SqlXmlCommand` class. This class is analogous to the ADO.NET `SqlParameter` class.
`SqlXmlAdapter`	`SqlXmlAdapter` is used to interact with the ADO.NET `DataSet` class. This class is analogous to the ADO.NET `SqlDataAdapter` class.

All the preceding classes can use the SQL Server OLEDB provider (SQLOLEDB) or the SQL Native Client to communicate with the underlying database. In the next few sections, you are going to learn how the SQLXML classes can be used in your .NET applications.

Executing SELECT Queries

Let's begin by developing an application that will allow you to execute `SELECT` queries against the SQL Server database. The application user interface is shown in Figure 10-2.

Figure 10-2. *Application for executing SELECT queries via SqlXmlCommand*

The application consists of a text box for entering `SELECT` queries. Note that these `SELECT` queries must use some mode of the `FOR XML` clause you learned earlier. The Execute button executes the query and displays the results in a Web Browser control. The `Click` event handler of the Execute button is shown in Listing 10-17.

Listing 10-17. *Using the SqlXmlCommand Class*

```
private void button1_Click(object sender, EventArgs e)
{
  string strConn =
    @"Provider=SQLOLEDB;server=.\sqlexpress;database=northwind;integrated ➥
security=SSPI";
  SqlXmlCommand cmd = new SqlXmlCommand(strConn);
  cmd.CommandText = textBox1.Text;
  Stream stream= cmd.ExecuteStream();
  StreamReader reader=new StreamReader(stream);
  StreamWriter writer =
    File.CreateText(Application.StartupPath + @"\sqlxmlresults.xml");
  writer.Write(reader.ReadToEnd());
  writer.Close();
  webBrowser1.Navigate(Application.StartupPath + @"\sqlxmlresults.xml");
}
```

■Note Make sure to change the database connection string to match your development environment before running the preceding code.

The code declares a string variable for storing the database connection string. Notice the Provider parameter of the connection string, which specifies the SQLOLEDB provider. Then the code creates an instance of the SqlXmlCommand class by passing the connection string in its constructor. The CommandText property of SqlXmlCommand is set to the SELECT query entered in the text box, and the query is executed by calling the ExecuteStream() method of the SqlXmlCommand class.

The ExecuteStream() method executes your query and returns a Stream object containing the XML results. This Stream can then be used further to read the data. In the preceding code, the Stream is fed to a StreamReader class. We could have read the Stream byte by byte, but the StreamReader class makes our job easy.

The CreateText() method of the File class creates a new XML file at the specified location and returns a StreamWriter pointing to it. The XML returned from the database is read by using the ReadToEnd() method of the StreamReader class and is then written to the XML file. Finally, the Navigate() method of the Web Browser control is called to show the user the XML file.

There is an alternative way to do the same task. Have a look at Listing 10-18.

Listing 10-18. *Using the ExecuteToStream() Method*

```
private void button1_Click(object sender, EventArgs e)
{
string strConn =
  @"Provider=SQLOLEDB;server=.\sqlexpress;database=northwind;integrated ➥
security=SSPI";
  SqlXmlCommand cmd = new SqlXmlCommand(strConn);
  cmd.CommandText = textBox1.Text;
  StreamWriter writer =
    File.CreateText(Application.StartupPath + @"\sqlxmlresults.xml");
  cmd.ExecuteToStream(writer.BaseStream);
  writer.Close();
  webBrowser1.Navigate(Application.StartupPath + @"\sqlxmlresults.xml");
}
```

The code in Listing 10-18 looks very similar to that in Listing 10-17. The difference is that it calls the ExecuteToStream() method instead of ExecuteStream(), and by doing so emits the XML output to an existing Stream. The BaseStream property of the StreamWriter class returns the underlying Stream, which is then supplied to the ExecuteToStream() method.

■Note You can also use the ExecuteXmlReader() method of the SqlXmlCommand class. This method is identical to the ExecuteXmlReader() method of the SqlCommand class that you learned about in Chapter 7.

Executing Parameterized SELECT Queries

It will be common for your SELECT queries to have some parameters, and the technique to execute parameterized queries is similar to ADO.NET. However, there are a few differences. First, a parameter is represented by the SqlXmlParameter class. Second, the SqlXmlCommand class doesn't have a Parameters collection as does the SqlCommand class, so you need to call the CreateParameter() method of the SqlXmlCommand class to create a new parameter that belongs to the command. The value of the parameter can then be set. To illustrate the use of the SqlXmlParameter class, we will create an application as shown in Figure 10-3.

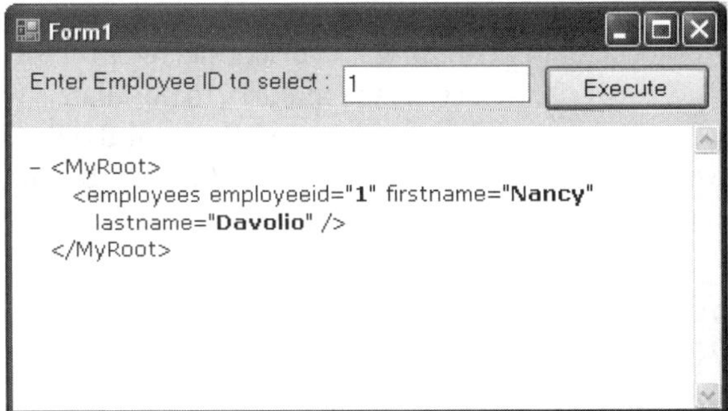

Figure 10-3. *Application for executing parameterized queries*

The application allows you to fetch details of only one employee whose EmployeeID is specified in the text box. The returned XML data is displayed in the Web Browser control as before. Listing 10-19 shows the Click event handler of the Execute button.

Listing 10-19. *Using the SqlXmlParameter Class*

```
private void button1_Click(object sender, EventArgs e)
{
  string strConn =
    @"Provider=SQLOLEDB;server=.\sqlexpress;database=northwind;integrated ➥
security=SSPI";
  string sql = "SELECT employeeid,firstname,lastname FROM employees
                WHERE employeeid=? FOR XML AUTO,ROOT('MyRoot')";
  SqlXmlCommand cmd = new SqlXmlCommand(strConn);
  cmd.CommandText = sql;
  SqlXmlParameter param = cmd.CreateParameter();
  param.Value = textBox1.Text;
  StreamWriter writer =
    File.CreateText(Application.StartupPath + @"\sqlxmlresults.xml");
  cmd.ExecuteToStream(writer.BaseStream);
  writer.Close();
  webBrowser1.Navigate(Application.StartupPath + @"\sqlxmlresults.xml");
}
```

Examine the `SELECT` query carefully. It has a `WHERE` clause with a parameter marked with a question mark (?). Further, the `CreateParameter()` method is called on the `SqlXmlCommand` class. The `CreateParameter()` method creates and returns a new `SqlXmlParameter`. You can then set the `Value` property of this `SqlXmlParameter` class. If your query has more than one parameter, you will need to call the `CreateParameter()` method once for each parameter. Note that the sequence of parameters in the query and the sequence in which you create `SqlXmlParameter` objects must be the same. After creating the required parameter, the XML output is saved to a `FileStream` by using the `ExecuteToStream()` method of `SqlXmlCommand`.

Filling a DataSet

A `DataSet` is one of the most commonly used objects for data binding and disconnected processing. It is obvious that the SQLXML object model must provide some mechanism to populate `DataSet` objects, and the `SqlXmlAdapter` fits the bill. It allows you to populate a `DataSet` and reflect the changes made to the `DataSet` back in the database. To illustrate the use of `SqlXmlAdapter` in populating a `DataSet`, you need to create an application as shown in Figure 10-4.

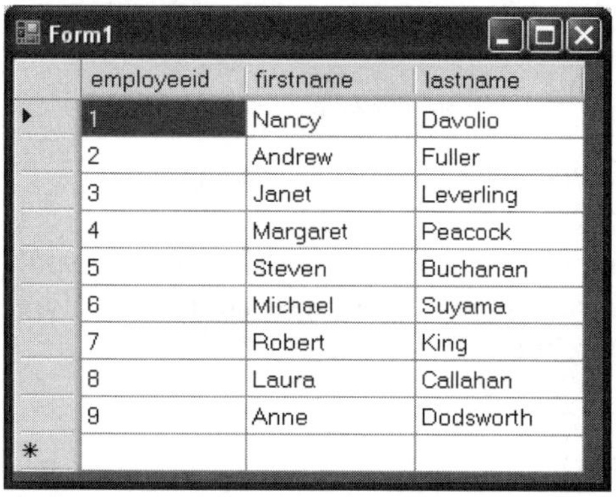

Form1

employeeid	firstname	lastname
1	Nancy	Davolio
2	Andrew	Fuller
3	Janet	Leverling
4	Margaret	Peacock
5	Steven	Buchanan
6	Michael	Suyama
7	Robert	King
8	Laura	Callahan
9	Anne	Dodsworth

Figure 10-4. *Application that fills a DataSet by using SqlXmlAdapter*

The application consists of a DataGridView control. When the form loads, a `DataSet` is filled with all the records from the `Employees` table and the resultant `DataSet` is bound to the DataGridView control. The `Load` event handler that does this job is shown in Listing 10-20.

Listing 10-20. *Filling a DataSet with SqlXmlAdapter*

```
private void Form1_Load(object sender, EventArgs e)
{
  string strConn =
    @"Provider=SQLOLEDB;server=.\sqlexpress;database=northwind;integrated ➥
```

```
security=SSPI";
  string sql = "SELECT employeeid,firstname,lastname FROM employees FOR XML AUTO";
  SqlXmlCommand cmd = new SqlXmlCommand(strConn);
  cmd.CommandText = sql;
  DataSet ds = new DataSet();
  SqlXmlAdapter da = new SqlXmlAdapter(cmd);
  da.Fill(ds);
  dataGridView1.DataSource = ds.Tables[0].DefaultView;
}
```

The code creates a `SqlXmlCommand` object as before. It then creates a new instance of the `DataSet` and `SqlXmlAdapter` classes. The `SqlXmlAdapter` accepts the `SqlXmlCommand` object as a parameter and thus the `SELECT` query (or stored procedure) is passed to it. The `Fill()` method of `SqlXmlAdapter` is then called by passing a `DataSet` object as a parameter. The `Fill()` method populates the `DataSet` with the results returned from the query. Finally, the `DataSet` is bound to the DataGridView control.

Updating a DataSet by Using SqlXmlAdapter

In the preceding example, we simply populated a `DataSet` with the help of the `SqlXmlAdapter` class. What if you make changes to the `DataSet` data and wish to save those changes in the database? The `SqlXmlAdapter` does provide the `Update()` method that updates the database with any changes to your `DataSet`. However, you need to do a bit more work than that. While filling the `DataSet`, you need to specify the XSD schema for the `DataTable` being created. This schema provides mapping between the `DataTable` column names and the actual table column names. In our example, we retrieve three columns of the `Employee` table: `EmployeeID`, `FirstName`, and `LastName`. The schema for this data structure is shown in Listing 10-21.

Listing 10-21. *Schema—Employees.xsd—for Our Data*

```
<?xml version="1.0" encoding="utf-8" ?>
<xs:schema xmlns:xs="http://www.w3.org/2001/XMLSchema">
  <xs:element name="Employees">
    <xs:complexType>
      <xs:sequence>
        <xs:element name="EmployeeID" type="xs:integer"/>
        <xs:element name="FirstName" type="xs:string"/>
        <xs:element name="LastName" type="xs:string"/>
      </xs:sequence>
    </xs:complexType>
  </xs:element>
</xs:schema>
```

The schema defines a root element called `<Employees>`, which has three child elements: `<EmployeeID>`, `<FirstName>`, and `<LastName>`. Note that the schema defines the columns as elements and not as attributes. To see the `SqlXmlAdapter` class in action, you need to develop an application as shown in Figure 10-5.

Figure 10-5. *Application for illustrating the Update() method of SqlXmlAdapter*

The application consists of a DataGridView control that displays all the employees from the `Employees` table. You can change the data in the DataGridView and click the Update button to save the changes back to the database. The complete code that makes this application work is shown in Listing 10-22.

Listing 10-22. *Saving Changes Made to a DataSet*

```
DataSet ds = new DataSet();
SqlXmlAdapter da;
SqlXmlCommand cmd;
string strConn =
  @"Provider=SQLOLEDB;server=.\sqlexpress;database=northwind;integrated ➥
security=SSPI";
```

```
private void Form1_Load(object sender, EventArgs e)
{
  cmd = new SqlXmlCommand(strConn);
  cmd.RootTag = "ROOT";
  cmd.CommandText = "Employees";
  cmd.CommandType = SqlXmlCommandType.XPath;
  cmd.SchemaPath = Application.StartupPath + @"\employees.xsd";
  ds = new DataSet();
  da = new SqlXmlAdapter(cmd);
  da.Fill(ds);
  dataGridView1.DataSource = ds.Tables[0].DefaultView;
}

private void button1_Click(object sender, EventArgs e)
{
  da.Update(ds);
}
```

The code in Listing 10-22 shows several interesting things. The `SqlXmlCommand`, `DataSet`, and `SqlXmlAdapter` variables are declared at the form level because we will be using them in more than one place. Notice the code marked in bold. It sets the `RootTag` property of the `SqlXmlCommand` property. The `AUTO` mode of the `FOR XML` clause doesn't return data along with a root element by default, so this property is used to indicate the name of the root element inside which the rest of the XML data will be wrapped.

The `CommandType` property is set to `XPath`, indicating that the `CommandText` property is an XPath expression. This means that this time the `CommandText` property is not a `SELECT` query but the XPath expression `Employees`, which will return various `<Employees>` elements.

The `CommandType` property of the `SqlXmlCommand` class is of type `SqlXmlCommandType`. The possible values of the `SqlXmlCommandType` enumeration are listed in Table 10-4.

Table 10-4. *Values of the SqlXmlCommandType Enumeration*

Value	Description
`DiffGram`	Indicates that `CommandText` is a DiffGram
`Sql`	Indicates that `CommandText` is a SQL statement (default)
`Template`	Indicates that `CommandText` is a template
`TemplateFile`	Indicates that `CommandText` is a template file
`UpdateGram`	Indicates that `CommandText` is an UpdateGram
`XPath`	Indicates that `CommandText` is a valid XPath expression

Further, the `SchemaPath` property specifies the path of the schema file that we created earlier. Then the `SqlXmlAdapter` populates a `DataSet`, which is bound to the DataGridView.

After the data is displayed in the DataGridView, you can modify it. After the modifications are complete, you need to click the Update button. The `Click` event of the Update button calls the `Update()` method of `SqlXmlAdapter`, which accepts the `DataSet` whose changes are to be reflected in the database. In Chapter 7, you learned that the `DataSet` class internally tracks the changes made to the data by using the DiffGram format. The same DiffGram is used by the `SqlXmlAdapter` class to propagate the changes back to the database.

Applying XSLT Templates

In Chapter 6, you learned to apply XSLT style sheets to XML data. You saw that XSLT allows you to transform XML data from one form to another. The same concept also can be applied in SQLXML, where you may wish to apply XSLT templates to whatever data you receive in your client application. This is accomplished by using the `XslPath` property of the `SqlXmlCommand` class. To demonstrate the use of `XslPath`, you need to develop an application as shown in Figure 10-6.

Figure 10-6. *Application to illustrate the use of the XslPath property*

The application consists of a Web Browser control. When the form loads, a `SELECT` query is executed by using `SqlXmlCommand`. An XSLT style sheet is then applied to the returned XML data to transform it into HTML. The resultant HTML document is then displayed in the Web Browser control.

Before you write any code, you must create an XSLT style sheet named `Employees.xslt` as shown in Listing 10-23.

Listing 10-23. *Employees.xslt Markup*

```
<?xml version="1.0" encoding="UTF-8" ?>
<xsl:stylesheet version="1.0" xmlns:xsl="http://www.w3.org/1999/XSL/Transform">
  <xsl:template match="/">
    <html>
      <body>
        <h1>Employee Listing</h1>
        <table border="1">
          <tr>
            <th>Employee ID</th>
            <th>First Name</th>
            <th>Last Name</th>
          </tr>
          <xsl:for-each select="root/employees">
            <tr>
              <td>
                <xsl:value-of select="@EmployeeID"/>
              </td>
              <td>
                <xsl:value-of select="@FirstName"/>
              </td>
              <td>
                <xsl:value-of select="@LastName"/>
              </td>
            </tr>
          </xsl:for-each>
        </table>
      </body>
    </html>
  </xsl:template>
</xsl:stylesheet>
```

The style sheet iterates through all the `<Employees>` elements and renders an HTML table. The HTML table displays the attribute values in various cells. Note that we will be using the `AUTO` mode of the `FOR XML` clause, which returns column values as XML attributes. That is why the style sheet uses attribute names (`@EmployeeID`, `@FirstName`, and `@LastName`). The code that actually executes the `SELECT` query and performs the transformation is shown in Listing 10-24.

Listing 10-24. *Applying an XSLT Style Sheet*

```
private void Form1_Load(object sender, EventArgs e)
{
string strConn =
  @"Provider=SQLOLEDB;server=.\sqlexpress;database=northwind;integrated ➥
security=SSPI";
  SqlXmlCommand cmd = new SqlXmlCommand(strConn);
  cmd.CommandText = "SELECT EmployeeID,FirstName,LastName
                     FROM employees FOR XML AUTO";
  cmd.RootTag = "root";
  cmd.XslPath = Application.StartupPath + @"\employees.xslt";
  StreamWriter writer =
    File.CreateText(Application.StartupPath + @"\sqlxmlresults.htm");
  cmd.ExecuteToStream(writer.BaseStream);
  writer.Close();
  webBrowser1.Navigate(Application.StartupPath + @"\sqlxmlresults.htm");
}
```

Notice the code marked in bold. This time the SELECT statement doesn't contain a ROOT clause. We could indeed have used it, but the code achieves the same thing with the help of the RootTag property of the SqlXmlCommand class. Recollect that in the absence of a ROOT clause in the FOR XML query, the returned XML data doesn't contain a root element. The RootTag property of SqlXmlCommand specifies the name of the root tag inside which the output of the SELECT query will be wrapped.

The XSLT style sheet to be used for transformation is specified via the XslPath property of the SqlXmlCommand class. This way, the SqlXmlCommand class knows which style sheet to apply to the returned XML data. The rest of the code should be familiar to you, as we discussed it in previous examples. It simply saves the transformed XML data into a disk file and displays that file in the Web Browser control.

Writing Template Queries

In the preceding example, we specified the SELECT query directly in code. There is an alternative to this too: you can store the queries in an XML file and specify the path of this XML file as the CommandText of the SqlXmlCommand class. These XML files are called *XML templates*. The structure of this XML file can be seen in Listing 10-25.

Listing 10-25. *Creating an XML Template*

```
<?xml version="1.0" encoding="utf-8" ?>
<ROOT xmlns:sql="urn:schemas-microsoft-com:xml-sql">
  <sql:header>
    <sql:param name='EmpID'>1</sql:param>
  </sql:header>
  <sql:query>
    SELECT EmployeeID,FirstName,LastName FROM Employees
    WHERE employeeid>@Empid FOR XML AUTO
  </sql:query>
</ROOT>
```

The root element `<ROOT>` is a user-defined element, but the namespace `urn:schemas-microsoft-com:xml-sql` is necessary. The `<ROOT>` element contains an optional section called `<sql:header>`, which is used to define parameters used by your query (if any). Each parameter is specified by using a `<sql:param>` element. The `name` attribute of the `<sql:param>` element indicates the name of the parameter, while the value of the parameter is stored within the `<sql:param>` and `</sql:param>` tags. The actual query is stored in the `<sql:query>` section. The query uses the parameter by prefixing its name with the `@` symbol.

To use this XML template file, you need to create an application as shown in Figure 10-7.

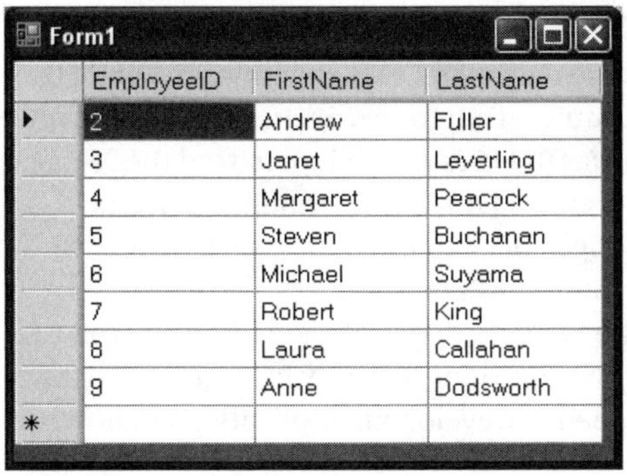

Form1

EmployeeID	FirstName	LastName
2	Andrew	Fuller
3	Janet	Leverling
4	Margaret	Peacock
5	Steven	Buchanan
6	Michael	Suyama
7	Robert	King
8	Laura	Callahan
9	Anne	Dodsworth

Figure 10-7. *Application that illustrates the use of XML templates*

The application consists of a DataGridView that displays all the records from the `Employees` table. The `Load` event of the form contains all the code necessary to use the XML template (Listing 10-26).

Listing 10-26. *Using XML Templates*

```
private void Form1_Load(object sender, EventArgs e)
{
  string strConn =
    @"Provider=SQLOLEDB;server=.\sqlexpress;database=northwind;integrated ➥
security=SSPI";
  SqlXmlCommand cmd = new SqlXmlCommand(strConn);
  cmd.CommandType = SqlXmlCommandType.TemplateFile;
  cmd.CommandText = Application.StartupPath + @"\querytemplate.xml";
  DataSet ds = new DataSet();
  SqlXmlAdapter da = new SqlXmlAdapter(cmd);
  da.Fill(ds);
  dataGridView1.DataSource = ds.Tables[0].DefaultView;
}
```

Notice the code marked in bold. This time the CommandType property of the SqlXmlCommand class is set to TemplateFile. This indicates that the CommandText property will be specifying the path of the XML template file. Then the CommandText property is set to the path of the XML template file we just created in Listing 10-25. The instance of SqlXmlAdapter is used as before to populate a DataSet. The DataSet is finally bound to the DataGridView control.

Updating Data with DiffGrams

In Chapter 7, you learned that DataSet objects can be serialized as XML documents. While serializing a DataSet object, we used an XmlWriteMode enumeration to specify how the data is to be written. Now, one of the options of XmlWriteMode was DiffGram, which persisted the DataSet contents in DiffGram format. Imagine that you have such a DiffGram containing inserts, updates, and deletes and you want to save these changes back to the database. One way to do this is to use DataSet and SqlXmlAdapter, which you've already seen.

There is another technique that also involves the SqlXmlCommand class. The SqlXmlCommand class can come in handy if you have a raw DiffGram that is not necessarily loaded in a DataSet. To illustrate the use of the SqlXmlCommand class, you need to develop an application as shown in Figure 10-8.

The application consists of a DataGridView control for displaying all the records from the Employees table. There are two buttons: Save DiffGram and Update DiffGram. The former saves the contents of the DataSet to a disk file in DiffGram format. The latter button reads the previously saved DiffGram and updates the database.

Figure 10-8. *Application for updating DiffGrams*

The Load event handler of the form contains the code shown in Listing 10-27.

Listing 10-27. *Filling a DataSet*

```
private void Form1_Load(object sender, EventArgs e)
{
  SqlXmlCommand cmd = new SqlXmlCommand(strConn);
  cmd.RootTag = "ROOT";
  cmd.CommandText = "Employees";
  cmd.CommandType = SqlXmlCommandType.XPath;
  cmd.SchemaPath = Application.StartupPath + @"\employees.xsd";
  SqlXmlAdapter da = new SqlXmlAdapter(cmd);
  da.Fill(ds);
  dataGridView1.DataSource = ds.Tables[0].DefaultView;
}
```

The code should be familiar to you, as you used it in previous examples. It simply populates a DataSet by using the SqlXmlAdapter class. The DataSet acts as DataSource for the DataGridView control. The code that saves this DataSet as a DiffGram goes in the Click event of the Save Diff-Gram button and is shown in Listing 10-28.

Listing 10-28. *Saving a DataSet as a DiffGram*

```
private void button2_Click(object sender, EventArgs e)
{
  StreamWriter writer=File.CreateText(Application.StartupPath + @"\employees.xml");
  ds.WriteXml(writer, XmlWriteMode.DiffGram);
  writer.Close();
}
```

The code calls the `WriteXml()` method of `DataSet` to save its contents to an XML file (`Employees.xml`). The `XmlWriteMode` parameter of `WriteXml()` indicates that DiffGram format is to be used while writing the data. This DiffGram is executed against the database when you click the Update DiffGram button. The `Click` event handler of the Update DiffGram button is shown in Listing 10-29.

Listing 10-29. *Updating a DiffGram in a Database*

```
private void button1_Click(object sender, EventArgs e)
{
  StreamReader reader = File.OpenText(Application.StartupPath + @"\employees.xml");
  SqlXmlCommand cmd = new SqlXmlCommand(strConn);
  cmd.CommandType = SqlXmlCommandType.DiffGram;
  cmd.CommandText = reader.ReadToEnd();
  cmd.SchemaPath = Application.StartupPath + @"\employees.xsd";
  cmd.ExecuteNonQuery();
  MessageBox.Show("DiffGram updated to database successfully!");
}
```

The code opens the `Employees.xml` file in a `StreamReader` object. It then creates an instance of the `SqlXmlCommand` class and sets the `CommandType` property of the `SqlXmlCommand` instance to `DiffGram`. This is how you tell `SqlXmlCommand` about your intention to update a DiffGram. When the `CommandType` is `DiffGram`, the `CommandText` property must contain the DiffGram itself. The `ReadToEnd()` method of `StreamReader` reads the complete DiffGram and assigns it to the `CommandText` property.

If you wish to update the database by using the DiffGram method, you must specify the `SchemaPath` property also. In this case, the schema is the same as we created in Listing 10-21 earlier. Finally, the `ExecuteNonQuery()` method of the `SqlXmlCommand` is called to save all the changes to the database. The `ExecuteNonQuery()` method is used for executing queries that do not return anything. In our example, we simply want to update the DiffGram to the database and hence we used the `ExecuteNonQuery()` method.

Note Just like DiffGram, the `SqlXmlCommand` object also allows you to update UpdateGrams. The UpdateGram format is similar to DiffGram in that it keeps the differential versions of the data. However, the `DataSet` class doesn't have any methods to serialize itself in UpdateGram format. You can think of DiffGram as a subset of UpdateGram.

The XML Data Type

Up until now, you've seen various features of SQL Server 2005 that provide a strong integration between relational and XML data. But that's not all. This section gives the next installment of the XML features of SQL Server 2005: the `XML` data type. Prior to SQL Server 2005, storing XML data in a table essentially meant that you had to use a `VARCHAR` or `TEXT` column for the data. From the point of view of storage, this was fine; but from a data-manipulation point of view, it was tedious. The XML data was treated just like any other text data. The new `XML` data type introduced in SQL Server 2005 is exclusively for storing XML documents and fragments.

Note An XML document is markup that contains the root element, whereas an XML fragment is markup without any root element. Remember that the `FOR XML` clause by default returns XML fragments and not documents.

As well as storing XML data, you can also execute XQuery operations and special XML data-manipulation statements on the data. The XML data can have an XSD schema attached to it so that data validations can be performed. You can also index tables on the basis of an XML column.

Note XQuery is a W3C proposed standard that deals with querying XML documents. You can think of XQuery as SQL for XML data. The XQuery syntax is based on XPath expression syntax.

To begin, let's see how to add a column of type `XML` to a SQL Server table.

Creating a Table with an XML Column

To see how a column of type `XML` can be added to a SQL Server table, you will create a new table in the `Northwind` database called `XMLDocs`. Figure 10-9 shows the `XMLDocs` table is design mode.

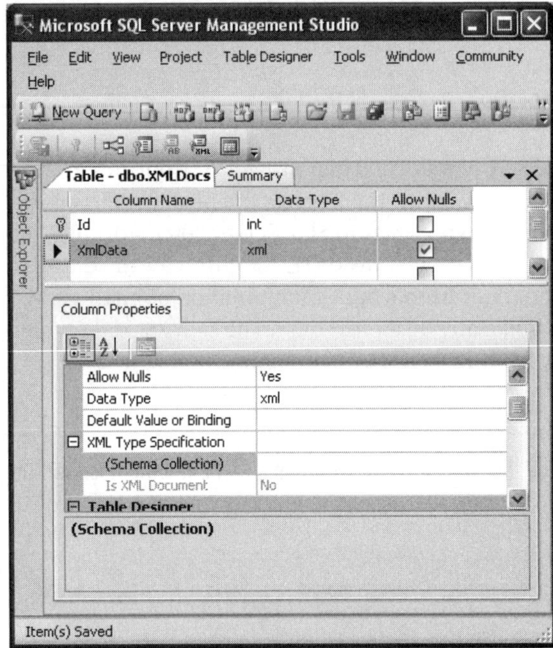

Figure 10-9. *Creating a table with an XML column*

The `XMLDocs` table consists of two columns: `Id` and `XmlData`. The former column is the primary and is marked as an identity column, and the latter is of type `XML`.

Inserting, Modifying, and Deleting XML Data

Inserting, modifying, or deleting XML data is similar to any other data type. However, there are some points to keep in mind. Listing 10-30 shows how to use `INSERT` and `UPDATE` statements against a column of type `XML`.

Listing 10-30. *Inserting and Updating XML Columns*

```
-- Here goes INSERT
INSERT INTO xmldocs(xmldata)
VALUES(
'<Employee EmployeeID="1">
<FirstName>Nancy</FirstName>
<LastName>Davolio</LastName>
</Employee>')

-- Here goes UPDATE
UPDATE xmldocs
SET xmldata='
<Employee EmployeeID="1">
<FirstName>Nancy</FirstName>
<LastName>Davolio</LastName>
</Employee>'
WHERE Id=1
```

As you can see, for an `INSERT` or an `UPDATE` against a column of the `XML` data type, you can use XML data in string format. You can also declare a variable of type `XML` in your Transact-SQL (T-SQL) scripts, as shown in Listing 10-31.

Listing 10-31. *Declaring a Variable of Type XML*

```
DECLARE @xmldata xml
SET @xmldata='
<Employee EmployeeID="2">
<FirstName>Nancy</FirstName>
<LastName> Davolio</LastName>
</Employee>'

UPDATE xmldocs
SET xmldata=@xmldata
WHERE Id=1
```

The script declares a variable called `xmldata` of type `XML` and stores some XML markup in it. The `xmldata` variable is then used in the `UPDATE` statement. If you wish to explicitly convert a string value into the `XML` data type, you can use the `CONVERT` function as shown in Listing 10-32.

Listing 10-32. *Converting String Values to an XML Data Type*

```
DECLARE @xmldata VARCHAR(255)
SET @xmldata='
<Employee EmployeeID="2">
<FirstName>Nancy</FirstName>
<LastName> Davolio</LastName>
</Employee>'

UPDATE xmldocs
SET xmldata=CONVERT(xml,@xmldata,0)
WHERE Id=1
```

The first parameter to the CONVERT function is the target data type. The second parameter is the source data to be converted, and the third parameter is the style. The value of 0 indicates that insignificant white spaces will be discarded. You might be wondering—if XML data can be represented as a string, why would we want to use XML variables at all? The answer is, using the XML data type is recommended because the XML data type checks that the XML data is well formed.

Methods of the XML Data Type

The XML data type provides some methods to query XML columns or variables. Some of these methods are listed in Table 10-5.

Table 10-5. *Methods of the XML Data Type*

Method	Description
query()	Queries an XML column or variable based on some XQuery expression and returns the results of the query
value()	Queries an XML column or variable and returns a scalar value of the SQL data type
exist()	Tells you whether the given XQuery expression returns any results
modify()	Modifies the content of an XML data type column or variable with the help of XML Data Modification Language, discussed later in this chapter
nodes()	Returns XML data as relational data

Some of these methods are discussed in the following sections.

Using the query() Method

The query() method is used to query XML data by using XQuery expressions. Listing 10-33 illustrates how this method is used.

Listing 10-33. *Using the query() Method*

```
SELECT xmldata.query('/Employee[@EmployeeID=2]') FROM xmldocs
```

```
<Employee EmployeeID="2">
<FirstName>Nancy</FirstName>
<LastName> Davolio</LastName>
</Employee>
```

The SELECT query uses the query() method on the XmlData column. The query() method accepts a valid XQuery expression and returns the matching nodes. In our example. we fetch the <Employee> element whose EmployeeID attribute value is 1. As you can see, the XQuery syntax is based on XPath syntax.

Using the value() Method

The value() method accepts an XQuery expression and returns a scalar (single) value. Listing 10-34 shows the use of this method.

Listing 10-34. *Using the value() Method*

```
SELECT xmldata.value('(/Employee/@EmployeeID)[1]','int') FROM xmldocs WHERE id=1
```

```
-----------
1
```

The value() method accepts two parameters:

- The first parameter is an XQuery.
- The second parameter is the target SQL Server data type.

In our example, we are trying to select the EmployeeID attribute value of the first employee. Note that the expression /Employee/@EmployeeID returns multiple rows and hence we specify the row index to access by using array notation. The EmployeeID scalar value is to be represented as an integer and hence the second parameter is int. Note that the data type name must be enclosed in quotes.

Using the exist() Method

The `exist()` method checks whether there are any nodes matching the supplied XQuery expression. Listing 10-35 illustrates the use of the `exist()` method.

Listing 10-35. *Using the exist() Method*

```
SELECT xmldata.exist('/Employee[@EmployeeID=1]') FROM xmldocs
```

The `exist()` method returns `1` if the XQuery expression returns at least one node, `0` if the XQuery expression returns zero nodes, and `NULL` if the `XML` column is null.

XML Data Modification Language (XML DML)

As SQL provides data-manipulation statements for relational data, so the XML DML introduced in SQL Server 2005 allows you to insert, replace, and delete data from an XML column. The XML DML statements are used along with the `modify()` method mentioned in Table 10-5. Listing 10-36 shows a script that inserts, replaces, and deletes XML data from the `XmlData` column of the `XMLDocs` table.

Listing 10-36. *Inserting, Replacing, and Deleting Content from an XML Column*

```
-- Here goes insert
UPDATE xmldocs
SET xmldata.modify
('
insert <Employee EmployeeID="3">
<FirstName>Janet</FirstName>
<LastName>Leverling</LastName>
</Employee> after (/Employee)[2]')

-- Here goes replace

UPDATE xmldocs
SET xmldata.modify
('
replace value of
(/Employee/@EmployeeID)[1] with "10"')

-- Here goes delete

UPDATE xmldocs
SET xmldata.modify
('
delete (/Employee[@EmployeeID=3])
')
```

The first UPDATE query uses the modify() method of the XML column to specify an insert XML DML statement that inserts a new <Employee> node at the end of the existing markup. Observe this syntax carefully. The whole insert statement is enclosed within quotes and acts as a parameter to the modify() method. The first expression in the insert statement is the new XML markup to be inserted followed by the after clause. In our example, we wish to insert the new <Employee> after the second <Employee> node and hence we specify (/Employee)[2]. You can also use before, as first, and as last clauses.

The second UPDATE query uses the modify() method along with the replace value of XML DML statement. The replace value of statement takes two expressions:

- The first specifies the markup to be replaced. In our example, we want to replace the EmployeeID attribute of the first <Employee> node.
- The second expression is the new value to be replaced. In our example, we want to assign a value of 10 to the EmployeeID attribute.

Finally, the third UPDATE statement uses the modify() method along with the delete XML DML statement. The delete statement takes the expression on the basis of which the markup is to be deleted. In our example, we want to delete an employee with EmployeeID equal to 3.

XQuery Support in the XML Data Type

While working with the XML data type, you saw that it heavily uses XQuery expressions. The XQuery expressions are in turn based on XPath syntax. In Chapter 4, you were introduced to XPath functions. The XQuery specifications support almost all the functions that you learned earlier.

Native Web Services

In Chapter 9, you learned to create web services by using the .NET Framework and Visual Studio. SQL Server 2005 has a built-in facility through which you can create web services native to the database. After the web services are created, they can be accessed from any client application over a network. To create and consume SQL Server 2005 native web services, you need to perform the following steps:

1. Create stored procedures or functions that you wish to make web callable.
2. Create HTTP endpoints on the SQL Server instance.
3. Expose stored procedures and functions as web methods.
4. Create a proxy for the native web service.
5. Consume the native web service by calling its web methods.

Let's perform these steps one by one and see how native web services work.

Creating a Stored Procedure

The first step in creating a native web service is to create stored procedures or functions that you want to make web callable. In our example, you need to create a stored procedure named `GetEmployees` that returns the `EmployeeID`, `FirstName`, and `LastName` columns of the `Employees` table. The complete script of the stored procedure is given in Listing 10-37.

Listing 10-37. *Creating the GetEmployees Stored Procedure*

```
CREATE PROCEDURE GetEmployees
AS
SELECT EmployeeID, FirstName, LastName FROM Employees
```

Creating an HTTP Endpoint

The next step is to create an HTTP endpoint for our stored procedure. An *endpoint* is an interface through which the client application can access the web service. To create an endpoint, T-SQL provides the `CREATE ENDPOINT` statement. Listing 10-38 shows the complete script that creates an HTTP endpoint.

Listing 10-38. *Creating an HTTP Endpoint*

```
CREATE ENDPOINT GetEmployeesEndPoint
STATE=STARTED
AS HTTP
(
PATH = '/SQL/GetEmployees',
AUTHENTICATION=(INTEGRATED),
PORTS = (CLEAR)
)
FOR SOAP
(
WEBMETHOD 'GetEmployees'
(
NAME='Northwind.dbo.GetEmployees',
SCHEMA=STANDARD),
WSDL=DEFAULT,
DATABASE='Northwind'
)
```

This script uses many options of the CREATE ENDPOINT statement:

- The STATE clause specifies the state of the endpoint. The possible states are STARTED, STOPPED, and DISABLED. Because we wish to use the web service, we specify it as STARTED.
- The AS HTTP clause specifies that this endpoint will be used over HTTP. Alternatively, we could have used TCP. Then the script gives some more information about the transport protocol:
  - The PATH indicates the URL that identifies the location of the endpoint on the host computer. In our case, we specify it as /sql/GetEmployees.
  - The AUTHENTICATION mode that will be used while consuming this endpoint will be INTEGRATED.
  - The PORTS clause specifies listening port types associated with the endpoint. The value of CLEAR indicates that the incoming request must come over HTTP. If you specify SSL instead, the request must come over HTTPS.
- The FOR SOAP clause indicates that the payload of the web service will be in SOAP format.
- The WEBMETHOD clause gives a name to the web method that we are exposing:
  - The WEBMETHOD clause must be accompanied by the NAME of the web method. The NAME is a three-part name (database.owner.stproc_name) of the stored procedure or function that you intend to expose as a web method.
  - The SCHEMA clause governs whether an inline schema will be returned in SOAP responses. The value of STANDARD indicates that the schema will not be returned.
- The WSDL clause specifies whether WSDL document generation is supported for this endpoint. If set to NONE, no WSDL response is generated. If set to DEFAULT, a default WSDL response is generated and returned for WSDL queries submitted to the endpoint.
- Finally, the DATABASE clause specifies the name of the database (Northwind in our case).

■ **Note** By default endpoints are created on port 80. If your machine is running any other application, say Internet Information Services (IIS), that is already using the same port, you will receive an error while creating the endpoint. If the application is IIS, you can stop the World Wide Web Publishing Service temporarily and then execute the CREATE ENDPOINT statement.

Execute the preceding script in Management Studio to create the GetEmployees endpoint.

Creating a Proxy for the Endpoint

Now that our `GetEmployees` endpoint is ready, we can create a proxy for it. The procedure for this is the same as the one in Chapter 9. You need to create a Windows application by using Visual Studio and then add a web reference to it. You might be wondering what URL you have to supply in the Add Web Reference dialog box. Assuming that SQL Server is running on your local machine, the URL will be `http://localhost/sql/GetEmployees?wsdl`. Remember that we specified `/sql/GetEmployees` as the `PATH` while creating the endpoint. At the end of the URL, you need to append the `wsdl` query string parameter. This way, SQL Server will return the WSDL document for your web service. Figure 10-10 shows the Add Web Reference dialog box with the URL entered.

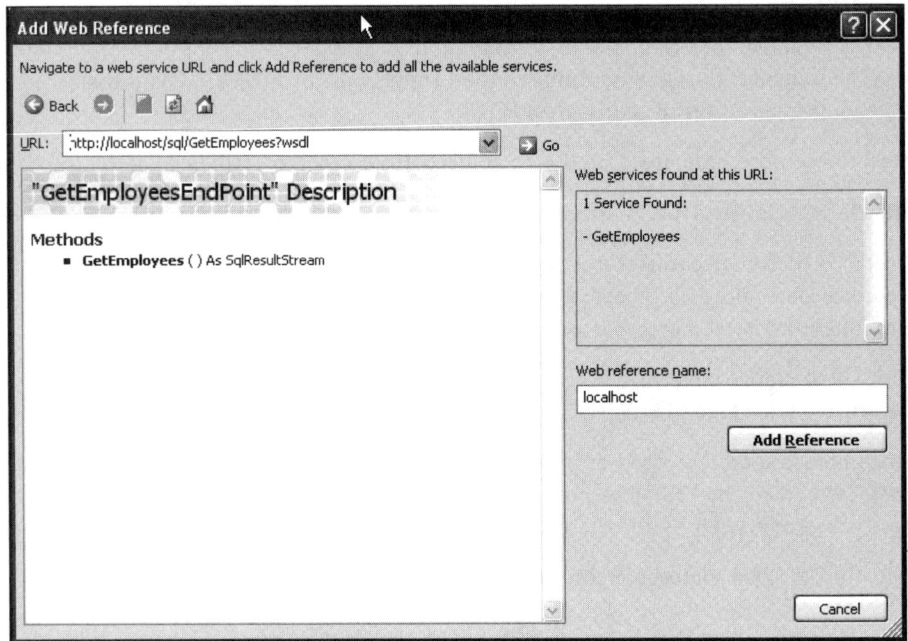

Figure 10-10. *Adding a web reference to the native web service*

Click the Add Reference button to create a proxy for the web service.

Consuming the Native Web Service

To consume the web service, you need to create a form as shown in Figure 10-11.

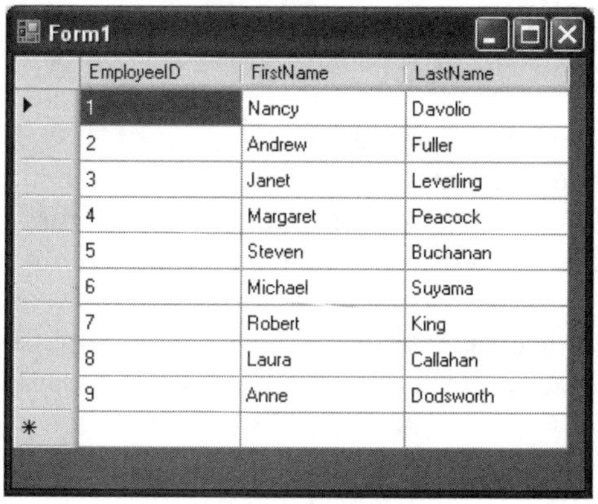

EmployeeID	FirstName	LastName
1	Nancy	Davolio
2	Andrew	Fuller
3	Janet	Leverling
4	Margaret	Peacock
5	Steven	Buchanan
6	Michael	Suyama
7	Robert	King
8	Laura	Callahan
9	Anne	Dodsworth

Figure 10-11. *Application that consumes the native web service*

The form consists of a DataGridView control. The records returned by the native web service are displayed in it. The code that calls the `GetEmployees` web method and binds the DataGridView with the results is shown in Listing 10-39.

Listing 10-39. *Calling Web Methods*

```
using WSClient.localhost;
using System.Net;

private void Form1_Load(object sender, EventArgs e)
{
  GetEmployeesEndPoint proxy = new GetEmployeesEndPoint();
  proxy.Credentials = CredentialCache.DefaultCredentials;
  object[] results=proxy.GetEmployees();
  dataGridView1.DataSource = ((DataSet)results[0]).Tables[0].DefaultView;
}
```

The code imports the namespace for the proxy class. In the Load event of the form, an object representing the proxy is created. Note that we have called our endpoint GetEmployeesEndPoint, so the same name is given to the proxy class. Then the Credentials property of the proxy class is set to the DefaultCredentials property of the CredentialCache class, which resides in the System.Net namespace and allows you to pass user credentials to the proxy. Recollect that while creating the endpoint, we specified the AUTHENTICATION mode as INTEGRATED. The DefaultCredentials property returns the Windows credentials of the current user.

Then the code calls the GetEmployees() method on the proxy. The return value of GetEmployees() is an object array, which contains two elements. The first element contains the actual return value as returned by the web method, and the second parameter is of type SqlRowCount. The SqlRowCount class contains a property called Count that tells you the number of rows returned by the web method.

The records returned by the SELECT query are received as a DataSet object in .NET applications. Hence the code type casts the first element of the array to DataSet. Finally, the DataSet is bound to the DataGridView.

Summary

SQL Server 2005 provides strong integration with XML. This chapter introduced you to many of the XML features of SQL Server 2005, which allows you to view relational data as XML. This is done with the help of the FOR XML clause of the SELECT statement. You can also look at XML data in a relational way by using the OPENXML function.

We also saw how SQL Server 2005 makes it easy to retrieve data in a client application over HTTP with the help of the SQLXML managed classes. These classes allow you to select data as a stream, an XmlReader, or a DataSet. They also allow you to update UpdateGrams and DiffGrams in the database. The newly added XML data type of SQL Server 2005 can be used to store whole XML documents or fragments and allows you to manipulate them via XML DML. You can expose stored procedures and functions as web methods by creating native web services. These native web services can be consumed by client applications in a way similar to their consuming .NET web services.

CHAPTER 11

Use of XML in the .NET Framework

Up until now, you have learned how to work with your own XML data. This includes reading, writing, validating, serializing, and querying XML data. However, Microsoft has used XML extensively in the .NET Framework. The most significant area where XML is used extensively is in application configuration. Further, ASP.NET makes heavy use of XML for representing server controls and data binding. Understanding the use of XML in the .NET Framework is therefore essential for any .NET developer. This chapter introduces you to many of these features. Specifically, you will learn about the following topics:

- Remoting
- How XML is used in a remoting configuration
- ASP.NET server controls
- Use of XML in representation of server controls
- The XML data source control
- Navigational controls of ASP.NET such as TreeView, Menu, and SiteMap
- The XML server control
- Website configuration files and XML

Note that although this chapter covers topics such as remoting and server controls, by no means does it give an exhaustive treatment to these topics. The focus here is to learn how XML is used in various areas of the .NET Framework.

Understanding Remoting

The concept of distributed applications is not new. For years companies have invented their own ways to develop distributed applications. As far as Microsoft is concerned, Distributed Component Object Model, or DCOM, was the main technology pillar for developing distributed applications during COM days. In the .NET Framework, they introduced remoting. You can think of remoting as the substitute for DCOM under the .NET Framework. However, remoting is much more flexible and powerful than DCOM for the following reasons:

- Remoting provides open architecture that allows you to customize and extend it easily.
- Remoting allows you to customize the format of communication.
- Remoting allows you to customize the communication channel on which the applications talk with each other.
- Remoting doesn't require a specific port range for communication.
- Remoting can be used easily in web-based scenarios also.

Now that you have brief idea about remoting, you're ready to try to understand its general architecture.

Remoting Architecture

The overall remoting architecture is shown in Figure 11-1.

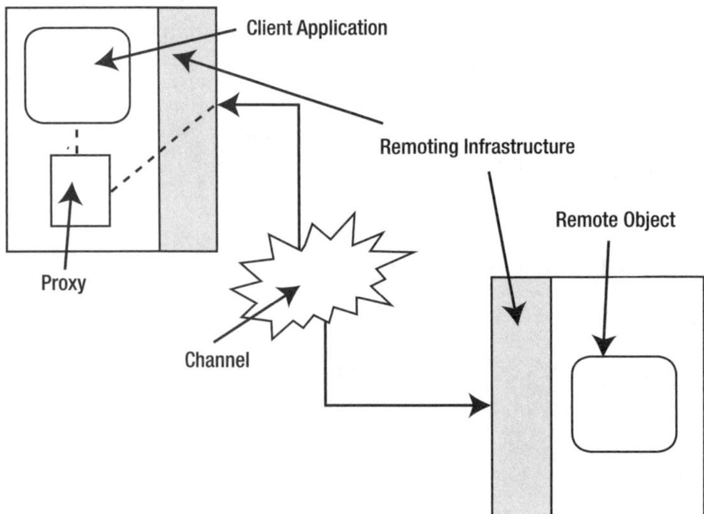

Figure 11-1. *Remoting architecture*

Every .NET application has a security and isolation boundary. Traditionally, this boundary is provided by the operating system in the form of a process. In the .NET Framework, however, this boundary is provided by the Common Language Runtime (CLR) and is called the *application domain,* or *app domain* for short. Two .NET app domains (or applications) cannot talk to each other directly for the sake of obvious security and isolation reasons. If you wish to communicate between two app domains, you need a proxy and marshalling infrastructure.

Fortunately, the .NET Framework provides all the necessary infrastructure to achieve this communication.

Figure 11-1 shows a remote object being consumed by a client application. The client application is loaded in its own app domain. Similarly, the server object is loaded in its own app domain. Before the remote object (often called a *server*) can be consumed, it must be activated on the server. Activation is a process by which the remote object is published and made available on a network, and the remoting infrastructure must be present at both ends of the .NET Framework. When the client wishes to call any method of the remote object, it does so via a proxy. The proxy marshals the method call to the remote server. The remote object then executes it and marshals the return value back. Again, the proxy acts as a middleman and conveys the results back to the client application. The data marshalled from one application to the other is transferred over a communication channel. Typically this channel will be TCP or HTTP.

Object Activation

In the preceding section, you learned that a remote object must be activated prior to consuming it. The term *activation* refers to how the objects are created and maintained on the server. There are two ways in which the remote objects can be activated:

- Server-activated objects: The lifetime of these remote objects is controlled by the server. These objects have a unique name (Uniform Resource Identifier, or URI) on the network and are often called *well-known objects*. Server-activated objects can be further classified as singleton or single call.
    - In the case of singleton objects, the server maintains only one instance of the remote object. The same instance serves all the clients. In other words, all the clients share the same object.
    - In the case of single-call objects, the server creates and destroys an object on a per-call basis. That means each method call gets its own instance to work with. After the method completes, the instance is destroyed.
- Client-activated objects: The lifetime of these remote objects is controlled by the client application. For each client, a separate object instance is created and maintained on the server.

It is worth noting that server activation is recommended for stateless objects, whereas client-side activation is good for stateful objects.

Channels and Formatters

Previously you learned that the proxy marshals data across the client and server over a channel. Thus a channel is responsible for carrying method calls and data across the network. The .NET Framework provides three built-in channels: Transmission Control Protocol (TCP), Hypertext Transfer Protocol (HTTP), and interprocess communication (IPC).

The marshalled data must be sent in a certain understandable format. This is the job of formatters. The .NET Framework comes with two formatters out of the box: a binary formatter and a SOAP formatter.

Note Recollect that in Chapter 8 you learned about serialization formats. The remoting framework internally uses the same serialization classes for marshalling the data.

By default the TCP channel uses a binary formatter, whereas the HTTP channel uses a SOAP formatter. However, this coupling is by no means rigid. You can use SOAP over TCP and binary over HTTP if you so wish. You can even develop custom channels and formatters.

Flavors of Marshalling

In the previous sections, you learned about the process of marshalling. The objects can be marshalled over a network by using two techniques:

Marshalling by value: A copy of the remote object is made and is serialized over the wire to the client application. A change to the copy doesn't affect the remote server. You mark classes for marshalling by value by using the `[Serializable]` attribute.

Marshalling by reference: The complete object is not sent to the client. Instead, a proxy for the remote object is created and is serialized over the network. Any change made on the proxy affects the remote server object (of course, depending on the activation model). To mark your classes for marshalling by reference, you need to make sure they inherit from the `MarshalByRefObject` base class.

Remoting Assemblies and Namespaces

All the functionality of the remoting infrastructure is available via an assembly, `System.Runtime.Remoting.dll`. The `System.Runtime.Remoting` namespace residing in this assembly contains classes that allow you to configure the client and server applications for remoting services. The `System.Runtime.Remoting.Channels` namespace provides classes that offer channel-related services. This namespace further contains sub-namespaces for individual channel type (`Tcp`, `Http`, `Ipc`, and so forth).

Creating a Remoting-Enabled Application

Any remoting-enabled application consists of three parts:

- The remote server
- An application that publishes the remote server
- A client that consumes the remote server

The remote server is typically created as a class library. In the class library, you need to create the classes that you wish to consume remotely. The remote server must be published over the network by selecting its activation model. This job is done by creating a console application, Windows application, or Windows service. After the remote server is activated, it can then be consumed in the client application.

The application that publishes the server and the client application require you to configure certain parameters of the remoting infrastructure at the respective ends. These configuration settings can be specified via code or via configuration files. We will be using the latter approach. The remoting configuration files are XML files that contain certain predefined elements and attributes. The advantage of using configuration files is that you can change the configuration parameters at any time without recompiling the application.

In the following sections, you will create an application that displays employee details based on the specified employee ID. The client calls a remote object called `Employee` to retrieve these details. The remote server returns the details in the form of a serializable class called `EmployeeDetails`. The remote server is published on the network by using a console application.

Creating the Remote Server

To create the remote server, you need to create a project of type class library in Visual Studio. Name the project `EmployeeServer`. This name is given by default to the output assembly and namespace. Then add two classes in the class library and name them `Employee` and `EmployeeDetails`, respectively. The `Employee` is the main remote object. The `EmployeeDetails` class is used to carry information about an employee from the `Employee` object to the client application. Listing 11-1 shows the `EmployeeDetails` class.

Listing 11-1. *EmployeeDetails Class*

```
[Serializable]
public class EmployeeDetails
{
        private int intID;
        private string strFName;
        private string strLName;
        private string strHPhone;
        private string strNotes;

        public int EmployeeID
        {
            get
            {
                return intID;
            }
            set
            {
                intID = value;
            }
        }

        public string FirstName
        {
            get
            {
                return strFName;
            }
            set
            {
                strFName = value;
            }
        }

        public string LastName
        {
            get
            {
                return strLName;
            }
            set
            {
                strLName = value;
            }
        }
```

```
        public string HomePhone
        {
            get
            {
                return strHPhone;
            }
            set
            {
                strHPhone = value;
            }
        }

        public string Notes
        {
            get
            {
                return strNotes;
            }
            set
            {
                strNotes = value;
            }
        }
}
```

The EmployeeDetails class consists of five private variables for storing the employee ID, first name, last name, home phone, and notes. These private variables are wrapped in respective public properties: EmployeeID, FirstName, LastName, HomePhone, and Notes. The important thing to notice about this class is that it is marked with the [Serializable] attribute. The [Serializable] attribute is necessary so that the objects of the EmployeeDetails class can be serialized over the wire. In other words, the EmployeeDetails class is a marshal-by-value type.

Listing 11-2 shows the complete Employee class.

Listing 11-2. *Employee Class*

```
public class Employee:MarshalByRefObject
{
        public Employee()
        {
            Console.WriteLine("Inside Employee Constructor...");
        }

        public EmployeeDetails GetEmployee(int empid)
```

```
        {
            string strConn = @"data source=.\sqlexpress;initial ➥
catalog=northwind;integrated security=true";
            EmployeeDetails emp = new EmployeeDetails();
            SqlConnection cnn = new SqlConnection(strConn);
            SqlCommand cmd =
              new SqlCommand("SELECT employeeid,firstname,lastname,homephone,notes
                             FROM employees WHERE employeeid=@id", cnn);
            SqlParameter p = new SqlParameter("@id", empid);
            cmd.Parameters.Add(p);
            cnn.Open();
            SqlDataReader reader = cmd.ExecuteReader();
            while (reader.Read())
            {
                emp.EmployeeID = reader.GetInt32(0);
                emp.FirstName = reader.GetString(1);
                emp.LastName = reader.GetString(2);
                emp.HomePhone = reader.GetString(3);
                emp.Notes = reader.GetString(4);
            }
            reader.Close();
            cnn.Close();
            return emp;
        }
}
```

■ **Note** Make sure to change the database connection string in Listing 11-2 to suit your development environment.

As mentioned earlier, any marshal-by-reference class must inherit from the `MarshalByRefObject` class. Hence the `Employee` class inherits from the `MarshalByRefObject` base class. The `Employee` class contains a single method named `GetEmployee()`, which accepts the employee ID of an employee, populates its details in an object of the `EmployeeDetails` class, and returns it back to the caller. To accomplish this, the code creates a `SqlConnection` and passes a connection string to its constructor. It then creates an instance of the `SqlCommand` class by passing a `SELECT` query and the `SqlConnection` instance that we just created.

The SELECT query fetches five columns from the Employees table of the Northwind database: EmployeeID, FirstName, LastName, HomePhone, and Notes. Then the database connection is opened for query execution by using the Open() method of the SqlConnection class. The ExecuteReader() method of the SqlCommand class executes the SELECT query and returns its results as a SqlDataReader. Then the code iterates through the SqlDataReader and sets various properties of the EmployeeDetails object. After the properties are set, the SqlDataReader and SqlConnection are closed. Finally, the EmployeeDetails instance is returned to the caller.

The class also has a public constructor, which simply emits a message on the console. The purpose of putting a message here will be clear when we develop and run the client application later in this chapter.

Creating an Application That Publishes the EmployeeServer

Now that you have completed the EmployeeServer class library, let's create a console application that publishes the EmployeeServer on the network. To do so, create a new project of type console application. Add references to the System.Runtime.Remoting and EmployeeServer assemblies by using the Add Reference dialog box.

At the top of the Main class, import two namespaces: System.Runtime.Remoting and EmployeeServer. Right-click on your project and add a new XML file named EmployeeServer.config. This XML file will contain markup necessary to configure the remoting infrastructure on the server side. Listing 11-3 shows the contents of the EmployeeServer.config configuration file.

Listing 11-3. *Configuring the Remoting Server*

```
<?xml version="1.0" encoding="utf-8" ?>
<configuration>
  <system.runtime.remoting>
    <application>
     <service>
        <wellknown type="EmployeeServer.Employee,EmployeeServer"
                   mode="SingleCall" objectUri="MyRemoteObject"></wellknown>
      </service>
      <channels>
        <channel port="8088" ref="tcp"></channel>
      </channels>
    </application>
  </system.runtime.remoting>
</configuration>
```

The root tag of the XML document is `<configuration>` because .NET Framework configuration files always have a root tag of `<configuration>`. Then comes the `<system.runtime.remoting>` section. This section encloses all the remoting-related configuration settings. The `<application>` section contains subsections related to application configuration.

The `<service>` section is used to configure server-activated objects. The `<wellknown>` tag specifies more details about the type being published. Remember that server-activated objects are also called *well-known objects* because they have a unique name over the network:

- The `type` attribute specifies the type being published as remotable. The format used to specify the type is `<fully_qualified_type_name>,<assembly_name>`. In our case, the fully qualified name of the `Employee` class is `EmployeeServer.Employee` and it resides in the `EmployeeServer` assembly.

- The `mode` attribute governs whether the type is to be published as `Singleton` or `SingleCall`. In our example, we are publishing it as `SingleCall`.

- The `objectUri` attribute specifies a unique URI for the type. The type is identified on the network with the help of this URI. In our example, the URI is `MyRemoteObject`.

The `<channels>` section is used to configure the channel of communication. The `<channel>` tag specifies more details about the transport channel:

- The `port` attribute specifies the port number at which the server will listen. Make sure to specify a port number that is not in use.

- The `ref` attribute indicates the channel to be used for the communication. There are three channels available out of the box: `Tcp`, `Http`, and `Ipc`.

After entering all the configuration information, save the file and add the code shown in Listing 11-4 in the `Main()` method.

Listing 11-4. *Loading the Remoting Configuration*

```
class Program
{
  static void Main(string[] args)
  {
    RemotingConfiguration.Configure(Environment.CurrentDirectory +
                                    @"\EmployeeServer.config",false);
    Console.WriteLine("Employee Server Published Successfully!");
    Console.WriteLine("Press ENTER to exit...");
    Console.ReadLine();
  }
}
```

The code calls the `Configure()` method of the `RemotingConfiguration` class, which accepts two parameters. The first is the filename of the `Remoting` configuration file (note the use of the `Environment` class to retrieve the current application folder). The second parameter indicates whether you wish to enforce security on the underlying channel.

Note The MSDN documentation of this method seems to be inadequate for the `ensureSecurity` parameter. If the `ensureSecurity` parameter is set to `true`, the remoting system determines whether the channel implements the `ISecurableChannel` interface. If it does, it enables encryption and digital signatures for the channel. In our example, we are not using any of these security features and hence set this parameter to `false`.

Then the code outputs a success message on the console. The server remains published only while this application is running. To accomplish this, we call the `ReadLine()` method, which blocks the current thread until the user presses the Enter key.

Creating the Client Application

In this section, we will develop a Windows application that acts as a client for the `EmployeeServer`. The application user interface is shown in Figure 11-2.

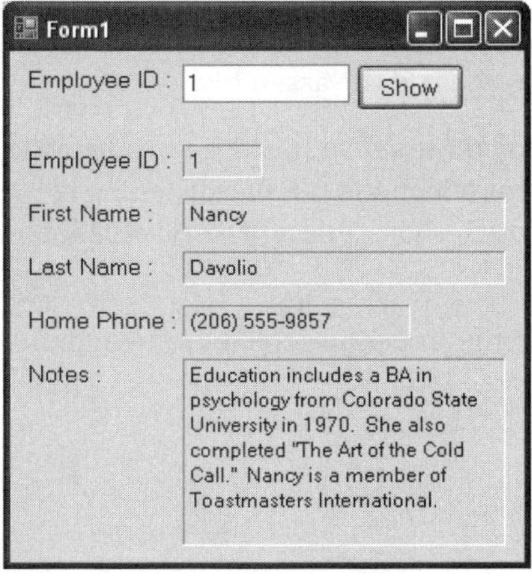

Figure 11-2. *Application that consumes the EmployeeServer*

The application consists of a text box for accepting the employee ID whose details are to be retrieved. Clicking the Show button calls the `GetEmployee()` method of the remote `Employee` object. The returned employee details are displayed in labels.

To begin developing the application, add a reference to the System.Runtime.Remoting and EmployeeServer assemblies. Also, import the System.Runtime.Remoting and EmployeeServer namespaces at the top of the form class. Now add a new XML file named EmployeeClient.config to the project. This configuration file will store the settings required to configure the remoting infrastructure at the client end. The complete markup of EmployeeClient.config is shown in Listing 11-5.

Listing 11-5. *Configuring the Remoting Client*

```
<?xml version="1.0" encoding="utf-8" ?>
<configuration>
  <system.runtime.remoting>
    <application>
      <client>
        <wellknown type="EmployeeServer.Employee,EmployeeServer"
                   url="tcp://localhost:8088/MyRemoteObject"></wellknown>
      </client>
    </application>
  </system.runtime.remoting>
</configuration>
```

Just like the server configuration file, the root node of the client configuration file is <configuration>, but the <application> section this time contains the <client> subsection. The <client> subsection contains a tag named <wellknown> that specifies details about the remote type. Its attributes are as follows:

- The tag attribute specifies the fully qualified type name and the assembly.
- The url attribute specifies the complete URL of the remote server. Because we are using the TCP channel, the URL protocol is tcp. The port at which the server is listening is mentioned just after localhost. Finally, the URI of the remote object (MyRemoteObject in our case) is specified.

Now we are ready to consume the remote object. Listing 11-6 shows the relevant code.

Listing 11-6. *Calling a Method of a Remote Object*

```
private void Form1_Load(object sender, EventArgs e)
{
  RemotingConfiguration.Configure(Environment.CurrentDirectory +
                                  @"\EmployeeClient.config", false);
}
```

```
private void button1_Click(object sender, EventArgs e)
{
  Employee emp = new Employee();
  EmployeeDetails ed= emp.GetEmployee(int.Parse(textBox1.Text));
  label7.Text = ed.EmployeeID.ToString();
  label8.Text = ed.FirstName;
  label9.Text = ed.LastName;
  label10.Text = ed.HomePhone;
  label11.Text = ed.Notes;
}
```

The `Configure()` method of the `RemotingConfiguration` class is called in the `Load` event handler of the form. This method is the same as the one we called in the console application. The code passes the full path of the client configuration file to the `Configure()` method. This call is needed just once and hence it has been put in the `Load` event and not in the `Click` event of the Show button.

Inside the `Click` event handler of the Show button, a new instance of the `Employee` class is created. Then the `GetEmployee()` method of the `Employee` class is called by passing the supplied employee ID. The `GetEmployee()` method returns an object of type `EmployeeDetails`. The details such as `EmployeeID`, `FirstName`, `LastName`, `HomePhone`, and `Notes` are then displayed in labels.

■ **Note** If you look at the code that consumes the remote server, you won't find anything different. This is how you consume any other class. This feature is often called *location transparency*.

That's it. You've just completed the three parts of a remoting application. To test the application, you need to follow a specific sequence:

1. Run the console application.
2. Run the client application.
3. Enter a valid employee ID and click the Show button.

Figure 11-3 shows the console application window after the `GetEmployee()` method call has been made. Notice the message that reads, "Inside Employee Constructor." We outputted this message from the constructor of the `Employee` class. After making a call to the `GetEmployee()` method, this message is shown in the console window. This proves that it was the remote component that was called and not the local copy.

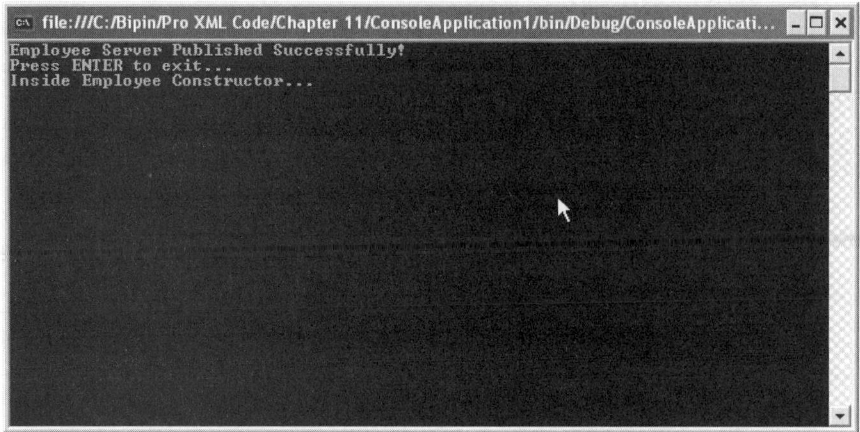

Figure 11-3. *The console application publishing the EmployeeServer*

Note You might be wondering why we referenced the `EmployeeServer` in the client application when it is to be consumed remotely. This is necessary because even though the method is to be called on a remote object, the client application still needs the server's metadata. There are ways to avoid this coupling, but they are not within the scope of this book. You may refer to the MSDN library for a description of a command-line tool called `soapsuds.exe`. This tool creates metadata-only assemblies that you can use in client applications in place of the actual server assembly.

Using XML in ASP.NET

ASP.NET is a technology for building dynamic and data-driven web applications. In ASP.NET, web pages are called *web forms*. Web forms use the `.aspx` extension and contain HTML markup, server control markup, and optionally code. Web forms are called so because they provide the same event-driven programming model as provided by Rapid Application Development (RAD) tools such as Visual Basic 6. Every web form is a class that inherits directly or indirectly from the `System.Web.UI.Page` base class.

Server controls are object-oriented wrappers over traditional HTML elements. They are processed by ASP.NET on the server side, which is why they are called server controls. They provide many advantages over traditional HTML controls, including rich functionality, data binding, object-oriented features, and many others. An ASP.NET website is a collection of web forms and related resources such as images, JavaScript files, and compiled components.

Web Form Code Models

You can develop web forms via two coding models:

- The single-file code model
- The code-behind model

The Single-File Code Model

In the single-file code model, you place HTML markup, server control markup, and code in a single physical file. This file has an extension of `.aspx`. Your code resides in a `<script runat="server"> </script>` block.

The Code-Behind Model

In the code-behind model, there are two distinct files per web form: one with an extension of `.aspx`, and the other with an extension of `.cs` if you are using C# or `.vb` if you are using VB.NET. This latter file is referred to as the code-behind file of the web form.

The .ASPX file contains the entire HTML and server control markup. The .CS file contains all the code including event handlers and user-defined functions. In our examples, we will be using the code-behind model for all our web forms.

XML and ASP.NET

ASP.NET uses XML in several places. Some of the main areas where XML is used extensively are as follows:

- Server control markup
- XML data source control
- Navigational controls such as TreeView, Menu, and SiteMap
- XML control
- Website configuration

You will learn about all these features in the following sections.

Server Control Markup

As mentioned previously, ASP.NET web forms consist of HTML and server control markup. The server control markup is actually a special vocabulary of XML. Each server control has a predefined tag name, tag prefix, and attributes. Some server controls are empty elements (they do not contain any child elements), whereas others can contain markup or text.

To better understand server controls, you will develop an ASP.NET website with one web form. The web form represents a typical Contact Us page. The page will be used by end users to contact you with any questions, feedback, or comments about your website.

Creating a Website

To create a new website by using Visual Studio, you need to choose the File ➤ New Web Site option. This option opens the New Web Site dialog box, as shown in Figure 11-4.

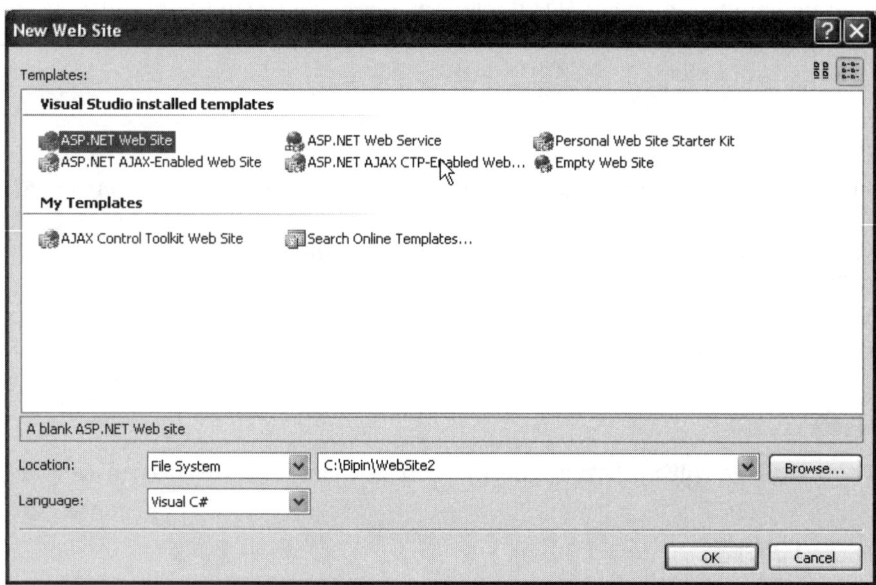

Figure 11-4. *Creating a new website*

The ASP.NET Web Site template allows you to create a website. The Location drop-down list indicates the target location where the website will be created. Possible locations are File System, IIS Virtual Root (HTTP), and FTP Folder (FTP). In our example, we will choose File System. The path specified after the Location drop-down is the target folder where the website will be created. Make sure to select Visual C# as the language. Click the OK button to create the website. Visual Studio will create the website with a single web form named `Default.aspx`.

Designing the Web Form

The next task is to design the Contact Us web form. To do so, choose Layout ➤ Insert Table from the menu and insert a table with 11 rows and 2 columns in the default web form. Now you need to drag and drop various controls and arrange them in the cells of this table, as detailed in the following steps. Figure 11-5 shows `Default.aspx` after designing the web form.

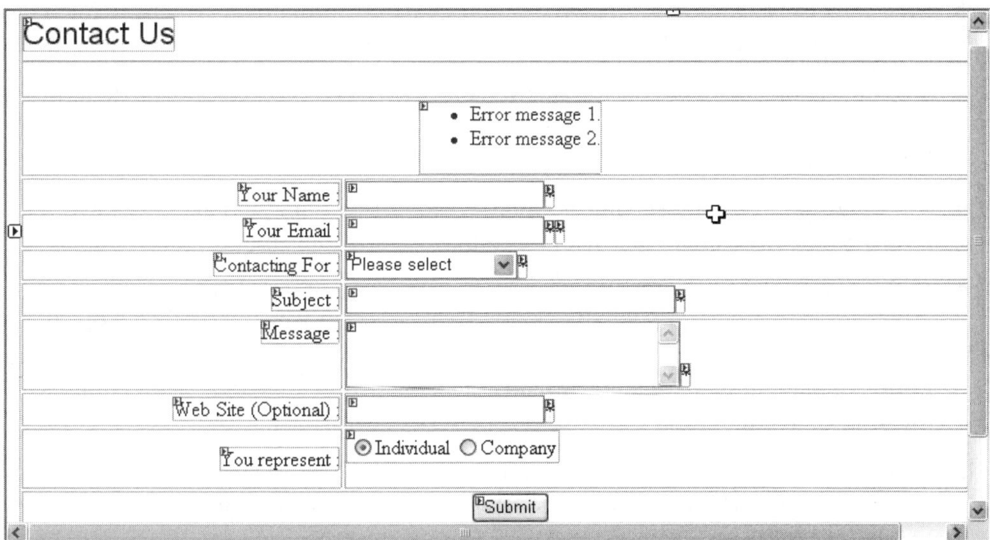

Figure 11-5. *Designing a web form*

The web form consists of many server controls such as Label, TextBox, DropDownList, RadioButtonList, Button, RequiredFieldValidator, RegularExpressionValidator, and ValidationSummary. To begin designing the web form, use the following steps:

1. Drag and drop a Label control to the first row of the table. Set its Text property to **Contact Us**. Set its Font property to your choice. Also, drag and drop a Horizontal Rule HTML control below the Contact Us label.

2. Drag and drop a ValidationSummary control in the second row. The ValidationSummary control is available in the Validation node of the toolbox and is used to display a consolidated list of validation errors from the current web form.

3. Drag and drop seven Label controls in rows 3 through 9. Set their Text properties to **Your Name :**, **Your Email :**, **Contacting For :**, **Subject :**, **Message :**, **Web Site (Optional) :**, and **You represent :**, respectively.

4. Drag and drop a TextBox control after the Your Name, Your Email, Subject, Message, and Web Site (Optional) labels, respectively. Set the TextMode property of the Message text box to **MultiLine**.

5. Drag and drop a DropDownList control after the Contacting For label.

6. Drag and drop a RadioButtonList after the You Represent label.

7. Drag and drop a Button control to row 10 and set its Text property to **Submit**.

8. Drag and drop a Label control to row 11 and set its Text property to a blank string. This label will be used to display a success message to the user.

9. Select the DropDownList control. Open its property window and locate the Items property. Add four items in the DropDownList: **Please Select**, **Sales Quotation**, **Technical Problem**, and **Other**.

10. Select the RadioButtonList control. Open its property window and locate the Items property. Add two items in the RadioButtonList: **Individual** and **Company**.

11. Drag and drop a RequiredFieldValidator control in front of the controls that accept name, email, reason for contact, subject, and message. The RequiredFieldValidator control is used to validate that the control to which it has been attached contains some value. Set the ControlToValidate property of all the RequiredFieldValidator controls to the ID property of the respective text boxes or **DropDownList**.

12. Set the InitialValue property of the RequiredFieldValidator attached to the Contacting For drop-down to **Please Select**. This way, the user will need to choose an option other than Please Select.

13. Drag and drop a RegularExpressionValidator control in front of the controls that accept email and website. The RegularExpressionValidator control validates the entered value for a specific pattern. The pattern is set by using regular expression syntax. Set the ControlToValidate property of both the RegularExpressionValidator controls to the ID property of the respective text boxes. Set the ValidationExpression property of the first RegularExpressionValidator control to **Internet Email Address**. Similarly, set the ValidationExpression property of the second RegularExpressionValidator control to **Internet URL**.

14. Set the Text property of all the validation controls (RequiredFieldValidator and RegularExpressionValidator) to *. This text will be displayed in place of the validation control whenever there is a validation error. Also, set the ErrorMessage property of all the validation controls to some meaningful error message. The ErrorMessage will be displayed in the ValidationSummary control in the event of any validation error.

Our web form design is now over. At the bottom of the web form designer, you will find a tab named Source. Click on it to see the markup generated for our web form. The relevant markup of `Default.aspx` is given in Listing 11-7.

Listing 11-7. *Server Control Markup from Default.aspx*

```
<%@ Page Language="C#" AutoEventWireup="true"
CodeFile="Default.aspx.cs" Inherits="_Default" %>

<!DOCTYPE html PUBLIC "-//W3C//DTD XHTML 1.0 Transitional//EN"
 "http://www.w3.org/TR/xhtml1/DTD/xhtml1-transitional.dtd">
```

```
...
<form id="form1" runat="server">
...
<asp:Label ID="Label1" runat="server" Font-Names="Arial"
Font-Size="X-Large" Text="Contact Us">
</asp:Label>
...
<asp:ValidationSummary ID="ValidationSummary1" runat="server" />
...
<asp:Label ID="Label2" runat="server" Text="Your Name :"></asp:Label>
...
<asp:TextBox ID="TextBox1" runat="server"></asp:TextBox>
<asp:RequiredFieldValidator
                 ID="RequiredFieldValidator1"
                 runat="server" ControlToValidate="TextBox1"
                 Display="Dynamic"
                 ErrorMessage="Please enter your name">*
</asp:RequiredFieldValidator>
...
<asp:Label ID="Label3" runat="server" Text="Your Email :"></asp:Label>
...
<asp:TextBox ID="TextBox2" runat="server"></asp:TextBox>
<asp:RequiredFieldValidator
                 ID="RequiredFieldValidator2" runat="server"
                 ControlToValidate="TextBox2"
                 Display="Dynamic"
                 ErrorMessage="Please enter your email">*
</asp:RequiredFieldValidator>
<asp:RegularExpressionValidator
                 ID="RegularExpressionValidator1"
                 runat="server"
                 ControlToValidate="TextBox2"
                 Display="Dynamic"
                 ErrorMessage="Please enter a valid email address"
               ValidationExpression="\w+([-+.']\w+)*@\w+([-.]\w+)*\.\w+([-.]\w+)*">*
            </asp:RegularExpressionValidator></td>
...
<asp:Label ID="Label4" runat="server" Text="Contacting For :"></asp:Label>
...
<asp:DropDownList ID="DropDownList1" runat="server">
<asp:ListItem Value=" Please select ">Please select</asp:ListItem>
<asp:ListItem Value=" Sales Quotation ">Sales Quotation</asp:ListItem>
<asp:ListItem Value=" Technical Problem ">Technical Problem</asp:ListItem>
<asp:ListItem Value=" Other ">Other</asp:ListItem>
</asp:DropDownList>
```

```
<asp:RequiredFieldValidator ID="RequiredFieldValidator3" runat="server"
ControlToValidate="DropDownList1" Display="Dynamic"
ErrorMessage="Please select a reason for contacting us"
InitialValue="PS">*
</asp:RequiredFieldValidator>
...
<asp:Label ID="Label5" runat="server" Text="Subject :"></asp:Label>
...
<asp:TextBox ID="TextBox3" runat="server" Columns="37"></asp:TextBox>
<asp:RequiredFieldValidator
ID="RequiredFieldValidator4" runat="server" ControlToValidate="TextBox3"
Display="Dynamic" ErrorMessage="Please enter subject">*
</asp:RequiredFieldValidator>
...
<asp:Label ID="Label6" runat="server" Text="Message :"></asp:Label>
...
<asp:TextBox ID="TextBox4" runat="server" Columns="30" Rows="3"
 TextMode="MultiLine"></asp:TextBox>
<asp:RequiredFieldValidator
ID="RequiredFieldValidator5" runat="server" ControlToValidate="TextBox4"
Display="Dynamic" ErrorMessage="Please enter message">*
</asp:RequiredFieldValidator>
...
<asp:Label ID="Label7" runat="server" Text="Web Site (Optional) :"></asp:Label>
...
<asp:TextBox ID="TextBox5" runat="server"></asp:TextBox>
<asp:RegularExpressionValidator
ID="RegularExpressionValidator2" runat="server" ControlToValidate="TextBox5"
Display="Dynamic" ErrorMessage="Please enter a valid URL"
ValidationExpression="http(s)?://([\w-]+\.)+[\w-]+(/[\w- ./?%&=]*)?">
*</asp:RegularExpressionValidator>
...
<asp:Label ID="Label8" runat="server" Text="You represent :"></asp:Label>
...
<asp:RadioButtonList ID="RadioButtonList1" runat="server"
RepeatDirection="Horizontal">
<asp:ListItem Selected="True" Value="Individual">Individual</asp:ListItem>
<asp:ListItem Value="ListItem">Company</asp:ListItem>
</asp:RadioButtonList>
...
<asp:Button ID="Button1" runat="server" OnClick="Button1_Click" Text="Submit" />
...
<asp:Label ID="Label9" runat="server" Font-Bold="True" ForeColor="Red"></asp:Label>
...
</html>
```

Observe the markup carefully. At the top you have a directive called @Page. A directive gives information about some entity to the ASP.NET processing engine. The @Page directive gives details about the current web form such as language of coding, code filename, and the class from the code file that represents this web form.

Next there is a <!DOCTYPE> declaration that indicates that this document is based on a DTD. The DTD in this case is a standard DTD from the W3C. The DTD indicates that this document is XHTML compliant.

Note XHTML markup is nothing but HTML markup that strictly follows the rules of XML grammar.

If you observe further, you will notice that every server control is represented by special XML markup. For example, a Label control is represented by an <asp:Label> tag, and a TextBox control is represented by an <asp:TextBox> tag. The part prior to the colon (:)—in other words, asp—is called a *tag prefix*. The part after the colon—Label or TextBox—is called a *tag name*.

Each server control has its ID attribute set to a unique value. The ID of a control is used to access it programmatically. Similarly, every server control has a runat attribute, which must have the value of server and indicates that the tag is server control markup. You will also observe that all the properties that you set via the property window are represented either as attributes or child elements in the server control markup. Thus ASP.NET server control markup is a special vocabulary of XML.

Writing Code

In this section, you will write some code so that when a user enters valid data and clicks the Submit button, the data is emailed to you. To accomplish this requirement, you need to handle the Click event of the Submit button. Listing 11-8 shows the web form class and the skeleton Click event handler. We'll fill that in next.

Listing 11-8. *Web Form Class and the Click Event Handler*

```
using System;
using System.Data;
using System.Configuration;
using System.Web;
using System.Web.Security;
using System.Web.UI;
using System.Web.UI.WebControls;
using System.Web.UI.WebControls.WebParts;
using System.Web.UI.HtmlControls;
```

```
public partial class _Default : System.Web.UI.Page
{
    protected void Button1_Click(object sender, EventArgs e)
    {

    }
}
```

The code-behind file contains a partial class named `_Default` that inherits from the `System.Web.UI.Page` base class, which provides basic functionality to your web form. Remember that the `@Page` directive has an attribute called `Inherits` that refers to this class. The `_Default` class is marked as partial because only when the markup file (`.aspx`) and code-behind file (`.cs`) are combined together, the complete class is generated. This merging happens at run time and is the job of the ASP.NET processing engine. Also, notice several namespaces that are imported at the top. All the namespaces that start with `System.Web` are physically located in an assembly, `System.Web.dll`.

■ **Note** Thorough discussion of ASP.NET server controls and related concepts is out of the scope of this book. If you are interested in ASP.NET web application development, consider *Pro ASP.NET 2.0 in C# 2005, Special Edition* by Matthew MacDonald and Mario Szpuszta (Apress, 2006) or *Pro ASP.NET 2.0 in VB 2005, Special Edition* by Laurence Moroney and Matthew MacDonald (Apress, 2006).

To code our functionality, you need to import two namespaces: `System.Net` and `System.Net.Mail`. The latter namespace provides classes for sending emails. Listing 11-9 shows the `Click` event handler after adding the necessary code.

Listing 11-9. *Sending Email from the Code-Behind File*

```
protected void Button1_Click(object sender, EventArgs e)
{
  SmtpClient client = new SmtpClient("localhost");
  client.Credentials = CredentialCache.DefaultNetworkCredentials;
  MailMessage msg = new MailMessage();
  msg.From = new MailAddress(TextBox2.Text);
  msg.To.Add("you@yourdomain.com");
  msg.Subject = TextBox3.Text;
  msg.Body =
    "[" + DropDownList1.SelectedItem.Text + "]" + TextBox4.Text + "\r\n" +
      TextBox1.Text + "\r\n" + TextBox5.Text;
  client.Send(msg);
  Label9.Text = "Your message has been sent. Thank you!";
}
```

The code declares an object of the `SmtpClient` class. The `SmtpClient` class allows you to send emails based on Simple Mail Transfer Protocol (SMTP). The constructor of the `SmltpClient` class accepts the IP address or name of the machine used for SMTP operations. In our example, it is assumed that you are using a local installation of IIS for sending emails and hence `localhost` is passed as the parameter. The `Credentials` property of the `SmtpClient` class indicates the network credentials of a user for authenticating the sender. The `DefaultNetworkCredentials` property of the `CredentialCache` class indicates the authentication credentials of the current Windows user.

After the credentials have been set, a new `MailMessage` is created. The `MailMessage` class represents an email message. The `From` and `To` properties of this class represent the sender and receiver, respectively, and are of type `MailAddress`. The `Subject` and `Body` properties indicate the subject and body of the email, respectively. All these properties are assigned by using the values entered in various web form controls. Finally, the `Send()` method of the `SmtpClient` class sends the supplied `MailMessage` to one or more recipients. A success message is displayed in a label informing the user that the message has been received.

Running the Web Application

To run the web application that you just finished, you need to choose the Debug ➤ Start Debugging menu option. Visual Studio asks whether you would like to turn on debugging (Figure 11-6). Simply keep the default selection and click OK.

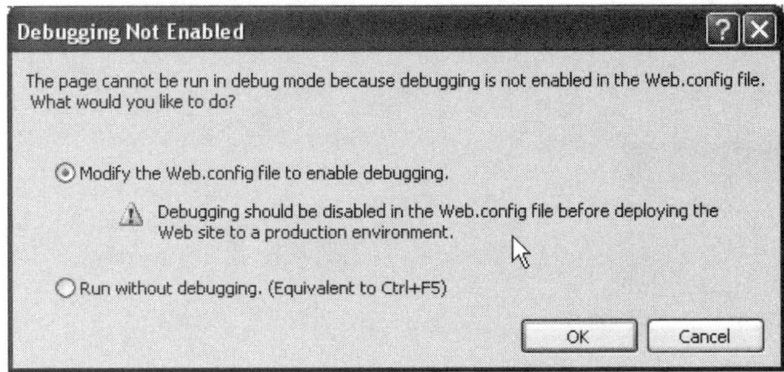

Figure 11-6. *Enabling debugging for your website*

■ **Note** After you click OK in the Debugging Not Enabled dialog box, Visual Studio will actually add a file called `web.config` to your website that enables debugging for your website. You will learn about the `web.config` file in later sections.

Visual Studio will launch the default development web server in the background and will host your website in it. It will also open the default browser and navigate to `Default.aspx`. Figure 11-7 shows the `Default.aspx` web form in the browser.

Figure 11-7. *Default.aspx in a browser*

If you try to click the Submit button without entering any values, you should see validation error messages, as shown in Figure 11-8.

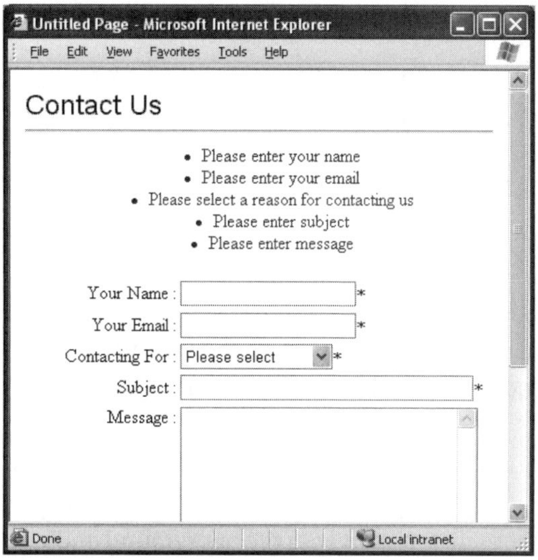

Figure 11-8. *Web form showing validation errors*

Notice how the ValidationSummary displays a collective list of error messages, whereas an asterisk is displayed in place of individual validation controls. If you enter valid values in the controls and click Submit, the code will send an email to your email address and will display a success message, as shown in Figure 11-9.

Figure 11-9. *Successful execution of the web form*

The XML Data Source Control

One of the strengths of server controls is their ability to perform data binding with relational or hierarchical data. ASP.NET data source controls are a set of web server controls that automate common data-access tasks such as fetching records and displaying them in other data bound controls. All of this is achieved without any code being written by the developer. As we are looking at XML in this book, it is the XML data source control we are interested in. This control is very useful when you are using controls such as TreeView that essentially display hierarchical data. Let's see how the XML data source control can be used along with a TreeView control.

Begin by creating a new website via Visual Studio. Add a new XML file to your website by using the Add New Item dialog box and name it `Navigation.xml`. The `Navigation.xml` file contains XML markup representing website navigation structure. The XML markup from `Navigation.xml` is shown in Listing 11-10.

Listing 11-10. *XML Markup from the Navigation.xml File*

```
<?xml version="1.0" encoding="utf-8" ?>
<node text="Home" url="default.aspx">
  <node text="Products" url="products.aspx">
    <node text="Product 1" url="product1.aspx"></node>
    <node text="Product 2" url="product2.aspx"></node>
    <node text="Product 3" url="product3.aspx"></node>
  </node>
  <node text="Services" url="services.aspx">
    <node text="Service 1" url="service1.aspx"></node>
    <node text="Service 2" url="service2.aspx"></node>
    <node text="Service 3" url="service3.aspx"></node>
  </node>
  <node text="About Us" url="about.aspx"></node>
  <node text="Contact Us" url="contact.aspx"></node>
</node>
```

The root tag of the document is <node>, which further contains various <node> tags. Each <node> element represents a node of the TreeView control and has two attributes, `text` and `url`:

- The `text` attribute specifies the text to be displayed in the TreeView node.
- The `url` attribute points to a URL where the user should be navigated.

The nesting of the <node> elements decides the nesting of the TreeView rendered. Thus the root node of the TreeView will be Home. The Home node will have four immediate children: Products, Services, About Us, and Contact Us. Similarly, the Products and Services nodes will have three children each.

Now drag and drop an XmlDataSource control from the toolbox onto the web form designer. Set its `DataFile` property to `Navigation.xml`. The `DataFile` property points to an XML file that will be supplying data to the XML data source control. Next, drag and drop a TreeView control onto the web form and set its `DataSourceID` property to the ID of the XmlDataSource control you just configured. Now locate the `DataBindings` property of the TreeView, and open the TreeView DataBindings Editor (Figure 11-10).

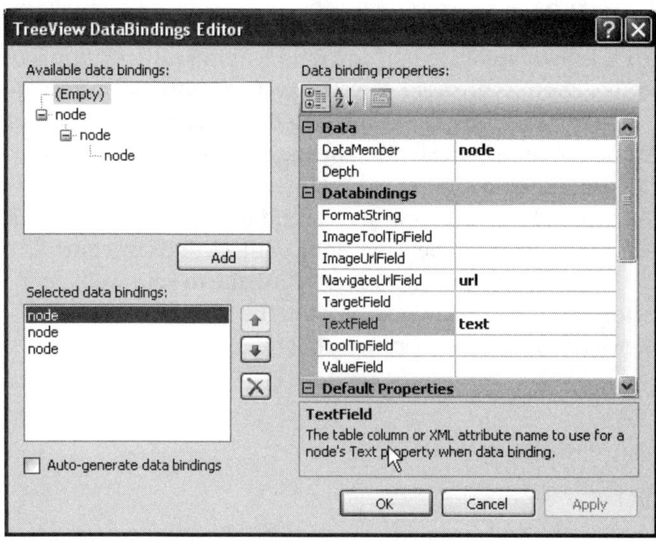

Figure 11-10. *TreeView DataBindings Editor*

In the Available Data Bindings area, you will see all the nodes at each level from the XML file. Select the node at each level and click the Add button. You will now have three entries in the Selected Data Bindings area. Select the first data binding and set its `TextField` and `NavigateUrlField` properties to `text` and `url`, respectively. As you might have guessed, `text` and `url` are the attributes of the <node> element. The `DataMember` property indicates the name of the element from the XML document that is supplying the data and is automatically set to node. Repeat the same process for the remaining two data bindings. Listing 11-11 shows the complete markup of Default.aspx.

Listing 11-11. *Markup Containing the XmlDataSource and the TreeView*

```
<%@ Page Language="C#" AutoEventWireup="true"  CodeFile="Default.aspx.cs"
Inherits="_Default" %>

<!DOCTYPE html PUBLIC "-//W3C//DTD XHTML 1.0 Transitional//EN"
"http://www.w3.org/TR/xhtml1/DTD/xhtml1-transitional.dtd">

<html xmlns="http://www.w3.org/1999/xhtml" >
  <head runat="server">
    <title>Untitled Page</title>
  </head>
  <body>
    <form id="form1" runat="server">
      <asp:XmlDataSource ID="XmlDataSource1" runat="server"
                         DataFile="~/Navigation.xml">
      </asp:XmlDataSource>
      <asp:TreeView ID="TreeView1" runat="server" AutoGenerateDataBindings="False"
                    DataSourceID="XmlDataSource1" Font-Bold="True" Font-Size="Large"
                    ShowLines="True">
        <DataBindings>
          <asp:TreeNodeBinding DataMember="node" NavigateUrlField="url"
                               TextField="text" />
          <asp:TreeNodeBinding DataMember="node" NavigateUrlField="url"
                               TargetField="text" />
          <asp:TreeNodeBinding DataMember="node" NavigateUrlField="url"
                               TargetField="text" />
        </DataBindings>
      </asp:TreeView>
    </form>
  </body>
</html>
```

As you can see, the XML data source control and the TreeView control are represented by the <asp:XmlDataSource> and <asp:TreeView> markup tags, respectively. Each TreeView node binding is represented by an <asp:TreeNodeBinding> tag. The DataMember, NavigateUrlField, and TextField attributes of the TreeNodeBinding element represent the properties that you assigned previously.

Now run the website as before and see how the TreeView control renders the various nodes based on the structure specified in the Navigation.xml file. Figure 11-11 shows a sample run of the web form.

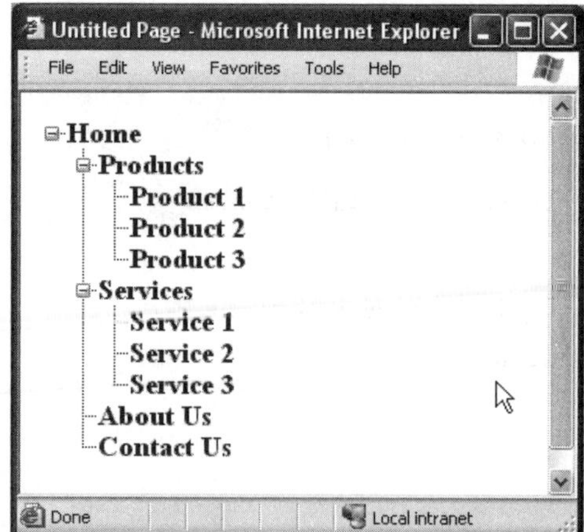

Figure 11-11. *A TreeView populated by using an XML data source control*

Applying Transformations

In the preceding example, you supplied the XML file as is to the XML data source control. What if you wish to apply an XSLT transformation to the XML file and then bind it with the TreeView? Fortunately, the XML data source control has a built-in facility to do just that: the `TransformFile` property, which points to an XSLT file. Before supplying the XML data to other controls such as a TreeView, the XSLT style sheet is applied to the XML data and then the transformed data is passed on. Suppose that you bound a TreeView control to an XML document as shown in Listing 11-12.

Listing 11-12. *XML Document to Be Bound to a TreeView*

```
<?xml version="1.0" encoding="utf-8"?>
<MenuItem Title="Home" URL="default.aspx">
  <MenuItem Title="Products" URL="products.aspx">
    <MenuItem Title="Product 1" URL="product1.aspx" />
    <MenuItem Title="Product 2" URL="product2.aspx" />
    <MenuItem Title="Product 3" URL="product3.aspx" />
  </MenuItem>
  <MenuItem Title="Services" URL="services.aspx">
    <MenuItem Title="Service 1" URL="service1.aspx" />
    <MenuItem Title="Service 2" URL="service2.aspx" />
    <MenuItem Title="Service 3" URL="service3.aspx" />
  </MenuItem>
  <MenuItem Title="About Us" URL="about.aspx" />
  <MenuItem Title="Contact Us" URL="contact.aspx" />
</MenuItem>
```

As you can see, this XML document uses the `<MenuItem>` element to represent a TreeView node. The `Title` and `URL` attributes represent the `Text` and `NavigateUrlField` properties of individual TreeView nodes. Now suppose that for some reason you want to bind the same TreeView to another XML document, as shown in Listing 11-13.

Listing 11-13. *XML Markup from the New XML File*

```
<?xml version="1.0" encoding="utf-8" ?>
<node text="Home" url="default.aspx">
  <node text="Products" url="products.aspx">
    <node text="Product 1" url="product1.aspx"></node>
    <node text="Product 2" url="product2.aspx"></node>
    <node text="Product 3" url="product3.aspx"></node>
  </node>
  <node text="Services" url="services.aspx">
    <node text="Service 1" url="service1.aspx"></node>
    <node text="Service 2" url="service2.aspx"></node>
    <node text="Service 3" url="service3.aspx"></node>
  </node>
  <node text="About Us" url="about.aspx"></node>
  <node text="Contact Us" url="contact.aspx"></node>
</node>
```

You might have noticed that this is the same XML file that we used in the previous example. To cater to the change, you need to reconfigure the TreeView node data bindings to suit the new XML document. If the underlying data binding has complex nesting, this may not be an easy task. This situation can be avoided if you apply an XSLT style sheet to the XML from Listing 11-13 and transform it to match the XML in Listing 11-12. The XSLT style sheet that can do this transformation is shown in Listing 11-14.

Listing 11-14. *An XSLT Style Sheet for Transforming the New XML Markup*

```
<?xml version="1.0" encoding="UTF-8" ?>
<xsl:stylesheet version="1.0" xmlns:xsl="http://www.w3.org/1999/XSL/Transform">
  <xsl:template match="/">
    <xsl:for-each select=".">
      <xsl:apply-templates/>
    </xsl:for-each>
  </xsl:template>
  <xsl:template match="node">
    <xsl:element name="MenuItem">
      <xsl:attribute name="Title">
        <xsl:value-of select="@text"/>
      </xsl:attribute>
```

```
      <xsl:attribute name="URL">
        <xsl:value-of select="@url"/>
      </xsl:attribute>
      <xsl:apply-templates />
    </xsl:element>
  </xsl:template>
</xsl:stylesheet>
```

The style sheet transforms a `<node>` element to a `<MenuItem>` element. Further, it transforms the `text` and `url` attributes to the `Title` and `URL` attributes, respectively.

To test how the `TransformFile` property works, you need to modify the preceding example by following these steps:

1. Add a new XSLT file named `Navigation.xsl` into the website.
2. Key in the markup shown in Listing 11-14.
3. Set the `TransformFile` property of the XML data source control to `Navigation.xsl`.
4. Open the TreeView DataBindings Editor of the TreeView and modify the data bindings to use the MenuItem node as `DataMember`, Title as `TextField`, and URL as `NavigateUrlField`.

This time, the TreeView DataBindings Editor looks like Figure 11-12.

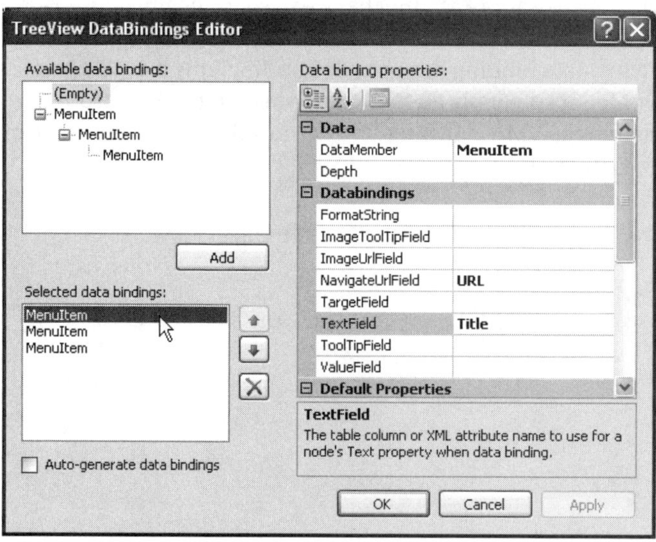

Figure 11-12. *TreeView DataBindings Editor showing transformed nodes*

You will observe that although the `DataFile` property is still `Navigation.xml`, the data bindings shown are as per the transformation specified in the XSLT style sheet. If you run the web form again, the output should be the same as in Figure 11-11 earlier.

Filtering Data by Using XPath Expressions

At times you may wish to filter the data from the source XML file and bind the filtered data to other controls. This is where the `XPath` property of the XML data source control comes in. The `XPath` property takes a valid XPath expression and applies it to the source XML data.

Suppose, for example, that you wish to display only product-related nodes in the TreeView. You can achieve this by setting the XPath property of the XML data source to `/node/node[@text="Products"]`. This way, only the product-related nodes (Products, Product 1, Product 2, and Product 3) will be filtered. The TreeView will have nesting up to two levels only (Products as the top node, and the other three nodes as child nodes). Figure 11-13 shows a sample run of the same web form after setting the `XPath` property.

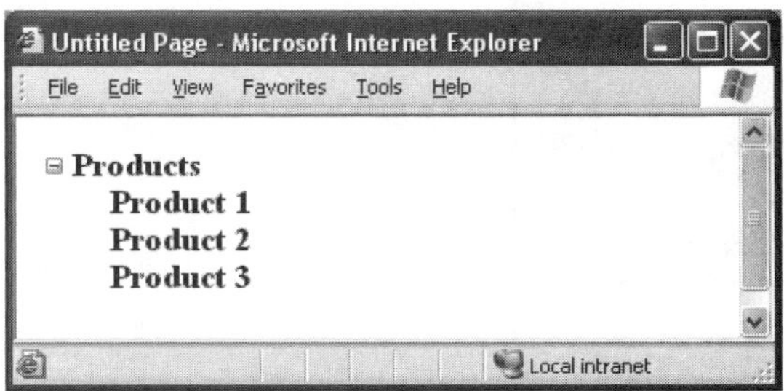

Figure 11-13. *TreeView after applying the XPath filter*

Binding an XML Data Source to a Menu Control

In the previous examples, you used a TreeView to display data supplied by an XML data source control. ASP.NET also provides a Menu control that can be used to display hierarchical data. The Menu control closely matches the TreeView control with respect to XML data binding. However, it differs in its look and feel. The Menu control renders dynamic pull-down menus in your web forms similar to traditional Windows applications. Let's see an example of how it can be used.

Create a new website in Visual Studio. Add the `Navigation.xml` file that you created previously to the website by using the Add Existing Item dialog box. Drag and drop an XmlDataSource control onto the default web form and set its `DataFile` property to `Navigation.xml`. Now drag and drop a Menu control onto the form and set its `DataSourceID` property to the ID of the XmlDataSource control you just configured.

Now, locate the Menu control's `DataBindings` property. Similar to the TreeView, the Menu control opens the Menu DataBindings Editor, wherein you can configure the data bindings.

The process of configuring data bindings is exactly the same as before. You need to select the required data bindings and set their `DataMember`, `TextField`, and `NavigateUrl` properties to `node`, `text`, and `url`, respectively. Figure 11-14 shows the Menu DataBindings Editor with required data bindings added.

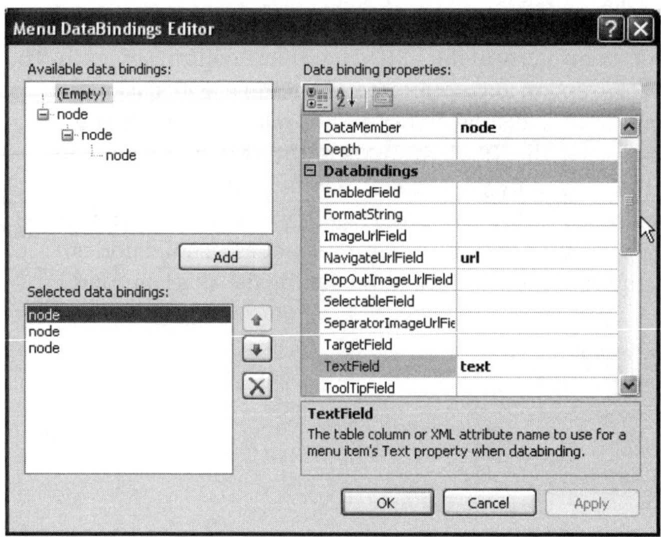

Figure 11-14. *Menu DataBindings Editor*

The complete markup of the web form is shown in Listing 11-15.

Listing 11-15. *Markup of the Menu Control*

```
<%@ Page Language="C#" AutoEventWireup="true"  CodeFile="Default.aspx.cs"
         Inherits="_Default" %>

<!DOCTYPE html PUBLIC "-//W3C//DTD XHTML 1.0 Transitional//EN"
"http://www.w3.org/TR/xhtml1/DTD/xhtml1-transitional.dtd">
<html xmlns="http://www.w3.org/1999/xhtml" >
  <head runat="server">
    <title>Untitled Page</title>
  </head>
  <body>
    <form id="form1" runat="server">
      <asp:XmlDataSource ID="XmlDataSource1" runat="server"
                         DataFile="~/Navigation.xml"></asp:XmlDataSource>
```

```
      <asp:Menu ID="Menu1" runat="server" BackColor="#E3EAEB"
                DataSourceID="XmlDataSource1"
        <DataBindings>
          <asp:MenuItemBinding DataMember="node" NavigateUrlField="url"
                               TextField="text" />
          <asp:MenuItemBinding DataMember="node" NavigateUrlField="url"
                               TextField="text" />
          <asp:MenuItemBinding DataMember="node" NavigateUrlField="url"
                               TextField="text" />
        </DataBindings>
      </asp:Menu>
    </form>
  </body>
</html>
```

As you can see, the Menu control is represented by the `<asp:Menu>` markup tag. The `<DataBindings>` section defines one or more data bindings, where each data binding is represented by an `<asp:MenuItemBinding>` element. Running the web form should render the menu as shown in Figure 11-15.

Figure 11-15. *The Menu control in action*

Working with Site Maps

A *site map* is an XML file that details the overall navigational layout of your website. You can then consume this site map file as required. The site map file has an extension of `.sitemap`. Let's examine site map files via an example. Have a look at Figure 11-16.

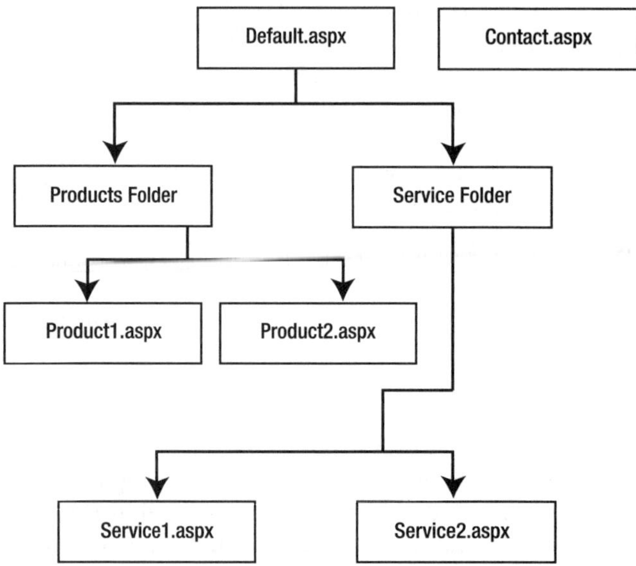

Figure 11-16. *Structure of a website*

Figure 11-16 shows the directory structure of a sample website. The home page (`Default.aspx`) and Contact Us page (`contact.aspx`) reside in the root folder of the website. There are two subfolders called `Products` and `Services`. Each of them contains two web forms—`Product1.aspx` and `Product2.aspx`, and `Service1.aspx` and `Service2.aspx`—respectively. Now let's represent this website structure by using a site map.

Create a new website by using Visual Studio. Add a new site map file by using the Add New Item dialog box (Figure 11-17). Name the site map file `Web.sitemap`.

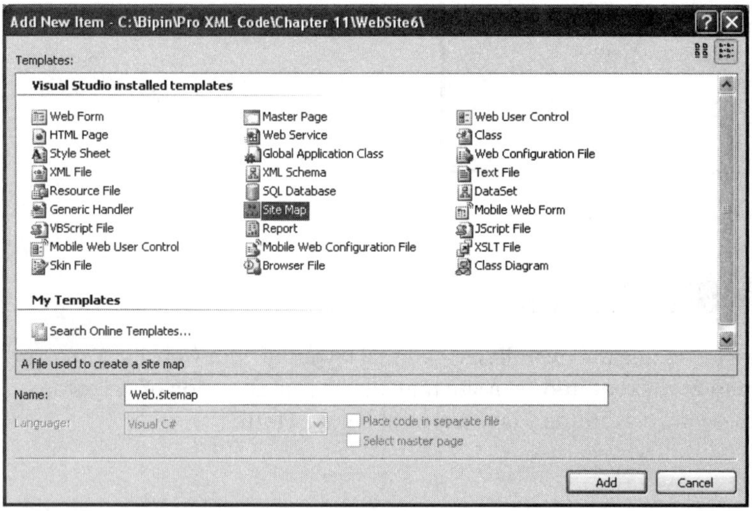

Figure 11-17. *Adding a new site map*

Now key in the XML markup shown in Listing 11-16 in the Web.sitemap file.

Listing 11-16. *Contents of the Web.sitemap File*

```
<?xml version="1.0" encoding="utf-8" ?>
<siteMap xmlns="http://schemas.microsoft.com/AspNet/SiteMap-File-1.0" >
<siteMapNode url="default.aspx" title="Home" description="My Web Site">
  <siteMapNode url="~/products/default.aspx" title="Products">
    <siteMapNode url="~/products/product1.aspx" title="First Product" />
    <siteMapNode url="~/products/product2.aspx" title="Second Product" />
  </siteMapNode>
  <siteMapNode url="~/services/default.aspx" title="Services">
    <siteMapNode url="~/services/service1.aspx" title="First Service" />
    <siteMapNode url="~/services/service2.aspx" title="Second Service" />
  </siteMapNode>
<siteMapNode url="contact.aspx" title="Contact Us" />
</siteMapNode>
</siteMap>
```

The site map file contains a set of predefined tags and attributes. The root node of a site map file is <siteMap>. It further contains several <siteMapNodes> tags depending on your website structure. The <siteMapNode> tag has four important attributes. They are listed in Table 11-1.

Table 11-1. *Attributes of a Site Map Node*

Attribute	Description
title	Indicates the title of the page. This attribute is often used by navigational controls to display the title for the URL.
url	Indicates the URL of the page that this node represents.
description	Specifies the description of the destination page. You can use this description to show ToolTips.
roles	While using security trimming, this attribute specifies the roles that are allowed to access this page.

■ Note *Security trimming* is a feature that implements role-based security by rendering only the nodes that are allowed for the current user. In other words, a particular <siteMapNode> will be accessible to a user only if the user's role is specified in the roles attribute of the <siteMapNode> element.

Site map files are often used to render some kind of navigational structure. There are two common ways in which you can consume the site map file you just created:

- In a SiteMapPath control
- In a SiteMapDataSource control

In the following sections, you are going to see both of them.

Using a SiteMapPath Control

The SiteMapPath control allows you to render what are often called *breadcrumbs*. Figure 11-18 shows what breadcrumbs are.

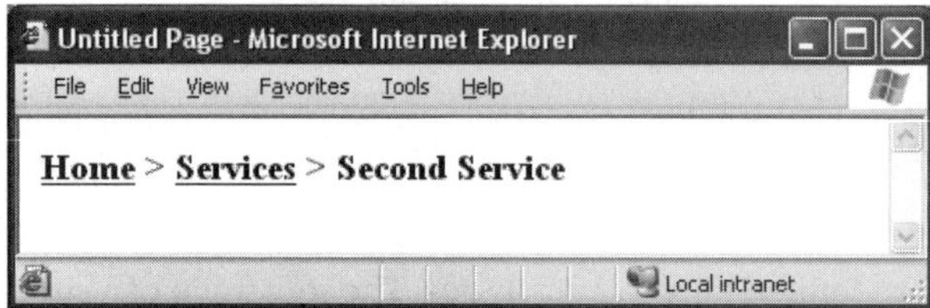

Figure 11-18. *Breadcrumbs*

The SiteMapPath control displays various levels of navigation. You can click on the parent or root levels to navigate back or to the top level. Before we delve into the details, let's first create the required directory structure and web forms. Begin by adding two folders to the website called `Products` and `Services`. Add the web forms as shown in Table 11-2.

Table 11-2. *Folders and Web Forms*

Web Form Name	Folder
`Default.aspx`	Root folder
`Contact.aspx`	Root folder
`Product1.aspx`	`Products`
`Product2.aspx`	`Products`
`Service1.aspx`	`Services`
`Service2.aspx`	`Services`

Now drag and drop a SiteMapPath control onto each web form. Run `Service2.aspx` in the browser, and you should see something similar to Figure 11-18. The SiteMapPath control automatically renders breadcrumbs for the current web form based on its location in the site map file.

Using a SiteMapDataSource Control

The use of site maps is not limited just to SiteMapPath controls. You can also attach the site map to navigational controls such as a TreeView. In this example, we will use the same site map file to bind to a TreeView.

Create a new website by using Visual Studio. Add the same `Web.sitemap` file to it. This time drag and drop a SiteMapDataSource control onto the web form. The SiteMapDataSource control automatically picks up the `Web.sitemap` file and supplies it to other controls. Further, drag and drop a TreeView control and set its `DataSourceID` property to the ID attribute of the SiteMapDataSource. That's it. Run the web form, and it should resemble Figure 11-19.

Figure 11-19. *TreeView bound with SiteMapDataSource control*

Using the XML Control

In Chapter 6, you learned to apply XSLT style sheets to XML data and transform them from one vocabulary to another. You achieved this by creating an instance of the `XslCompiledTransform` class. You then loaded an XSLT style sheet into it by using its `Load()` method. Finally, you did the transformation by using its `Transform()` method. ASP.NET provides an easy alternative to this manual coding: the XML control. The XML control accepts an XML document and XSLT style sheet. It then applies the style sheet to the XML data and renders the content on the web page. The most common use of the XML control is to transform XML data into HTML, though of course it doesn't have to be HTML.

To illustrate the use of the XML control, create a new website. Add a new XML file named `Employees.xml` and key in the markup shown in Listing 11-17.

Listing 11-17. *XML File That Supplies Data to the XML Control*

```
<?xml version="1.0" encoding="utf-8" ?>
<?xml-stylesheet type="text/xsl" href="Employees4.xslt"?>
<!-- This is list of employees -->
<employees>
  <employee employeeid="1">
    <firstname>Nancy</firstname>
    <lastname>Davolio</lastname>
    <homephone>(206) 555-9857</homephone>
    <notes>
      <![CDATA[includes a BA in psychology from Colorado State University in 1970.
She also completed "The Art of the Cold Call." Nancy is a member of
Toastmasters  International.]]>
  </notes>
  </employee>
  <employee employeeid="2">
    <firstname>Andrew</firstname>
    <lastname>Fuller</lastname>
    <homephone>(206) 555-9482</homephone>
    <notes>
      <![CDATA[Andrew received his BTS commercial in 1974 and a Ph.D. in
international marketing from the University of Dallas in 1981.  He is fluent in
French and Italian and reads German. He joined the company as a sales
representative, was promoted to sales manager in January 1992 and to vice
president of sales in March 1993. Andrew is a member of the Sales Management
Roundtable, the Seattle Chamber of Commerce, and the Pacific Rim Importers
Association.]]>
    </notes>
  </employee>
  <employee employeeid="3">
    <firstname>Janet</firstname>
    <lastname>Leverling</lastname>
    <homephone>(206) 555-3412</homephone>
    <notes>
      <![CDATA[Janet has a BS degree in chemistry from Boston College (1984).
She has also completed a certificate program in food retailing management.
Janet was hired as a sales associate in 1991 and promoted to sales
representative in February 1992.]]>
    </notes>
  </employee>
</employees>
```

Similarly, add a new XSLT style sheet named `Employees.xsl` and key in the markup shown in Listing 11-18.

Listing 11-18. *XSLT Style Sheet to Be Applied*

```
<?xml version="1.0" encoding="UTF-8" ?>
<xsl:stylesheet version="1.0" xmlns:xsl="http://www.w3.org/1999/XSL/Transform">
  <xsl:template match="/">
    <html>
      <body>
        <h1>Employee Listing</h1>
        <table border="1">
          <tr>
            <th>Employee ID</th>
            <th>First Name</th>
            <th>Last Name</th>
            <th>Home Phone</th>
            <th>Notes</th>
          </tr>
          <xsl:for-each select="employees/employee">
            <tr>
              <td>
                <xsl:value-of select="@employeeid"/>
              </td>
              <td>
                <xsl:value-of select="firstname"/>
              </td>
              <td>
                <xsl:value-of select="lastname"/>
              </td>
              <td>
                <xsl:value-of select="homephone"/>
              </td>
              <td>
                <xsl:value-of select="notes"/>
              </td>
            </tr>
          </xsl:for-each>
        </table>
      </body>
    </html>
  </xsl:template>
</xsl:stylesheet>
```

■ **Note** These are the same files that you used in Chapter 6. If you wish, you can add them to your website instead of re-creating them.

Now drag and drop an XML control onto the default web form. Set its `DocumentSource` property to `Employees.xml` and its `TransformSource` property to `Employees.xsl`. The former property points to the XML file that is to be transformed, whereas the latter property points to the XSLT style sheet that is to be applied to the DocumentSource. Now run the web form and you should see something similar to Figure 11-20.

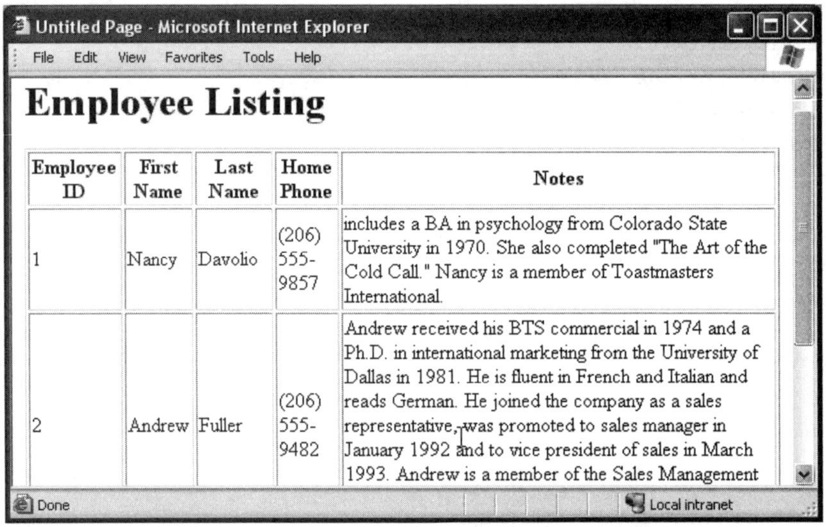

Figure 11-20. *XML data transformed to HTML by using the XML control*

Using the .NET Framework Configuration System

The .NET Framework's configuration system is based purely on XML. When you install the .NET Framework on a machine, an XML file named `Machine.config` is installed in the installation folder. The `Machine.config` file is the master configuration file and contains configuration settings that are applied to all .NET applications running on that machine. Though this file is in XML format and can be edited directly, you should do so with caution. Any change made to this file is going to affect all the applications running on that machine. Figure 11-21 shows a view of `Machine.config`.

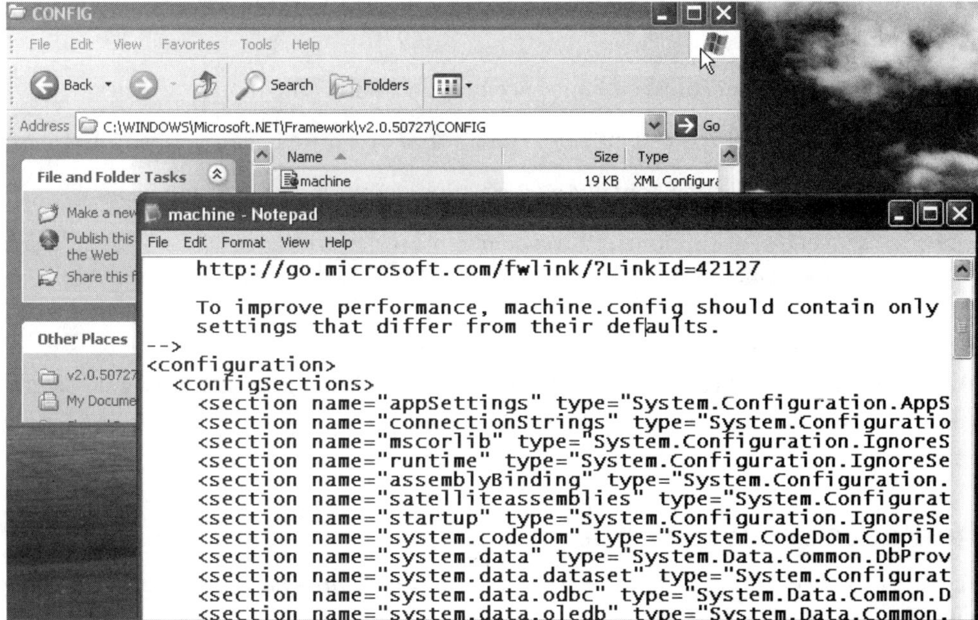

Figure 11-21. *Machine.config*

To override settings specified in the `Machine.config` file, you need to create application configuration files. Application configuration files are also XML files containing special XML markup. For Windows-based applications, the application configuration file is of the form `<exe_name>.exe.config`, where `exe_name` is the name of the application executable. For web applications and services, the application configuration filename must be `web.config`. In the following sections, you are going to learn more about the `web.config` file and the XML vocabulary used therein.

Structure of the web.config File

Listing 11-19 shows the general structural outline of a `web.config` file.

Listing 11-19. *Structural Outline of web.config*

```
<configuration>
     <appSettings />
     <connectionStrings />
     <system.web />
</configuration>
```

As you can see, the root node of the `web.config` file is `<configuration>`, and there are three main subsections:

- The `<appSettings>` section is used to specify application configuration settings.
- The `<connectionStrings>` section is used to store one or more database connection strings.
- The `<system.web>` section contains all the settings applicable to web applications.

All of these sections are optional. However, in most real-world cases you will have at least the `<system.web>` section.

■ **Note** The `web.config` file contains many configuration sections. It isn't possible to cover every section here. I am going to discuss some commonly used sections only.

Inheritance and web.config

The `web.config` file exhibits what is often referred to as *inheritance behavior*. In a single web application, there can be one or more `web.config` files in different folders. The settings of one `web.config` file are applied to the folder in which it resides and all the subfolders. However, if the subfolders contain a `web.config` of their own, the settings specified in that `web.config` take precedence.

Common Configuration Tasks

Now that we have a basic understanding of how `web.config` works, let's see how to perform some common configuration tasks. We are going to cover the following tasks in particular:

- How to store and retrieve application configuration settings
- How to store and retrieve your database connection strings
- How to work with membership, roles, and profile features
- How to provide custom error pages in your website

Storing and Retrieving Application Configuration Settings

Avoiding hard-coding values is a mandatory requirement in many real-world applications. Earlier in this chapter, we developed a Contact Us web form that sends messages from users to a specified email address. In that example, we hard-coded an email address in the code-behind file. What if the email address changes after deployment? Obviously, you need to change the source code to match the new email address and redeploy the application. This is not a recommended practice for real-world applications. Wouldn't it be nice if we could isolate the email address from the application, store it in an external location, and retrieve it inside your code? In VB6 or Visual C++, developers achieved this by using .INI files or the registry. In .NET you have a nice alternative: the application configuration section of configuration files.

The `<appSettings>` section of `web.config` allows you to store such application-specific settings. You can then read these settings in your source code. Tomorrow if the settings change, you need to change just the `web.config` file and not the source code. Let's modify our Contact Us web form to use application configuration settings.

Open the same website by choosing File ➤ Open Web Site from the menu. Open the `web.config` file in the IDE and modify the `<appSettings>` section as shown in Listing 11-20.

Listing 11-20. *Storing Values in the <appSettings> Section*

```
<appSettings>
    <add key="host" value="localhost"/>
    <add key="email" value="you@yourdomain.com"/>
</appSettings>
```

The `<appSettings>` section can contain one or more `<add>` elements. The `<add>` element has two attributes:

- The `key` attribute defines a key with which the value will be accessed in the code.
- The `value` attribute specifies the actual value of the key.

In our example, we defined two keys: `host` and `email`. The former key stores the value of the SMTP host, and the latter stores your email address. Now open the code-behind web form and modify the `Click` event handler of the Submit button as shown in Listing 11-21.

Listing 11-21. *Retrieving Values from the <appSettings> Section*

```
protected void Button1_Click(object sender, EventArgs e)
{
  string host = ConfigurationManager.AppSettings["host"];
  string email = ConfigurationManager.AppSettings["email"];
  SmtpClient client = new SmtpClient(host);
  client.Credentials = CredentialCache.DefaultNetworkCredentials;
  MailMessage msg = new MailMessage();
  msg.From = new MailAddress(TextBox2.Text);
  msg.To.Add(email);
  msg.Subject = TextBox3.Text;
  msg.Body =
    "[" + DropDownList1.SelectedItem.Text + "]" + TextBox4.Text + "\r\n" +
      TextBox1.Text + "\r\n" + TextBox5.Text;
  client.Send(msg);
  Label9.Text = "Your message has been sent. Thank you!";
}
```

Observe the code marked in bold. The code uses a class called `ConfigurationManager`, which resides in the `System.Configuration` namespace. By default `System.Configuration` is imported in the code-behind. The `AppSettings` property of the `ConfigurationManager` class exposes the entire `<appSettings>` section as a `NameValueCollection`. You can access individual values by using an index or a key name, though it is more common to access them by using key names.

The code retrieves the values of two keys—`host` and `email`—and stores them in a string variable. The constructor of the `SmtpClient` class now accepts the value stored in the `host` string variable instead of a hard-coded value. Similarly, the `Add()` method accepts the value stored in the `email` string variable and not a hard-coded value. If you run the application, you should get the results as before, but now you are free to change the host name and email address without touching the source code.

Storing and Retrieving Database Connection Strings

Storing database connection strings outside the source code is probably the most common configuration task. ASP.NET provides a special section of `web.config` to store database connection strings called `<connectionStrings>`. The `<connectionStrings>` section allows you to store one or more database connection strings that can be retrieved later in your code. To retrieve the connection strings stored in the `<connectionStrings>` section, you again need to use the `ConfigurationManager` class.

To illustrate the use of the `<connectionStrings>` section, you will develop a simple employee listing web form. The web form will display a list of employees in a GridView control. To begin, create a new website by using Visual Studio. Add a `web.config` file to the website by using the Add New Item dialog box (Figure 11-22).

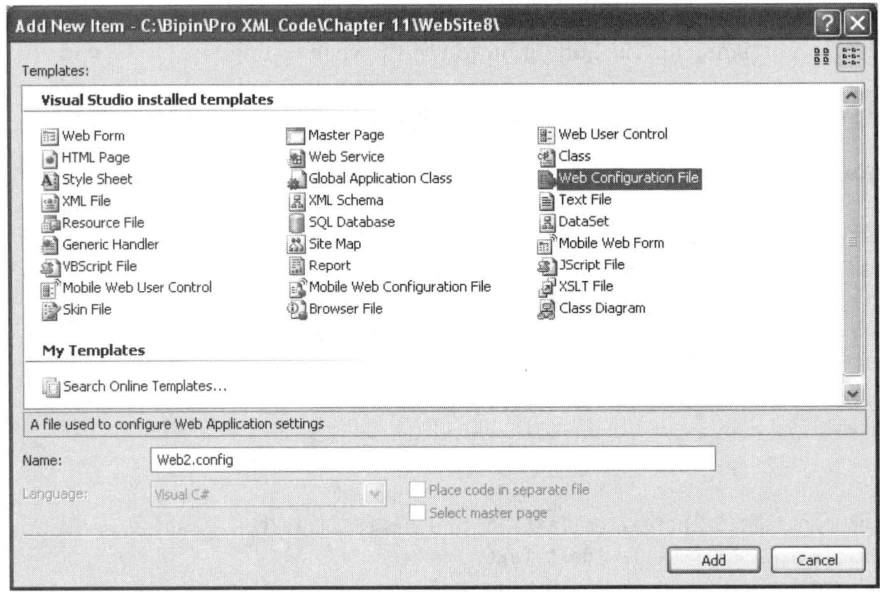

Figure 11-22. *Adding a web.config file*

Open the `web.config` file in the IDE and modify the `<connectionStrings>` section as shown in Listing 11-22.

Listing 11-22. *Adding a Connection String to the <connectionStrings> Section*

```
<connectionStrings>
  <add name="connectionstring"
       connectionString="data source=.;initial catalog=Northwind;
       integrated security=true"
       providerName="System.Data.SqlClient"/>
</connectionStrings>
```

The `<connectionStrings>` section can contain one or more `<add>` elements, each defining a database connection string:

- The `name` attribute of the `<add>` element defines a name for that connection string. This name is used later to access the connection string.
- The `connectionString` attribute specifies the actual database connection string.
- Finally, the `providerName` attribute indicates the .NET data provider that can be used to communicate with the database.

Now open the default web form and drag and drop a GridView control onto it. Then key in the code shown in Listing 11-23 in the `Page_Load` event of the web form.

Listing 11-23. *Retrieving the Connection String*

```
protected void Page_Load(object sender, EventArgs e)
{
  string strConn=
    ConfigurationManager.ConnectionStrings["connectionstring"].ConnectionString;
  SqlDataAdapter da =
    new SqlDataAdapter("SELECT EmployeeID,FirstName, LastName FROM Employees",
                       strConn);
  DataSet ds = new DataSet();
  da.Fill(ds, "employees");
  GridView1.DataSource = ds;
  GridView1.DataBind();
}
```

The code uses the `ConfigurationManager` class to retrieve the connection string value. The `ConnectionStrings` collection can be accessed by using an index or a connection string name. In our example, we access it with a name.

Each connection string stored in the `<connectionStrings>` section is represented by a `ConnectionStringSettings` class, and the `ConnectionString` property of this class returns the actual connection string. The connection string is then used as the second parameter of the `SqlDataAdapter` constructor, the first parameter being the `SELECT` query.

A `DataSet` is then filled by using the `Fill()` method of the `SqlDataAdapter` class. The `DataSet` thus created acts as a `DataSource` to the GridView control. The `DataBind()` method of the GridView control binds the data from the `DataSet` to the GridView. If you run the web form after writing the code, you should see something similar to Figure 11-23.

Figure 11-23. *Web form displaying an employee listing*

The ASP.NET Provider Model

Prior to ASP.NET 2.0, a data store was never an integrated and built-in part of the application framework. As a developer, you used to do all the work to use a database. ASP and ASP.NET 1.*x* did not provide a direct interaction with the database for framework-level services. However, ASP.NET 2.0 comes with a host of new features such as membership, roles, and profile management that require a database to store data involved in the functioning of a particular feature. This database can be Microsoft SQL Server, Microsoft Office Access, or anything else.

To isolate a specific database from the ASP.NET infrastructure, ASP.NET brings in the concept of the provider model. Figure 11-24 illustrates how the provider model works.

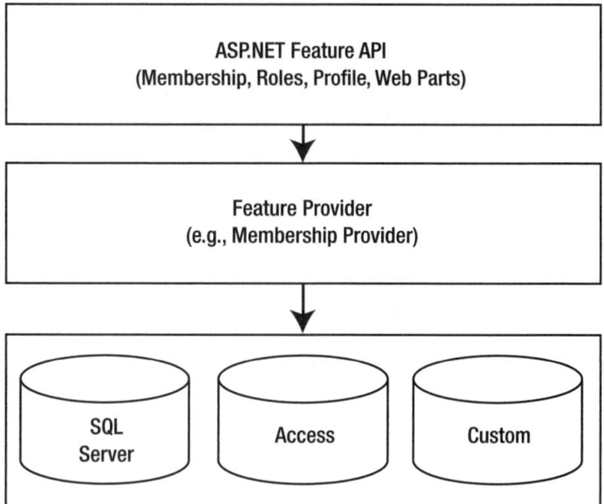

Figure 11-24. *ASP.NET provider model*

As you can see, at the bottom you have the physical data store such as SQL Server or Access. The data store stores all the data required for proper functioning of the feature under consideration. ASP.NET deals with the data store through a set of classes called *provider classes*—for example, the membership provider. Different features have different providers. For example, for membership features with SQL Server, the class used is `SqlMembershipProvider`. If you wish, you can also build your own provider. Finally, the actual feature-level APIs communicate with the provider to get the data in and out of the actual data store. Out of the box, ASP.NET comes with two providers:

- `AspNetSqlProvider`
- `AspNetAccessProvider`

AspNetSqlProvider

As you might have guessed, `AspNetSqlProvider` uses the SQL Server database as a data store. This is the default provider in ASP.NET. In the default mode when you use any of the features that require a provider to store data, ASP.NET automatically creates a SQL Server Express database and adds it to the `App_Data` folder of your website. You can of course configure your website to use a different SQL Server database, or even a non–SQL Server database.

AspNetAccessProvider

`AspNetAccessProvider` uses the Access (Jet) database for storing information. Generally, Access is not used in real-world heavy-duty applications, but you can certainly use it if the application calls for it.

Services Offered by the Provider Model

The three frequently used implementations of the provider model are membership, roles, and profile services:

- The membership services deal with user management. By using membership services, you can create, manage, and authenticate users of your website.
- The roles services deal with role-based authentication. By using roles services, you can check whether a user belongs to a specific role. You can also create and manage roles.
- The profile services deal with personalization. A *profile* is nothing but an extended set of information about a user. For example, you may capture details such as birth date, address, and full name while the user is registering with your website. These details are stored as the profile of that user.

Using Membership, Roles, and Profile Services

Now that you have an idea about the ASP.NET provider model, let's develop an application that configures membership, roles, and profile providers and then uses these features in a website. The general steps that you need to follow are as follows:

- Configure a database for supporting membership, roles, and profile services.
- Enable website security.
- Configure membership, roles, and profile providers.
- Define application-specific roles.
- Create a user registration and login page.
- Add users to roles.
- Capture profile information.

Configure a Database for Supporting Membership, Roles, and Profile Services

Membership, roles, and profile data must be stored in a database. In our example, we will use the Northwind database as a data store. To store membership, roles, and profile data in the Northwind database, it must contain certain predefined tables and stored procedures. To create these tables and stored procedures, the .NET Framework provides a tool called aspnet_regsql.exe. The tool consists of a wizard that guides you through the necessary steps:

1. Open Visual Studio Command Prompt from the Visual Studio program group and run the aspnet_regsql.exe tool from there. Figure 11-25 shows the first step of the wizard.

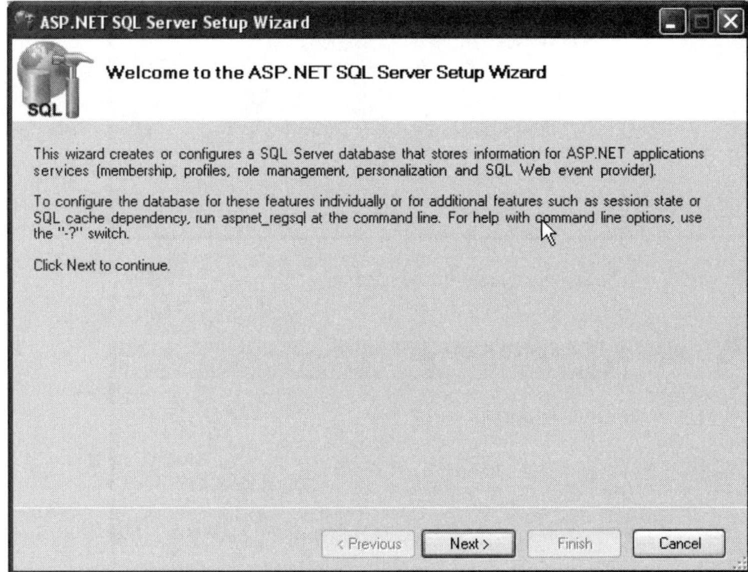

Figure 11-25. *Step 1 of the aspnet_regsql.exe tool*

2. Step 1 of the wizard is just a welcome step. Click Next to go to step 2 (Figure 11-26).
3. The second step allows you to specify whether you want to configure the database for application services or remove the configuration. Keep the default selection as it is and click Next. The screen shown in Figure 11-27 appears.
4. Step 3 of the wizard accepts database connectivity-related details such as server name, authentication mode, and database name. Make sure that you specify Northwind as the database to configure. Click Next to finish the wizard.

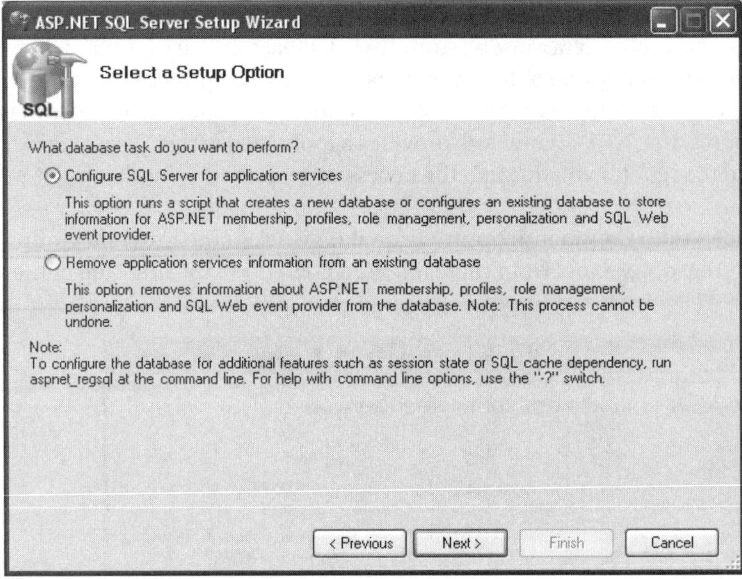

Figure 11-26. *Step 2 of the aspnet_regsql.exe tool*

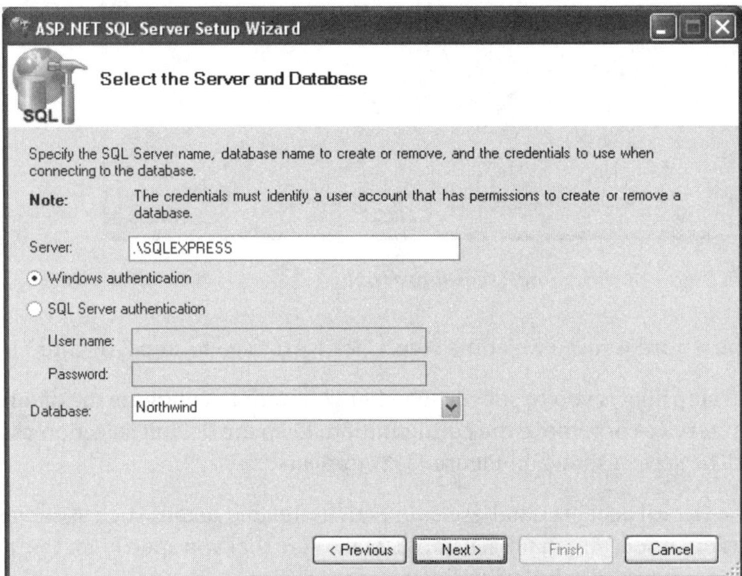

Figure 11-27. *Step 3 of the aspnet_regsql.exe tool*

Now your database is ready to consume membership, roles, and profile features.

Enable Website Security

Now you need to tell ASP.NET about the security scheme you wish to apply. In this example, we will be using forms-based security. This security scheme can be applied by entering the markup shown in Listing 11-24 under the `<system.web>` section in `web.config`.

Listing 11-24. *Applying a Forms-Based Security Schema*

```
<authentication mode="Forms">
  <forms loginUrl="login.aspx"></forms>
</authentication>
<authorization>
  <deny users="?"/>
</authorization>
```

The `mode` attribute of the `<authentication>` section specifies the security scheme to be applied. In our example, we set it to `Forms`. The sub-element `<forms>` has an attribute called `loginUrl` that points to our login page. This way, ASP.NET can automatically redirect unauthenticated users to the login page.

The `<authorization>` section is used to grant or deny website access to specific users or roles. The `<deny>` element denies access. The `users` attribute is set to a ? indicating that our application should ban all anonymous users.

Configure Membership, Roles, and Profile Providers

The membership, roles, and profile providers are configured by using the `<membership>`, `<roleManager>`, and `<profile>` sections, respectively. Enter the markup shown in Listing 11-25 that configures these providers to use the `Northwind` database as a data store.

Listing 11-25. *Configuring Membership, Roles, and Profile Providers*

```
<connectionStrings>
  <add name="connectionstring" connectionString="data source=.;initial ➥
catalog=Northwind;integrated security=true" providerName="System.Data.SqlClient"/>
</connectionStrings>

<system.web>
...
  <membership defaultProvider="mp">
    <providers>
      <add name="mp" connectionStringName="connectionstring"
           type="System.Web.Security.SqlMembershipProvider"/>
    </providers>
  </membership>
```

```
  <roleManager enabled="true" defaultProvider="rp">
    <providers>
      <add name="rp" connectionStringName="connectionstring"
           type="System.Web.Security.SqlRoleProvider"/>
    </providers>
  </roleManager>
  <profile defaultProvider="pp">
    <providers>
      <add name="pp" connectionStringName="connectionstring"
           type="System.Web.Profile.SqlProfileProvider"/>
    </providers>
    <properties>
      <add name="FullName"/>
      <add name="DOB" type="System.DateTime"/>
      <group name="Address">
        <add name="Street"/>
        <add name="State"/>
        <add name="Country"/>
        <add name="PostalCode"/>
      </group>
    </properties>
  </profile>
...
```

The markup first specifies a database connection string in the `<connectionString>` section. It points to the `Northwind` database and is named `connectionstring`. The `<membership>` tag configures the membership provider. The `<providers>` section of `<membership>` can contain one or more providers specified by the `<add>` element, which has the following attributes:

- The `name` attribute indicates the name of this provider entry. This name is specified in the `defaultProvider` attribute of the `<membership>` tag.
- The `connectionStringName` attribute specifies the name of the connection string from the `<connectionStrings>` section that is to be used.
- The `type` attribute specifies the fully qualified name of the membership provider. The `SqlMembershipProvider` is the default membership provider for SQL Server databases.

The `<roleManager>` section is similar to the `<membership>` section with a couple of differences. First, the `enabled` attribute of the `<roleManager>` tag must be set to `true` to enable the roles feature. Second, the `type` attribute of the `<add>` tag specifies the `SqlRoleProvider` class.

The `<profiles>` section consists of two subsections: `<providers>` and `<properties>`. The use of the former is the same as for the `<membership>` and `<roleManager>` sections. The type used to deal with profiles is `SqlProfileProvider`. The `<properties>` section defines profile properties and groups. A *profile property* is a single piece of information that you want to capture from users, whereas a *group* is a set of profile properties.

Let's say we want to capture full name, birth date, street address, state, country, and postal code from the end users. Thus our example defines `FullName` and `DOB` as profile properties and `Address` as a group. The `Address` group further contains four properties: `Street`, `State`, `Country`, and `PostalCode`. By default the data type of profile properties is assumed to be a string. You can specify any other data type by using the `type` attribute of the `<add>` tag.

This completes the configuration of membership, roles, and profile providers.

Define Application-Specific Roles

The next step is to define application-specific roles. Let's assume that our application needs two groups: manager and salesperson. To define these roles, Visual Studio provides a built-in tool called the Web Site Administration tool. Follow these steps to use the tool:

1. Invoke the Web Site Administration tool by choosing Website ➤ ASP.NET Configuration from the Visual Studio menu. Figure 11-28 shows this tool.

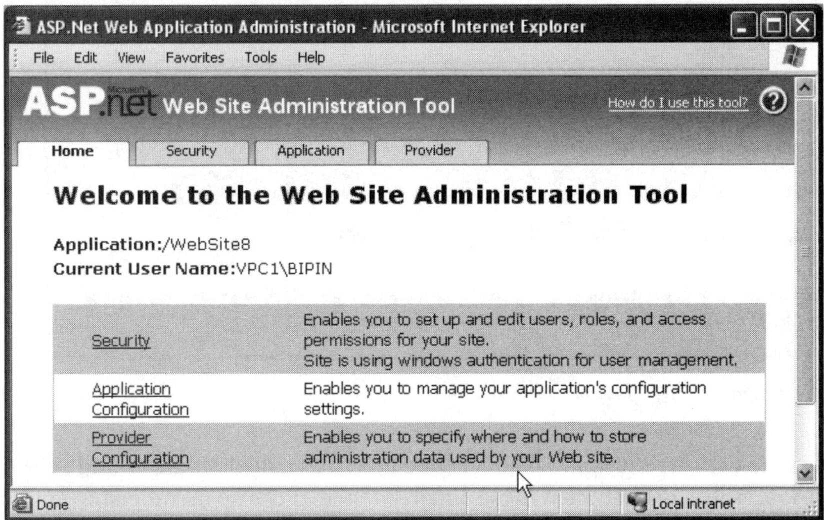

Figure 11-28. *The Web Site Configuration tool*

2. Click the Security tab so that your browser will show the screen in Figure 11-29.

Figure 11-29. *The Security tab of the Web Site Administration tool*

3. Click the Create or Manage Roles link so that your browser window resembles Figure 11-30.

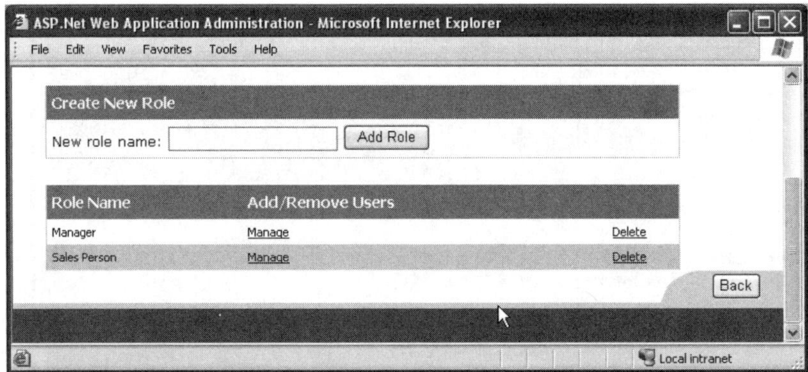

Figure 11-30. *Creating roles*

4. Using the Create New Role section, create two roles called **Manager** and **Sales Person**. This tool reads your `web.config` file and from there picks up membership and roles provider information. Thus the newly created roles will be saved in the `Northwind` database.

Create a User Registration and Login Page

Now add a new web form named `Login.aspx` to your website. This web form is going to be your login and registration page. Traditionally, developers needed to manually design login and registration pages. ASP.NET simplifies this job by providing ready-made controls called Login and CreateUserWizard. Drag and drop Login and CreateUserWizard controls onto the web form. Your web form should look like Figure 11-31.

Figure 11-31. *Login.aspx in design mode*

The CreateUserWizard control refers to the membership provider specified in the `web.config` file and stores the user data in the specified database. Similarly, the Login control uses the membership provider specified in the `web.config` file for validating the user during the login process.

Run `Login.aspx` and create two users—Nancy and Andrew—by using the CreateUserWizard control (Figure 11-32).

Untitled Page - Microsoft Internet Explorer
File Edit View Favorites Tools Help
Sign Up for Your New Account
User Name: Nancy
Password: ●●●●●●●●●●
Confirm Password: ●●●●●●●●●●
E-mail: nancy@somedomain.com
Security Question: What is your pet's name?
Security Answer: Tom
Create User
Start downlo. Local intranet

Figure 11-32. *Creating new users by using the CreateUserWizard control*

Add Users to Roles

Now that you have created two users, it's time to add them to a role. To do so, you will again invoke the Web Site Administration tool. This time you need to click the Manage Users link from the Security tab. You can then edit the required users and add them to the required roles (Figure 11-33).

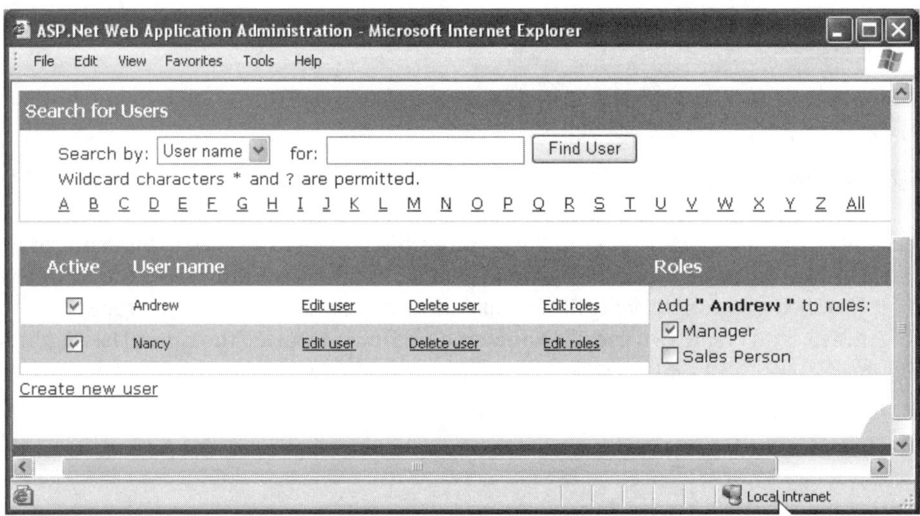

Figure 11-33. *Assigning roles to the users*

Add the user Nancy to the Sales Person role, and Andrew to the Manager role.

Capture Profile Information

Now the users can log in to the website, but we have not yet captured their profile information. To do so, you need to design the `Default.aspx` as shown in Figure 11-34.

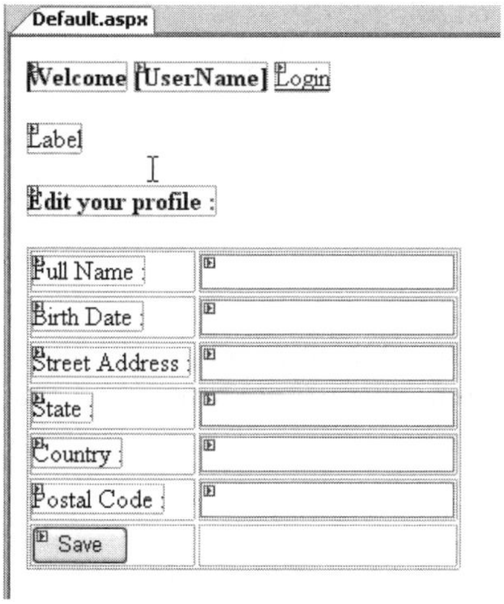

Figure 11-34. *Default.aspx in design mode*

The web form consists of two more login-related controls at the top: UserName and LoginStatus. The former control displays the user name of the logged-in control on the form, whereas the latter displays the login status of the user (logged in or not logged in). Below the UserName and LoginStatus controls there is a label that will display the roles to which the user belongs. Finally, there is a set of text boxes for capturing all the profile properties. Clicking the Save button will save the profile information.

The `Page_Load` event handler of `Default.aspx` is shown in Listing 11-26.

Listing 11-26. *Displaying Information About User Roles*

```
protected void Page_Load(object sender, EventArgs e)
{
  string[] roles=Roles.GetRolesForUser();
  Label2.Text = "Your are registered as " + string.Join(",", roles);
  if (!IsPostBack)
  {
    GetProfile();
  }
}
```

The code retrieves all the roles to which the current user belongs by using the `GetRolesForUser()` method of the `Roles` object. `Roles` is a built-in object implicitly available to all ASP.NET applications. The `GetRolesForUser()` method returns all the roles as a string array. The roles' names are joined together by using the `Join()` method of the string class and then displayed in a Label control.

Next, the code checks the `IsPostBack` property of the web form. The `IsPostBack` property tells you whether you are in the `Page_Load` event handler because of a fresh request or because of some post-back operation. If the user is visiting the page as a fresh request, the `GetProfile()` helper method is called. The `GetProfile()` method retrieves the profile properties of the user and displays them in the respective text boxes. This method is discussed shortly.

The `Click` event handler of the Save button is shown in Listing 11-27.

Listing 11-27. *Saving Profile Values*

```
protected void Button1_Click(object sender, EventArgs e)
{
  SetProfile();
}
```

This simply calls a helper method—`SetProfile()`—that sets the profile properties as per the values entered in various text boxes. The `GetProfile()` and `SetProfile()` helper methods are shown in Listing 11-28.

Listing 11-28. *Saving and Retrieving Profile Properties*

```
private void SetProfile()
{
  Profile.FullName = TextBox1.Text;
  Profile.DOB = DateTime.Parse(TextBox2.Text);
  Profile.Address.Street = TextBox3.Text;
  Profile.Address.State = TextBox4.Text;
  Profile.Address.Country = TextBox5.Text;
  Profile.Address.PostalCode = TextBox6.Text;
}

private void GetProfile()
{
  if (Profile.FullName != "")
  {
    TextBox1.Text = Profile.FullName;
    TextBox2.Text = Profile.DOB.ToShortDateString();
    TextBox3.Text = Profile.Address.Street;
    TextBox4.Text = Profile.Address.State;
    TextBox5.Text = Profile.Address.Country;
    TextBox6.Text = Profile.Address.PostalCode;
  }
}
```

The `SetProfile()` method uses the `Profile` object to assign profile property values. Just like the `Roles` object, the `Profile` object is a built-in object accessible to all web applications. Notice how the profile properties defined in the `web.config` file appear as properties of the `Profile` object. Also, note that the `DOB` property is of type `DateTime` and hence type conversion is necessary. The profile properties from the group (`Address`) can be accessed by using the familiar nested property notation.

The `GetProfile()` method retrieves profile property values and assigns them back to the text boxes.

That's it. You are now ready to run and test your web forms. To test the application, you can follow these steps:

1. Run `Login.aspx`.
2. Log in to the website by using any of the user credentials that you created earlier.
3. You will be taken to `Default.aspx`, where you can enter all profile details. Notice how role information is displayed.
4. Enter all the profile values and click the Save button.
5. Click the Logout link rendered by the LoginStatus control so that you will be logged out and redirected to `Login.aspx` again.
6. Sign in again with the same user credentials. This time you will see the text boxes already populated with the previously entered profile values.

Figure 11-35 shows a sample run of the application.

Figure 11-35. *Sample run of Default.aspx*

Displaying Custom Error Pages

Even after taking great care during the coding phase, errors can crop up at run time in your website. Users make typos in page URLs, try to access areas that are restricted, network failures can happen, and so on. As a robust programming practice, you should make provisions to trap all such unexpected errors. In classic ASP, developers used to set custom error pages for web-server-level errors (file not found, access denied, and so on) in IIS. This required physical access to the web server. Thankfully, ASP.NET allows you to specify such custom error pages in the `web.config` file. Let's see how.

Create a new website in Visual Studio. Add a new folder in it called `Admin`. This folder is supposed to contain administrative pages, and users are unauthorized to access it. Add five web forms as shown in Table 11-3.

Table 11-3. *Web Forms Arrangement*

Web Form	Folder	Description
`Default.aspx`	Root	The default page of the website
`FileNotFound.aspx`	Root	Custom error page that is displayed for HTTP error code 404
`UnAuthorized.aspx`	Root	Custom error page that is displayed for HTTP error code 403
`GlobalErrorPage.aspx`	Root	Custom error page that is displayed for any other unhandled error in code or otherwise
`Default.aspx`	`Admin`	Represents the default page of the `Admin` folder

Now design `Default.aspx` from the root folder as shown in Figure 11-36.

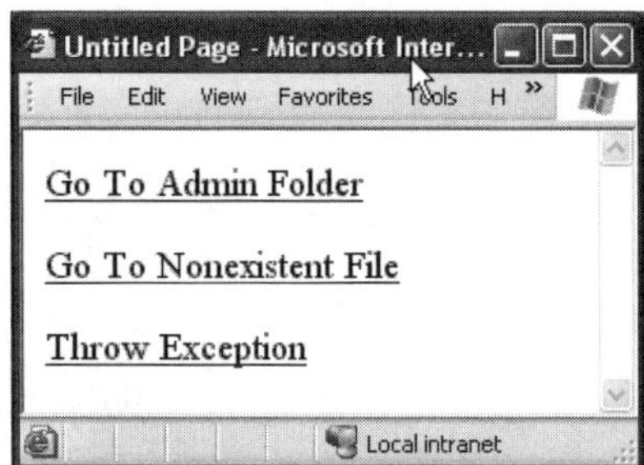

Figure 11-36. *Design of Default.aspx*

`Default.aspx` contains two hyperlink controls titled Go to Admin Folder and Go to Nonexistent File, respectively. Set the `NavigateUrl` property of these hyperlink controls to `~/admin/default.aspx` and `~/notexists.aspx`, respectively. Note that we are deliberately setting `NavigateUrl` of the second hyperlink to a nonexistent file. Now drag and drop a LinkButton control and set its `Text` property to `Throw Exception`. Add the code shown in Listing 11-29 in its `Click` event handler.

Listing 11-29. *Throwing an Exception*

```
protected void LinkButton1_Click(object sender, EventArgs e)
{
  throw new Exception("Unexpected Error");
}
```

The code simply throws a new exception. Because this is an unhandled exception, we will get a chance to trap it by using a custom error page. Now add a Label and a HyperLink control each on FileNotFound.aspx, UnAuthorized.aspx, and GlobalErrorPage.aspx. Set the Text property of the Label controls to a friendly error message. Point the HyperLink to Default.aspx so that users can easily navigate back to the home page.

Add the code shown in Listing 11-30 in the Page_Load event of the Admin/Default.aspx web form.

Listing 11-30. *Throwing an HttpException*

```
protected void Page_Load(object sender, EventArgs e)
{
  throw new HttpException(403, "Unauthorized");
}
```

The code raises an HttpException with a status code of 403 and a string message. The HttpException class represents an HTTP-specific exception. This way, we trigger an exception with status code 403 (unauthorized access).

Now open web.config in the IDE and add the markup shown in Listing 11-31 under the <system.web> section.

Listing 11-31. *Specifying Custom Error Pages*

```
<customErrors mode="On" defaultRedirect="GlobalErrorPage.aspx">
  <error statusCode="403" redirect="~/UnAuthorized.aspx"/>
  <error statusCode="404" redirect="~/FileNotFound.aspx"/>
</customErrors>
```

The <customErrors> section allows you to specify custom error pages for your website. The mode attribute has three possible values:

- If the mode is On, custom error pages are enabled for all the machines browsing the website.
- If the mode is Off, custom error pages are disabled for all the machines.
- If the mode is RemoteOnly, the custom errors are enabled only for remote machines browsing the website, but they are turned off for local browsers.

During development, most commonly your web server and the browser will be running on the same machine and hence you should set the mode to On.

The defaultRedirect attribute points to a web page that is to be displayed in case there is any application-wide unhandled error.

The <customErrors> section can have a number of <error> tags. The statusCode attribute of the <error> tag specifies the web-server-level HTTP error code. The redirect attribute specifies the web page to be displayed in the event of that error. In our example, we configure two custom error pages: one for status code 403 (UnAuthorized.aspx) and the other for status code 404 (FileNotFound.aspx).

Now run `Default.aspx` and click all three links, one by one. You will notice that instead of displaying the default error page, this time ASP.NET displays the custom error pages as specified in `web.config`. Figure 11-37 shows one sample run of the website.

Figure 11-37. *Custom error page for status code 403*

Documenting XML Code

Documenting your source code is a common requirement in any professional development. Everybody knows the importance of well-documented code. However, documenting your source code is just one part of the story. You also need to generate professional help files that ship along with your application and are used by the end users.

There are various ways of creating documentation and help files. Most of them are manual in that somebody (the developer or technical writer) needs to key in the help text in HTML or PDF format. Then a tool (such as Microsoft HTML Help Workshop) is used to compile the source files into a .CHM file. That means there is duplication of work. First, developers need to write comments in the source code. Then the same information is repeated in the help files.

Fortunately, the .NET Framework and Visual Studio support a feature called XML comments. By using this feature, you can add comments to your source code by using a specific XML vocabulary. Later you can extract these XML comments in a separate XML file, which is then converted into a .CHM file. Thus documentation of code is automated and avoids duplication.

In C#, XML comments are indicated by three forward slashes (`///`). There are several XML tags that you can use in XML comments. In the following sections, you will learn many of them.

Creating a Class Library

To begin, you need to create a class library named `Calculator.dll`. This class library represents a simple mathematical calculator and consists of a single class called `SimpleCalculator`. The `SimpleCalculator` class allows you to add, subtract, divide, and multiply numbers. Though this example may sound too simple (and indeed it is), your aim here is to learn XML commenting syntax.

Create a new class library project in Visual Studio. Name the project `Calculator` and the class `SimpleCalculator`. Key in the code from Listing 11-32 in the `SimpleCalculator` class.

Listing 11-32. *The SimpleCalculator Class*

```
public class SimpleCalculator
{
  public int Add(int a, int b)
  {
    return (a + b);
  }
  public int Subtract(int a, int b)
  {
    return (a - b);
  }
  public int Divide(int a, int b)
  {
    return (a / b);
  }
  public int Multiply(int a, int b)
  {
    return (a * b);
  }
}
```

The class consists of four methods: `Add()`, `Subtract()`, `Divide()`, and `Multiply()`. Each method accepts two parameters and performs the corresponding action on them. The result of the calculation is returned to the caller. Now that you have the class ready, let's add XML documentation comments to it.

Documenting the Summary and Remarks

To describe your classes and members therein, you can use two tags: `<summary>` and `<remarks>`. The `<summary>` tag is used to describe a type or its members. The `<remarks>` tag is used to specify additional information about the type or member other than that specified in `<summary>`. Listing 11-33 shows the `SimpleCalculator` class after adding `<summary>` and `<remarks>` tags.

Listing 11-33. *Adding <summary> and <remarks>*

```
/// <summary>
/// This is a class that represents
/// a simple mathematical calculator.
/// </summary>
/// <remarks>
/// This class is developed on .NET 2.0
/// </remarks>
public class SimpleCalculator
{
...
```

Adding Paragraphs

The summary or remarks may consist of multiple paragraphs of text. Each paragraph is represented by a <para> tag. Note that a <para> tag is always a child element of <summary> or <remarks>. Listing 11-34 shows the use of a <para> tag.

Listing 11-34. *Using a <para> Tag*

```
/// <summary>
/// This is a class that represents
/// a simple mathematical calculator.
/// <para>
/// You can use it to add, subtract,
/// divide and multiply integers and
/// fractional numbers.
/// </para>
/// </summary>
/// <remarks>
/// This class is developed on .NET 2.0
/// </remarks>
```

Documenting Method Parameters and Return Values

Methods often take one or more parameters. They might also return some value to the caller. Parameters are represented by <param> tags, whereas return values are represented by <return> tags. The <param> tag has one attribute—name—that indicates the name of the parameter. Listing 11-35 shows the use of both of these tags on the Add() method.

Listing 11-35. *Documenting Parameters and Return Values*

```
/// <summary>
/// This method adds two integers.
/// </summary>
/// <param name="a">The first number</param>
/// <param name="b">The second number</param>
/// <returns>An integer representing addition of a and b</returns>
public int Add(int a, int b)
{
  return (a + b);
}
```

Specifying Scope and Permissions

Your class may contain private, protected, or public members. The scope of these members can be indicated by using the `<permission>` tag. The `<permission>` tag has one attribute—`cref`—that specifies the name of the member in the given context. Listing 11-36 shows an example of using the `<permission>` tag.

Listing 11-36. *Using the <permission> Tag*

```
/// <summary>
/// This method adds two integers.
/// </summary>
/// <param name="a">The first number</param>
/// <param name="b">The second number</param>
/// <returns>An integer representing addition of a and b</returns>
/// <permission cref="Add">Public method</permission>
public int Add(int a, int b)
{
  return (a + b);
}
```

Specifying Links to Other Members

You may need to cross-reference members of your class. The MSDN library itself is a good example of this. At many places, documentation of one class points to another related class. Also, at the bottom of the documentation page, there appears a section called See Also. You can achieve the same thing for your documentation by using the `<see>` and `<seealso>` tags. The `<see>` tag must be used inside the `<summary>` or `<remarks>` tags. The `<seealso>` tag has an attribute called `cref` that points to another member and can be used outside the `<summary>` tag. Listing 11-37 illustrates the use of the `<seealso>` tag as an example.

Listing 11-37. *Using the <seealso> Tag*

```
/// <summary>
/// This method adds two integers.
/// </summary>
/// <param name="a">The first number</param>
/// <param name="b">The second number</param>
/// <returns>An integer representing addition of a and b</returns>
/// <permission cref="Add">Public method</permission>
/// <seealso cref="Subtract"/>
public int Add(int a, int b)
{
  return (a + b);
}
```

Adding Lists

Your documentation may need bulleted or numbered lists. This can be achieved by using three tags: `<list>`, `<item>`, and `<listheader>`. The `<item>` and `<listheader>` tags must appear inside the `<list>` tag. The `<list>` tag has an attribute named `type` that can take a value of `bullet`, `number`, or `table`. The `<listheader>` tag serves the purpose of supplying a header for the list. Finally, the `<item>` tag encapsulates a single item of the list. Listing 11-38 shows the use of these tags.

Listing 11-38. *Using the <list>, <item>, and <listheader> Tags*

```
/// <summary>
/// This is a class that represents
/// a simple mathematical calculator.
/// <para>
/// You can use it to add, subtract,
/// divide and multiply integers and
/// fractional numbers.
/// </para>
/// <list type="bullet">
/// <listheader>Supported Operations</listheader>
/// <item>Addition</item>
/// <item>Subtraction</item>
/// <item>Division</item>
/// <item>Multiplication</item>
/// </list>
/// </summary>
/// <remarks>
/// This class is developed on .NET 2.0
/// </remarks>
public class SimpleCalculator
{
...
```

Generating Documentation

Generating documentation is a two-step process:

1. Generate XML documentation from the comments.
2. Generate .CHM documentation from XML documentation.

Generating XML Documentation from Comments

To generate XML documentation from source code comments, you need to open the project properties dialog box (Figure 11-38).

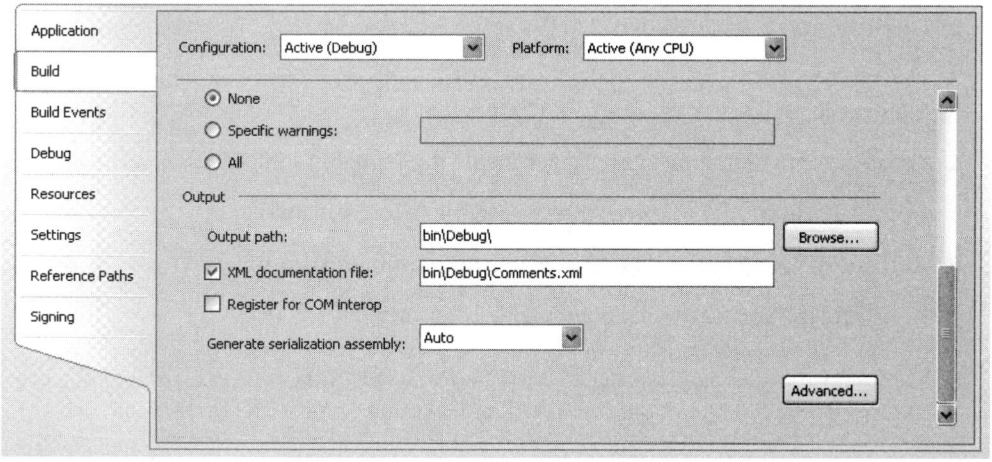

Figure 11-38. *Generating XML documentation*

The Output section of the Build tab allows you to specify whether to generate XML documentation and the filename. Specify the filename as `Comments.xml` and build the Calculator class library. As a result of the compilation, you will get `Calculator.dll` and `Comments.xml`.

Generating .CHM Documentation from XML Documentation

This step is a bit tricky. There is no built-in tool in Visual Studio to compile XML documentation files into a .CHM file. One option is to apply your own style sheets to the output XML file and get HTML documentation. The HTML files thus generated can be further fed to HTML Help Workshop to generate a .CHM file. Luckily, Microsoft has developed a command-line tool called Sandcastle that simplifies your job.

■ **Note** The Sandcastle tool is still in beta. You can download it from `http://msdn.microsoft.com`. Currently this tool is not integrated with the Visual Studio IDE. It would be nice to see it integrated in the IDE at some future date.

Sandcastle requires that you have HTML Help Workshop installed. HTML Help Workshop can be downloaded free from Microsoft's website. Using Sandcastle involves the following multiple steps:

1. Go to the installation folder of Sandcastle.
2. Go to the `Examples` subfolder.
3. Run the `SetPath.bat` file from the `Examples` folder to set the `PATH` variables to use the Sandcastle tools.
4. Create a subfolder named `Calculator` inside the `Examples` subfolder.
5. Copy `Calculator.dll` and `Comments.xml` to the `Calculator` folder.
6. Run the following commands one by one at a command prompt:

```
MRefBuilder Calculator.dll /out:reflection.org

XslTransform /xsl:..\..\ProductionTransforms\AddOverloads.xsl reflection.org
/xsl:..\..\ProductionTransforms\AddGuidFilenames.xsl /out:reflection.xml

XslTransform /xsl:..\..\ProductionTransforms\ReflectionToManifest.xsl
reflection.xml /out:manifest.xml

call ..\..\Presentation\vs2005\copyOutput.bat

BuildAssembler /config:sandcastle.config manifest.xml

XslTransform /xsl:..\..\ProductionTransforms\ReflectionToChmProject.xsl
reflection.xml /out:Output\Calculator.hhp

XslTransform /xsl:..\..\ProductionTransforms\ReflectionToChmContents.xsl
reflection.xml /arg:html=Output\html /out:Output\Calculator.hhc

XslTransform /xsl:..\..\ProductionTransforms\ReflectionToChmIndex.xsl ➥
reflection.xml
/out:Output\Calculator.hhk
```

Note Running so many commands might be tedious, but as of this writing, that is what is available in Sandcastle. Detailed descriptions of each command and command-line switch are outside the scope of this book. You can obtain more information about the tool from `https://blogs.msdn.com/sandcastle/`.

---

7. As a result of the preceding commands, you will get the `Calculator.hhp` file in the `Output` subfolder of the `Calculator` folder. The .HHP files are HTML Help Workshop project files.

8. Open the `Calculator.hhp` file in HTML Help Workshop (Figure 11-39).

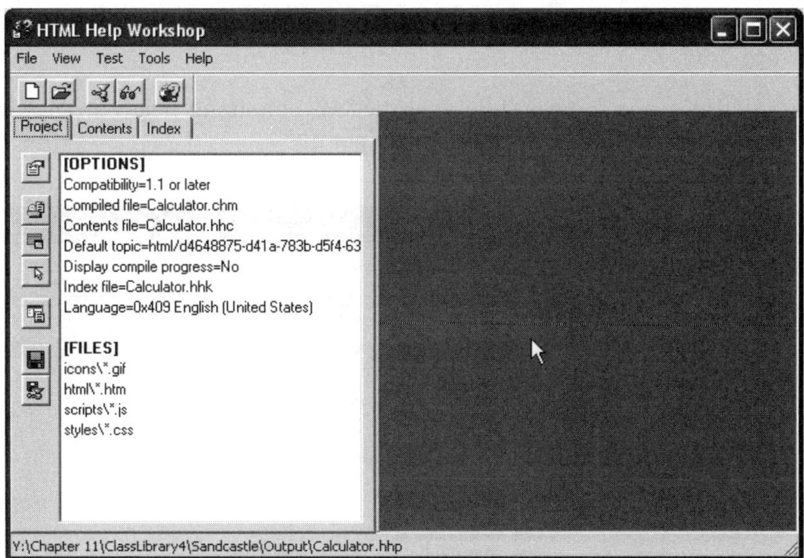

Figure 11-39. *Loading Calculator.hhp in HTML Help Workshop*

9. Click the project properties icon to open the Options dialog box, as shown in Figure 11-40.

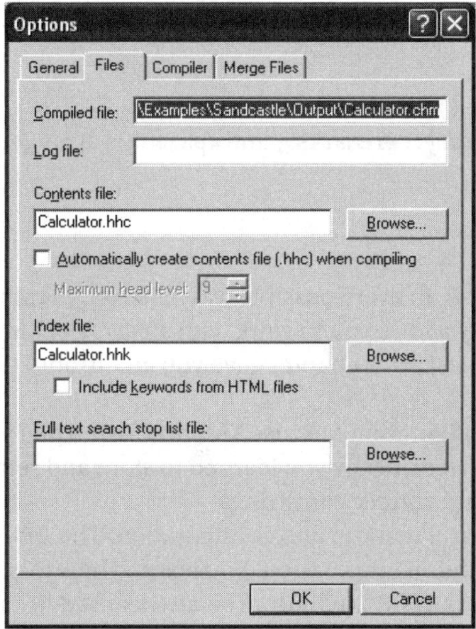

Figure 11-40. *Help project properties*

10. Ensure that the `Contents` file is pointing to `Calculator.hhc`, and the `Index` file to `Calculator.hhk` (these files are generated when you run the preceding commands).

11. Compile the help project by choosing File ➤ Compile from the menu to create `Calculator.chm`.

12. Open `Calculator.chm` and you should see the XML comments neatly arranged in the help file. Figure 11-41 shows the `Calculator.chm` file.

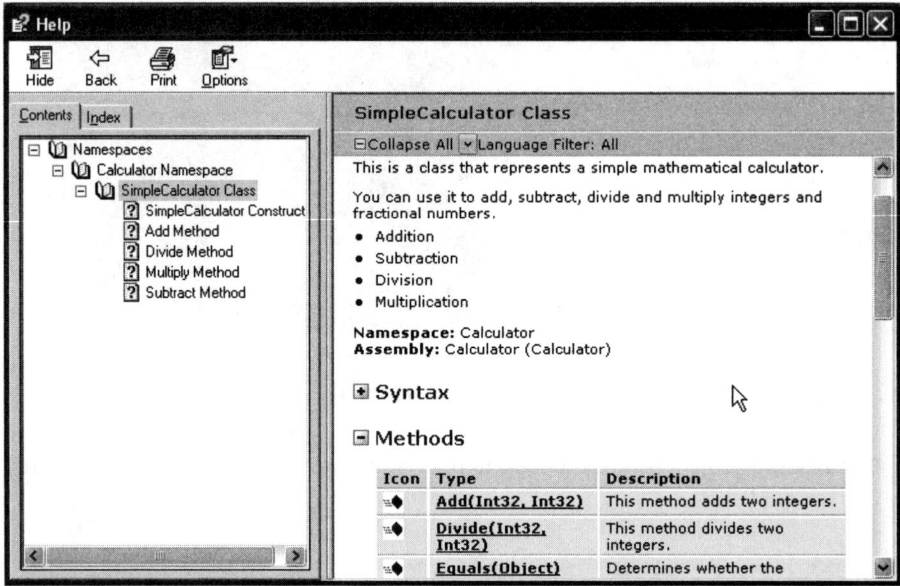

Figure 11-41. *Calculator.chm*

Note how the text from tags such as `<summary>`, `<remarks>`, and `<param>` is arranged.

Summary

Microsoft has tried to harness the power of XML in every possible way. The .NET Framework is no exception. The .NET Framework not only allows you to work with an array of XML technologies, but also uses them at many places itself. This chapter gave you an introduction to these areas.

You started with remoting, where the configuration files use XML markup. Then you learned about application configuration files. Specifically you learned to store and retrieve application configuration settings and database connection strings.

ASP.NET uses XML heavily for server control markup and configuration. The `web.config` file is an XML file that stores ASP.NET configuration information. You learned how to configure membership, roles, and profile providers by using XML markup. You also learned to configure custom error pages for unexpected errors in your website. Finally, you generated .CHM help files by using XML documentation syntax.

CHAPTER 12

■ ■ ■

Creating Services by Using Windows Communication Foundation

Chapter 9 introduced you to web services, and Chapter 11 introduced you to remoting—both of which allow you to develop distributed applications. Web services are mainly used when you wish to communicate across the Internet, whereas remoting is preferred in intranet scenarios. However, in most real-world cases, you need to decide between web services and remoting well in advance because your choice affects your development process. For example, if you decide to use web services, their proxies and XML serialization come into the picture, whereas if you decide to use remoting, activation type and binary serialization come into the picture. At times these differences can prove to be painful. Imagine, for example, that you begin the development with remoting in mind and the application is developed and deployed in a production environment. After a few months, you want to replace remoting components with web services. Can you do that without changing anything in the client application? In most cases, the answer will be a resounding no.

Recognizing the need to bridge the gap between various component technologies, Microsoft developed what is known as the *Windows Communication Foundation (WCF)*. WCF is a part of .NET Framework 3.0 and provides a unified model for developing service-oriented software components. Under WCF you can employ the same piece of software regardless of whether you are using it over the Internet or an intranet. You can design and develop your software initially for TCP networks and later use it over HTTP. This can be achieved with no changes to the client or component source code. Moreover, WCF heavily uses XML as the data transfer format. That means data that is sent between the client and the server is in XML format. You can also customize how your objects are serialized on the wire. This chapter introduces you to the following topics:

- Common terms used in relation to WCF
- Creating a WCF service
- Hosting a WCF service
- Consuming a WCF service
- The role of XML in WCF services

Understanding WCF Vocabulary

In Chapter 9, you learned about the Web Services Description Language (WSDL). WSDL uses terms such as *port, message, service type, binding,* and *service.* WCF vocabulary is very similar to WSDL with a few differences. In this section, you will learn the WCF vocabulary:

Service model: The model provided by WCF to build software components is often called a service model.

Channel layer: The channel layer is that part of WCF that deals with low-level network programming. The classes from the channel layer are used by high-level classes of WCF.

Service: A service is a piece of software that responds to communication over a network. A service has one or more endpoints. Communication with the service is redirected to one of these endpoints.

Endpoint: An endpoint is where the actual request for a service is redirected. An endpoint consists of an address, a binding, and a contract.

Address: An address is nothing but the unique location of the underlying service on a network. Clients use this address to talk with the service. An address takes the form of a Uniform Resource Locator (URL)—for example, `http://localhost:8000/MyService`.

Binding: An address is just a URL where the service can be located. However, that's not enough. You also need to know the protocol used for communication such as TCP or HTTP. This is specified with the help of a binding. The binding specifies the protocol for encoding the request and response as well as the protocol for transporting them over the network.

Contract: A contract is a set of operations that are exposed by the service. In other words, a contract is a set of operations available at a given endpoint. At the code level, a contract is defined with the help of an interface.

Service type: A service type is a class that implements a contract.

■Note You must have the final version of .NET Framework 3.0 installed on your machine in order to work with the examples discussed in this chapter. You can download it at `http://msdn.microsoft.com`. As far as examples in this chapter are concerned, you need not have the .NET Framework software development kit (SDK) as such; the .NET Framework runtime is sufficient.

Creating and Consuming a WCF Service

To create and consume WCF services, you essentially need to develop three pieces of software:

- One or more service types
- A host application that publishes the services exposed by the service types on a network
- A client application that consumes the services exposed by the service types

All the core functionality of WCF is available in the `System.ServiceModel.dll` assembly. The `System.ServiceModel` namespaces contain many classes and attributes related to WCF. In all the projects that we discuss in this chapter, you must reference this assembly and import the `System.ServiceModel` namespace. In the next few sections, you will learn how to develop each of the three parts listed.

Creating the Service

Creating a WCF service requires the following steps:

1. Define a contract for the service.
2. Implement the service contract.
3. Define the data structures (if any) to carry data from the service to the client.

Now that you have a brief idea about creating WCF services, let's create our own service. Begin by creating a new class library project named `EmployeeLibrary`. After you create the project, add a reference to the `System.ServiceModel` assembly by using the Add Reference dialog box. Add an interface to it by using the Add New Item dialog box and name it `IEmployeeService` (Figure 12-1).

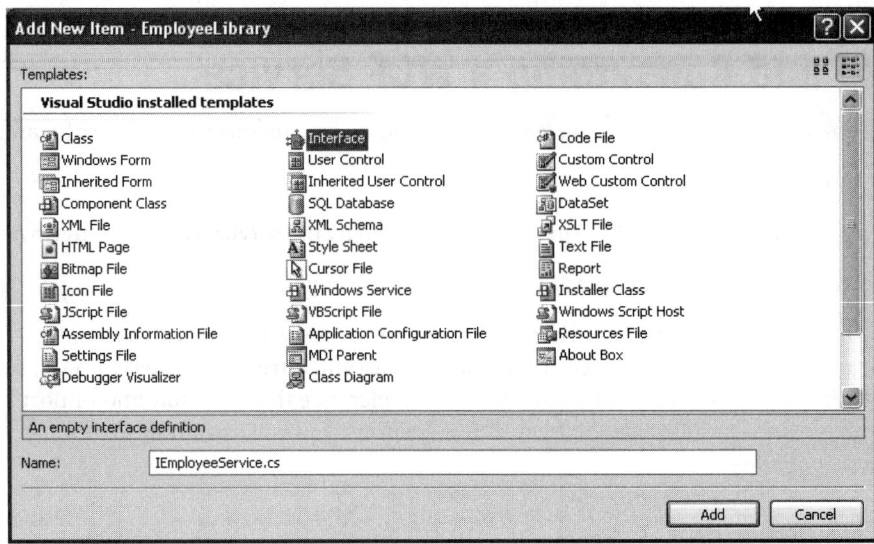

Figure 12-1. *Adding a new interface*

Import the `System.ServiceModel` namespace at the top of the interface file and add the code shown in Listing 12-1 in the interface.

Listing 12-1. *Creating the IEmployeeService Interface*

```
using System;
using System.Collections.Generic;
using System.Text;
using System.ServiceModel;
using System.Data;

namespace EmployeeLibrary
{
    [ServiceContract]
    public interface IEmployeeService
    {
        [OperationContract]
        DataSet GetEmployees();
```

```
        [OperationContract]
        Employee GetEmployee(int id);

    }
}
```

The IEmployeeService interface acts as a WCF contract. A contract of a WCF service is defined by an interface, which you define in the normal fashion. The IEmployeeService interface defines two methods: GetEmployees() and GetEmployee(). The former method when implemented will return a DataSet filled with a list of all the employees from the Employees table of the Northwind database. The latter method when implemented will return an Employee object containing details of a specified employee. The Employee class is defined later in this section. Notice two things about the IEmployeeService interface:

- The interface must be decorated with the [ServiceContract] attribute. This attribute indicates that the interface decorated by it is a WCF service contract.
- Each method signature in the interface must be marked with the [OperationContract] attribute, which indicates that the method decorated by it will be exposed as a part of the service. Methods are referred to as *operations* in WCF terms.

After you define a contract, you need to implement it. You do this by creating a class that implements the contract interface. You need not do anything special with the service type apart from implementing the service contract. In our example, the next step is to create the Employee class. This class will be used to carry details of an employee from the service to the client. Add a reference to the System.Runtime.Serialization assembly. Import the System.ServiceModel and System.Runtime.Serialization namespaces at the top of the Employee class. Listing 12-2 shows the complete code that makes up the Employee class.

Listing 12-2. *The Employee Class*

```
using System;
using System.Collections.Generic;
using System.Text;
using System.ServiceModel;
using System.Runtime.Serialization;
using System.Data;

namespace EmployeeLibrary
{
    [DataContract]
    public class Employee
    {
        private int intID;
        private string strFName;
        private string strLName;
```

```
        [DataMember]
        public int EmployeeID
        {
            get
            {
                return intID;
            }
            set
            {
                intID = value;
            }
        }

        [DataMember]
        public string FirstName
        {
            get
            {
                return strFName;
            }
            set
            {
                strFName = value;
            }
        }

        [DataMember]
        public string LastName
        {
            get
            {
                return strLName;
            }
            set
            {
                strLName = value;
            }
        }
    }
}
```

The Employee class consists of three public properties: EmployeeID, FirstName, and LastName. Notice how the class is marked with the [DataContract] attribute, and individual properties with the [DataMember] attribute. This way, the class and its state information are serialized to the client. If you wish to return custom classes from your service methods, you need to mark such classes with the [DataContract] attribute. Further, each member of the class that will be transferred to the client must be marked with the [DataMember] attribute. You may notice that the use of the [DataContract] attribute is similar to the [Serializable] attribute.

The last step in creating our service is to implement the service contract in a class called EmployeeService. Listing 12-3 shows the complete code of the EmployeeService class.

Listing 12-3. *The EmployeeService Class*

```
using System;
using System.Collections.Generic;
using System.Text;
using System.Data;
using System.Data.SqlClient;

namespace EmployeeLibrary
{
    public class EmployeeService:IEmployeeService
    {

        public DataSet GetEmployees()
        {
            SqlDataAdapter da =
          new SqlDataAdapter("SELECT employeeid,firstname,lastname FROM employees",
          @"data source=.\sqlexpress;initial catalog=northwind;integrated ➥
security=true");
            DataSet ds = new DataSet();
            da.Fill(ds,"employees");
            return ds;
        }

        public Employee GetEmployee(int id)
```

```
        {
            SqlConnection cnn =
              new SqlConnection(@"data source=.\sqlexpress;initial ➥
catalog=northwind;integrated security=true");
            SqlCommand cmd = new SqlCommand();
            cmd.Connection = cnn;
            cmd.CommandText =
              "SELECT employeeid,firstname,lastname
               FROM employees WHERE employeeid=@id";
            SqlParameter p = new SqlParameter("@id", id);
            cmd.Parameters.Add(p);
            cnn.Open();
            SqlDataReader reader = cmd.ExecuteReader();
            Employee emp = new Employee();
            while (reader.Read())
            {
                emp.EmployeeID = reader.GetInt32(0);
                emp.FirstName = reader.GetString(1);
                emp.LastName= reader.GetString(2);
            }
            reader.Close();
            cnn.Close();
            return emp;
        }

    }
}
```

The EmployeeService class implements the IEmployeeService interface. The GetEmployees() method fills a DataSet with a list of all the employees (including the EmployeeID, FirstName, and LastName columns) and returns it to the caller.

The GetEmployee() method accepts an employee ID. It then fetches details of that employee from the database and adds them to an Employee object. The Employee instance is then returned to the caller.

Compile the EmployeeService class library so as to create the EmployeeLibrary.dll assembly.

Hosting the Service

Now that you have created the service type, it's time to think about hosting it. Hosting the service will allow client applications to consume it. To host the service, you have three options:

- Create a console application and use it as a host.
- Host the WCF service in IIS.
- Host the WCF service in a Windows service application.

In this example, we will use a console application as a host. In later sections, you will learn to use IIS to host WCF services.

Add a new project of the type console application in the same solution as the service and name it `EmployeeServiceHostConsole`. Add a reference to the `System.ServiceModel` and `EmployeeLibrary` assemblies. Add an application configuration file to the project by using the Add New Item dialog box (Figure 12-2).

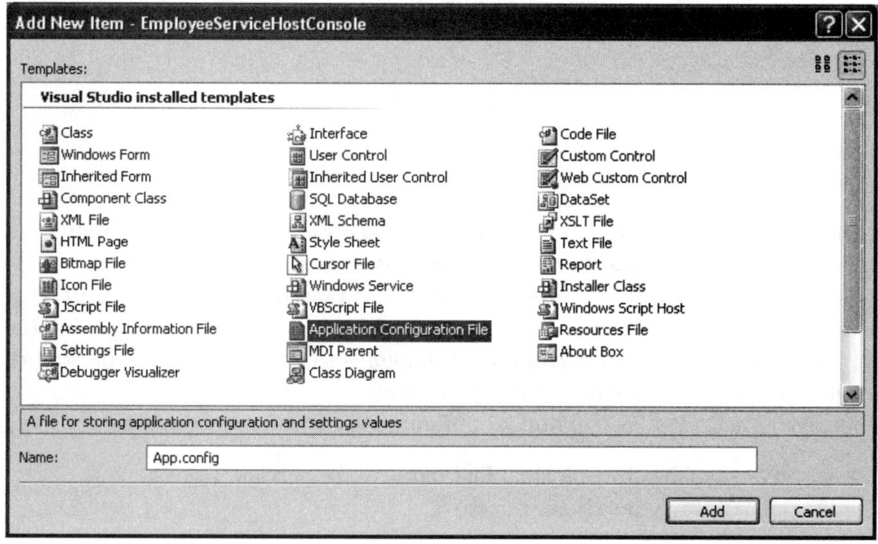

Figure 12-2. *Adding an application configuration file*

You need this configuration file to configure the service. Open the `App.config` file in Visual Studio and enter the markup shown in Listing 12-4.

Listing 12-4. *Configuring the Service*

```
<?xml version="1.0" encoding="utf-8" ?>
<configuration>
  <system.serviceModel>
    <services>
      <service name="EmployeeLibrary.EmployeeService"
               behaviorConfiguration="EmployeeServiceBehavior">
        <endpoint address="EmployeeService" binding="netTcpBinding"
                  contract="EmployeeLibrary.IEmployeeService" />
        <endpoint address="EmployeeService" binding="basicHttpBinding"
                  contract="EmployeeLibrary.IEmployeeService" />
      </service>
    </services>
    <behaviors>
      <serviceBehaviors>
        <behavior name="EmployeeServiceBehavior">
          <serviceMetadata httpGetEnabled="True"/>
        </behavior>
      </serviceBehaviors>
    </behaviors>
  </system.serviceModel>
</configuration>
```

The `<system.serviceModel>` section of the configuration file contains all the configuration settings related to WCF services. There are two subsections: `<services>` and `<behaviors>`. The former contains configuration information about one or more services in terms of name, endpoints, and addresses. The latter contains configuration information about behavior exhibited by the services defined in the `<services>` section. A *behavior* is a class that modifies or extends the service or client functionality. It can also modify channel settings.

Each service from the `<services>` section is configured via a `<service>` section:

- The `name` attribute specifies the fully qualified name of the service type (`EmployeeLibrary.EmployeeService` in our case).
- The `behaviorConfiguration` attribute points to the name of the service behavior as defined in the `<serviceBehaviors>` section.
- The `<endpoint>` element details one or more endpoints where the service is available.
    - The `address` attribute of the `<endpoint>` element specifies the address of the service.
    - The `binding` attribute specifies the protocol to be used for communication. The two commonly used bindings are `net.tcp` for TCP and `basicHttpBinding` for HTTP. There are several other bindings provided such as `NetMsmqBinding`, `NetNamedPipeBinding`, and so on.
    - Finally, the `contract` attribute specifies the fully qualified name of the interface that provides the service contract.

In our example, we created two endpoints: one for TCP-based communication and one for HTTP-based communication.

The `<serviceBehaviors>` section contains one or more `<behavior>` elements:

- The `name` attribute of the `<behavior>` element specifies the name of that behavior. This name is used in the `behaviorConfiguration` attribute of the `<service>` element.
- The `<serviceMetadata>` element indicates that the metadata of the service can be retrieved by using an HTTP `GET` request. You will find this feature analogous to web services, where you retrieve WSDL by using a query string (that is, a `GET` request).

Now open the `Main()` method of the console application and key in the code shown in Listing 12-5.

Listing 12-5. *Hosting the WCF Service*

```
using System;
using System.Collections.Generic;
using System.Text;
using System.ServiceModel;
using EmployeeLibrary;

namespace ServiceHostConsole
{
    class Program
    {
        static void Main(string[] args)
        {

            Type t = typeof(EmployeeService);
            Uri tcp = new Uri("net.tcp://localhost:8010/EmployeeService");
            Uri http = new Uri("http://localhost:8000/EmployeeService");
            ServiceHost host = new ServiceHost(t, tcp, http);
            host.Open();
            Console.WriteLine("Published");
            Console.ReadLine();
            host.Close();
        }
    }
}
```

The code retrieves the `Type` of the service type class by using the `typeof()` statement. It then creates two instances of the `Uri` class: one pointing to the TCP-based URL where the service is to be published and the other pointing to the HTTP-based URL. Note how the port numbers are set as 8000 and 8010 for TCP and HTTP URLs, respectively.

Then an instance of the `ServiceHost` class is created. The `ServiceHost` class hosts the service by publishing the service type at the specified URIs. Note that the constructor of the

ServiceHost class takes a parameter array of URIs. In our example, we have passed two, but you can pass more if you so wish. The following constructor signature will make it clear:

```
public ServiceHost ( Type serviceType, params Uri[] baseAddresses)
{
  ...
}
```

The Open() method of the ServiceHost class is then called. This method actually hosts the service depending on the configuration information. The service will remain published so long as the host application is live. That is why the ReadLine() method of the Console class is called. It keeps the application live until the user presses the Enter key. Finally, the Close() method of the ServiceHost class is called. This completes the host application.

Consuming the Service

In this section, you will create a client application that consumes the EmployeeService we created previously. To begin, you need to create a Windows application as shown in Figure 12-3.

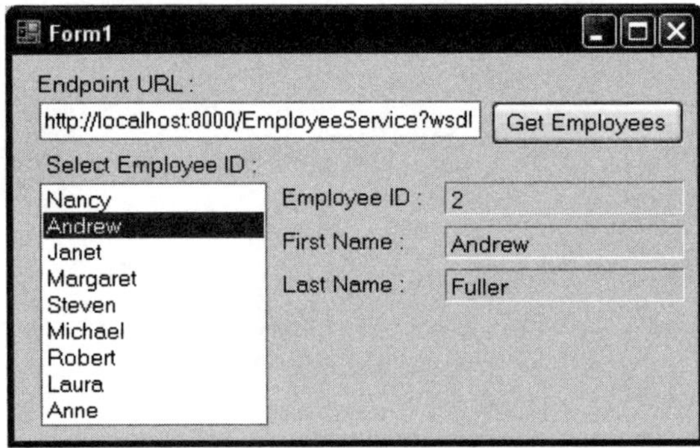

Figure 12-3. *The client consuming the WCF service*

The application consists of a text box for entering the URL where the EmployeeService is available. After you enter the URL and click the Get Employees button, a list of employees is displayed in a list box. Clicking a particular employee will display their details in Label controls. Listing 12-6 shows the Click event handler of the Get Employees button.

Listing 12-6. *Retrieving the List of Employees*

```
private void button1_Click(object sender, EventArgs e)
{
  Uri uri = new Uri(textBox1.Text);
  ServiceEndpointCollection endpts =
    MetadataResolver.Resolve(typeof(IEmployeeService), uri,
                             MetadataExchangeClientMode.HttpGet);
  foreach (ServiceEndpoint obj in endpts)
  {
    IEmployeeService proxy =
     new ChannelFactory<IEmployeeService>(obj.Binding, obj.Address).CreateChannel();
    DataSet ds = proxy.GetEmployees();
    listBox1.DataSource = ds.Tables[0].DefaultView;
    listBox1.DisplayMember = "FirstName";
    listBox1.ValueMember = "EmployeeID";
    ((IChannel)proxy).Close();
  }
}
```

The code creates a new instance of the `Uri` class by passing the supplied URL of the `EmployeeService`. Then the `Resolve()` static method of the `MetadataResolver` class is called. This class is used to retrieve and import the metadata of the service into one or more `ServiceEndpoint` objects. The `Resolve()` method takes three parameters: the type of service contract, the URI where the service is available, and `MetadataExchangeClientMode`. The `MetadataExchangeClientMode` enumeration has two possible values: `HttpGet` and `MetadataExchange`. The former is used when you wish to retrieve metadata by using a plain `GET` request, whereas the latter is used with WS-MetadataExchange to retrieve the metadata of a service.

■ **Note** WCF implements the WS-MetadataExchange specifications to retrieve the XML schema, WSDL, and WS-Policy of a service.

The Resolve() method returns the endpoints as a ServiceEndpointCollection. The code then iterates through the ServiceEndpointCollection. To call the service, you need to create a proxy for it. This is accomplished by using the ChannelFactory class. The CreateChannel() method of the ChannelFactory class accepts the binding and address of the endpoint and returns a proxy for the service. Notice the use of generics in the ChannelFactory class. After the proxy is retrieved, you can call any method on it. In our example, we call GetEmployees(). The returned DataSet is then bound to the ListBox control. After we've finished with the proxy, we call its Close() method.

When a user clicks on any of the employees listed in the ListBox, details of that employee are to be displayed in the Label controls. This is done in the Click event handler of the ListBox (Listing 12-7).

Listing 12-7. *Retrieving the Details of an Employee*

```
private void listBox1_Click(object sender, EventArgs e)
{
  Uri uri = new Uri(textBox1.Text);
  ServiceEndpointCollection endpts =
    MetadataResolver.Resolve(typeof(IEmployeeService), uri,
                             MetadataExchangeClientMode.HttpGet);
  foreach (ServiceEndpoint obj in endpts)
  {
    IEmployeeService proxy =
     new ChannelFactory<IEmployeeService>(obj.Binding, obj.Address).CreateChannel();
    Employee emp = proxy.GetEmployee(int.Parse(listBox1.SelectedValue.ToString()));
    label5.Text = emp.EmployeeID.ToString();
    label6.Text = emp.FirstName;
    label7.Text = emp.LastName;
    ((IChannel)proxy).Close();
  }
}
```

The code is very similar to what you saw earlier. This time it calls the GetEmployee() method on the proxy by passing the selected EmployeeID. The GetEmployee() method returns an instance of the Employee class filled with the required details. The details such as EmployeeID, FirstName, and LastName are then displayed in respective labels.

Testing the Host and Client

Now that you have coded all three parts (service, host, and client), let's test them. First, compile all the projects from the solution. Then navigate to the .EXE of the console application and run it. If everything goes well, you should see a command prompt as shown in Figure 12-4.

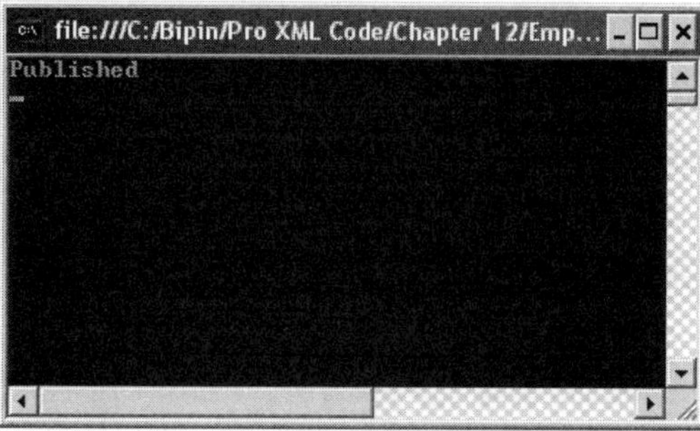

Figure 12-4. *Running the host application*

Next open Internet Explorer and enter the URL of the service endpoint (`http://localhost:8000/EmployeeService`) in the address bar. You should get a web page as shown in Figure 12-5.

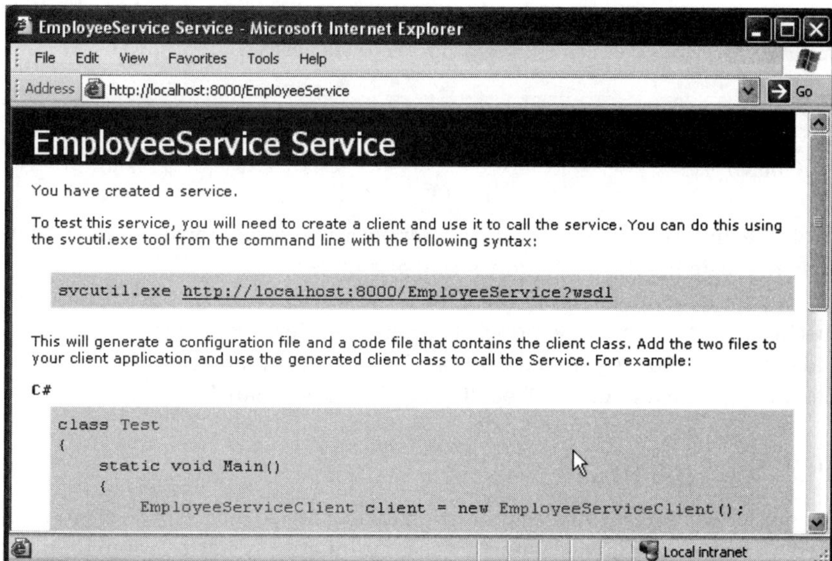

Figure 12-5. *Testing to see whether the service is hosted properly*

If you get this page, the service is hosted correctly. Click on the URL specified at the top of the web page and you should see the WSDL of the service, as shown in Figure 12-6.

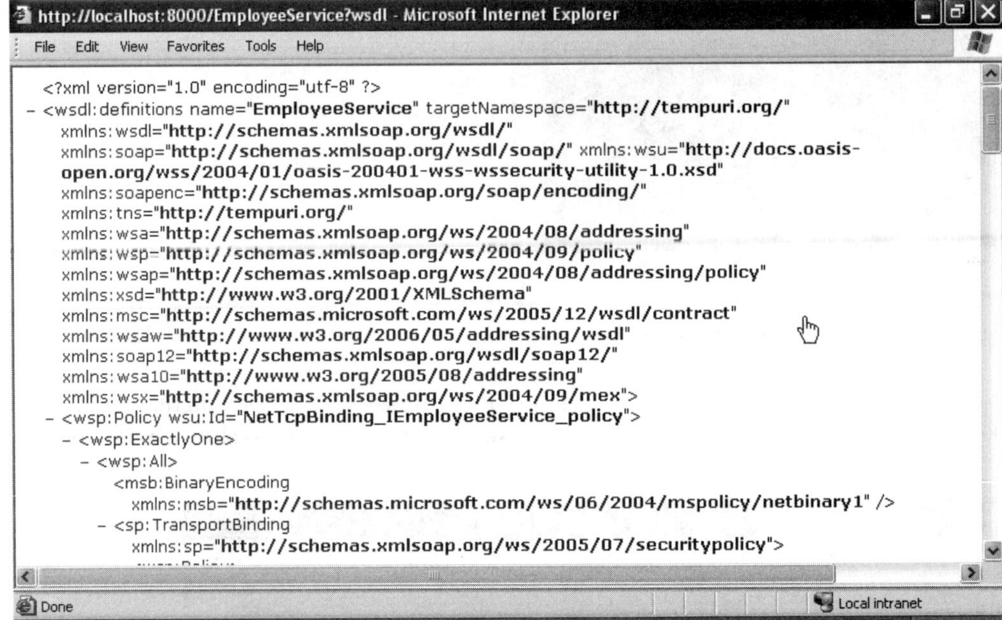

Figure 12-6. *WSDL of the service*

You will find this mechanism very similar to web services, where you retrieved the WSDL of a web service just by specifying the `wsdl` query string parameter.

Now run the client application and enter the URL of the service's WSDL. You can simply copy and paste the URL from the browser window of Figure 12-6. Next, click the Get Employees button. You should see the ListBox populated with the list of all the employees. Click on individual employee names, and their details will be displayed in various labels.

Hosting a WCF Service in IIS

In the preceding example, we used a console application to host our service. However, you can also use IIS to host WCF services. This way, your service is automatically started when IIS starts and you get all the security features of IIS for your service.

To begin, create a new website by using Visual Studio. Because you will be hosting the service in IIS, make sure to create an HTTP-based website (Figure 12-7).

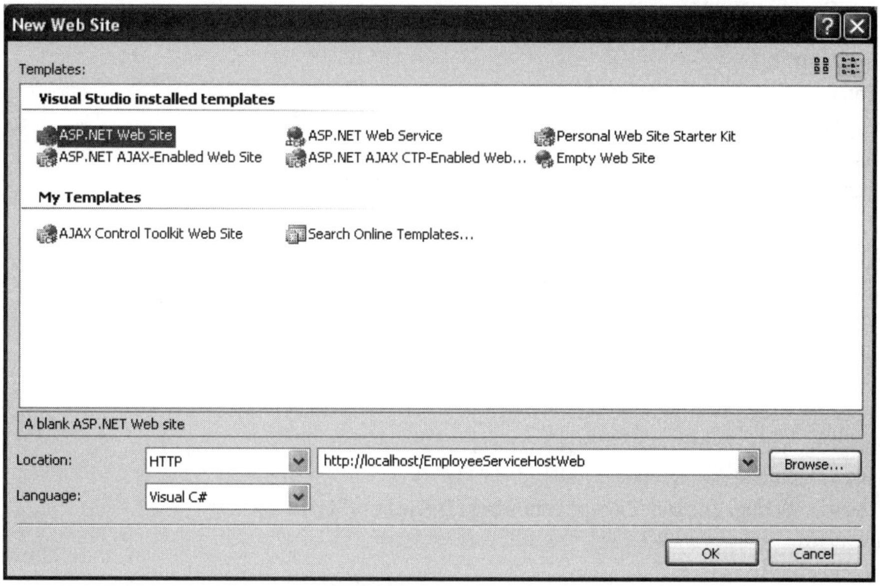

Figure 12-7. *Creating an HTTP-based website*

This way, an IIS application will be created for the newly created website. Remove the default web form from the site. Add a new text file to the site and name it `EmployeeServiceHost.svc`. This file essentially hosts the service inside IIS. Add a reference to `EmployeeLibrary.dll` so that it gets copied to the `Bin` folder of your website. Now key in the markup inside the .SVC file as shown in Listing 12-8.

Listing 12-8. *Adding the ServiceHost Directive*

```
<%@ServiceHost Service="EmployeeLibrary.EmployeeService" %>
```

The `@ServiceHost` directive indicates that the file is a WCF service host. The `Service` attribute specifies the fully qualified name of the service type. Now add a `web.config` file to the website and key in the markup shown in Listing 12-9.

Listing 12-9. *Configuring the Host*

```
<?xml version="1.0"?>
<configuration>
  <system.serviceModel>
    <services>
      <service name="EmployeeLibrary.EmployeeService"
               behaviorConfiguration="EmployeeServiceBehavior">
        <endpoint address="" binding="basicHttpBinding"
                  contract="EmployeeLibrary.IEmployeeService"></endpoint>
      </service>
    </services>
    <behaviors>
      <serviceBehaviors>
        <behavior name="EmployeeServiceBehavior">
          <serviceMetadata httpGetEnabled="True"/>
          <serviceDebug includeExceptionDetailInFaults="true"/>
        </behavior>
      </serviceBehaviors>
    </behaviors>
  </system.serviceModel>
</configuration>
```

It is essentially the same markup that you specified for the console host. The only difference is that the `address` attribute of the `<endpoint>` element is an empty string. This is because for an IIS-hosted service, the address is the same as the URI of the .SVC file hosting the service.

To access the `EmployeeService` hosted in IIS, the endpoint URL will be `http://localhost/EmployeeServiceHostWeb/EmployeeServicerHost.svc?wsdl`. Observe that the URL points to the .SVC file and contains the `wsdl` query string parameter. Everything else in the client application remains the same.

Understanding the Role of XML in WCF Services

From what you have learned up until now, it is clear that WCF uses XML for configuring various pieces of services. However, there is more to the story. Internally WCF services heavily rely on XML.

When a WCF service call is made by a client application, the call is converted into a message, which is represented by a class called `Message`. Internally, the client request is stored in a special XML format called InfoSet. When the client call is sent to the service, it is serialized in a format decided by the binding. For example, if the client is a non-WCF client, the message is encoded in XML format, whereas if the client is a WCF client, it is represented in an optimized binary format. When the message reaches the service, it is deserialized back into an InfoSet. A `Message` object is created and then handed over to the service along with the InfoSet. The service then executes the method call and returns the data in a similar fashion.

Using the XmlFormatter and XmlSerializer Classes

Internally, the WCF framework uses two classes for XML manipulation:

- `XmlFormatter` is new to .NET Framework 3.0 and is used by default in WCF communication. You have very little control on how `XmlFormatter` serializes the XML data.
- You learned about the `XmlSerializer` class in Chapter 8. You can also use `XmlSerializer` for WCF communication. Doing so will give you more control of how the data is serialized. You can customize the serialization process by using various attributes such as `[XmlAttribute]` and `[XmlElement]`. However, `XmlFormatter` will be a better solution in terms of performance.

Using XmlSerializer Instead of XmlFormatter

To instruct the WCF framework that it should use `XmlSerializer` instead of `XmlFormatter`, all you need to do is decorate the service contract interface with the `[XmlSerializerFormat]` attribute. The `IEmployeeService` interface after applying the `[XmlSerializerFormat]` attribute is shown in Listing 12-10.

Listing 12-10. *Applying the [XmlSerializerFormat] Attribute*

```
[ServiceContract]
[XmlSerializerFormat]
public interface IEmployeeService
{
        [OperationContract]
        DataSet GetEmployees();

        [OperationContract]
        Employee GetEmployee(int id);
}
```

Summary

Windows Communication Foundation (WCF) provides a unified programming model for developing service-oriented applications. This chapter gave you an overview of WCF. You saw the basic vocabulary of WCF along with parts of a typical WCF-enabled application. You created a WCF service, host, and client application. WCF services can be hosted in a console application, on IIS, or as a Windows service. WCF relies heavily on XML for data transmission. The `XmlFormatter` and `XmlSerializer` classes can take part in the serialization process, `XmlFormatter` being the default.

APPENDIX A

Creating Custom XmlReader and XmlWriter Classes

In Chapter 3, you learned about the XmlReader and XmlWriter classes. The abstract classes XmlReader and XmlWriter can be used in three ways:

- To call the Create() method of the respective classes that returns an instance of the generic XmlReader or XmlWriter classes
- To use the concrete classes XmlTextReader and XmlTextWriter provided by the .NET Framework
- To create custom classes that inherit from the XmlReader and XmlWriter classes

You are already familiar with the first two approaches. In the following sections, you are going to learn how to create custom readers and writers from the abstract base classes XmlReader and XmlWriter.

Creating a Custom Implementation of XmlReader

In this section, you will create a custom implementation of the XmlReader class. The SqlCommand class provides the ExecuteXmlReader() method that returns an instance of XmlReader to the caller. This works fine if your database is SQL Server, but what if your database is Microsoft Office Access or any other OLEDB-compliant database? Moreover, XML extensions such as the FOR XML clause may not be available for all databases. Does that mean that you cannot retrieve the data and read it by using an XmlReader? Of course not.

There is no out-of-the-box solution for this problem, but you can build your own mechanism to overcome this limitation, by creating a custom class that inherits from the XmlReader abstract class. You can then override the required properties and methods as per your need. The requirements for the custom XmlReader class are summarized here:

- It should accept the database connection string and table name to read.
- The column values should be treated as attribute values.
- It should allow iterating through the table to read each row.
- The column values should be accessible by specifying a column index or name.

Inheriting from XmlReader

The XmlReader class is an abstract class and provides several properties and methods that you need to override when you inherit from it. Listing A-1 shows signatures of these properties and methods.

Listing A-1. *Properties and Methods of the XmlReader Class*

```
public abstract int AttributeCount;
public abstract string BaseURI
{
  get;
}
public abstract void Close();
public abstract int Depth
{
  get;
}
public abstract bool EOF
{
  get;
}
public abstract string GetAttribute(int i);
public abstract string GetAttribute(string name, string namespaceURI);
public abstract string GetAttribute(string name);
public abstract bool HasValue
{
  get;
}
public abstract bool IsEmptyElement
{
  get;
}
public abstract string LocalName
{
  get;
}
public abstract string LookupNamespace(string prefix);
public abstract bool MoveToAttribute(string name, string ns);
public abstract bool MoveToAttribute(string name);
public abstract bool MoveToElement();
public abstract bool MoveToFirstAttribute();
public abstract bool MoveToNextAttribute();
public abstract XmlNameTable NameTable
{
  get;
}
```

```
public abstract string NamespaceURI
{
  get;
}
public abstract XmlNodeType NodeType
{
  get;
}
public abstract string Prefix
{
  get;
}
public abstract bool Read();
public abstract bool ReadAttributeValue();
public abstract ReadState ReadState
{
  get;
}
public abstract void ResolveEntity();
public abstract string Value
{
  get;
}
```

You can override these properties and methods and write your own data-manipulation logic. If you do not want to override a particular property or method, you still need to have its empty implementation. A better way is to throw an exception in such properties and methods so that the caller knows that these properties and methods are not implemented by you. I will not discuss every property here because you are already familiar with many of them (see Chapter 3 for more information).

Creating a TableReader Class

Now that you are familiar with the `XmlReader` abstract class, let's create our own implementation. To do so, create a new project of type class library by using Visual Studio. Add a class named `TableReader`. Make sure that references to the `System.Xml` and `System.Data` assemblies are added to the project. Import the namespaces as shown in Listing A-2 at the top of the `TableReader` class and ensure that the `TableReader` class inherits from the `XmlReader` class.

Listing A-2. *Importing Namespaces and Setting Inheritence*

```
using System.Xml;
using System.Data;
using System.Data.OleDb;

class TableReader:XmlReader
{
...
```

You need to add an implementation of each property and method mentioned. Visual Studio provides a shortcut for adding empty implementations of these members. Right-click on the XmlReader class in the class definition and choose the Implement Abstract Class menu option (Figure A-1).

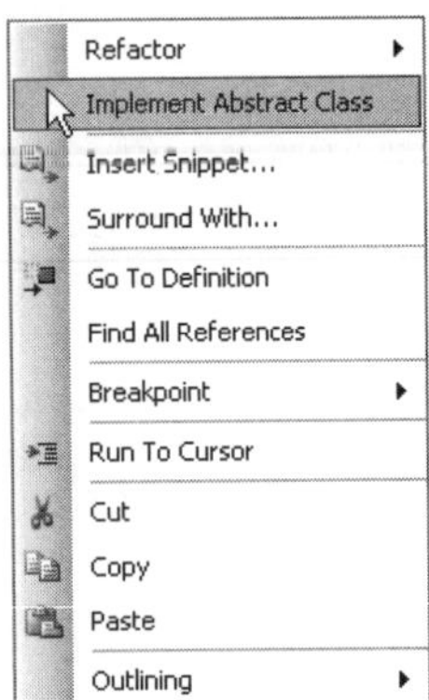

Figure A-1. *Adding empty implementations of properties and methods*

This will add dummy signatures of all the properties and methods that need to be overridden. Notice how the dummy implementation throws an exception by using the throw keyword. This way, if somebody tries to use unimplemented members, an exception will be thrown indicating that "the method or operation is not implemented." Code the TableReader class as shown in Listing A-3.

Listing A-3. *The TableReader Class*

```
public class TableReader:XmlReader
{
        private OleDbConnection cnn;
        private OleDbCommand cmd;
        private OleDbDataReader reader;
        private int intColumnIndex = -1;
        private string strValue;

        public TableReader(string connectionString,string tableName)
        {
            cnn = new OleDbConnection(connectionString);
            cmd = new OleDbCommand();
            cmd.Connection = cnn;
            cmd.CommandText = tableName;
            cmd.CommandType = CommandType.TableDirect;
            cnn.Open();
            reader = cmd.ExecuteReader();
        }
```

```
public override int AttributeCount
{
    get
    {
        return reader.FieldCount;
    }
}

public override void Close()
{
    reader.Close();
    cnn.Close();
}

public override int Depth
{
    get
    {
        return reader.Depth;
    }
}

public override string GetAttribute(int i)
{
    return reader.GetValue(i).ToString();
}

public override string GetAttribute(string name)
{
    return reader.GetValue(reader.GetOrdinal(name)).ToString();
}

public override bool MoveToAttribute(string name)
{
    intColumnIndex = reader.GetOrdinal(name);
    return true;
}

public override bool MoveToElement()
{
    intColumnIndex = -1;
    return true;
}
```

```
public override bool MoveToFirstAttribute()
{
    intColumnIndex = 0;
    return true;
}

public override bool MoveToNextAttribute()
{
    intColumnIndex++;
    if (intColumnIndex > reader.FieldCount - 1)
    {
        return false;
    }
    else
    {
        return true;
    }
}

public override bool Read()
{
    intColumnIndex = -1;
    strValue = "";
    return reader.Read();
}

public override bool HasValue
{
    get
    {
        return reader.IsDBNull(intColumnIndex);
    }
}

public override bool ReadAttributeValue()
{
    if (intColumnIndex < reader.FieldCount)
    {
        strValue = reader.GetValue(intColumnIndex).ToString();
        return true;
    }
    else
    {
        return false;
    }
}
```

```
        public string Name
        {
            get
            {
                if (intColumnIndex == -1)
                {
                    return cmd.CommandText;
                }
                else
                {
                    return reader.GetName(intColumnIndex);
                }
            }
        }

        public override string Value
        {
            get
            {
                return strValue;
            }
        }
...
}
```

In the following text, we will dissect the code step by step.

Declaring Class-Level Variables

```
private OleDbConnection cnn;
private OleDbCommand cmd;
private OleDbDataReader reader;
private int intColumnIndex = -1;
private string strValue;
```

The TableReader class declares private variables of type OleDbConnection, OleDbCommand, and OleDbDataReader classes at the class level:

- The OleDbConnection class is used to establish a connection with OLEDB-compliant databases such as Access.
- The OleDbCommand class is used to execute any query, SQL query, or stored procedures against a database.
- The OleDbDataReader class allows you to iterate through a result set in a cursor-oriented manner.

The intColumnIndex integer variable keeps track of the current column index whose value is to be read. Similarly, the strValue string variable stores the value from the column indicated by intColumnIndex.

Initializing the Variables

```
public TableReader(string connectionString,string tableName)
{
   cnn = new OleDbConnection(connectionString);
   cmd = new OleDbCommand();
   cmd.Connection = cnn;
   cmd.CommandText = tableName;
   cmd.CommandType = CommandType.TableDirect;
   cnn.Open();
   reader = cmd.ExecuteReader();
}
```

The constructor of the TableReader class accepts two parameters: the database connection string and the name of the table whose data is to be read. Using the connection string, the OleDbConnection is instantiated. The Connection property of the OleDbCommand class is set to the OleDbConnection class we just instantiated. The CommandText property of the OleDbCommand class is set to the name of the table whose data is to be read.

Have a look at the CommandType property. It is set to TableDirect, which returns all the rows from the table indicated by the CommandText property. In effect, it works as if we have specified SELECT * FROM <tableName> as the query. The database connection is then opened. The ExecuteReader() method of OleDbCommand is called and an OleDbDataReader is retrieved.

Retrieving the Total Number of Attributes

```
public override int AttributeCount
{
   get
   {
      return reader.FieldCount;
   }
}
```

The TableReader class is going to return column values as attributes in the resultant XML data. Hence, the AttributeCount read-only property returns the total number of columns in the underlying table. The total number of columns in the table is obtained by using the FieldCount property of the OleDbDataReader class.

Closing the Reader

```
public override void Close()
{
   reader.Close();
   cnn.Close();
}
```

```
public override int Depth
{
   get
   {
      return reader.Depth;
   }
}
```

The Close() method closes the OleDbDataReader as well as the OleDbConnection. The Depth property returns the Depth of the OleDbDataReader.

Reading Attributes

```
public override string GetAttribute(int i)
{
   return reader.GetValue(i).ToString();
}

public override string GetAttribute(string name)
{
   return reader.GetValue(reader.GetOrdinal(name)).ToString();
}
```

The column values can be retrieved by using two overloads of the GetAttribute() method. The first overload accepts the attribute index. In our case, the attribute index is the same as the column index. The GetValue() method of the OleDbDataReader class accepts the column index and returns the column value as an object. The ToString() method returns a string representation of the object to the caller. The second overload accepts an attribute name. The GetOrdinal() method of OleDbDataReader accepts the column name and returns its index. The returned index is then passed to the GetValue() method as before.

Navigating Between the Attributes

```
public override bool MoveToAttribute(string name)
{
   intColumnIndex = reader.GetOrdinal(name);
   return true;
}

public override bool MoveToElement()
{
   intColumnIndex = -1;
   return true;
}
```

```
public override bool MoveToFirstAttribute()
{
   intColumnIndex = 0;
   return true;
}

public override bool MoveToNextAttribute()
{
   intColumnIndex++;
   if (intColumnIndex > reader.FieldCount - 1)
   {
      return false;
   }
   else
   {
      return true;
   }
}
```

The `MoveToAttribute()`, `MoveToFirstAttribute()`, `MoveToNextAtribute()`, and `MoveToElement()` methods allow you to navigate within the available attributes:

- The `MoveToAttribute()` method accepts the name of the column (which is the same as the attribute name) and sets the column index variable to the index of that column.
- The `MoveToFirstAttribute()` method sets the current column index to `0`, whereas `MoveToNextAttribute()` increments it so that the next column value can be read.
- The `MoveToElement()` method simply sets the current column index to `-1`, indicating that no column value can be read. The `MoveToElement()` method is intended to move the reader to the element node from any of its attributes. By setting the column index to `-1`, we reset the column index counter and mimic this behavior.

Advancing the Reader

```
public override bool Read()
{
   intColumnIndex = -1;
   strValue = "";
   return reader.Read();
}
```

The Read() method allows you to iterate through the table. It calls the Read() method of the OleDbDataReader class and returns a Boolean value indicating whether the read operation was successful. As the record pointer is moving on to a new record, the current column index and value are reset.

Checking Whether the Value Is Empty

```
public override bool HasValue
{
   get
   {
      return reader.IsDBNull(intColumnIndex);
   }
}
```

The HasValue property indicates whether the TableReader contains any value. If the column contains a NULL value, HasValue should return false. The IsDbNull() method of the OleDbDataReader class accepts a column index and returns true if the column contains a NULL value.

Reading Values

```
public override bool ReadAttributeValue()
{
   if (intColumnIndex < reader.FieldCount)
   {
      strValue = reader.GetValue(intColumnIndex).ToString();
      return true;
   }
   else
   {
      return false;
   }
}
```

The ReadAttributeValue() method returns the value of the current column. It does so by using the GetValue() method of the OleDbDataReader class as before.

Returning the Table or Column Name

```
public string Name
{
   get
   {
      if (intColumnIndex == -1)
      {
         return cmd.CommandText;
      }
      else
      {
         return reader.GetName(intColumnIndex);
      }
   }
}
```

The `Name` property returns either the underlying table name or column name. This is useful to see which column is being read. The table name is obtained from the `CommandText` property of the `OleDbCommand` class, whereas the column name is obtained from the `GetName()` method of the `OleDbDataReader` class.

Returning Values

```
public override string Value
{
   get
   {
      return strValue;
   }
}
```

Finally, the `Value` property simply returns the value stored in the `strValue` variable. Note that `strValue` gets assigned in the `ReadAttributeValue()` method.

The remaining properties and methods are not implemented by the `TableReader` class. Compile the class library and you should get an assembly, `TableReader.dll`. This assembly can be used in client applications to work with OLEDB databases and XML.

Using the TableReader Class

To consume the `TableReader` class, you need to create a Windows application as shown in Figure A-2.

The application consists of text boxes for entering the database connection string and table name, respectively. After you click the Read button, the `TableReader` class is instantiated. It reads the table data and writes it to an XML file. The XML file thus created is displayed in a Web Browser control. The `Click` event handler of the Read button contains the code shown in Listing A-4.

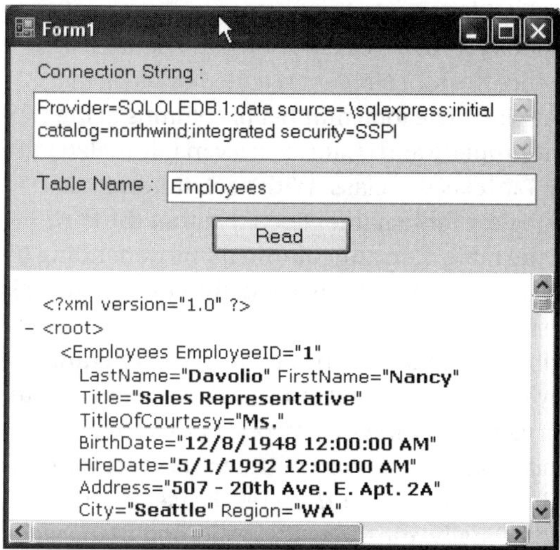

Figure A-2. *Application that consumes TableReader class*

Listing A-4. *Using the TableReader Class*

```
private void button1_Click(object sender, EventArgs e)
{
  TableReader tr = new TableReader(textBox1.Text, textBox2.Text);
  XmlTextWriter writer =
    new XmlTextWriter(Application.StartupPath + @"\temp.xml", null);
  writer.WriteStartDocument();
  writer.WriteStartElement("root");
  int count = tr.AttributeCount;
  while (tr.Read())
  {
    writer.WriteStartElement(tr.Name);
    for (int i = 0; i < count; i++)
    {
      tr.MoveToAttribute(i);
      tr.ReadAttributeValue();
      writer.WriteAttributeString(tr.Name, tr.Value);
    }
    writer.WriteEndElement();
  }
  writer.WriteEndElement();
  tr.Close();
  writer.Close();
  webBrowser1.Navigate(Application.StartupPath + @"\temp.xml");
}
```

Before you write the preceding code, add a reference to `TableReader.dll` in the Windows application and import the namespace at the top. The code creates an instance of the `TableReader` class by passing the database connection string and table name to its constructor. Then an XmlTextWriter is created that writes data to a temporary XML file called temp.xml. The TableReader class will return only the fragmented XML data; hence the root element is added by using the WriteStartElement() method of the XmlTextWriter class. The total number of columns in the supplied table is retrieved by using the AttributeCount property and is stored in a variable for later use.

A while loop calls the Read() method of the TableReader class. With each iteration, an element is added to the file with the same name as the table name. Recollect that the Name property of the TableReader class returns either the table name or column name depending on the current column index. Because we have just called the Read() method, the column index is going to be -1 and hence the table name will be returned.

Next, a for loop iterates through all the attributes—that is, columns. With each iteration of the for loop, the value of the attribute is read by using the ReadAttributeValue() method. An attribute is then written to the file along with its value by using the WriteAttributeString() method of the XmlTextWriter class. The WriteEndElement() method of the XmlTextWriter class writes end tags for the nearest open element. The TableReader and XmlTextReader are then closed by using their respective Close() methods. Finally, the Navigate() method of the web browser control shows the user the XML file.

Creating a Custom XmlWriter

Now that you have created a custom implementation of XmlReader, let's move further and see how to create a custom XmlWriter. As an example, we will create an RSS writer that emits RSS feeds.

Really Simple Syndication (RSS) is a standard way to share your website content with others. It is nothing but standardized XML markup that describes the content you want to share. Because RSS is a widely accepted format, your content immediately becomes ready to be consumed by others. Listing A-5 illustrates an RSS document.

Listing A-5. *Sample RSS Markup*

```
<rss version="2.0">
  <channel>
    <title>DotNetBips.com Latest Articles</title>
    <link>www.dotnetbips.com</link>
    <description>DotNetBips.com Latest Articles</description>
    <copyright>Copyright (C) DotNetBips.com. All rights reserved.</copyright>
    <generator>www.dotnetbips.com RSS Generator</generator>
    <item>
      <title>Using WebRequest and WebResponse</title>
      <link>http://www.dotnetbips.com/displayarticle.aspx?id=239</link>
      <description>Description here</description>
      <pubDate>Sun, 25 Jan 2004 12:00:00 AM GMT</pubDate>
    </item>
  </channel>
</rss>
```

Let's look at each markup tag closely:

- <rss> forms the root tag and has a version attribute. The latest version is 2.0.
- <channel> contains tags such as <title>, <link>, and <item> nodes. A channel represents metadata information from a particular source. It essentially acts as a container for the rest of the tags. An RSS document can contain one or more channels.
- <title> represents the title of this RSS feed.
- <link> represents the URL of the website providing the RSS feed.
- <description> details more information about this feed.
- <copyright> specifies copyright information.
- <generator> specifies the application that generated this feed.

In addition to the preceding tags, there can be one or more <item> tags, each of which represents an actual item that you want to share (for example, an article or a blog entry). Each <item> tag further contains the following subnodes:

- <title> represents the title of this item (for example, the article title).
- <link> represents the URL of this item (for example, the article URL).
- <description> contains the description of the item (for example, a summary of the article).
- <pubDate> contains the publication date of the item. A typical date format is Sun 28 Dec 2003 12:00:00 AM GMT.

■ **Note** The RSS markup shown here is the basic markup. You may need to add additional tags to incorporate additional information. You can obtain more information about RSS at http://en.wikipedia.org/wiki/RSS_(file_format).

In the absence of any out-of-the-box solution for generating RSS feeds in your website, you need to use classes such as XmlTextWriter yourself. You also need to remember the allowed tag names. To overcome this problem, we will create a custom class called RssWriter. The RssWriter class will inherit from XmlWriter and allow you to emit RSS feeds easily.

To create RssWriter, you need to create a class library project. As before, be sure to add a reference to the System.Xml assembly.

Inheriting from XmlWriter

To create a custom implementation of XmlWriter, you need to inherit from it and override the properties and methods shown in Listing A-6.

Listing A-6. *Properties and Methods of the XmlWriter Class*

```
public abstract void Close();
public abstract void Flush();
public abstract string LookupPrefix(string ns);
public abstract void WriteBase64(byte[] buffer, int index, int count);
public abstract void WriteCData(string text);
public abstract void WriteCharEntity(char ch);
public abstract void WriteChars(char[] buffer, int index, int count);
public abstract void WriteComment(string text);
public abstract void
  WriteDocType(string name, string pubid, string sysid, string subset);
public abstract void WriteEndAttribute();
public abstract void WriteEndDocument();
public abstract void WriteEndElement();
public abstract void WriteEntityRef(string name);
public abstract void WriteFullEndElement();
public abstract void WriteProcessingInstruction(string name, string text);
public abstract void WriteRaw(string data);
public abstract void WriteRaw(char[] buffer, int index, int count);
public abstract void
  WriteStartAttribute(string prefix, string localName, string ns);
public abstract void WriteStartDocument(bool standalone);
public abstract void WriteStartDocument();
public abstract void WriteStartElement(string prefix, string localName, string ns);
public abstract WriteState WriteState
{
  get;
}
public abstract void WriteString(string text);
public abstract void WriteSurrogateCharEntity(char lowChar, char highChar);
public abstract void WriteWhitespace(string ws);
```

Many of these properties and methods should be familiar to you because we discussed them in Chapter 3.

Creating the RssWriter Class

To begin, we need to specify that the `RssWriter` class inherits from the `XmlWriter` base class. As shown in Figure A-1, add dummy definitions of the properties and methods that implement the abstract base class `XmlWriter`. Then add a couple of variables and a constructor to the `RssWriter` class as shown in Listing A-7.

Listing A-7. *The Constructor of RssWriter*

```
public class RssWriter:XmlWriter
{
  private XmlWriter writer;
  private Stream objStream;
  public RssWriter(Stream stream)
  {
    objStream = stream;
    writer = XmlWriter.Create(objStream);
  }
```

The code declares class-level variables of `XmlWriter` and `Stream` types, respectively. The constructor takes a parameter of type `Stream`. This stream acts as an output stream for emitting the RSS feeds. An instance of the `XmlWriter` is constructed by using the `Create()` method of the `XmlWriter` class. The stream passed to the constructor is supplied to the `Create()` method so that the newly created instance of `XmlWriter` writes to that stream.

Coding Stream-Related Operations

The stream needs to be closed and flushed to ensure that the emitted data is saved correctly. The two overridden methods—`Close()` and `Flush()`—do just that. Listing A-8 shows these methods.

Listing A-8. *The Close() and Flush() Methods*

```
public override void Close()
{
  objStream.Close();
  writer.Close();
}
public override void Flush()
{
  writer.Flush();
}
```

The `Close()` method calls the `Close()` method of the underlying stream as well as that of the `XmlWriter`. Similarly, the `Flush()` method calls the `Flush()` method of the `XmlWriter` so that data is flushed to the stream.

Defining Enumerations for RSS-Specific Tags

It would be nice to readily provide RSS tag and attribute names so that you need not remember them. This is achieved by creating two enumerations: `RssElements` and `RssAttributes`. The enumerations are shown in Listing A-9.

Listing A-9. *Enumerations for Representing RSS Tags and Attributes*

```
public enum RssElements
{
  Rss,Channel,Title,Description,Link,Copyright,Generator,Item,PubDate
}
public enum RssAttributes
{
  Version
}
```

The RssElements enumeration contains values for representing RSS elements. The RssAttributes enumeration contains just one value—Version—that represents the version attribute of the <rss> element.

Writing Elements

To emit the RSS feed, you need to write elements such as <rss> and <item> onto the output stream. We will create three methods for this purpose: WriteElement(), WriteElementString(), and WriteEndElement(). The complete code of these methods is shown in Listing A-10.

Listing A-10. *Writing Elements*

```
public void WriteStartElement(RssElements element)
{
  string elementName = "";
  switch (element)
  {
    case RssElements.Channel:
      elementName = "channel";
      break;
    case RssElements.Copyright:
      elementName = "copyright";
      break;
    case RssElements.Description:
      elementName = "description";
      break;
    case RssElements.Generator:
      elementName = "generator";
      break;
    case RssElements.Item:
      elementName = "item";
      break;
```

```
    case RssElements.Link:
      elementName = "link";
      break;
    case RssElements.PubDate:
      elementName = "pubDate";
      break;
    case RssElements.Rss:
      elementName = "rss";
      break;
    case RssElements.Title:
      elementName = "title";
      break;
  }
  writer.WriteStartElement(elementName);
}

public void WriteElementString(RssElements element, string value)
{
  string elementName = "";
  switch (element)
  {
    case RssElements.Channel:
      elementName = "channel";
      break;
    case RssElements.Copyright:
      elementName = "copyright";
      break;
    case RssElements.Description:
      elementName = "description";
      break;
    case RssElements.Generator:
      elementName = "generator";
      break;
    case RssElements.Item:
      elementName = "item";
      break;
    case RssElements.Link:
      elementName = "link";
      break;
    case RssElements.PubDate:
      elementName = "pubDate";
      break;
```

```
    case RssElements.Rss:
      elementName = "rss";
      break;
    case RssElements.Title:
      elementName = "title";
      break;
  }
  writer.WriteElementString(elementName, value);
}

public override void WriteEndElement()
{
  writer.WriteEndElement();
}
```

The WriteStartElement() method accepts a parameter of type RssElements that indicates the element name to be written. It contains a switch statement that checks the supplied element name against various values from the RssElements enumeration. The name of the element is stored in a string variable. Finally, the WriteStartElement() method of XmlWriter is called by supplying the element name stored in the variable.

The WriteElementString() method accepts two parameters: RssElements and the value of the element. It contains a similar switch statement as in the previous method and stores the element name in a variable. The WriteElementString() method of the XmlWriter class is called by passing the element name and its value. Note that WriteStartElement() and WriteElementString() are new methods—that is, they are not defined by the XmlWriter base class.

The WriteEndElement() method simply calls the WriteEndElement() method of the XmlWriter instance so that the end tag of the nearest element is emitted.

Writing Attributes

Just as we added methods for writing elements, we also need to add methods for emitting attributes. Three methods—WriteStartAttribute(), WriteAttributeString(), and WriteEndAttribute()—will do that job. Listing A-11 shows these methods.

Listing A-11. *Writing Attributes*

```
public void WriteStartAttribute(RssAttributes attb)
{
  if (attb == RssAttributes.Version)
  {
    writer.WriteStartAttribute("version");
  }
}
```

```
public void WriteAttributeString(RssAttributes attb, string value)
{
  if (attb == RssAttributes.Version)
  {
    writer.WriteAttributeString("version",value);
  }
}

public override void WriteEndAttribute()
{
  writer.WriteEndAttribute();
}
```

The `WriteStartAttribute()` method accepts a parameter of type `RssAttributes`. Inside it checks whether the attribute to be emitted is `Version`, and if so, calls the `WriteStartAttribute()` method of the `XmlWriter` instance to write the attribute.

The `WriteAttributeString()` method accepts two parameters: `RssAttributes` and the value of the attribute. It then calls the `WriteAttributeString()` method of the `XmlWriter` instance by passing the supplied value and `version` as the attribute name.

The `WriteEndAttribute()` method simply calls the `WriteEndAttribute()` method of the `XmlWriter` instance.

Writing Data

Though the methods that we created for writing elements will take care of most of the RSS feed generation, you may need additional methods to emit comments, character data, white spaces, and so on. To accomplish this task, we will write a set of methods as shown in Listing A-12.

Listing A-12. *Methods for Writing Data*

```
public override void WriteCData(string text)
{
  writer.WriteCData(text);
}

public override void WriteChars(char[] buffer, int index, int count)
{
  writer.WriteChars(buffer, index, count);
}

public override void WriteComment(string text)
{
  writer.WriteComment(text);
}
```

```
public override void WriteWhitespace(string ws)
{
  writer.WriteWhitespace(ws);
}

public override void WriteString(string text)
{
  writer.WriteString(text);
}
```

These methods do not contain much code. They simply call the corresponding method on the `XmlWriter` instance. For example, the `WriteCData()` method accepts a string and calls the `WriteCData()` method of the `XmlWriter` by passing the string. The `WriteChars()`, `WriteComment()`, `WriteWhitespace()`, and `WriteString()` methods also call the respective methods of the `XmlWriter` instance.

Writing an XML Declaration

An RSS feed is an XML document and from that point of view should contain an XML declaration. The methods `WriteStartDocument()` and `WriteEndDocument()` emit an XML declaration with a version of 1.0. These methods are shown in Listing A-13.

Listing A-13. *Writing an XML Declaration*

```
public override void WriteStartDocument()
{
  writer.WriteStartDocument();
}
public override void WriteStartDocument(bool standalone)
{
  writer.WriteStartDocument(standalone);
}
public override void WriteEndDocument()
{
  writer.WriteEndDocument();
}
```

The `WriteStartDocument()` method has two overloads. The one with a Boolean parameter emits a stand-alone attribute. Both the methods call respective overloads of the `WriteStartDocument()` method on the `XmlWriter` instance. The `WriteEndDocument()` method simply calls the `WriteEndDocument()` method of the `XmlWriter` instance.

That's it: the `RssWriter` class is now ready. Compile the class library to get its output assembly.

Consuming the RssWriter Class

To consume the RssWriter class we just created, you will need to create a new website in Visual Studio. Add a reference to the assembly in which RssWriter resides. Open the default web form in the IDE and write the code shown in Listing A-14 in its Page_Load event handler.

Listing A-14. *Using the RssWriter Class*

```
protected void Page_Load(object sender, EventArgs e)
{
  Response.ContentEncoding = System.Text.Encoding.UTF8;
  Response.ContentType = "text/xml";
  RssWriter writer = new RssWriter(Response.OutputStream);
  writer.WriteStartElement(RssElements.Rss);
  writer.WriteAttributeString(RssAttributes.Version, "2.0");
  writer.WriteStartElement(RssElements.Channel);
  writer.WriteElementString(RssElements.Title, "DotNetBips.com");
  writer.WriteElementString(RssElements.Link, "http://www.dotnetbips.com");
  writer.WriteElementString(RssElements.Description,
                            "Latest Articles from DotNetBips.com");
  writer.WriteElementString(RssElements.Copyright,
                            "Copyright (C) DotNetBips.com. All rights reserved.");
  writer.WriteElementString(RssElements.Generator, "Pro XML RSS Generator");
  writer.WriteStartElement(RssElements.Item);
  writer.WriteElementString(RssElements.Title, "DotNetBips.com");
  writer.WriteElementString(RssElements.Link,
                "http://www.dotnetbips.com/Articles/displayarticle.aspx?id=242");
  writer.WriteElementString(RssElements.Description,
                   "This article explains how to create and consume RSS feeds.");
  writer.WriteElementString(RssElements.PubDate,
                            "Sun, 25 Jan 2004 12:00:00 AM GMT");
  writer.WriteEndElement();
  writer.WriteEndElement();
  writer.WriteEndElement();
  writer.Close();
  Response.End();
}
```

The code sets the ContentEncoding property of the Response object to UTF-8 (that is, ASCII). It also sets the ContentType property to text/xml. This way, the browser knows that the response is XML data rather than HTML. A new instance of the RssWriter class is then created. The OutputStream of the Response object is passed as a parameter to the constructor of the RssWriter class. This way, the XML data will be written directly on the response stream.

Then, one by one, RSS tags are emitted so as to output an RSS feed, as shown in Listing A-5 earlier. Notice how the `RssElements` enumeration has made our job easy. Various methods such as `WriteElementString()` and `WriteStartElement()` make extensive use of the `RssElements` enumeration. After the writing of the feed is over, the `RssWriter` instance is closed. Finally, the `End()` method of the `Response` object is called so that the response stream is flushed off to the client.

Note For the sake of simplicity, the code emits hard-coded values. In most real-world cases, you will retrieve data such as the title, URL, and publication date from a database table.

If you run the web form after writing the code, it should look similar to Figure A-3.

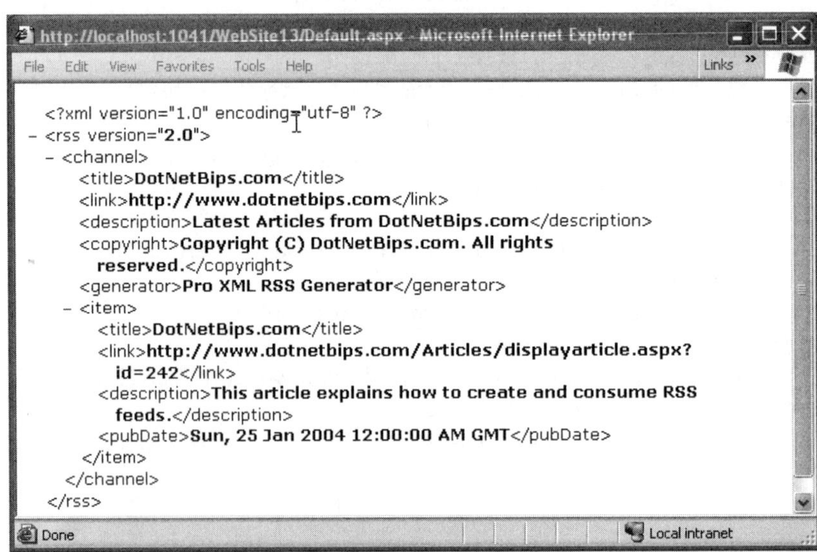

Figure A-3. *RSS feed displayed in the browser*

Summary

In this appendix, you learned to create custom implementations of the `XmlReader` and `XmlWriter` classes. The `XmlReader` and `XmlWriter` classes are abstract classes. To create custom readers and writers, you need to inherit from them and override various properties and methods. This way, you can easily extend the out-of-the-box functionality exposed by these classes for a specific scenario.

APPENDIX B

Case Study: A Web Service–Driven Shopping Cart

In Chapter 9, you learned about web services. In the sections to follow, you are going to learn how web services can be put to use in a real-world scenario. As an example, we are going to develop a shopping cart driven entirely by web services. The business scenario under consideration is as follows:

Acme Inc. is a company marketing and selling electric and electronic items. As an aggressive marketing strategy, they wish to tie up with various leading websites to increase their sales and reach. To attract website owners, Acme launches an affiliate program through which website owners can sell Acme products on their respective websites. The websites will not ship or distribute any products themselves. They will simply grab orders from their visitors and then submit the orders to Acme for fulfillment. In return, the websites will earn a commission on each order. Acme wants to develop a web service–based solution that is easy to implement, cross-platform, and industry accepted.

Considering this scenario, we can define the requirements of the solution as follows:

- The solution must be platform independent.
- The individual websites will not maintain a product database themselves.
- Acme will expose the functionality of the shopping cart (addition, modification, and removal of products from the cart) in the form of a web service.
- Acme will expose their product database via a web service so that individual websites can display product catalogs on their respective sites.
- When the visitors of individual websites place an order, the data is saved directly into the Acme database.

Creating the Database

To begin, you need to create a SQL Server database. You can do so with the help of Server Explorer. Open Server Explorer by choosing View ➤ Server Explorer from the menu. Then right-click on the Data Connection node of Server Explorer and choose Create New SQL Server Database. Clicking this option will pop up the dialog box shown in Figure B-1.

Figure B-1. *Creating a new database by using Server Explorer*

The dialog box essentially allows you to specify a database server, authentication mode, and database name. Name the database `Database`.

Note You can also create the database via a `CREATE DATABASE` T-SQL statement. To do so, you can open a query window of SQL Server Management Studio by clicking the New Query toolbar button and then execute a `CREATE DATABASE` database statement. This will create a new database named `Database` with default settings.

After you create the database, you need to create four tables in it: `Products`, `ShoppingCart`, `Orders`, and `OrderDetails`. The structure of these tables should match the details shown in Table B-1.

Table B-1. *Table Structures*

Table Name	Column Name	Data Type	Description
`Products`	`Id`	`int`	Product ID and primary key
`Products`	`Name`	`varchar(50)`	Name of the product
`Products`	`Description`	`varchar(MAX)`	Description of the product
`Products`	`UnitPrice`	`money`	Unit price of the product
`ShoppingCart`	`Id`	`int`	Identity column and primary key
`ShoppingCart`	`CartID`	`varchar(255)`	A unique identifier (say, GUID) of a shopping cart

Table Name	Column Name	Data Type	Description
ShoppingCart	ProductID	int	Product ID of an item
ShoppingCart	Qty	int	Quantity of ProductID
Orders	Id	int	Primary key
Orders	CartID	varchar(255)	Cart ID for which this order has been placed
Orders	OrderDate	dateTime	Date and time at which the order was placed
Orders	Amount	money	Total amount of the order
Orders	Street	varchar(50)	Street address where the order is to be shipped
Orders	Country	varchar(50)	Country of shipment
Orders	State	varchar(50)	State of shipment
Orders	City	varchar(50)	City of shipment
Orders	PostalCode	varchar(50)	Postal code of shipment
OrderDetails	Id	int	Primary key
OrderDetails	CartID	varchar(255)	A unique cart ID
OrderDetails	ProductID	int	Product ID from the Products table
OrderDetails	Qty	int	Quantity of a selected product

Creating the Web Service

Now that you have the database ready, you can proceed to create the web service. To do so, choose File ➤ New Web Site from the menu to open the New Web Site dialog box. Name the web service project ECommerceService.

Creating the SqlHelper Class

Right-click on the App_Code folder and choose the Add New Item option. Add a new class named SqlHelper. This class will act as a data access layer and will take the data in and out of the database. The complete code of the SqlHelper class is shown in Listing B-1.

Listing B-1. *SqlHelper Class*

```
using System;
using System.Configuration;
using System.Data;
using System.Data.SqlClient;

public class SqlHelper
{
    private static string strConn;
```

```
static SqlHelper()
{
    strConn =
    ConfigurationManager.ConnectionStrings["connectionstring"].ConnectionString;
}

public static int ExecuteNonQuery(string sql, SqlParameter[] p)
{
    SqlConnection cnn = new SqlConnection(strConn);
    SqlCommand cmd = new SqlCommand(sql, cnn);
    for (int i = 0; i < p.Length; i++)
    {
        cmd.Parameters.Add(p[i]);
    }
    cnn.Open();
    int retval = cmd.ExecuteNonQuery();
    cnn.Close();
    return retval;
}

public static object ExecuteScalar(string sql, SqlParameter[] p)
{
    SqlConnection cnn = new SqlConnection(strConn);
    SqlCommand cmd = new SqlCommand(sql, cnn);
    for (int i = 0; i < p.Length; i++)
    {
        cmd.Parameters.Add(p[i]);
    }
    cnn.Open();
    object obj = cmd.ExecuteScalar();
    cnn.Close();
    return obj;
}

public static DataSet GetDataSet(string sql,SqlParameter[] p)
{
    SqlConnection cnn = new SqlConnection(strConn);
    SqlCommand cmd = new SqlCommand(sql, cnn);
    if (p != null)
    {
        for (int i = 0; i < p.Length; i++)
        {
            cmd.Parameters.Add(p[i]);
        }
```

```
        }
        SqlDataAdapter da = new SqlDataAdapter();
        da.SelectCommand = cmd;
        DataSet ds = new DataSet();
        da.Fill(ds);
        return ds;
    }
}
```

Before you start coding the SqlHelper class, make sure to import the System.Data and System.Data.SqlClient namespaces. The SqlHelper class consists of a static constructor and three static methods: ExecuteNonQuery(), ExecuteScalar(), and ExecuteDataSet().

The constructor of SqlHelper reads the database connection string from the <connectionStrings> section of the web.config file and stores it in a private static variable. This is done with the help of the ConfigurationManager class.

The ExecuteNonQuery() method is intended for executing action queries such as INSERT, UPDATE, and DELETE. The method takes two parameters: the SQL query to be executed and an array of the SqlParameter class representing parameters of the query. Then the method creates an instance of SqlConnection and SqlCommand. The SqlParameters are added to the Parameters collection. The database connection is then opened and the query is executed by using the ExecuteNonQuery() method of the SqlCommand object, which returns the number of records affected by the query and is returned to the caller.

The ExecuteScalar() method is used to execute SELECT queries that return just one value. It takes two parameters: the SQL query to be executed and an array of the SqlParameter class representing parameters of the query. The pattern is then the same as before: the method creates an instance of SqlConnection and SqlCommand, and SqlParameters are added to the Parameters collection. The database connection is then opened and the query is executed by using the ExecuteScalar() method of the SqlCommand object, which returns the result of the query as an object. This object is returned to the caller.

The ExecuteDataSet() method is used to execute SELECT queries and retrieve the result set as a DataSet. It takes two parameters: the SQL query to be executed and an array of the SqlParameter class representing parameters of the query. The novel part of this method instantiates a SqlDataAdapter. The SelectCommand property of the SqlDataAdapter is set to the SqlCommand instance that we just created. The SqlDataAdapter then fills a DataSet with the help of the Fill() method. The filled DataSet is then returned to the caller.

Specifying the Connection String in web.config

The database connection used by SqlHelper needs to be stored in the web.config file. Add a web.config file by using the Add New Item dialog box of Visual Studio and specify the connection string in its <connectionStrings> section. Listing B-2 shows how this is done.

Listing B-2. *Specifying the Connection String in web.config*

```
<connectionStrings>
<add name="connectionstring"
connectionString="Data Source=.\SQLEXPRESS;Initial Catalog=Database;
Integrated Security=True;User Instance=True"
providerName="System.Data.SqlClient"/>
</connectionStrings>
```

Creating the Web Methods

The EcommerceService consists of several web methods. Before you code these web methods, you must import System.Data and System.Data.SqlClient namespaces. The web methods of ECommerceService are listed in Table B-2.

Table B-2. *Web Methods of ECommerceService*

Web Method Name	Description
GetProducts()	Returns a list of products from the Products table
AddItem()	Adds an item to the shopping cart
UpdateItem()	Updates an item from the shopping cart
RemoveItem()	Removes an item from the shopping cart
GetCart()	Returns all the items from a specified shopping cart
GetCartAmount()	Returns the total amount of a specified shopping cart
PlaceOrder()	Places an order for a specified shopping cart

Each of the web methods is described next.

Retrieving the List of Products

The GetProducts() web method is designed to return a list of products from the Products table. The method is shown in Listing B-3.

Listing B-3. *The GetProducts() Method*

```
[WebMethod]
public DataSet GetProducts()
{
  DataSet ds = SqlHelper.GetDataSet("SELECT * FROM products",null);
  return ds;
}
```

The GetProducts() web method simply selects all the products from the Products table by using the GetDataSet() method of the SqlHelper class and returns the DataSet to the caller. This method can be used to create a product catalog in the client application.

Adding Items to the Shopping Cart

When an end user adds various items, they should be stored in the ShoppingCart table. This is accomplished with the help of the AddItem() web method, shown in Listing B-4.

Listing B-4. *Adding Items to the Shopping Cart*

```
[WebMethod]
public int AddItem(string cartid,int productid,int qty)
{
  string sql = "INSERT INTO shoppingcart(cartid,productid,qty)
              VALUES(@cartid,@productid,@qty)";
  SqlParameter[] p = new SqlParameter[3];
  p[0] = new SqlParameter("@cartid", cartid);
  p[1] = new SqlParameter("@productid", productid);
  p[2] = new SqlParameter("@qty", qty);
  return SqlHelper.ExecuteNonQuery(sql, p);
}
```

The AddItem() method accepts a unique cart identifier, product ID, and quantity. It then executes an INSERT query against the ShoppingCart table by using the SqlHelper class. If the item is added successfully, the ExecuteNonQuery() method of the SqlHelper class will return 1. This return value is passed back to the client application. This value can be used to display success or failure messages.

Updating Items in the Shopping Cart

The end users may change the quantity of a selected item and hence there must be a provision to update already-selected items. The UpdateItem() web method does just that and is shown in Listing B-5.

Listing B-5. *Updating Items from the Shopping Cart*

```
[WebMethod]
public int UpdateItem(string cartid, int productid,int qty)
{
  string sql = "UPDATE shoppingcart SET qty=@qty
              WHERE cartid=@cartid AND productid=@productid";
  SqlParameter[] p = new SqlParameter[3];
  p[0] = new SqlParameter("@qty", qty);
  p[1] = new SqlParameter("@cartid", cartid);
  p[2] = new SqlParameter("@productid", productid);
  return SqlHelper.ExecuteNonQuery(sql, p);
}
```

The UpdateItem() web method accepts a unique cart identifier, product ID, and quantity. It then issues an UPDATE statement with the help of the SqlHelper class. As in the previous case, the return value of the ExecuteNonQuery() method is sent back to the client.

Removing Items from the Shopping Cart

At times users may want to remove previously selected items from the shopping cart. This is done with the help of the RemoveItem() web method, shown in Listing B-6.

Listing B-6. *Removing Items from the Shopping Cart*

```
[WebMethod]
public int RemoveItem(string cartid, int productid)
{
  string sql = "DELETE FROM shoppingcart
               WHERE cartid=@cartid AND productid=@productid";
  SqlParameter[] p = new SqlParameter[2];
  p[0] = new SqlParameter("@cartid", cartid);
  p[1] = new SqlParameter("@productid", productid);
  return SqlHelper.ExecuteNonQuery(sql, p);
}
```

The RemoveItem() web method accepts a unique cart identifier and product ID to be removed. It then executes a DELETE statement against the ShoppingCart table by using the SqlHelper class. As before, the return value of the ExecuteNonQuery() method is sent back to the client.

Retrieving Shopping Cart Items

The client application may need to display a complete list of items selected by a user in their shopping cart. This is accomplished with the help of the GetCart() web method, shown in Listing B-7.

Listing B-7. *Retrieving Shopping Cart Items*

```
[WebMethod]
public DataSet GetCart(string cartid)
{
  string sql = "SELECT * FROM shoppingcart c,products p
               WHERE c.productid=p.id AND c.cartid=@cartid";
  SqlParameter[] p = new SqlParameter[1];
  p[0] = new SqlParameter("@cartid", cartid);
  DataSet ds = SqlHelper.GetDataSet(sql, p);
  return ds;
}
```

The GetCart() web method accepts the shopping cart identifier and returns all the items from that cart to the caller in the form of a DataSet. Notice that the SELECT query is based on two tables—ShoppingCart and Products—because the product name and unit price also need to be sent back to the client application.

Retrieving the Shopping Cart Amount

Often shopping cart web pages need to display the total amount of the cart. This is achieved by a web method named GetCartAmount(), shown in Listing B-8.

Listing B-8. *Retrieving the Cart Amount*

```
 [WebMethod]
public decimal GetCartAmount(string cartid)
{
  string sql1 = "SELECT SUM(c.Qty * p.UnitPrice) AS Total FROM Products AS p
                 INNER JOIN ShoppingCart AS c ON p.Id = c.ProductID
                 WHERE c.CartID = @cartid";
  SqlParameter[] p1 = new SqlParameter[1];
  p1[0] = new SqlParameter("@cartid", cartid);
  object obj = SqlHelper.ExecuteScalar(sql1, p1);
  if (obj != DBNull.Value)
  {
    decimal amount = (decimal)obj;
    return amount;
  }
  else
  {
    return 0;
  }
}
```

The GetCartAmount() web method accepts a unique cart identifier and returns the total amount for that cart. Inside it executes a SUM() aggregate query. If the query returns NULL, a value of 0 is returned to the caller. Otherwise, the actual cart total is returned as a decimal value.

Placing Orders

When an order is placed, the Orders table should have an entry for that order. Moreover, all the items from the shopping cart must be moved to the OrderDetails table. This is accomplished with the help of the PlaceOrder() web method, shown in Listing B-9.

Listing B-9. *Placing an Order*

```
 [WebMethod]
public int PlaceOrder(string cartid,string street,string city,string state,
                      string country,string postalcode)
{
  string sql1 = "SELECT SUM(c.Qty * p.UnitPrice) AS Total FROM Products AS p
                 INNER JOIN ShoppingCart AS c ON p.Id = c.ProductID
                 WHERE c.CartID = @cartid";
```

```
    SqlParameter[] p1 = new SqlParameter[1];
    p1[0] = new SqlParameter("@cartid", cartid);
    object obj=SqlHelper.ExecuteScalar(sql1, p1);
    decimal amount = (decimal)obj;
    string sql2 = "INSERT INTO
                Orders(cartid,orderdate,amount,street,
                       country,state,city,postalcode)
                VALUES(@cartid,@orderdate,@amount,@street,
                       @country,@state,@city,@postalcode)";
    SqlParameter[] p2 = new SqlParameter[8];
    p2[0] = new SqlParameter("@cartid", cartid);
    p2[1] = new SqlParameter("@orderdate", DateTime.Now);
    p2[2] = new SqlParameter("@amount", amount);
    p2[3] = new SqlParameter("@street", street);
    p2[4] = new SqlParameter("@country", country);
    p2[5] = new SqlParameter("@state", state);
    p2[6] = new SqlParameter("@city", city);
    p2[7] = new SqlParameter("@postalcode", postalcode);
    int i=SqlHelper.ExecuteNonQuery(sql2, p2);

    string sql3 = "INSERT INTO orderdetails(cartid,productid,qty)
                SELECT cartid,productid,qty FROM shoppingcart
                  WHERE cartid=@cartid";
    SqlParameter[] p3 = new SqlParameter[1];
    p3[0] = new SqlParameter("@cartid", cartid);
    SqlHelper.ExecuteNonQuery(sql3, p3);

    string sql4 = "DELETE FROM shoppingcart WHERE cartid=@cartid";
    SqlParameter[] p4 = new SqlParameter[1];
    p4[0] = new SqlParameter("@cartid", cartid);
    SqlHelper.ExecuteNonQuery(sql4, p4);
    return i;
}
```

The `PlaceOrder()` method accepts six parameters. These parameters essentially capture the unique cart identifier and shipping address. Inside, the method retrieves the total amount of the cart. The shopping cart ID and shipping address are stored in the `Orders` table. Then product details such as product ID and quantity are added to the `OrderDetails` table. The link between the `Orders` and `OrderDetails` tables is `CartID`. The records are then deleted from the `ShoppingCart` table.

This completes the web service. Compile it to ensure that there are no syntactical errors.

Creating the Shopping Cart

Now that you have created the Ecommerce web service, you are ready to consume it in a client application. To do so, add a new website to the web service project you just created. Add three web forms to the website: Default.aspx, ShoppingCart.aspx, and Success.aspx. The Default.aspx web form will act as a product catalog and displays a list of products. Users can add items from the product catalog to their shopping cart. The shopping cart is displayed on ShoppingCart.aspx. Users can add, modify, or remove selected items here. When the order is placed successfully, the Success.aspx web form displays a success message to the end user.

Adding the Web Reference

To consume the web service, you need to add a web reference to it first. This is done by right-clicking on the website and choosing Add Web Reference. In the dialog box that appears, you can either specify the complete URL of EcommerceService.asmx or use the Services from This Solution option. Figure B-2 shows this dialog box.

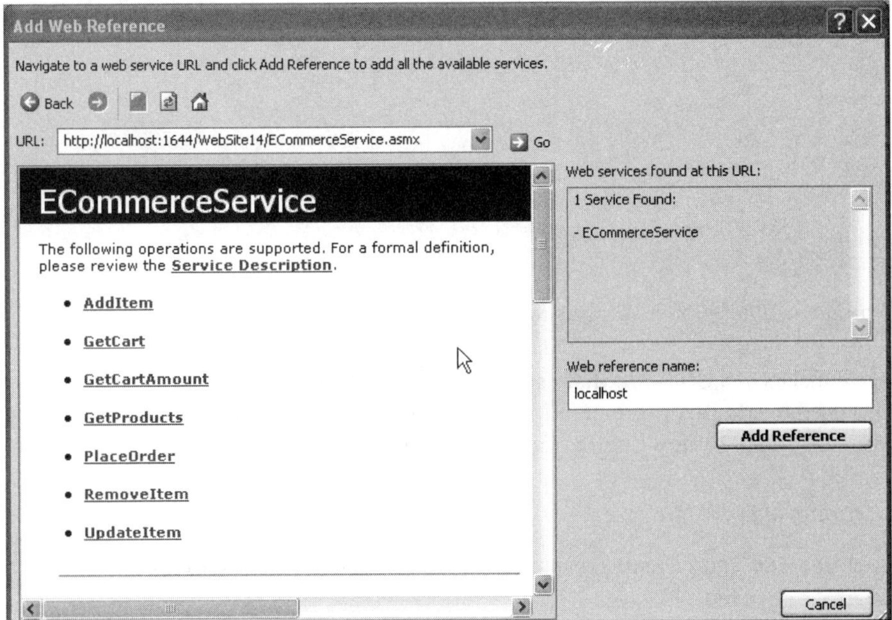

Figure B-2. *Adding a web reference to ECommerceService.asmx*

Keep the web reference name to the default value of `localhost` and click the Add Reference button. Visual Studio will add the `App_WebReferences` folder to your website and will store the web reference files in it.

Displaying the Product Catalog

Figure B-3 shows `Default.aspx` in design mode.

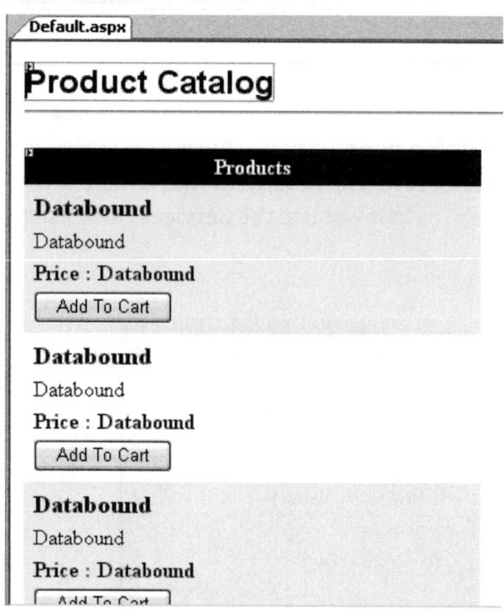

Figure B-3. *Product catalog page in design mode*

The page consists of a GridView that lists all the products in a template field. The Add to Cart button is used to add that product to the shopping cart. It also contains an Object Data Source control. Listing B-10 shows the complete markup of `Default.aspx`.

Listing B-10. *Markup of Default.aspx*

```
<%@ Page Language="C#" AutoEventWireup="true"  CodeFile="Default.aspx.cs"
         Inherits="_Default" %>

<!DOCTYPE html PUBLIC "-//W3C//DTD XHTML 1.0 Transitional//EN"
"http://www.w3.org/TR/xhtml1/DTD/xhtml1-transitional.dtd">

<html xmlns="http://www.w3.org/1999/xhtml" >
<head runat="server">
  <title>Untitled Page</title>
</head>
<body>
  <form id="form1" runat="server">
    <div>
```

```
<asp:Label ID="Label1" runat="server" Font-Bold="True" Font-Names="Arial"
           Font-Size="X-Large" Text="Product Catalog"></asp:Label><br />
<hr />
<br />
<asp:GridView ID="GridView1" runat="server" AutoGenerateColumns="False"
              CellPadding="4" DataSourceID="ObjectDataSource1"
              ForeColor="#333333" GridLines="None"
              OnSelectedIndexChanged="GridView1_SelectedIndexChanged"
              DataKeyNames="Id" Width="341px">
  <FooterStyle BackColor="#990000" Font-Bold="True" ForeColor="White" />
  <Columns>
    <asp:TemplateField HeaderText="Products">
      <ItemTemplate>
        <table style="width: 100%">
          <tr>
            <td nowrap="noWrap">
              <asp:Label ID="Label2" runat="server" Font-Bold="True"
                         Text='<%# Eval("Name") %>'
                         Font-Size="Large"></asp:Label>
            </td>
          </tr>
          <tr>
            <td style="height: 21px" nowrap="noWrap">
              <asp:Label ID="Label3" runat="server"
                         Text='<%# Eval("Description") %>'></asp:Label>
            </td>
          </tr>
          <tr>
            <td nowrap="noWrap">
              <asp:Label ID="Label5" runat="server" Font-Bold="True"
                         Text="Price :"></asp:Label>
              <asp:Label ID="Label4" runat="server"
                         Text='<%# Eval("UnitPrice","{0:C}") %>'
                         Font-Bold="True"></asp:Label>
            </td>
          </tr>
          <tr>
            <td nowrap="nowrap">
              <asp:Button ID="Button1" runat="server"
                          CommandArgument='<%# Eval("Id") %>'
                          CommandName="Select" Text="Add To Cart" />
            </td>
          </tr>
        </table>
      </ItemTemplate>
    </asp:TemplateField>
  </Columns>
```

```
        <RowStyle BackColor="#FFFBD6" ForeColor="#333333" />
        <SelectedRowStyle BackColor="#FFCC66" Font-Bold="True" ForeColor="Navy" />
        <PagerStyle BackColor="#FFCC66" ForeColor="#333333"
                    HorizontalAlign="Center" />
        <HeaderStyle BackColor="#990000" Font-Bold="True" ForeColor="White" />
        <AlternatingRowStyle BackColor="White" />
      </asp:GridView>
    </div>
    <asp:ObjectDataSource ID="ObjectDataSource1" runat="server"
                          SelectMethod="GetProducts"
                          TypeName="localhost.ECommerceService">
    </asp:ObjectDataSource>
    <br />
    <asp:HyperLink ID="HyperLink1" runat="server" Font-Bold="True"
                   NavigateUrl="~/ShoppingCart.aspx">Go To Shopping ➥
Cart</asp:HyperLink>
  </form>
</body>
</html>
```

Notice the use of the Eval() data-binding expression in binding columns such as Id, Name, UnitPrice, and Description to various labels. To configure the Object Data Source control, you need to set its TypeName property to localhost.ECommerceService. Also, set its SelectMethod property to GetProducts(). At run time the Object Data Source control creates an instance of the class specified by the TypeName property and calls SelectMethod on it. The returned data is then supplied to the GridView. There is a hyperlink at the bottom of the web form that points to ShoppingCart.aspx. This way, the user can navigate to the shopping cart.

Now go to the code-behind file of the web form and import the localhost namespace. Remember that localhost is the web reference name that you specified while creating the web service proxy.

Each user should have a unique shopping cart ID. Though you can use any unique ID, it is best to use Globally Unique Identifiers (GUIDs) so you are sure that the cart has a unique value globally. The code that generates a GUID for a user is shown in Listing B-11.

Listing B-11. *Creating a Unique Shopping Cart Identifier*

```
protected void Page_Load(object sender, EventArgs e)
{
  if (Session["cartid"] == null)
  {
    Session["cartid"]= Guid.NewGuid().ToString();
  }
}
```

In the Page_Load event, we check whether a session variable named cartid already exists. If not, we create a new GUID by using the NewGuid() method of the Guid class. The GUID is then stored in the cartid session variable. This variable is used further while calling various web methods.

Whenever a user clicks the Add to Cart button, we should add that product to the user's shopping cart. This is done in the SelectedIndexChanged event handler, as shown in Listing B-12.

Listing B-12. *Adding a Product to the Shopping Cart*

```
protected void GridView1_SelectedIndexChanged(object sender, EventArgs e)
{
  ECommerceService proxy = new ECommerceService();
  proxy.AddItem(Session["cartid"].ToString(),
              Convert.ToInt32(GridView1.SelectedValue), 1);
}
```

The code creates an instance of the ECommerceService proxy class. Then the AddItem() method of the proxy class is called. The shopping cart identifier stored in the session is passed to the AddItem() method along with the product ID. Because we set the DataKeyNames property of the GridView to Id, the SelectedValue property returns the value of the Id column for the selected row. The quantity is passed as 1.

Creating the Shopping Cart Page

The shopping cart page consists of two parts. One part is the shopping cart itself, and the other part is a panel for collecting the shipping address. Figures B-4 and B-5 show these parts in design mode.

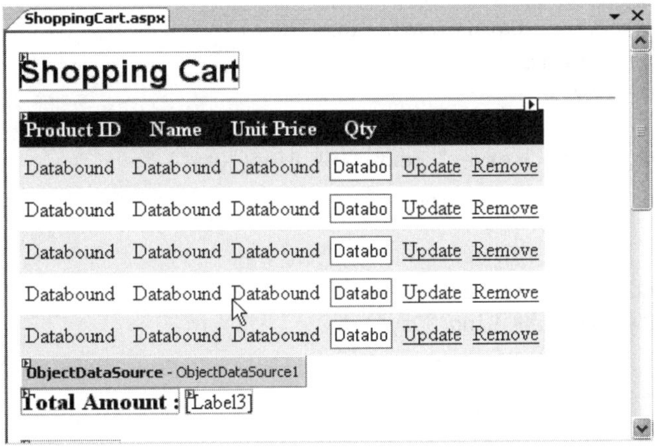

Figure B-4. *Shopping cart in design mode*

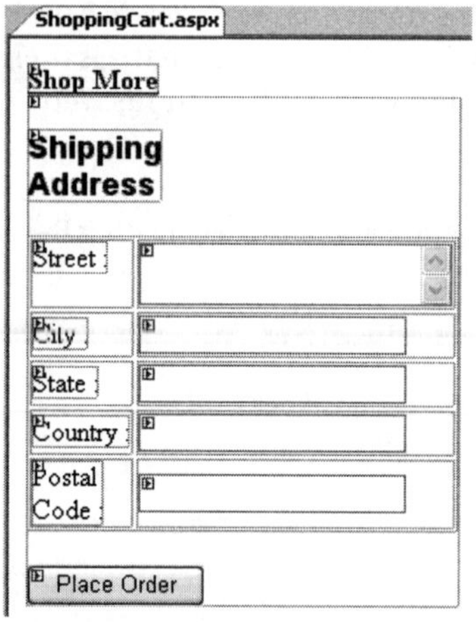

Figure B-5. *Shipping address panel in design mode*

The complete markup of the GridView is shown in Listing B-13.

Listing B-13. *Markup of the GridView*

```
<asp:GridView ID="GridView1" runat="server" AutoGenerateColumns="False"
              CellPadding="4" DataSourceID="ObjectDataSource1" ForeColor="#333333"
              GridLines="None" OnRowCommand="GridView1_RowCommand">
  <FooterStyle BackColor="#990000" Font-Bold="True" ForeColor="White" />
  <Columns>
    <asp:BoundField DataField="productid" HeaderText="Product ID" />
    <asp:BoundField DataField="Name" HeaderText="Name" />
    <asp:BoundField DataField="UnitPrice" DataFormatString="{0:c}"
                    HeaderText="Unit Price" />
    <asp:TemplateField HeaderText="Qty">
      <EditItemTemplate>
        <asp:TextBox ID="TextBox1" runat="server" Text='<%# Bind("Qty") %>'>
        </asp:TextBox>
      </EditItemTemplate>
      <ItemTemplate>
        <asp:TextBox ID="TextBox2" runat="server"
                     Columns="2" Text='<%# Bind("Qty") %>'>
        </asp:TextBox>
      </ItemTemplate>
    </asp:TemplateField>
    <asp:ButtonField CommandName="UpdateItem" Text="Update" />
    <asp:ButtonField CommandName="RemoveItem" Text="Remove" />
  </Columns>
```

```
  <RowStyle BackColor="#FFFBD6" ForeColor="#333333" />
  <EmptyDataTemplate>
    <asp:Label ID="Label2" runat="server" Font-Bold="True" ForeColor="Red"
             Text="Your shopping cart is empty"></asp:Label>
  </EmptyDataTemplate>
  <SelectedRowStyle BackColor="#FFCC66" Font-Bold="True" ForeColor="Navy" />
  <PagerStyle BackColor="#FFCC66" ForeColor="#333333" HorizontalAlign="Center" />
  <HeaderStyle BackColor="#990000" Font-Bold="True" ForeColor="White" />
  <AlternatingRowStyle BackColor="White" />
</asp:GridView>
```

The GridView consists of three bound fields for displaying the `ProductID`, `Name`, and `UnitPrice`, respectively. There is a template field that displays quantity. The user can also edit the quantity. The last two columns—`Update` and `Remove`—are button fields. The `CommandName` property of these button fields is set to `UpdateItem` and `RemoveItem`, respectively.

The complete markup of the shipping address panel is shown in Listing B-14.

Listing B-14. *Markup of the Shipping Address Panel*

```
<asp:Panel ID="panel1" runat=server>
  <br />
  <asp:Label ID="Label5" runat="server" Font-Bold="True" Font-Names="Arial"
           Font-Size="Large" Text="Shipping Address"></asp:Label><br />
  <br />
  <table>
    <tr>
      <td style="width: 100px" valign="top">
        <asp:Label ID="Label6" runat="server" Text="Street :"></asp:Label>
      </td>
      <td style="width: 100px">
        <asp:TextBox ID="TextBox3" runat="server" TextMode="MultiLine">
        </asp:TextBox>
      </td>
    </tr>
    <tr>
      <td style="width: 100px">
        <asp:Label ID="Label7" runat="server" Text="City :"></asp:Label>
      </td>
      <td style="width: 100px">
        <asp:TextBox ID="TextBox4" runat="server"></asp:TextBox>
      </td>
    </tr>
    <tr>
      <td style="width: 100px">
        <asp:Label ID="Label8" runat="server" Text="State :"></asp:Label>
      </td>
```

```
        <td style="width: 100px">
          <asp:TextBox ID="TextBox5" runat="server"></asp:TextBox>
        </td>
      </tr>
      <tr>
        <td style="width: 100px">
          <asp:Label ID="Label9" runat="server" Text="Country :"></asp:Label>
        </td>
        <td style="width: 100px">
          <asp:TextBox ID="TextBox6" runat="server"></asp:TextBox>
        </td>
      </tr>
      <tr>
        <td style="width: 100px">
          <asp:Label ID="Label10" runat="server" Text="Postal Code :"></asp:Label>
        </td>
        <td style="width: 100px">
          <asp:TextBox ID="TextBox7" runat="server"></asp:TextBox>
        </td>
      </tr>
    </table>
    <br />
    <asp:Button ID="Button1" runat="server" OnClick="Button1_Click"
                Text="Place Order" />
</asp:Panel>
```

The panel consists of text boxes for capturing street address, country, state, city, and postal code. At the bottom there is a button titled Place Order.

An Object Data Source supplies data to the GridView, the complete markup of which is shown in Listing B-15.

Listing B-15. *Markup of the Object Data Source Control*

```
<asp:ObjectDataSource ID="ObjectDataSource1" runat="server" SelectMethod="GetCart"
                      TypeName="localhost.ECommerceService">
  <SelectParameters>
    <asp:SessionParameter Name="cartid" SessionField="cartid" Type="String" />
  </SelectParameters>
</asp:ObjectDataSource>
```

As before, the `TypeName` property specifies the proxy class name. This time the `SelectMethod` property is set to `GetCart`. The `GetCart()` web method expects the shopping cart ID as a parameter, which is supplied from the session variable `cartid`.

`ShoppingCart.aspx` needs to display the total amount of the cart at a given point. To achieve this, you need to create a helper method called `DisplayTotal()`. The code of the `DisplayTotal()` method is shown in Listing B-16.

Listing B-16. *DisplayTotal() Method*

```
private void DisplayTotal()
{
  ECommerceService proxy = new ECommerceService();
  decimal total=proxy.GetCartAmount(Session["cartid"].ToString());
  if (total == 0)
  {
    panel1.Visible = false;
  }
  Label3.Text = "$" + total ;
}
```

As before, make sure to import the `localhost` namespace before you proceed. The `DisplayTotal()` method creates an instance of the web service proxy class. It then calls the `GetCartAmount()` web method by passing the cart ID from the session variable. The returned value is displayed in a Label control. The first place where the `DislayTotal()` method is called is the `Page_Load` event handler (Listing B-17).

Listing B-17. *The Page_Load Event Handler of ShoppingCart.aspx*

```
protected void Page_Load(object sender, EventArgs e)
{
  if (!IsPostBack)
  {
    DisplayTotal();
  }
}
```

The `RowCommand` event handler of the GridView is where removal and modification of items selected in the shopping cart are done. The `RowCommand` event handler is shown in Listing B-18.

Listing B-18. *Removing and Updating Shopping Cart Items*

```
protected void GridView1_RowCommand(object sender, GridViewCommandEventArgs e)
{
  ECommerceService proxy = new ECommerceService();
  GridViewRow row = GridView1.Rows[Convert.ToInt32(e.CommandArgument)];
  int productid = Convert.ToInt32(row.Cells[0].Text);
  if (e.CommandName == "RemoveItem")
  {
    proxy.RemoveItem(Session["cartid"].ToString(),productid);
  }
  if (e.CommandName == "UpdateItem")
  {
    int qty = Convert.ToInt32(((TextBox)row.FindControl("TextBox2")).Text);
    if (qty <= 0)
```

```
    {
      throw new Exception("Quantity must be greater than 0");
    }
    proxy.UpdateItem(Session["cartid"].ToString(),productid,qty);
  }
  GridView1.DataBind();
  DisplayTotal();
}
```

The code creates an instance of the web service proxy class. It then retrieves a reference to the current row from the Rows collection with the help of the CommandArgument property of GridViewCommandEventArgs, which returns the row index of the GridView row that triggered the event. The product ID of the product to be removed or updated is then retrieved from the first column of the GridView. The two if conditions check the CommandName property of the GridViewCommandEventArgs class. If the CommandName is RemoveItem, the RemoveItem() web method is called by passing the cart ID and the product ID. Similarly, if the CommandName is UpdateItem, the UpdateItem() web method is called by passing the cart ID, the product ID, and the new quantity. The GridView is then bound with the new cart details by calling its DataBind() method. Finally, the DisplayTotal() helper method is called to reflect the changed amount.

After the user has decided to place the order, the user needs to enter the shipping address and click the Place Order button. The Click event handler of the Place Order button contains the code shown in Listing B-19.

Listing B-19. *Placing an Order*

```
protected void Button1_Click(object sender, EventArgs e)
{
  ECommerceService proxy = new ECommerceService();
  proxy.PlaceOrder(Session["cartid"].ToString(), TextBox3.Text, TextBox4.Text,
                   TextBox5.Text, TextBox6.Text, TextBox7.Text);
  Response.Redirect("success.aspx");
}
```

Again, an instance of the web service proxy class is created. This time the PlaceOrder() web method is called by passing the cart ID and shipping address information. Finally, the user is taken to the Success.aspx web form, wherein a success message is displayed.

Testing the Website

Now that you have created the web service and the client application, let's test it. First, add a few records to the Products table. If you wish, you can use the sample T-SQL script provided along with the code download to add a few records for you.

Run Default.aspx in the browser. You should see something similar to Figure B-6.

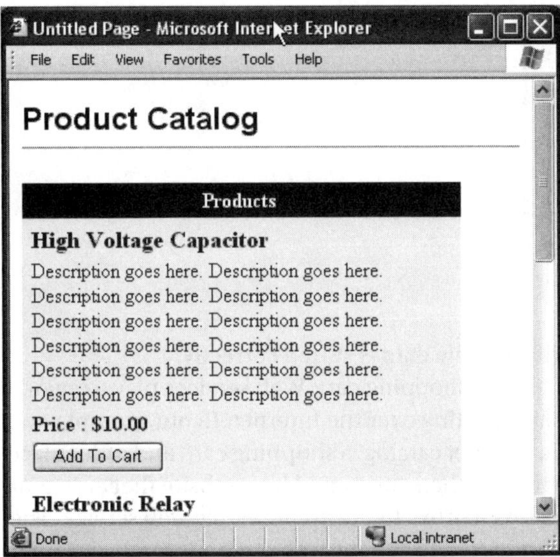

Figure B-6. *Product catalog*

Now select a few items by clicking the Add to Cart button and then click the Go to Shopping Cart button. The `ShoppingCart.aspx` web form should be displayed as shown in Figure B-7.

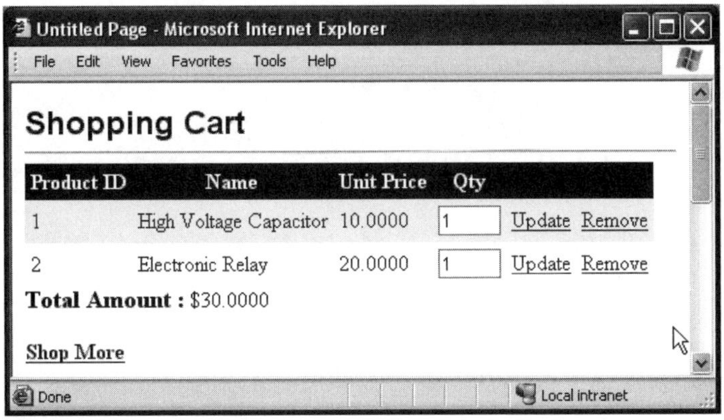

Figure B-7. *Shopping cart*

Try modifying the quantity or removing some items. Then enter the shipping address and click the Place Order button. You should see a success message as shown in Figure B-8.

Figure B-8. *Order placed successfully*

Also, open the database tables and verify that the data is stored correctly.

That's it—we've created a web service–driven shopping cart. Web services play a major role when the client and the server are communicating over the Internet. In our example, we exposed e-commerce functionality such as a product catalog, a shopping cart, and order placement via a single web service. The web service was then consumed in a website that acts as an e-commerce storefront. You did that by creating a proxy to the e-commerce web service. The controls such as Object Data Source were configured to call the web methods for the required functionality. Though we didn't use XML data directly, behind the scenes the data transfer from web service to website was in XML format.

APPENDIX C

Resources

The following resources will help you learn more about XML, .NET, and web services:

W3C website for XML specifications

http://www.w3.org/XML

W3C website for XML schema specifications

http://www.w3.org/XML/Schema

W3C website for XPath-related information

http://www.w3.org/TR/xpath

W3C website for XSL-related information

http://www.w3.org/Style/XSL/

XML Developer's Center—Microsoft's website for XML-related resources and information

http://msdn.microsoft.com/xml/default.aspx

MSDN newsgroups for XML

http://msdn.microsoft.com/newsgroups/ ➥
default.aspx?dg=microsoft.public.xml&lang=en&cr=US
http://msdn.microsoft.com/newsgroups/ ➥
default.aspx?dg=microsoft.public.dotnet.xml&lang=en&cr=US
http://msdn.microsoft.com/newsgroups/ ➥
default.aspx?dg=microsoft.public.sqlserver.xml&lang=en&cr=US
http://msdn.microsoft.com/newsgroups/ ➥
default.aspx?dg=microsoft.public.xsl&lang=en&cr=US

Web Service Developer's Center

http://msdn.microsoft.com/webservices/

SQL Server Developer's Center

http://msdn2.microsoft.com/en-us/sql/default.aspx

.NET Framework Developer's Center

http://msdn2.microsoft.com/en-us/netframework/default.aspx

W3Schools.com—tutorials on XML and allied technologies

http://msdn2.microsoft.com/en-us/netframework/default.aspx

Wikipedia—XML section

http://en.wikipedia.org/wiki/XML

Articles and code samples in ASP.NET, XML, web services, and .NET development in general

http://www.dotnetbips.com
http://www.binaryintellect.net

XML Notepad—XML editor from Microsoft

http://www.microsoft.com/downloads/ ➥
details.aspx?FamilyID=72D6AA49-787D-4118-BA5F-4F30FE913628&displaylang=en

Sandcastle—MSDN style help creator

http://www.microsoft.com/downloads/ ➥
details.aspx?FamilyId=E82EA71D-DA89-42EE-A715-696E3A4873B2&displaylang=en

SQLXML programming

http://msdn2.microsoft.com/en-us/library/ms171779.aspx

Index

Symbols

A

D

G

H

I

N

O

P

U

V

W

eBookshop

ASP Today

Apress®
THE EXPERT'S VOICE™